La Jolla Cooks

Favorite Recipes
from La Jolla
Country Day School

La Jolla Country Day School Parents Association

La Jolla, California

Cover design: Caroff/Reiken, New York
Graphic design and typesetting: La Jolla Mailing Service, La Jolla
Printing: R.R. Donnelley & Sons, Chicago

First Printing   August 1985
Second Printing   December 1985

Published by
La Jolla Country Day School Parents Association
9490 Genesee Avenue
La Jolla, California 92037

ISBN 0-9614176-0-9

Printed in the United States of America

Library of Congress Cataloging in Publication Data
Main entry under title:

La Jolla cooks.

   Edited by: Gloria Andújar.
   Includes index.
   1. Cookery, American—California style. 2. La Jolla
(Calif.)—Social life and customs. 3. Cookery—
California—La Jolla. I. Andújar, Gloria. II. La Jolla
Country Day school.
TX715.J755 1985   641.5   85-8084
ISBN 0-9614176-0-9

To the children of La Jolla Country Day—yesterday's, today's and tomorrow's.

EDITORIAL STAFF

Gloria Andújar
Joyce Aftahi
Valerie Bauer
Margi Bingham
Kathy Burns
Janis Butcher
Libby Clemmer
Carol Garcia
Melody Gentry
Alyce Gibbs
Kathy Glick

Lyda Goldsmith
Estelle Graff
Patita Hasse
Lyn Heller
Karen Kessler
Helen Mayer
Kerry Myers
Brooke Peterson
Jeannie Riley
Carol Vadnais
Catherine van Sonnenberg

A special word of thanks to the many friends who contributed and tested recipes.

For additional copies of **La Jolla Cooks** use order blanks in the back of the book or write directly to:

La Jolla Cooks
La Jolla Country Day School
9490 Genesee Avenue
La Jolla, California 92037

Checks should be made payable to LJCDS Parents Association for the amount of $14.95 plus $2.00 for postage and handling per book. California residents please add 6% sales tax.

Profits from the sale of **La Jolla Cooks** will benefit La Jolla Country Day School.

CONTENTS

PREFACE

Southern California's rich culinary heritage evolved from early Spanish and Indian foundations and has been bountifully enhanced by a continuous flow of diverse people and cultures. This fine blend of ethnic traditions reflects a sophisticated mixture of heritages we proudly call our own. **La Jolla Cooks** is an outstanding collection of nearly 800 recipes which represent the diversity of our community and appeal to a wide variety of tastes. Within its pages you will discover practical, simple dishes as well as elegant gourmet fare. We make no claims to originality, only to tried and true favorites. Each recipe has been tested and carefully edited in an attempt to clarify instructions and ingredients.

Cooking can be an enjoyable and effective tool to promote a child's natural curiosity and creativity. "Just For Kids" features fun and delicious treats children will enjoy cooking and eating. Emphasize kitchen safety rules and supervise young chefs at all times.

Interest in foreign dishes and their authentic preparation inspired our chapter on foods "From Around The World". We are fortunate to count among us people from all four corners of the world, as well as those who have gathered exciting recipes from personal travels. From Japan to Spain and Thailand to Austria, the cuisine of nearly 20 countries is represented in "From Around The World". Southern California cookery claims a variety of dishes which might be classified as Mexican elsewhere in the United States. These, however, are common on our tables and an integral part of our local bill of fare. Therefore, guacamole, chicken enchiladas, carne asada burritos and the like have been incorporated throughout their corresponding chapters.

San Diego is fast becoming a center of international gastronomical acclaim with an extraordinary array of superb restaurants. "From Around The Town" features exclusive recipes from over 30 leading restaurants. Try these simplified recipes with confidence and discover that the mystique of cordon bleu meals can be recreated in your own kitchen.

Sharing a meal with family or guests has been a traditional and meaningful way of expressing friendship. We invite you to share the joy of our treasured recipes and hope some will become your new favorites. We are confident that **La Jolla Cooks** will serve as a permanent reference for delicious recipes and become a cherished member of your kitchen library.

Gloria Andújar
Editor, **La Jolla Cooks**

1

Appetizers

Artichoke Nibbler

Serves 12-16

INGREDIENTS:

1 small onion, finely chopped
1 garlic clove, minced
2 6-ounce jars marinated artichoke
  hearts, chopped
4 eggs, lightly beaten
¼ cup bread crumbs (or finely
  crushed Ritz crackers)

¼ teaspoon salt
2 tablespoons parsley, minced
⅛ teaspoon pepper
⅛ teaspoon oregano
⅛ teaspoon hot sauce
½ pound sharp cheddar cheese,
  grated

PROCEDURE:

Preheat oven to 325°. Sauté onion and garlic in marinade of one jar artichoke
hearts. Drain second jar, finely chop all hearts and set aside. Mix all ingredients
well and pour into a greased 8″ by 8″ baking dish. Bake for 30 minutes. Cut
into 1″ squares and serve either hot or cold.

Geri Caceres   *Betty Shaffer*
Sherry Cook   *Marilyn Wells*

Asparagus Bits

Serves 20

INGREDIENTS:

20 slices thin white bread, crusts
  trimmed
3 ounces blue cheese, softened
8 ounces cream cheese, softened

1 egg, beaten
20 asparagus spears, fresh or
  frozen
½ pound butter, melted

PROCEDURE:

Preheat oven to 400°. Flatten bread with a rolling pin. Blend cheeses and egg
well. Spread about 1 tablespoon of cheese mixture per bread slice. Steam
asparagus until crisp. Roll a spear inside each bread slice securing with a
toothpick. Dip each roll in melted butter to coat. Place on a cookie sheet and
freeze. When firm, slice into bite size pieces (about 75) and bake for 25
minutes or until golden brown.

Margi Bingham

1

Hot Artichoke Appetizer

Yields 2½ cups

INGREDIENTS:

1 8½-ounce can water-packed
  artichoke hearts
1 6-ounce jar marinated artichoke
  hearts
1 4-ounce can green chiles, diced

6 tablespoons mayonnaise
2 cups Monterey jack cheese,
  grated
1 package tortilla chips

PROCEDURE:

Preheat oven to 350°. Drain and finely chop artichokes. Distribute evenly across bottom of a well-greased 7½" by 11" baking dish. Scatter chiles on top and spread the mayonnaise carefully over all. Sprinkle with cheese and bake for 15 minutes or until bubbly. Serve with tortilla chips.

This delicious appetizer can be prepared in advance, refrigerated and baked right before guests arrive. Make sure to allow a little extra cooking time if cold.

Carol Davis
Patty MacIntyre

Artichoke Delight

Serves 6

INGREDIENTS:

1 8½-ounce can artichoke hearts,
  drained and chopped
1 cup mayonnaise
1 cup Parmesan cheese

garlic salt to taste (optional)
Worcestershire sauce to taste
  (optional)

PROCEDURE:

Preheat oven to 350°. Combine all ingredients well. Pour into ovenproof serving dish. Bake 30 minutes until bubbly and golden brown. Serve warm with your favorite crackers.

This surprisingly simple recipe is always a hit with young and old. Double all ingredients for a larger crowd and use any leftovers to fill a breakfast omelette the next day!

Sally Peters Davidson
Jackie Hassler
Adelaide Regan

Sauerkraut Rolls

Yields 30-40

INGREDIENTS:

½ pound cooked turkey, coarsely ground
½ pound cooked ham, coarsely ground
½ pound cooked beef, coarsely ground
3 eggs, beaten
1 cup sauerkraut, chopped and squeezed dry

½ cup process cheese spread
1 small onion, minced
salt to taste
pepper to taste
1 cup bread crumbs (or cracker meal)

PROCEDURE:

Combine turkey, ham and beef. Add eggs, sauerkraut, cheese, onion, salt and pepper. Mix well. Shape into 1" balls and roll in bread crumbs. Deep fry balls, a few at a time, in very hot oil until golden brown (20-40 seconds).

Anne Coleman

Appetizer Pecan Pie

Serves 12

INGREDIENTS:

8 ounces cream cheese, softened
½ cup sour cream
2 tablespoons milk
2½-ounce package sliced chipped beef, finely chopped
⅓ cup green onion, finely chopped

3 tablespoons green pepper, finely chopped
1 tablespoon pimiento, chopped
⅛ teaspoon pepper
¼ cup pecans, coarsely ground

PROCEDURE:

Preheat oven to 350°. Combine cheese, sour cream and milk. Add beef, onion, green pepper, pimiento and pepper. Mix well. Place in 8" ovenproof dish, sprinkle pecans on top. Bake 15 minutes or until hot and bubbly. Serve warm with crackers.

Gets raves every time.

Margi Bingham

3

Crispy Fried Walnuts

Serves 4-6

INGREDIENTS:

4 cups water
6 ounces raw walnuts (or cashews)
5 tablespoons sugar

4 tablespoons honey
5 cups oil

PROCEDURE:

Boil nuts in 2 cups water. Drain. Add nuts to 2 cups of water, sugar and honey.
Cook over low heat for 6 minutes and drain. Deep fry nuts in oil 7 minutes
or until golden brown. Cool before serving.

Dolly Woo

Deviled Squares

Yields 40 squares

INGREDIENTS:

1 package refrigerator biscuits
¼ cup butter (or margarine)

1 4½-ounce can deviled ham
¼ cup Parmesan cheese, grated

PROCEDURE:

Preheat oven to 400°. Snip each biscuit into quarters. Arrange in two 8″ round
baking dishes. Melt butter and blend in ham. Pour over biscuit pieces. Sprinkle
with cheese. Bake 15 minutes or until golden brown.

Jo Anne Keesee

Ham And Cheese Wheels

Serves 6-8

INGREDIENTS:

8 ounces cream cheese, at room
  temperature
1 tablespoon mayonnaise
  (or butter)

3 green onions, finely chopped
¼ teaspoon pepper
7 slices boiled ham

PROCEDURE:

Blend cheese, mayonnaise, onions and pepper until spreadable. Apply thinly to each ham slice and roll into cylinders. Wrap in foil and freeze. Cut each roll into 6-8 bite-size slices and serve on crackers or thin bread circles.

For a slightly different taste, substitute 1 teaspoon horseradish instead of onions and pepper.

Linda Bird
Jean Mitchell

King Crab Pâté

Yields 3 cups

INGREDIENTS:

1 8-ounce package frozen crab (or
  7½-ounce can, drained)
½ cup butter, softened
½ cup mayonnaise
2 tablespoons lemon juice
⅓ cup Parmesan cheese, grated
3 eggs, hard boiled

1½ teaspoons horseradish
½ teaspoon salt
¼ teaspoon garlic powder
¼ teaspoon white pepper
¼ cup onion, minced
¼ cup parsley, chopped

PROCEDURE:

Chop drained crab, reserving one leg piece for garnish. Whip butter and lemon juice until fluffy. Beat in mayonnaise, cheese, chopped egg yolks and seasonings. Add finely chopped egg whites, crab, onion and parsley. Pack into small serving bowl or crock. Chill several hours. Garnish with crab leg and serve with crackers.

Anne Coleman
Jackie Hassler

Country Pâté

Serves 16-20

INGREDIENTS:

2 tablespoons salad oil
¼ pound mushrooms, chopped
1 medium onion, minced
1 garlic clove, minced
¼ cup dry sherry
1 teaspoon salt
½ teaspoon pepper
1 teaspoon thyme

½ teaspoon nutmeg
½ pound ground pork
½ pound ground chicken
¼ cup pistachios, shelled and
  chopped
1 egg
⅓ cup parsley, chopped
½ pound sliced bacon

PROCEDURE:

Preheat oven to 350°. Over medium heat cook oil, mushrooms, onion and garlic until tender. Add sherry, salt, pepper, thyme and nutmeg and bring to boil. Simmer 5 minutes. In bowl, combine mushroom mixture, pork, chicken, pistachios, egg and 2 tablespoons parsley. Mix thoroughly with wooden spoon. Line 8½″ by 4½″ loaf pan with bacon, allowing to hang over sides of pans. Spoon mixture into pan, packing to press out air pockets. Fold bacon ends over mixture. Bake 1¼ hours. Cover with foil-wrapped cardboard. Place cans on top to weigh down pâté. Chill thoroughly. Just before serving, dip pan in hot water 15 seconds, run metal spatula around sides of pan and invert. Scrape off excess fat. Garnish with reserved parsley and serve with your favorite cracker.

Can be prepared up to a week ahead.

Silvia A. Smith

Pâté A´ La Boyde

Serves 8

INGREDIENTS:

1 pound chicken livers, chopped
½ pound bacon, chopped
1 onion, chopped
5 garlic cloves, chopped

2 tablespoons butter (or margarine)
pepper to taste
salt to taste
rosemary to taste

PROCEDURE:

Preheat oven to 325°. Combine livers, bacon, onion, garlic and butter. Bake for 25 minutes or until soft. Reduce oven to 250°. Blend all ingredients until smooth, adding seasonings to taste. Replace in oven for "setting", approximately 10 minutes.

Gloria Márquez Sterling

Chicken Liver Pâté

Serves 12

INGREDIENTS:

15 chicken livers
5 eggs
4 slices of bread, cubed
½ teaspoon salt
½ teaspoon white pepper

¼ pound butter (or margarine)
16 ounces milk
Pam
parsley (for garnish)
olives (for garnish)

PROCEDURE:

Wash and soak livers in water for ½ hour, then soak in milk for 2 hours. Strain. In blender or food processor, combine livers, bread, salt and pepper. Melt butter and combine all ingredients into a Pam-sprayed double boiler. Cover and bring to boil. Simmer for 1½ hours. Transfer to serving dish, garnish with parsley and olives, and accompany with thin toast points or crackers.

Susana Deicas

Cheese Nuggets

Yields 4 dozen

INGREDIENTS:

1 pound sharp cheddar cheese,
    at room temperture
¼ pound butter, at room
    temperature

1 cup sifted flour
48 small stuffed green olives

PROCEDURE:

Preheat oven to 350°. Blend cheese with butter. Add flour and mix well.
Roll into 1″ balls, indent and fill with olive. Reshape into balls. Place 2″
apart on cookie sheet and refrigerate for 15 minutes. Bake 15-18 minutes.

*These crowd-pleasers can be frozen days ahead and
baked right before serving.*

Laurie Marcus

Pesto Cheese

Serves 12-15

INGREDIENTS:

2 3½-ounce cartons Rondelé
    herb and garlic cheese, softened
2 3½-ounce cartons Rondelé onion
    cheese, softened
⅓ cup pine nuts

4 basil leaves, chopped
parsley to taste, chopped
Pam
3 basil leaves (for garnish)

PROCEDURE:

Combine all ingredients well. Place in small shaped mold sprayed with Pam.
Refrigerate several hours or overnight. Arrange whole basil leaves on serving plate and unmold cheese on top. Fabulous with French bread rounds.

Merel Nissenberg

Cheese Boxes

Serves 12-15

INGREDIENTS:

1 loaf white unsliced sandwich
   bread
½ pound margarine, softened
½ pound cheddar cheese, grated

½ teaspoon salt
1 tablespoon cream
dash of paprika
1 egg white, unbeaten

PROCEDURE:

Preheat oven to 450°. Trim and discard bread crust. Slice loaf into 1½″ cubes. Thoroughly mix remaining ingredients until spreadable. Apply a thin layer of cheese mixture on all but bottom side of each bread cube. Bake on lightly greased cookie sheet for approximately 10 minutes. Serve warm.

Messy to make, but simply wonderful. Can be frozen and baked as needed.

Linda Goodwin

Chile Cheese Squares

Serves 12

INGREDIENTS:

10 eggs, beaten
½ cup flour
1 teaspoon baking powder
dash of salt
½ cup butter

8 ounces green chiles, chopped
16 ounces cottage cheese
1 pound Monterey jack cheese,
   grated

PROCEDURE:

Preheat oven to 400°. Blend eggs, flour, baking powder and salt. Melt butter. Add chiles and cheeses to butter. Blend all ingredients together and pour into a greased 13″ by 9″ by 2″ pan. Bake 15 minutes, then reduce to 325° for 35-40 minutes. Cool slightly and cut into bite-size squares. Serve warm.

Valdene Ramrus

Hot Cheese Rounds

Serves 6

INGREDIENTS:

10 ounces extra sharp cheddar
  cheese, grated
2 tablespoons onion, grated
1 cup mayonnaise

1 4½-ounce can ripe olives, sliced
  or diced
party rye rounds

PROCEDURE:

Preheat oven to 350°. Blend ingredients thoroughly and let stand.
Spread on party rye rounds and bake 10 minutes or until bubbly.

So easy to prepare yet always a party favorite. Can be made several days ahead.

Ruth Lischke

Cheese Stuffed Mushrooms

Serves 15-20

INGREDIENTS:

¾ pound fresh mushrooms,
  cleaned
7 tablespoons salad oil
1 tablespoon onion, minced

¼ cup salami, finely chopped
¼ cup smoked cheese spread
1 tablespoon catsup
soft buttered bread crumbs

PROCEDURE:

Preheat oven to 425°. Remove stems from mushrooms. Set aside ⅓ cup stems, chopped. Brush caps lightly with 5 tablespoons oil. Sauté chopped stems and onions in remaining oil. Stir salami, cheese spread and catsup. Spoon mixture into mushroom cavities and arrange in shallow baking pan. Sprinkle with bread crumbs. Bake for approximately 6-8 minutes.

May be prepared in advance and refrigerated.

Joy Charney

Cheese and Shrimp Roll

Serves 12-20

INGREDIENTS:

16 ounces Velveeta cheese,
  softened
8 ounces cream cheese, softened
14 ounces sour cream

1 4¼-ounce can small/medium
  shrimp
salsa to taste

PROCEDURE:

Roll Velveeta flat between wax paper. Mix remaining ingredients until smooth. Pour into center of flattened cheese. Fold up sides, seal and flip into serving platter. (It helps to roll cheese out on a cutting board to facilitate flipping the end result).

Cindy Small

Pâte Choux Au Fromage

Yields 35

INGREDIENTS:

1 cup cold water
6 tablespoons butter
1 teaspoon salt
dash of cayanne pepper
dash of pepper (black or white)

scraping of nutmeg
1 cup all-purpose flour, sifted
4 eggs
1 cup Swiss cheese, coarsely
  grated

PROCEDURE:

Preheat oven to 425°. Combine and bring to boil water, butter and seasonings. Gradually beat in flour until smooth, stirring constantly. Quickly beat in eggs one at a time, fold in cheese. (Batter can be frozen at this time). Squeeze from pastry bag (or drop by teaspoon) on a lightly buttered cookie sheet. Bake 20 minutes, then slit puffs. Return to turned-off oven for 10 minutes leaving door ajar. Serve hot.

For a yummy dessert puff, substitute sugar for the pepper and cheese.
Pipe custard or whipped cream into each slit.

Estelle Graff

11

Curry Cheese Ball

Serves 10-12

INGREDIENTS:

8 ounces cream cheese, softened
1 cup cooked chicken, finely
  chopped
¾ cup toasted almonds, finely
  chopped

⅓ cup mayonnaise
2 tablespoons chutney
1 tablespoon curry poweder
¼ teaspoon salt
flaked coconut

PROCEDURE:

Combine all ingredients except coconut. Chill several hours. Shape into a ball and roll in coconut flakes.

For a great holiday gift, stick a sprig of holly in the center, wrap in plastic, tie with a colorful ribbon and set atop a box of foil-wrapped crackers.

Libby Clemmer

Elgin Cheese Ball

Serves "lots"

INGREDIENTS:

1 5-ounce jar Roka cheese
1 5-ounce jar Old English cheese
4 ounces cheddar cheese, shredded
8 ounces cream cheese, softened

1 onion, dried
1 teaspoon Worcestershire sauce
1 teaspoon paprika
chopped nuts

PROCEDURE:

Combine all ingredients thoroughly. Refrigerate 12 hours. Shape into ball. Sprinkle with or roll in nuts.

Betty Davis

Blue Cheese Ball

Serves 8

INGREDIENTS:

¼ pound butter, softened
8 ounces cream cheese, softened
4½-ounces stuffed green olives,
  chopped

4 ounces blue cheese (or to taste)
½ cup pecans (or walnuts),
  chopped

PROCEDURE:

Blend all ingredients except nuts until smooth. Shape into a ball and roll in nuts. Refrigerate at least one hour.

Karen Stewart

Chutney Cheese Ball

Serves 10-12

INGREDIENTS:

16 ounces cream cheese, softened
2 tablespoons curry powder (or to
  taste)

½ cup peanuts, chopped
1 9-ounce jar chutney
  (preferably Major Grey's)

PROCEDURE:

Combine cheese with curry. Chill until ready to handle. Shape into ball on wax paper and chill overnight. Roll in peanuts before serving, then pour chutney over the top. Serve with crackers, or apple or pear slices.

Jackie Hassler

No-Crust Quiche

Serves 15

INGREDIENTS:

1 pound Monterey jack cheese, grated
1 pound cheddar cheese, grated
4 eggs, beaten
1 cup evaporated milk

2 tablespoons flour
1 7-ounce can green chiles, chopped
1 8-ounce can tomato sauce

PROCEDURE:

Preheat oven to 325°. Arrange cheese in greased 9″ by 13″ glass baking dish. Combine eggs, milk and flour. Pour over cheese. Spread chiles on top. Pour tomato sauce over all. Bake for 50 minutes. Reduce oven to 225° and bake an additional 10 minutes. Let stand before slicing into small squares.

Cut into larger squares and accompany with a hearty green salad for a buffet supper or carry to a picnic with cut, crisp vegetables.

Carol Hinrichs

Mini Quiches

Yields 24

INGREDIENTS:

1 package refrigerated (or butter flake) dinner rolls
1 4½-ounce can shrimp, drained (or 1 cup fresh shrimp, cleaned)
1 egg, beaten
½ cup whipping cream

2 tablespoons green onion, chopped
1 tablespoon brandy
½ teaspoon salt
dash of pepper
1½ ounces Gruyère cheese, sliced

PROCEDURE:

Preheat oven to 375°. Grease 2 dozen 1¾″ muffin pans. Divide rolls into 24 segments. Press into muffin pans, approximately ¼-½″ high around the edges. Place shrimp on each shell. Combine egg, cream, onion, brandy, salt and pepper. Spoon evenly over shells. Divide cheese into 24 portions and top each appetizer. Bake for 15 minutes or until light golden brown. Under-bake if freezing. Rewarm frozen appetizers at 375° for 7-10 minutes.

These freeze well and are practical to keep on hand especially over the holidays. Try substituting ham, bacon, or your favorite vegetable for the shrimp.

Michelle Benson
Alma Hertweck

Ceviche

Serves 6-8

INGREDIENTS:

1½ pounds firm, fresh white fish
(seabass, sole, snapper, flounder)
1 cup lemon juice
3 limes juiced
2 tomatoes, peeled and diced
½ cup onion, mined
2 mild green chiles, minced
1 teaspoon salt

1 teaspoon cilantro, minced
½ teaspoon fresh ground pepper
½ teaspoon mashed garlic
1 teaspoon olice oil
lettuce leaves, tomato and
avocado slices and olives
(for garnish)

PROCEDURE:

Dice fish into ½" pieces and toss in citrus juices. Cover and refrigerate for 6 hours or until white. Drain and mix with all ingredients. Refrigerate for at least 1 hour. Serve on lettuce leaves garnished with avocado slices, tomatoes and olives.

This elegant and tasty dish may be served as an appetizer with crackers, a first course in champagne glasses, or a side salad. For a slightly different flavor, try adding ½ pound of scallops and/or small shrimp.

Nina Calhoun
Melanie Fields
Linda Morefield

Seafood Shells

Serves 6-8

INGREDIENTS:

1 large onion, minced
¼ cup butter
3 6½-ounce cans clams, drained
1 4¼-ounce can shrimp, drained
   and chopped
1 8-ounce can Italian flavored
bread crumbs

dash of Worcestershire sauce
3" anchovy paste
minced garlic (optional)
minced bacon, uncooked

PROCEDURE:

Preheat oven to 450°. Brown onion in butter. Combine clams, shrimp, bread-crumbs, Worcestershire sauce, anchovy paste and garlic. Pile lightly in flat sea shells. Sprinkle bacon on top. Heat 15-20 minutes or until lightly browned.

Mabel Ericson

Caviar Mousse

Serves 12

INGREDIENTS:

6 eggs, hard boiled, chopped
1 medium onion, chopped
1 cup mayonnaise
1 teaspoon Worcestershire sauce

1 package unflavored gelatine
2 tablespoons lemon juice
8 ounces black caviar
fresh dill (for garnish)

PROCEDURE:

Purée eggs, onion, mayonnaise and Worcestershire sauce in blender or food processor. Over low heat, melt gelatine in 2 tablespoons of water and lemon juice. Fold into egg mixture. Stir in 4 ounces caviar. Place in greased mold and refrigerate 6 hours. Unmold and decorate with remaining caviar and sprigs of dill. Serve with party rye or Bremmer wafers.

Will elicit rave compliments from caviar lovers.

Grace Bowman

16

Caviar Pie

Serves 15

INGREDIENTS:

4 eggs, hard boiled, finely chopped   1½ cups sour cream
½ teaspoon shallots, chopped   chopped parsley
8 ounces black caviar

PROCEDURE:

Combine eggs with onions. Pat firmly into pie pan or fluted quiche mold.
Drain caviar and gently pat it dry. Spread over egg mixture. Cover entire
pie with sour cream except rim. Border with a chopped ring of parsley. Serve
with crackers or party rye.

Mary Landa

Crab Mold

Serves 12

INGREDIENTS:

1½ tablespoons gelatine   ½ large green pepper, diced
1 10¾-ounce can tomato soup   1 cup celery, chopped
8 ounces cream cheese, softened   1 4½-ounce can crabmeat
1 medium onion, diced   1 cup mayonnaise

PROCEDURE:

Dissolve gelatine in tomato soup in a double boiler. Using a wisk, work in
cream cheese until creamy and smooth. Cool slightly and add remaining
ingredients. Pour into 1-quart mold, chill until set. Garnish with lemon
wedges and snow crab legs. Serve with crackers.

Libby Clemmer

Escargots Bourgignon

Serves 4-6

INGREDIENTS:

1 dozen snail shells
1 dozen whole escargots
2¼ sticks butter
7½ teaspoons garlic, minced
6 tablespoons parsley, chopped

7½ teaspoons shallots, chopped
¼ teaspoon salt
dash of pepper
dash of nutmeg

PROCEDURE:

Preheat oven to 450°. Wash each escargot well. Cream the butter and garlic. Mix the parsley, shallots and seasonings. Place a small amount of butter mixture in each shell, insert an escargot and cover the opening with mixture. Arrange filled shells, opening side up, on a heatproof serving dish. Bake 10-15 minutes or until butter bubbles. Serve immediately with French bread.

This is a favorite recipe of true escargot fans.

Estelle Graff

Seafood Spread

Serves 6

INGREDIENTS:

3 ounces cream cheese, softened
1 tablespoon Roquefort or blue
   cheese, crumbled
¼ cup sour cream
½ garlic clove, crushed

1 tablespoon green onion, finely
   chopped
2 teaspoons lemon juice
1 6½-ounce can lobster (or crab),
   drained

PROCEDURE:

Blend all ingredients except seafood until smooth. Stir in seafood and chill several hours or overnight. Serve on miniature rye or pumpernickel bread. Garnish with green onions.

Laurie Marcus

Danish Herring

Serves 10

INGREDIENTS:

6 herrings in brine
½ cup sugar
½ cup oil
1 teaspoon mustard powder
1 cup vinegar

¼ teaspoon pepper
1 6-ounce can tomato paste
1 cup onion, chopped
1 cup apple, chopped

PROCEDURE:

Skin and bone herring. Cover with equal parts water and milk. Refrigerate for 24 hours. Drain and slice herring into ¼" strips. Combine all remaining ingredients, add the herring slices and marinate overnight. Serve cold.

Jan Borkum

French Stuffed Eggs

Serves 6

INGREDIENTS:

6 eggs, hard boiled
½ cup cooked shrimp, diced
3 tablespoons mayonnaise
½ teaspoon salt
dash of pepper

dash of Tabasco sauce
6 crisp lettuce leaves
parsley (for garnish)

PROCEDURE:

Slice eggs in half lengthwise, remove yolks. Mash yolks of 4 eggs and combine with shrimp, mayonnaise and seasonings. Refill egg whites mixture and arrange on lettuce leaves on serving platter. Force remaining yolks through a fine sieve, sprinkle over eggs. Garnish with parsley.

Julie Teel Regan

Super Nachos

Serves 10-15

INGREDIENTS:

½ pound lean ground beef
½ pound chorizo sausage
1 large onion, chopped
salt to taste
Tabasco sauce to taste
2 16-ounce cans refried beans
1 4-ounce can whole green chiles,
  seeded
3 cups Monterey jack cheese,
  shredded

¾ cup prepared taco sauce
¼ cup green onions, chopped
1 cup ripe olives, sliced
1 ripe avocado, mashed
  (or guacamole)
1 cup sour cream
red pickled pepper to taste
fresh cilantro to taste
8 cups tortilla chips

PROCEDURE:

Preheat oven to 400°. Crumble and brown meats with onion. Discard fat, season with salt and Tabasco to taste. Spread beans in a shallow 10″ by 15″ baking dish. Cover evenly with browned meat. Sprinkle chiles on top, then cheese, and drizzle with taco sauce. (Cover and chill at this point if made in advance). Bake uncovered for 25 minutes. Quickly garnish with chopped onions and olives. Mound avocado in center, top with sour cream and sprinkle with pickled pepper and cilantro. Tuck tortilla chips all around edges to form a petaled flower effect and use to scoop up mixture.

Always a hit! If chorizo is not available at your local markets, substitute for another ½ pound of ground beef.

Kim Jenkins

Mexican Casserole

Serves 18-20

INGREDIENTS:

1 pound ground beef
1 30-ounce can spicy refried beans
1 4-ounce can whole green chiles, chopped
1 16-ounce can chile dip
1½ cups Monterey jack cheese, grated

1½ cups cheddar cheese, grated
sour cream (for garnish)
guacamole (for garnish)
sliced black olives (for garnish)

PROCEDURE:

Preheat oven to 350°. Brown and drain meat. In a 9″ by 12″ shallow casserole dish, layer beans, chiles, dip, meat, jack and cheddar cheese. Bake for 20 minutes. Garnish with sour cream, guacamole and sliced black olives. Serve with tortilla chips.

Michelle Benson

Chile Con Queso

Serves 12-15

INGREDIENTS:

1 large onion, minced
1 garlic clove, minced
4 tablespoons butter
1 13-ounce can tomatoes, chopped
1 14-ounce can peeled green chiles, rinsed of seeds and chopped

1 cup evaporated milk
2 tablespoons flour
salt to taste
Tabasco sauce to taste
½ pound cheddar (or Monterey jack cheese), diced

PROCEDURE:

Cook onion and garlic in 2 tablespoons butter until soft. Add tomatoes and simmer until thick (about 1 hour). Add chiles. Melt remaining butter. Add milk and flour. Stir over medium heat until smooth and thick. Combine this sauce with tomato mixture, season to taste. Just before serving, stir in cheese until melted. Serve warm from a chafing dish with chips for dipping.

Sherry Cook

Chile Con Chips

Serves 12

INGREDIENTS:

1 15-ounce can chile con carne
   without beans
1 4-ounce can green chiles,
   chopped

1 tablespoon chile powder
1 small can sliced ripe olives
8 ounces cream cheese

PROCEDURE:

Blend all ingredients over low heat. Serve warm with tortilla chips.

Quick and easy. Can be prepared ahead and reheated.

Judy Lewis

Tortilla Rings

Serves 4-6

INGREDIENTS:

8 ounces cream cheese, softened
2 tablespoons sour cream
garlic salt to taste
1 4-ounce can green chiles,
   chopped

1 tablespoon onion, chopped
alfalfa sprouts
1 large flour tortilla

PROCEDURE:

Blend together first 5 ingredients. Sprinkle sprouts on tortilla, spread with mixture, roll and chill. Cut into bite-size slices and garnish with more sprouts.

Cynthia Moyers

Mexican Layer Pie

Serves 8

INGREDIENTS:

2 avocadoes, mashed
Worcestershire sauce to taste
lemon juice to taste
⅛ teaspoon salt
1 cup sour cream

1 cup chile dip
3 tomatoes, seeded, chopped
  and drained
¼ cup onion, chopped
1½ cups cheddar cheese, grated

PROCEDURE:

Mix avocadoes, Worcestershire sauce, lemon juice and salt. Spread in a 9″ pie or quiche plate. Top with layer of sour cream, then chile dip. Sprinkle tomatoes, onions, and end with cheese. Cover and refrigerate until ready to serve. Use tortilla chips as dippers.

Pretty in a glass dish where you can see the layers.

Terry Cohler

Guacamole

Yields 2 cups

INGREDIENTS:

2-3 ripe avocadoes, mashed
salt to taste
2 tablespoons lemon juice
½ cup green onions, finely
  chopped

1 ripe tomato, peeled and diced
3 tablespoons green chiles,
  chopped
fresh cilantro to taste

PROCEDURE:

Combine avocadoes with salt and lemon juice. Stir in onions, tomato and chiles. Mix well. (Place avocado pits on top to prevent discoloring). Cover and chill. Garnish with cilantro and serve with tortilla chips.

Michelle Benson
Kim Jenkins

23

Shrimply Divine

Yields 1½ cups

INGREDIENTS:

3 ounces cream cheese, softened
1 cup sour cream
2 teaspoons lemon juice
½ 1⅝-ounce package Italian salad
  dressing mix

½ cup fresh cooked shrimp, finely
  chopped (add more to taste)

PROCEDURE:

Blend all ingredients thoroughly. Chill 2 hours or more before serving with
crackers.

Joyce Aftahi

Super Shrimp Dip

Serves 8-10

INGREDIENTS:

8 ounces cream cheese, softened
3 tablespoons chile sauce
½ teaspoon onion juice
½ cup mayonnaise

1 teaspoon lemon juice
¼ teaspoon Worcestershire sauce
4½ ounces tiny shrimp

PROCEDURE:

Beat cream cheese until smooth. Add chile sauce, onion juice, mayonnaise,
lemon juice and Worcestershire sauce. Fold in shrimp. Serve with toast points
or elegant crackers.

An absolute favorite!

Retta Dwyer

24

Fruit Of The Sea Dip

Serves 10-12

INGREDIENTS:

8 ounces cream cheese, softened
¼ cup mayonnaise
3 tablespoons milk
¼ teaspoon salt
¼ teaspoon bottled hot sauce

⅛ teaspoon garlic powder
dash of dill weed
¼ teaspoon lemon juice
1 cup crab or lobster (or ½ cup
   each)

PROCEDURE:

Combine all ingredients until smooth, adding seafood last. Chill well before serving.

Easy to make ahead.

Alice Sweeney

Clam Cave

Serves a group

INGREDIENTS:

2 sheepherder's bread, uncut
16 ounces cream cheese
3 6½-ounce cans minced clams,
   drain but save juice of one can

6 drops Tabasco sauce
2 teaspoons Worcestershire sauce
2 tablespoons lemon juice
2 tablespoons onion, grated

PROCEDURE:

Preheat oven to 225°. Carve out center of one bread, saving top. Cut other into bit-size pieces. Combine remaining ingredients over low heat until smooth. Pour into hollowed bread and cover. Wrap in foil, bake for 3-4 hours. Use bite-size bread pieces for dipping.

Be sure to eat bread bowl when dip is gone, it's the best part!

Cindy Small

25

Manhattan Clam Dip

Serves 6-8

INGREDIENTS:

8 ounces sour cream
¼ cup chile sauce
1 6½-ounce can minced clams,
  drained

¼ cup mayonnaise
1 tablespoon green onion,
  finely chopped
1 teaspoon lemon juice

PROCEDURE:

Combine, mix well and chill. Garnish as desired. Good with vegetables or water biscuits.

Andy Meyer

Hot Clam Dip

Serves a crowd

INGREDIENTS:

2 7½-ounce cans minced clams
  (drain and reserve juice)
2 teaspoons lemon juice
1 onion, chopped
1 green pepper, chopped
¼ cup parsley, chopped
¼ cup clam juice

¼ pound butter
1 tablespoon oregano
2 teaspoons Tabasco sauce
¼ teaspoon seasoned pepper
¾ cup seasoned bread crumbs
⅛ cup cheddar cheese, grated
⅛ cup Parmesan cheese, grated

PROCEDURE:

Preheat oven to 325°. Simmer drained clams with lemon juice. Blend (in blender or food processor) onion, pepper, parsley and clam juice. Add to clams with butter and oregano. After butter melts, stir in remaining ingredients except cheeses. Mix until oatmeal consistency. Transfer to ramekin, sprinkle with cheeses. Bake 15-20 minutes. Can be frozen, but bring to room temperature before baking. Serve with Triscuits.

A little work, but well worth the effort!

Carol Garcia

Tasty Veggies Dip

Serves 10-12

INGREDIENTS:

1 cup mayonnaise
1 egg, hard boiled and chopped
½ teaspoon ginger
1 garlic clove, minced
½ teaspoon salt

2 tablespoons scallions (or shallots), finely chopped
2 tablespoons lemon juice
1 teaspoon curry

PROCEDURE:

Combine all ingredients. Chill and surround with crisp, colorful vegetables.

Jackie Hassler

Not-A-Drip Dip

Serves 10-12

INGREDIENTS:

½ cup mayonnaise
12 ounces cream cheese, softened
½ cup parsley, chopped
2 eggs, hard boiled and chopped

2 tablespoons onion, chopped
1 garlic clove, minced
1 tablespoon anchovy paste
pepper to taste

PROCEDURE:

Combine all ingredients. Serve with fresh vegetables of your choice or use to fill celery.

Karen Stewart

Dilly Dip

Serves 10-12

INGREDIENTS:

1 cup sour cream
1 cup mayonnaise
½-1 tablespoon dill weed

1 tablespoon instant onion flakes
1 teaspoon dry parsley
1 teaspoon Beau Monde seasoning

PROCEDURE:

Blend together. Refrigerate overnight to bring out flavor.

Super!

Estelle Graff

Cheese Dunking Bowl

Serves a crowd

INGREDIENTS:

1 cup half and half
12 ounces creamed cottage cheese
Tabasco sauce to taste

1 teaspoon onion powder
3 ounces cream cheese, cubed
½ pound cheddar cheese, cubed

PROCEDURE:

At high speed, blend cream, cottage cheese and seasonings. Slowly add small amounts of cheddar and cream cheese until thick and creamy. Chill and serve with crisp raw vegetables and/or sliced apples.

Any leftovers are great over baked potatoes!

Paula Russell

Always Popular Bacon Dip

Yields 3 cups

INGREDIENTS:

1½ cups creamed cottage cheese,
  sieved
1 cup sour cream
horseradish to taste
¼ teaspoon garlic salt

dash of cayenne pepper
3 tablespoons green onion,
  chopped
6 slices bacon, crisply cooked and
  crumbled

PROCEDURE:

Blend all ingredients, adding onion and bacon last.

Nice, easy, quick and delicious!

Patricia Hasse

Spinach Bowl

Serves 20

INGREDIENTS:

1 2¾-ounce box Knorr vegetable
  soup mix
1 10-ounce package frozen
  spinach, thawed, drained and
  squeezed
1 cup sour cream (or plain yogurt)

1 cup mayonnaise
1 cup water chestnuts, drained
  and chopped
2 green onions, chopped
chopped pimientos (optional)

PROCEDURE:

Blend all ingredients well. Chill for at least 4 hours, or up to 24 hours.
Serve in a hollowed out sheepherder's bread bowl or artichoke shell.
Also great with cubed bread, vegetables or crackers.

Margi Bingham
DiAnn Hjermstad
Peggy Turley

29

Notes

2

Soups & Sandwiches

Tomato And Yogurt Soup

Serves 4-6

INGREDIENTS:

2 tablespoons butter
2 cups onion, chopped
2 cups cucumber, peeled
and chopped
3 cups tomatoes, peeled
and chopped

3 basil leaves (or 1 teaspoon dried)
2 cups chicken broth
2 cups yogurt
salt to taste
1 teaspoon mint

PROCEDURE:

Melt butter in large pan. Sauté onion for 10 minutes, but do not brown. Add cucumbers, tomatoes, basil and broth. Cook for 30 minutes, stirring often. Blend yogurt and salt. Add to soup. Purée all in blender or food processor. Chill. Garnish with mint.

Carol Garcia

Artichoke Heart Soup

Serves 6

INGREDIENTS:

2 8½-ounce cans water-packed
artichoke hearts, drained
2 10¾-ounce cans chicken broth
salt to taste

4 tablespoons fresh parsley, minced
1 cup heavy cream
¾ cup Chablis
6 lemon slices

PROCEDURE:

Combine artichoke hearts and broth, bit by bit, in blender. Purée until almost smooth but still slightly coarse. Pour into pan. Add salt to taste and parsley. Heat until very hot. Add cream. Do not boil! Remove from heat. Add Chablis. Serve with floating lemon slice.

Prepare a day ahead. Chill and slowly reheat just before serving. Always a hit!

Nancy Lischke

31

Avocado And Crab Soup

Serves 4-6

INGREDIENTS:

¼ cup flour
4¼ cups chicken broth
6-8 ounces crab (fresh, frozen
   or canned)
2 avocadoes, peeled and puréed

½ cup half and half
1 teaspoon dill weed
1 teaspoon oregano
1 tablespoon chives, chopped

PROCEDURE:

Blend flour with ¼ cup broth. Add remaining broth and bring to a boil, stirring constantly. Simmer until slightly thickened. Remove from heat. Add crab, avocadoes and half and half. Chill. Combine dill, oregano and chives. Sprinkle as garnish.

Wonderful with a splash of lemon!

Naomi Kurtz

Cascadilla

Serves 4-6

INGREDIENTS:

1 cucumber, chopped
1 scallion, chopped
1 garlic clove, crushed
1 tablespoon honey
½ teaspoon dill weed
salt to taste
pepper to taste

4 cups tomato juice (or V-8)
1 cup yogurt (or sour cream)
1 sweet pepper, chopped
6-8 fresh mushrooms, cleaned
   and thinly sliced
croutons (optional)

PROCEDURE:

Combine all ingredients. Chill. Serve with croutons.

Perfect with warm French bread.

Laura Galinson

Cold Cucumber Soup

Serves 4

INGREDIENTS:

2 cucumbers, peeled
1 cup sour cream
1 can consommé madrilène,
  chilled

dash of onion juice
salt to taste
pepper to taste
thyme (or marjoram) to taste

PROCEDURE:

Purée cucumbers. Add remaining ingredients. Mix well. (If chilled consommé won't mix easily, place in blender with sour cream). Chill.

Cool and light. Easy and delicious. Keeps for several days, too.

Catherine van Sonnenberg

Gazpacho

Serves 6-8

INGREDIENTS:

1 garlic clove
1 medium onion, chopped
1 cucumber, chopped
3 tomatoes, peeled and chopped
1 green pepper, seeded
  and chopped
4 eggs
⅛ teaspoon salt
⅛ teaspoon cayenne pepper
¼ cup vinegar

¼ cup olive oil
¾ cup tomato juice
GARNISH
1 cup bread cubes
2 tablespoons olive oil
1 garlic clove, minced
1 cucumber, diced
1 onion, chopped
1 green pepper, chopped

PROCEDURE:

Purée garlic, onion, cucumber, tomatoes, pepper and eggs. Mix in salt, cayenne, vinegar, oil and tomato juice. Chill. Brown bread cubes in oil with garlic. Sprinkle soup with croutons, diced cucumber, onion and pepper just before serving. Serve ice cold in chilled bowls.

So easy and hearty. A light and refreshing summer dinner with your favorite crusty bread. Try a dash of red pepper for extra kick!

Catherine van Sonnenberg

33

Iced Avgolemono

INGREDIENTS:

3 cups canned, condensed
    chicken broth
3 cups water
⅓ cup rice
1 teaspoon salt (optional)

3 egg yolks
⅓ cup fresh lemon juice
½ teaspoon MSG (optional)
lemon wedges
snipped pimiento

PROCEDURE:

Bring broth, water, rice and salt to a boil in a large pot. Reduce heat, cover and simmer until rice is cooked (approximately 20 minutes). Remove from heat. Beat yolks lightly. Add lemon juice and MSG. Slowly whisk in 2 cups hot broth. Gradually pour egg mixture back into soup. Return to heat and cook, stirring constantly, until steaming. Do not boil. Cool. Refrigerate at least 4 hours. Serve in chilled bowls garnished with lemon and snipped pimiento.

For a delicious sauce over meats, fish or vegetables, simply reduce broth and water to 1½ cups each, strain to remove rice and then proceed as above.

Judie Dresser

Ice Box Soup

Serves 6-8

INGREDIENTS:

1 32-ounce can tomatoes, chopped
1 46-ounce can tomato juice
½ green pepper, sliced
½ cup celery, finely sliced
½ cup cucumber, finely sliced
½ onion, thinly sliced

3 tablespoons olive oil
juice of ½ lemon
2 limes, sliced
salt to taste
pepper to taste
Worcestershire sauce to taste

PROCEDURE:

Mix all ingredients by hand. Refrigerate for 12-24 hours.

Linda Morefield

Creamy Broccoli Soup

Serves 4

INGREDIENTS:

1 10¾-ounce can chicken broth
1 9-ounce package frozen broccoli
1 teaspoon onion, minced
1 teaspoon nutmeg (or curry)

1 tablespoon butter
1 10¾-ounce can cream
 of mushroom soup
1 cup sour cream

PROCEDURE:

Combine broth, broccoli, onion, nutmeg and butter in saucepan. Simmer for 5 minutes. Cool slightly. Purée in blender (or processor) and add mushroom soup and sour cream. May be served well-chilled or hot. (Do not boil while reheating).

Helen Russell

Creamed Broccoli Mushroom Soup

Serves 4-6

INGREDIENTS:

3 large spears fresh broccoli,
 peeled and chopped
3 tablespoons onion, chopped
2 teaspoons instant chicken
 bouillon in 1½ cups water
¼ pound fresh mushrooms,
 cleaned and sliced

3 tablespoons butter
 (or margarine)
2 tablespoons flour
1½ cups milk
1 cup sour cream
fresh parsley, chopped

PROCEDURE:

Combine broccoli, onion and stock in medium pan. Cover. Simmer 15 minutes or until broccoli is tender. Cool. Melt butter in medium skillet over medium heat. Stir in mushrooms and cook until soft (about 3 minutes). Stir in flour, cooking to brown. Add milk in slow, steady stream, stirring and cooking until smooth and thick. Add mushroom mixture to cooled broccoli stock. Purée in blender or processor (steel blade) in small batches. Heat in Dutch oven over low to medium heat. Add sour cream, salt and pepper. Heat to steaming. Garnish with parsley.

This is a thick, rich, tasty and filling soup. Double the recipe and freeze some for quick lunches.

Brooke Peterson

Fresh Carrot Soup

Serves 4-6

INGREDIENTS:

6 tablespoons butter
  (or margarine)
½ cup onion, chopped
2 cups carrots, thinly sliced
1 teaspoon salt

3 chicken bouillon cubes
2 cups water
¼ cup uncooked rice
2 cups milk

PROCEDURE:

Melt butter in pan. Lightly brown onion. Add carrots and salt; toss to coat with butter. Cook, lightly covered, over low heat for 20 minutes. Stir occasionally. Add bouillon cubes, water and rice. Cover. Simmer 45 minutes, stirring occasionally. Cool slightly and purée until smooth. Return to pan, add milk and heat through. Serve hot.

Uva Márquez Sterling

Creamy Cauliflower Soup

Serves 4-6

INGREDIENTS:

1 small cauliflower head
1 large leek (white part only)
2 tablespoons butter
2 tablespoons flour

3½ cups boiling water
salt to taste
pepper to taste
½ cup heavy cream
1 cup croutons

PROCEDURE:

Break cauliflower into florets. Drop into boiling water for 1 minute. Drain immediately and rinse in ice water. Wash leek and slice into small rounds. Melt butter. Sauté leek until soft and golden. Add flour. Mix well and cook a few minutes. Slowly add boiling water, mixing thoroughly with wire whisk to avoid lumps. Add cauliflower, season to taste and simmer 20 minutes. Purée soup in blender (or processor). Stir in cream and adjust seasonings. Top with croutons.

Perfect for a cold winter's day or "apres ski."

Janine Ryder

White Corn Chowder

Serves 6-8

INGREDIENTS:

6-8 ears white corn
pale green interior husk of all ears
4 tablespoons butter
1 medium onion, diced
¾-1½ teaspoons salt (or to taste)
4 tablespoons flour
fresh ground white pepper to taste

3-4 cups corn stock
3 cups heavy cream
¼ teaspoon cayenne pepper
    to taste
¼ teaspoon sugar to taste
1 red bell pepper, roasted
1 yellow pepper, roasted
cilantro (for garnish)

PROCEDURE:

Fill a pot, just large enough to hold corn and husks, with water and bring to boil. Add corn and husks. Remove corn after one minute. Continue to cook husks for ½ hour at slow boil. Discard husk, cool stock. Refrigerate or freeze until needed. When corn is cool, remove kernels and reserve. (They may be frozen up to six months). Melt butter in 3 or 4 quart pan. Add onion, sauté until golden. Add salt and pepper. Mix in flour. Cook roux for 2 or 3 minutes. Add stock. Bring to boil. Boil 5 minutes. Simmer for 30 minutes, add cream and simmer 30 more minutes. Season with cayenne, sugar and more salt. Before serving bring to a simmer, add corn kernels and cook 15 minutes or until hot. Thin soup if necessary with small spoonfuls of cream. Garnish with pepper strips and cilantro leaves. To roast peppers: place on heavy foil in upper middle of oven. Broil, turning as each side is charred. When entirely charred, place in plastic bag. Seal. Let rest 15 minutes. Peel, seed, remove ribs and cut in fine strips. Cilantro leaves: wash cilantro, roll in paper towels. Refrigerate until needed. Use 5 leaves or so to garnish.

Lyn Heller

Cream Of Mushroom Soup

Serves 8

INGREDIENTS:

¾ pound mushrooms
¼ cup butter
4 tablespoons flour
3 13¾-ounce cans chicken broth
   (5 cups)

2 cups heavy cream
salt to taste
white pepper (optional)

PROCEDURE:

Clean mushrooms. Trim stems. Reserve one mushroom, sliced, for garnish. Chop remainder coarsely. Heat butter in 3-quart pan. Sauté mushrooms for 5 minutes. Sprinkle with flour. Add broth gradually, stirring constantly. Bring to a boil. Remove from heat. Stir in cream. Whirl in blender, add salt and pepper to taste; reheat but do not boil.

Can be prepared a day ahead. Easy to make and very flavorful.

Emma Van Campen

Creamy Mushroom Soup

Serves 12

INGREDIENTS:

1 pound fresh mushrooms,
   cleaned
½ cup onions, chopped
1 teaspoon Beau Monde seasoning
1 teaspoon salt
6 cups chicken stock

½ pound butter (not margarine)
1 cup flour
1 quart heavy cream, warm
¾ cup Chablis
small whole mushrooms
or parsley (optional)

PROCEDURE:

Purée mushrooms, onions, Beau Monde, salt and stock to a paste. Set aside. Melt butter, add flour and mix to a roux. Slowly add cream, stirring constantly. Cook and stir 5 minutes. Add puréed ingredients, wine and more salt if desired. Cover. Simmer 20 minutes. Garnish with sautéed mushrooms or fresh parsley.

This can be made ahead and frozen. To serve: thaw completely, heat on low but do not boil.

Suzie Desmarais

Mushroom Bisque

Serves 4

INGREDIENTS:

¼ cup butter
2 tablespoons green onions, chopped
¼ teaspoon dry mustard
¼ teaspoon salt
¼ cup flour, sifted
2 cups half and half

1 4¼-ounce can shrimp, deveined (or fresh)
1 8-ounce can mushrooms, drained and sliced
1 egg yolk
1 tablespoon dry sherry

PROCEDURE:

Cook onion in butter until soft. Blend in mustard, salt and flour. Slowly stir in half and half. Cook and stir until boiling and thickened. Add shrimp and mushrooms. Beat egg yolk with sherry. Stir a little hot soup mix into egg, then return egg mix to pot of soup. Heat slowly until hot.

Yummy!

Rhonda Read

Onion Soup

Serves 6

INGREDIENTS:

6 large yellow onions, thinly sliced
4 tablespoons butter
1 teaspoon sugar
1 tablespoon flour
⅓ cup Chablis
1 quart beef stock (or 2 cans consommé and 2 cans water)

6 slices French bread
2 cups Swiss cheese, grated
½ cup fresh Parmesan cheese, grated
Worcestershire sauce (optional)

PROCEDURE:

Melt butter in heavy-bottomed pan. Slowly brown onions. Add sugar. Cook until onions are dark brown, about 30 minutes. Occasionally scrape brown crust from bottom of pan, using wooden spoon. Add flour. Cook and stir 2 or 3 minutes. Add wine, dash of Worcestershire sauce and cook 2-3 minutes. Add stock. Simmer, partially covered, 1 hour.

To serve: Heat oven to 350°. Ladle soup into bowls or casseroles. Cover with bread, generous amounts of Swiss and a sprinkling of Parmesan. Bake covered for 15 minutes. Uncover, bake 10 more minutes.

A good, full-bodied beef stock can make this classic truly remarkable.

Ann Poovey

Hearty Beef Stock

2-3 quarts

INGREDIENTS:

4 pounds meaty beef bones
(shank, neckbones, etc.)
⅓ cup vegetable oil
4 cups yellow onions,
finely chopped
2 leeks (white part only), sliced
8 carrots, peeled and chopped
1 parsnip, peeled and chopped

1½ tablespoons dried thyme
4 bay leaves
6 whole cloves
12 black peppercorns
6 parsley sprigs
1 tablespoon salt
1 6-ounce can tomato paste
water, as needed

PROCEDURE:

Preheat oven to 400°. Spread beef bones in a single layer in a baking pan. Bake for 1½ hours. Meats should be very brown. Turn pieces occasionally and drain rendered fat as necessary. Heat the oil in a large pot. Add the onions, leeks, carrots and parsnip and cook over high heat, stirring often, until well browned, about 25 minutes. Add bones to the vegetables, along with remaining ingredients. Deglaze baking pan in which bones were browned by pouring 1 cup water into the pan and set it over high heat. Stir and scrape up any carmelized particles from the bottom and sides. Pour this liquid into the pot with the vegetables and bones. Add additional water to cover all ingredients well and set pot over medium heat. When the stock reaches a boil, skim, reduce heat so liquid simmers, partially cover, and simmer 4 hours. Skim occasionally. Strain out and discard the solids, and chill stock. Before using chilled stock, or before freezing same, remove any fat that has solidified on top.

Helen Mayer

Pumpkin Soup

Serves 4-6

INGREDIENTS:

3 tablespoons melted butter
¼ cup green onions, chopped
2 cups pumpkin (canned or fresh)
1 10¾-ounce can chicken broth

½ teaspoon salt
⅛ teaspoon pepper
1 fresh tomato, peeled and diced
1 cup half and half

PROCEDURE:

Melt butter. Sauté onions until soft. Add pumpkin, broth, salt, pepper and tomato. Heat through until steaming, but not boiling. Beat for 15 minutes with electric beater. Stir in half and half. Serve hot.
If using fresh pumpkin, cut in half to scoop out seeds and all stringy flesh. Preheat oven to 350°. Place halves, cut side up, on baking sheet covering and sealing each half with foil. Bake until flesh is very tender, about 1½ hours. Scoop out flesh and purée in processor or mash with potato masher.

A great way to use "ye old jack o' lantern" before he spoils.

Kathy Burns

Arizona Mountain Soup

Serves 12

INGREDIENTS:

3 cups cooked pinto beans
1 cup garbanzo beans
1 or 2 cups cooked rice
3 large tomatoes, skinned
  and diced
1 pound bacon, diced

3 small onions, sliced
2 garlic cloves, peeled
  and chopped
½ teaspoon paprika
¼ teaspoon pepper
4 cups water or stock

PROCEDURE:

In large, heavy pot, combine beans, rice and tomatoes. Fry bacon, onion and garlic. Add to bean mixture, including bacon drippings. Add seasonings and 2 cups liquid. Simmer, covered, for several hours. Stir occasionally. Add liquid as needed.

This is a very hearty soup, an excellent winter dish or after skiing warm-up.

Viviane Pratt

Tuscan Tomato Soup

Serves 6

INGREDIENTS:

2 tablespoons unsalted butter
¼ cup olive oil
2 carrots, peeled and minced
¼ cup onion, chopped
¼ cup celery, chopped
10 large tomatoes, skinned and seeded (or 2 quarts canned)

pinch of sugar
½ cup fresh basil leaves, chopped
salt to taste
pepper to taste
Parmesan cheese, freshly grated (optional)
croutons (optional)

PROCEDURE:

Heat butter and oil in large, heavy pot. Add carrots, celery and onion. Cook on medium-low for 20 minutes, until soft. Do not brown. Add tomatoes, sugar and half the basil. Cook 15-20 minutes. Stir in remaining basil, season with salt and pepper. Serve immediately. Garnish with cheese and croutons. (Sauté French bread cubes in olive oil with garlic clove until brown and crusty).

Kathy Glick

Cream Of Tomato Soup

Serves 4-6

INGREDIENTS:

2 pounds very ripe tomatoes, peeled and halved
1 ounce butter
2 onions, sliced
1 large carrot, peeled and sliced
1 tablespoon flour, rounded
1½ pints light chicken stock
bouquet garni
coarse salt to taste
black pepper to taste
sugar to taste
1 tablespoon cornstarch
light cream (optional)
chives (optional)

PROCEDURE:

Squeeze tomatoes over strainer to remove seeds. Discard seeds, save juice. Melt butter, add onions and carrot. Cook gently until just golden. Remove from heat. Stir in flour. Add tomatoes, juice and stock. Bring to boil, add bouquet garni, salt, pepper and sugar. Simmer, covered, 30 minutes. Remove bouquet garni. Purée soup and return to rinsed pan. Bring to boil, add cornstarch, which has been slaked with a little cold water, and stir quickly with wooden spoon. One tablespoon light cream may be stirred into each bowl. Garnish with snipped chives.

To make bouquet garni: take cheesecloth, place 1 teaspoon each of dried thyme, marjoram and basil, 1 crumbled bay leaf and 5 black peppercorns in center. Tie closed. Drop into soup.

Helen Mayer

Chicken Soup

Serves 12

INGREDIENTS:

1 3½-4 pound chicken, cleaned
12 cups cold water
2 onions, quartered
2 carrots, scraped
1 parsnip, scraped and sliced
1 leek (white part only), sliced
2 celery stalks, sliced

4-5 sprigs fresh parsley
coarse salt to taste
black pepper to taste
1 tablespoon dried thyme
1 tablespoon dried marjoram
1 tablespoon dried basil

PROCEDURE:

Place chicken and water in large stainless or enamel pot. Bring to boil on high. When boiling, skim scum with large spoon. Skim until water is clear. Add vegetables, spices and herbs. Simmer on lowest possible heat, tightly covered, 3-4 hours. Cool slightly. Strain into glass, glazed ceramic or stainless container. Discard chicken and vegetables. Cool. Cover tightly and refrigerate overnight. Remove fat from surface. Freeze or heat and serve.

Use fresh vegetables for best results. This soup is wonderful plain or with steamed julienne vegetables or fine noodles floating in it.

Helen Mayer

Clam Chowder

Serves 15

INGREDIENTS:

1 pound bacon, finely diced
2 onions, finely diced
4 or 5 medium potatoes, diced
3 cups boiling water
1 cup canned tomatoes
3 pounds canned clams, minced
  or whole

3 cups clam juice
1 pint half and half
1 teaspoon salt
1 teaspoon celery salt
pinch of pepper
dash of Tabasco sauce
2 teaspoons butter

PROCEDURE:

In large pan, fry bacon. Remove bacon, drain and reserve drippings. Cook onion in drippings until transparent. Do not brown. Add potatoes, boiling water and tomatoes. Bring to boil, reduce heat, cover and cook until potatoes are tender, about 10 minutes. Drain clams. Reserve liquid. Add milk if necessary to make 3 cups. Stir into potatoes. Heat slowly to boiling. Add clams, bacon, cream and seasonings. Heat thoroughly. Season to taste.

Beth Dowding

Spicy Clam Soup

Serves 4

INGREDIENTS:

¼ cup olive oil
1 pound hot Italian sausage
  (remove casings)
1 pound mushrooms, coarsely
  chopped
2 medium onions, thinly sliced
1 28-ounce can tomatoes
  (undrained), chopped

1 cup dry white wine
1 cup clam juice
2 teaspoons dried basil
½ tablespoon fresh garlic, minced
1¼ cups fresh parsley, chopped
2-3 dozen clams, scrubbed

PROCEDURE:

Heat oil in large, heavy pan over medium heat. Add sausage, mushrooms and onion. Cook, break up sausage and stir frequently until meat loses pink color (about 12 minutes). Stir in tomatoes. Bring to a boil. Reduce heat to low. Simmer 5 minutes. Add wine and clam juice. Heat to boiling. Cover, simmer on low for 20 minutes stirring occasionally. Add basil and garlic. Cook 5 minutes. (May be covered and refrigerated at this point, for one day). Before serving, bring to a boil, add 1 cup parsley and clams. Reduce heat to medium-high. Cover. Simmer 10 minutes or until clams open. Discard any unopened clams. Ladle soup into bowls; garnish with parsley.

Di Ann Hjermstad

Crab Bisque

Serves 8-12

INGREDIENTS:

2 10¾-ounce cans pea soup
2 10¾-ounce cans beef consomme
2 10¾-ounce cans tomato soup
1 pint whipping cream

1 pound cooked crab (fresh
  or frozen)
sherry to taste

PROCEDURE:

Combine soups in pan over low heat. Stir in cream then crab. Add sherry to taste. Do not boil. Stir and serve.

This soup has an interesting texture. It can be frozen and reheated.

Bobbi Susselman

Baked Minestrone Soup

Serves 12

INGREDIENTS:

2 pounds beef stew, cubed small
1 large onion, sliced
2 tablespoons oil
1 cup water
1 cup carrots, sliced
1 cup celery, sliced
1 cup zucchini, sliced
1 small green pepper, in strips
3 16-ounce cans stewed tomatoes
3 cups cabbage, shredded

½ teaspoon salt
½ teaspoon sugar
½ teaspoon rosemary
½ teaspoon basil
½ teaspoon thyme
¼ teaspoon pepper
3 14-ounce cans beef broth
3 cups cooked (6 ounces dry)
   shell macaroni
Parmesan cheese (for garnish)

PROCEDURE:

Preheat oven to 400°. Place beef, onion and oil in large casserole or Dutch oven. Bake, uncovered, for 40 minutes stirring occasionally. Add water. Cover. Reduce heat to 350°. Bake for 1 hour. Add vegetables, seasonings and broth. Cover. Bake for 1½ hours. Stir in macaroni just before serving. Garnish with Parmesan.

Elizabeth Wheelock

Pasta And Sausage Soup

Serves 8-12

INGREDIENTS:

1½ pounds hot or sweet Italian
  sausage
¼ cup water
3 medium green peppers, cut into
  ¼″ strips
2 medium onions, chopped
1 small garlic clove, minced

1 28-ounce can tomatoes
1 8-ounce bag bowtie macaroni
1 tablespoon Worcestershire sauce
2 chicken bouillon cubes
  (or envelopes)
6 cups water

PROCEDURE:

Bring sausage and water to a boil in 5-quart pan. Cover. Simmer 5 minutes.
Uncover. Cook, turning sausages frequently, until water evaporates and
sausages are well browned, about 20 minutes. Drain sausage on paper towels
and cut into ¼″ slices. Sauté peppers, onions and garlic in pan drippings
until tender, stirring occasionally. Add sausage, tomatoes and liquid,
macaroni, sugar, Worcestershire, bouillon cubes and water. Bring to a boil.
Reduce to low, cover and simmer 25 minutes. Stir occasionally. Skim off
any fat.

*This soup, a fresh green salad, garlic bread and spumoni for dessert
constitute one of our family's preferred menus!*

Janice Przonek

Hodge Podge Soup

Serves 8

INGREDIENTS:

2 pounds lean ground beef,
    browned and drained
¾ cup onion, chopped
1½ cups celery, chopped
½ teaspoon garlic powder

3 10¾-ounce cans minestrone soup
1 8-ounce can baked beans
1 tablespoon Worcestershire sauce
½ teaspoon dried oregano
3 cups water

PROCEDURE:

Combine all ingredients. Cover. Simmer slowly about an hour.

Always popular with youngsters!

Judith Rosenberg

Split Pea Soup

Serves 6-8

INGREDIENTS:

1 16-ounce bag split peas
2 quarts cold water
1 large ham bone
½ cup onion, chopped
½ cup carrots, grated
1 cup potatoes, finely chopped

½ cup celery, chopped
2 tablespoons wine vinegar
2 tablespoons sugar
salt to taste
pepper to taste

PROCEDURE:

Soak peas overnight in water to cover. Rinse. Combine 2 quarts water, peas and ham. Simmer 2 hours. Remove bone, leaving any ham pieces. Add onion, carrots, potatoes and celery. Simmer until tender, 15-20 minutes. Remove from heat, add vinegar, sugar, salt and pepper. Serve piping hot.

Irene Kasmarik

49

Lentil Soup

Serves 4-6

INGREDIENTS:

¼ cup cooking oil
3 cups cooked ham, diced
¾ pound sweet Polish sausage,
  sliced
2 large onions, chopped
1 garlic clove, crushed
2 cups celery with leaves, chopped

2 large tomatoes, peeled and cut
  in wedges
1 16-ounce package lentils
4 cups water
½ teaspoon Tabasco sauce
1½ teaspoons salt
1 9-ounce package frozen
  chopped spinach, thawed

PROCEDURE:

In large kettle, heat oil. Add ham, sausage, onion and garlic. Cook 5 minutes. Add celery, tomatoes, lentils, water, Tabasco and salt. Cover. Simmer for 2 hours. Add spinach. Cook 10 more minutes.

Good with pumpernickel bread. Freezes well. A nutritious meal in itself!

Karen Stewart

Crab Sandwiches

Serves 6

INGREDIENTS:

1 tablespoon butter
1 tablespoon flour
pinch of salt
¼ cup (scant) half and half

¼ cup sauterne
1 egg, beaten
1 cup cheese, grated
½ pound crab (fresh or frozen)

PROCEDURE:

Melt butter. Add flour and salt. Cook for 1 minute. Stir in half and half and wine. Thicken over medium heat. Add egg and cheese. Heat on low until cheese melts, then add crab. Serve as hot, open-faced or cold, filled sandwiches.

Helen Russel

Hot Beef Sandwiches

Serves 4-6

INGREDIENTS:

1 pound or more chuck roast
¼ cup onions, sliced
¼ cup celery, diced
¼ cup green pepper, diced

water to cover
salt to taste
pepper to taste

PROCEDURE:

Combine all ingredients in pan. Simmer on low until meat shreds, about 2-3 hours. Skim fat. Serve on Italian rolls with hot peppers on the side, or potato rolls or bakery egg buns.

Leftover pot roast can be used, just shorten cooking time. Good with potato salad. Also makes tasty burritos.

Agnes Burns

Super Bowl Beef Treats

Yields 70

INGREDIENTS:

1 pound ground chuck
1 pound ground pork sausage
1 teaspoon oregano
1 teaspoon basil

¼ teaspoon garlic salt
1 pound Velveeta cheese
2 loaves cocktail rye
    bread (about 70 slices)

PROCEDURE:

Fry beef with sausage until no longer pink. Drain grease. Add spices and cheese. Heat until cheese melts. Mound on rye slices. Place on cookie sheet. Broil 3 minutes or until hot and bubbly. To make ahead, freeze quickly on cookie sheet. Remove. Double bag in freezer bags and refreeze. Before serving, heat on cookie sheet in 350° oven 8-10 minutes until bubbly. No need to thaw!

Great to always have on hand for unexpected company. Very tasty "lifesavers".

Mary Helen Cahill

51

Reuben Miniatures

Yields 35

INGREDIENTS:

1 loaf party rye (35 slices)
1 8-ounce bottle Russian dressing
1 8-ounce can sauerkraut

35 small slices corned beef
35 small slices Swiss cheese

PROCEDURE:

Heat oven to 350°. Spread each slice of bread with dressing, 1 teaspoon sauerkraut, corned beef and Swiss cheese. Heat until cheese melts.

Debbie Prudden

Hot Tuna Rolls

Serves 6-8

INGREDIENTS:

⅓ cup mayonnaise
3 tablespoons sweet relish
1 tablespoon Dijon mustard
¼ teaspoon garlic powder
⅛ teaspoon black pepper, ground
1 6½-ounce can tuna, drained
1 cup cheddar cheese, shredded

¼ cup green pepper, chopped
¼ cup celery, chopped
¼ cup green onion, thinly sliced
3 tablespoons stuffed green olives, chopped
6-8 onion (or kaiser) rolls

PROCEDURE:

Preheat oven to 325°. Combine mayonnaise, relish, mustard, garlic and pepper. Mix well. Add tuna, cheese, green pepper, celery, onions and olives. Mix well. Split rolls in half. Spread equal amounts of tuna mix on bottoms of roll. Cover with tops. Wrap in foil. (Chill at this point if not used immediately). Bake for 20 minutes or until cheese melts and rolls are heated through. (Chilled rolls should bake 30-35 minutes).

Keep on hand for quick hot lunches.

Debbie Greenfield

Tuna Biscuits

Serves 2-3

INGREDIENTS:

1 6¾-ounce can tuna, drained and flaked
⅓ cup mayonnaise
¼ cup celery, diced

1 carrot, grated
2 tablespoons sweet relish
1 package refrigerator biscuits

PROCEDURE:

Preheat oven to 375°. Mix tuna, mayonnaise, celery, carrot and relish. Roll biscuits into flat circles on lightly floured surface. Spoon tuna mixture onto 5 circles and top with remaining 5. Press edges to seal. Bake for 20 minutes.

Great hot or cold. Keep a batch in your freezer and pop into oven as needed.

Julie Harris

Pork Turnovers

Serves 4-6

INGREDIENTS:

2 tablespoons butter
½ cup onion, finely chopped
½ cup green pepper, finely chopped
2 cups cooked pork, cubed
1 8-ounce jar applesauce

2 tablespoons prepared mustard
½ teaspoon ginger
½ teaspoon salt
12 refrigerator biscuits
1 egg
sesame seeds (optional)

PROCEDURE:

Heat oven to 400°. Melt butter in pan. Sauté onion and green pepper until tender. Stir in pork, applesauce, mustard, ginger and salt. Roll biscuits into 5" circles. Spread pork mixture on 6 biscuits, within ½" of edge. Top with remaining dough rounds. Press edges together, using fork tines. Brush with beaten egg, sprinkle with sesame seeds and bake 15 minutes.

My answer to the "what to do with those leftover porkchops" question.
Good alongside your favorite soup.
Gloria Andújar

53

Stuffed Buns

Yields 8

INGREDIENTS:

1 pound ground beef
½ pound cheddar cheese, grated
¼ cup black olives, sliced
2 tablespoons onion, grated
1½ cups tomato sauce

¼ teaspoon chile powder
salt to taste
pepper to taste
8 hot dog buns

PROCEDURE:

Preheat oven to 350°. Brown meat. Drain. Add remainder of ingredients and heat. Scoop out soft insides from buns. Stuff with filling. Wrap each in foil and bake for 20 minutes. Open foil to brown lightly.

For variety, try Italian, French or kaiser rolls.

Mary Stolberg

Olive Cheese Rolls

Yields 12

INGREDIENTS:

¼ cup oil
1 onion, finely chopped
1½ cups green pepper, finely
 chopped

1 pint green (or black) olives,
 chopped
3 hard boiled eggs, chopped
1 pound cheddar cheese, grated
12 French rolls

PROCEDURE:

Preheat oven to 350°. Heat oil in pan. Cook onions and pepper until tender. Add olives and eggs. Remove from heat. Add cheese, mix well. Slice rolls in half lengthwise. Remove some bread in center of roll to make a pocket. Fill with olive/cheese mixture and wrap in foil. Heat 15-20 minutes.

Those who like hot sauce can add a little to their rolls for a zestier taste.

Libby Clemmer

Sandwich Loaf

Serves 10-12

INGREDIENTS:

1 16-ounce loaf bread, unsliced
3 sandwich fillings (your
   favorites or see below)

2 8-ounce packages cream
   cheese, softened
⅓ cup cream

PROCEDURE:

Cut bread lengthwise into 4 slices. Place one slice on serving platter, spread with first filling. Repeat with second and third slices. Top with fourth slice. Mix cream cheese and cream until spreadable. Frost all sides of loaf like a cake. Chill 1 hour. Wrap in damp cloth and chill again several hours. To serve, remove cloth and slice.

SUGGESTED FILLINGS

   taramosalata or salmon mousse
   guacamole or mashed avocadoes with lemon juice
   liverwurst spread sprinkled with chopped green olives
   chicken liver pâté
   ham salad
   egg salad sprinkled with red or black caviar
   deviled ham

Gail Pfeifle

Notes

3

Meats

Steak Au Poivre Flambé

Serves 4

INGREDIENTS:

4 fillet steaks
2 tablespoons black (or green)
  peppercorns, crushed
2 ounces butter

½ cup cognac (or Armagnac)
1 cup crème fraîche (or
  heavy cream)
watercress (for garnish)

PROCEDURE:

Roll steaks in peppercorns and panfry in hot butter over moderately high heat to desired doneness. Transfer steaks to a heated platter and keep hot. Deglaze the pan juices with cognac; blaze. Blend in crème fraîche and cook quickly to reduce sauce by half. Pour over steaks, decorate with watercress and serve immediately.

Janine Ryder

Teriyaki Steak

Serves 4-6

INGREDIENTS:

MARINADE
¼ cup soy sauce
2 tablespoons salad oil
2 tablespoons (or more) honey
1 tablespoon wine vinegar

1 garlic clove, mashed
1 teaspoon fresh ginger, minced
  (or ½ teaspoon ground ginger)

1 large (2-3 pound) beef steak

PROCEDURE:

Combine all marinade ingredients, pour over steak and marinate for several hours. Remove from marinade and broil or charcoal broil to desired doneness.

Connie Galluzzi

57

Bœuf Barone

Serves 6-12

INGREDIENTS:

4-7 rib prime rib of beef, dressed
    (have butcher remove bones
    and tail, tie bones back
    onto meat)
onion juice (fresh or prepared)
1½-2-ounces dry mustard

salt to taste
freshly ground pepper to taste
4 8-ounce cans beef broth
28 ounces dry sherry (or ½ sweet,
    ½ dry)

PROCEDURE:

Bring meat to room temperature. Prick meat with a fork, rub liberally with onion juice and sprinkle with dry mustard to form a paste. Salt and generously pepper meat; let stand 30-45 minutes. Preheat oven to 450°. (Follow procedure to cook 7-rib roast medium-rare; for 4-rib roast reduce total cooking time 30-45 minutes, or use oven thermometer). Place meat in a large roasting pan and roast, fat side up, 1 hour. Mix broth with sherry and heat to boiling. Remove meat from oven; turn, fat side down, add broth mixture to pan, reduce heat to 375° and roast 1 hour. Turn again, fat side up, reduce heat to 350° and roast ¾-1 hour, basting once or twice. Remove meat for carving. Skim fat from broth, pour into a gravy boat and serve with sliced prime rib.

You may want to parboil new potatoes and carrots and add to pan last hour of cooking. Sensational prime rib!

Robert and Mary Barone

Fillet Strips

Serves 8

INGREDIENTS:

4 tablespoons butter
½ cup soy sauce
2 garlic cloves, crushed
2 tablespoons powdered ginger

4 tablespoons lemon juice
2 tablespoons sugar
2 beef fillet strips (about 2 pounds
    each)

PROCEDURE:

Mix together all ingredients except fillets and simmer until thick. Spread over meat and let stand for several hours. If refrigerated, bring meat and sauce to room temperature. Preheat oven to 350°. Place fillets in a shallow roasting pan, keeping them well spaced, and roast 45 minutes.

Nancy Knox

Pepper Steak

Serves 4

INGREDIENTS:

¼ cup soy sauce
1 tablespoon water
3½ teaspoons cornstarch
¼ teaspoon pepper
2 garlic cloves, crushed
1 pound lean flank steak
(or top round)

2½ cups green peppers, seeded and diced
2 tablespoons polyunsaturated oil
2 large tomatoes, cut in wedges (or canned tomatoes, broken up)
3 cups hot cooked rice

PROCEDURE:

Blend soy sauce, water, cornstarch, pepper and garlic in a medium-size bowl. Thinly slice steak diagonally across the grain; stir into soy sauce mixture. Sauté green peppers in heated oil in a large skillet, stirring until almost tender. Mix in drained meat, cook and stir about 5 minutes until meat loses its redness. Stir in tomatoes and soy sauce mixture and simmer until tender. Serve over hot cooked rice.

Joyce Aftahi

Good French Stew

Serves 6

INGREDIENTS:

2 pounds lean stewing beef, cubed
½ cup flour
1 teaspoon salt
1 teaspoon pepper
bacon drippings (or cooking oil)
1 garlic clove, chopped
1 large onion, chopped
2 cups consommé
1 cup red wine

1 bay leaf
peppercorns
small bunch parsley
small bunch celery leaves
12 small carrots, halved
12 (or more) pearl onions, peeled
¼-½ pound fresh mushrooms, sliced
sherry to taste

PROCEDURE:

Preheat oven to 325°. Dredge beef with a mixture of flour, salt and pepper. Brown in drippings with garlic and onion. Transfer to a casserole; add enough consommé and wine to cover. Tie bay leaf, peppercorns, parsley and celery leaves into a cheesecloth bag; drop in casserole, cover and bake 2 hours. Lightly sauté carrots and pearl onions in pan drippings, add to stew and bake 1½ hours. Discard cheesecloth bag. Sauté mushrooms in pan drippings and incorporate them into stew. Add sherry to taste.

Even better made a day ahead as stew ages so well.

Nancy Hatch

Barbecued Flank Steak

Serves 4-6

INGREDIENTS:

MARINADE
½ cup barbecue sauce
½ cup red wine
dash of Worcestershire sauce

dash of angostura bitters

1 2-3 pound flank steak (or eye round)

60

PROCEDURE:

Combine all marinade ingredients. Pour over steak, cover and refrigerate 24 hours. Remove from marinade, place on barbecue and grill to desired doneness. Slice diagonally across the grain and serve.

Elouise and Larry Potomac

Carne Asada Burritos

Serves 4

INGREDIENTS:

FILLING
2 pounds lean beef steak (sirloin, London broil)
1 large onion, sliced
1 10-ounce can tomatoes, undrained, chopped
1 4-ounce can diced green chiles, undrained
1 teaspoon garlic powder
1 teaspoon (or more) cumin powder
large flour tortillas

TOPPINGS
1 16-ounce can refried beans, heated
Monterey jack cheese, shredded
cheddar cheese, shredded
black olives, sliced (optional)
green chile salsa
iceberg lettuce, shredded
fresh tomatoes, chopped
green onions, chopped
diced green chiles, drained (optional)
guacamole or avocado slices
sour cream

PROCEDURE:

Slice steak thinly across the grain; pierce with a fork or pound with meat mallet. Combine with remaining filling ingredients, mix well and refrigerate 3 days in a tightly sealed container; pierce meat and stir occasionally. Stir-fry meat mixture quickly in a skillet over moderately high heat, adding a little water if mix is dry. Remove meat with slotted spoon. Warm a tortilla on a medium-hot, ungreased griddle or in a heavy skillet or microwave. Place scoop of meat on tortilla; if desired, add beans, cheese, olives and salsa. Roll up tortilla and heat thoroughly. Serve burrito with a scattering of toppings: lettuce, tomatoes, onions, cheeses, olives, chiles, guacamole and a dollop of sour cream. Pass salsa and refried beans.

A snap for a fast, hearty snack or meal — all the work's in the preparation.

Dona J. Nickel

Sherried Steak Casserole

Serves 6-8

INGREDIENTS:

½-1 pound fresh mushrooms, sliced
butter
3 pounds sirloin tip, trimmed, cut in bite-size pieces

2 10½-ounce cans cream of mushroom soup, undiluted
1 1⅜-ounce envelope dry onion soup mix
1 cup sherry

PROCEDURE:

Preheat oven to 325°. Sauté mushrooms in butter until lightly brown. Combine all ingredients in a large casserole, cover and bake 3 hours or until tender. Serve over steamed rice or noodles.

Goes great with a tossed green or vegetable salad. An easy make-ahead casserole especially good for parties. Do not freeze.

Nancy Amiel

Eggplant With Beef

Serves 12

INGREDIENTS:

2 medium-size eggplants, peeled, sliced ½″ thick
oil
4 medium white onions, sliced
1 tablespoon turmeric
1 teaspoon cinnamon

½ teaspoon saffron
5-6 pounds lean stewing beef (or rump roast), cut in 1½″ cubes
water
2 8-ounce cans tomato sauce

PROCEDURE:

Fry eggplant in oil over medium heat until browned on both sides, adding oil as needed. Set eggplant aside. Brown onions in 8 tablespoons oil in Dutch oven over medium/high heat, stirring often. Add seasonings, then beef. Brown very well on all sides. Add just enough water to cover; stir in tomato sauce, cover and simmer 1½ hours. Carefully place eggplant over meat, cover and simmer 1 more hour; skim off surface oil. Serve over white steamed rice.

A treasured Persian dish.

Housh Aftahi

Oven Beef Stew

Serves 15

INGREDIENTS:

¼-½ pound fresh mushrooms, sliced
butter
lemon juice
2½ pounds boneless stewing beef,
 cut in 1″ cubes
1 28-ounce can tomatoes,
 undrained, crushed
1 cup celery, coarsely chopped
4 medium carrots, sliced
3 medium potatoes, peeled and
 cubed
3 medium onions, chopped
2 cups beef bouillon

1 10-ounce package frozen peas
 (or green beans)
1 tablespoon salt
1 tablespoon sugar (optional)
freshly ground black pepper
 to taste
⅛ teaspoon ground thyme
⅛ teaspoon rosemary
⅛ teaspoon ground marjoram
¼ cup red wine
4-5 drops bottled brown bouquet
 sauce
1 10¼-ounce can brown gravy
3-4 tablespoons quick-cooking
 tapioca (or flour)

PROCEDURE:

Preheat oven to 250°. Sauté mushrooms in butter and lemon juice. Combine all ingredients in a 5-quart casserole, cover and simmer in oven 5 hours, stirring well after 3½ hours. If desired, thicken with tapioca and/or flour.

Serve with dumplings or a good, interesting bread.
More flavorful if made a day ahead. Freezes well.

Susan K. Bennett

Crocked Stew

Serves 20

INGREDIENTS:

2-3 carrots, very thinly sliced
2-3 potatoes, peeled or unpeeled, diced
1-2 onions, halved and thinly sliced
3-4 pounds rump roast, trimmed, cut in bite-size pieces
1 envelope brown gravy mix (or spaghetti sauce mix with mushrooms)
⅛ cup catsup

oregano to taste
parsley flakes to taste
pepper to taste
paprika to taste
  tarragon leaves to taste
Accent to taste
Lawry's seasoned salt to taste
3 cups dry Chablis (or white wine)
1 bay leaf
1 teaspoon Worcestershire sauce

PROCEDURE:

Place carrots in bottom of crock pot; add layer of potatoes, then onions and top with meat. Combine all remaining ingredients except bay leaf in a mixing bowl and blend well with portable mixer. Pour over meat, add bay leaf, cover and cook on low 8-12 hours, longer time recommended to insure doneness. Do not remove lid during cooking period; stir only when ready to serve. To cook on stovetop or in oven: cut meat and vegetables in larger chunks; brown beef if desired; combine all and cook about 3 hours or until tender, replenishing liquid as needed. If desired, thicken with flour-water paste.

Goes well with a tossed green salad and garlic bread. Equally good if made ahead and reheated. Freezes well.

Jerry K. Remmers

Bœuf Bourguignon

Serves 6

INGREDIENTS:

2½ pounds boneless stewing beef, cut in 1½" cubes
butter
3 tablespoons brandy
½ pound small white onions, peeled (about 12)
½ pound small fresh mushrooms
2½ tablespoons cornstarch
2-2½ teaspoons Bovril (or beef extract)

2 tablespoons tomato paste
1½ cups Burgundy
¾ cup dry sherry
¾ cup ruby port
1 10½-ounce can condensed beef broth, undiluted
⅛ teaspoon pepper
1 bay leaf
parsley (for garnish)

64

PROCEDURE:

Preheat oven to 350°. Brown beef well, about ¼ at a time, in 2 table-spoons hot butter in Dutch oven over moderately high heat; add butter as needed. Return all browned beef to pot. Heat 2 tablespoons brandy in small saucepan, ignite and pour over beef; remove meat to another pan. Sauté onions in 2 tablespoons butter in pot; cover and cook, stirring occasionally, over low heat until lightly browned. Add mushrooms; cook, stirring, 3 minutes. Remove vegetables with slotted spoon. Off heat, blend in corn-starch, Bovril and tomato paste; stir in Burgundy, sherry, port and broth and bring just to a boil. Add beef, vegetables, pepper, bay leaf and remain-ing tablespoon brandy and mix well. Transfer to oven, cover and cook 1½ hours, or until beef is fork tender, stirring occasionally. Garnish with parsley and serve.

Even better made a day ahead, refrigerated and reheated gently,
thinning with wine as needed.

Joyce Aftahi

Brisket Of Beef, Pot Roasted

Serves 6-8

INGREDIENTS:

1½ tablespoons peanut oil
1 3½-4 pound brisket of beef
½ cup water
8 medium onions, sliced
2 garlic cloves, slivered

2 tablespoons coarse salt
½ teaspoon black pepper (or more)
1 tablespoon sweet paprika
1 cup dark beer (optional)
  or water

PROCEDURE:

Heat oil in heavy pot over medium heat, add brisket and brown on both sides; remove to a platter. Deglaze pot with water, then stir in onions. Cut small slits in the surface of the meat, insert garlic and return meat to pot. Season with half the salt, pepper and paprika; pour beer over all, cover tightly and simmer over very low heat 45 minutes. Turn meat, sprinkle with re-maining seasoning, cover and simmer 2 hours or until fork tender. Slice brisket diagonally across the grain; top with sauce and onions and serve.

Excellent served with noodles or potato pudding. Best if allowed to mellow
in refrigerator for 24 hours.

Helen Mayer

Exotic Pot Roast

Serves 6-8

INGREDIENTS:

1 4-pound rump roast (or top round), boned and rolled
unseasoned natural meat tenderizer
3 tablespoons vegetable oil
1 garlic clove, minced
½ cup onion, chopped
1 teaspoon salt
1 16-ounce can tomato sauce
1 1-ounce square unsweetened chocolate, melted

½ cup dry red wine
2 teaspoons chili powder
1 teaspoon orange peel, grated
¼ teaspoon cinnamon
¼ teaspoon nutmeg
½ teaspoon oregano, crushed
1 16-ounce can baby carrots, drained
1 16-ounce can onions, drained
¼ cup blanched, slivered almonds

PROCEDURE:

Treat meat with tenderizer according to package directions. Brown pot roast in hot oil in Dutch oven; drain excess oil. Add garlic, onion and salt and stir until lightly browned. Combine remaining ingredients except carrots, onions and almonds; pour over meat, cover and simmer 3 hours or until tender. Add carrots and onions; cover and simmer until heated through. Remove pot roast to platter; wreathe with vegetables and sauce, sprinkle with almonds and serve.

Judie Dresser

Chier Family Brisket

Serves 6

INGREDIENTS:

1 4-pound center cut beef brisket, trimmed
salt to taste
pepper to taste
onion powder to taste
garlic powder to taste
Lawry's seasoned salt

2 onions, diced
½ cup catsup
2 tablespoons prepared mustard
1 tablespoon Worcestershire sauce
½ pound mushrooms, sliced (optional)

PROCEDURE:

Preheat oven to 350°. Sprinkle both sides of meat heavily with seasonings. Brown brisket, fat side down, in a large, heavy pot over medium/high heat; turn and brown with the onions alongside. Combine catsup, mustard and Worcestershire; spread over top of brisket. Add enough hot water around, but not on top of meat to almost cover; do not disturb layer of sauce. Bring to simmer, transfer to oven and cook, covered, 2½ hours, turning meat over after 1½ hours. Replenish water as needed. Remove brisket from pot; cool briefly, then carve ¼" thick slices across the grain. Return brisket to pot, add mushrooms, cover and simmer atop stove 30-60 minutes. Top sliced brisket with gravy and serve with potato pancakes or mashed potatoes.

Delicious accompanied with sweet and sour cabbage.

Olivia Chier

Marinated Beef Brisket

Serves 8-10

INGREDIENTS:

MARINADE
1 cup catsup
1 cup water
2 tablespoons vinegar
1 tablespoon instant onion

1 tablespoon prepared mustard
¼ teaspoon pepper
1 tablespoon prepared horseradish

1 4-5 pound beef brisket (or
  bottom round)

PROCEDURE:

Combine all marinade ingredients and pour over brisket. Cover and refrigerate overnight or 24 hours, turning meat once or twice. Preheat oven to 300°. Place brisket and marinade in a large pan, cover and simmer 4 hours or until tender. Slice meat diagonally across the grain and serve.

Elouise and Larry Potomac

Braised Short Ribs

Serves 6

INGREDIENTS:

4½ pounds beef short ribs
water
1 teaspoon salt
½ teaspoon pepper
4 celery stalks, diced
2 medium onions, diced
1 garlic clove, diced

1 28-ounce can tomatoes,
  undrained, crushed
2 cups beef stock
1 6-ounce can tomato paste
1 tablespoon Worcestershire sauce
½ cup red wine
4 carrots, sliced diagonally

PROCEDURE:

Preheat oven to 375°. Place ribs in a large, covered kettle, cover with water and bring to a boil. Drain, rinse and bone ribs. Place in Dutch oven; add salt and pepper. Cover with celery, onions and garlic and bake, uncovered, 30 minutes. Mix together remaining ingredients except carrots and pour over meat. Arrange carrots over all and bake, covered, 1 hour or until tender. Uncover and bake 30 minutes more.

Carol Vadnais

Sweet And Sour Short Ribs

Serves 8

INGREDIENTS:

5 pounds short ribs (or cross ribs),
  cut into 2" pieces
½ cup flour
2 teaspoons salt
pepper to taste
2 cups onions, chopped
¾ cup catsup

2 tablespoons vinegar
2 tablespoons Worcestershire
  sauce
4 tablespoons soy sauce
½ cup brown sugar
¾ cup water

PROCEDURE:

Preheat oven to 300°. Roll ribs in a mixture of flour, salt and pepper. Place in a casserole and cover with onions. Mix remaining ingredients, pour over ribs, cover and braise 3 hours. Serve ribs with sauce to accompany rice, dumplings or noodles.

Good with pot roast, too.

Nancy Levy

Barbecued Meat Balls

Serves 4

INGREDIENTS:

1½ pounds extra lean ground beef
Lawry's seasoned salt to taste
1 6-ounce can V-8 juice
 (or tomato juice)

½ cup hickory-flavored barbecue
 sauce
1 large tomato, cut in eighths

PROCEDURE:

Shape beef into 1″ balls; place in skillet, sprinkle with salt and brown well over medium/high heat; drain off fat. Pour juice over all and top each meat ball with a dollop of barbecue sauce. Scatter tomato around meat balls, cover and simmer 45 minutes.

Fabulous with rice or noodles and a crisp green salad. An easy, make-ahead dish.

Merel Nissenberg

Sweet And Sour Meat Balls

Serves 6-8

INGREDIENTS:

2 pounds ground beef
½ cup bread crumbs
2 eggs, beaten
garlic salt to taste
pinch of dry mustard
salt to taste

pepper to taste
minced onion to taste (optional)

SAUCE
1 12-ounce jar Welch's grape jam
1 12-ounce bottle Heinz chili
 sauce

PROCEDURE:

Combine all ingredients except the sauce and shape into balls. Set aside. Blend jam and chili sauce in skillet and heat through to blend. Add meat balls, cover and simmer 2-3 hours. Good over fluffy white rice.

Makes deliciously easy bite-size appetizers, too. Can be made a day ahead.

Estelle Graff

Meat Balls Hawaiian

Serves 4

INGREDIENTS:

MEAT BALLS
1¼ pounds ground beef chuck
¼ cup milk
1 8-ounce can water chestnuts,
  drained, finely chopped
3 garlic cloves, finely chopped
½ cup bread crumbs
1 egg, beaten
1 tablespoon soy sauce
salt to taste
pepper to taste
butter

SWEET AND SOUR SAUCE
3 tablespoons cornstarch
1 cup vinegar
1 cup sugar
4-5 dashes Tabasco sauce
2 tablespoons soy sauce
1 tablespoon prepared mustard
1 large green pepper, seeded and
  sliced diagonally
1 large red pepper, seeded and
  sliced diagonally
1 20-ounce can pineapple chunks,
  undrained

PROCEDURE:

Combine all meat ball ingredients and shape into balls; brown in butter and drain. Mix cornstarch, vinegar and sugar; cook, stirring, until clear. Add remaining ingredients and simmer slowly until pepper is crisp tender. Add meat balls and heat through. Serve over rice.

Suzie Desmarais

Meat Loaf

Serves 6

INGREDIENTS:

2 eggs, beaten
1 cup bread crumbs
1 6-ounce can V-8 juice
½ cup onion, chopped
½ cup celery, chopped
salt to taste

pepper to taste
3 pounds ground beef sirloin
1 tablespoon butter (or margarine)
1 12-ounce bottle chile sauce (or
  condensed tomato soup,
  undiluted)

PROCEDURE:

Preheat oven to 350°. Mix eggs and bread crumbs; add V-8 juice, onions, celery, salt and pepper. Combine with meat and mix very well; shape into a buttered loaf pan, cover with chile sauce and bake 1 hour. Variation: omit chile sauce, arrange 3 strips uncooked bacon over loaf and bake.

Janet Belport

Best Meat Loaf

Serves 6

INGREDIENTS:

1 pound ground beef
½ cup quick-cooking oatmeal
1 small onion, finely chopped
1 garlic clove, pressed
4 tablespoons grated Parmesan
　cheese
2 teaspoons parsley, chopped

1 8-ounce can tomato sauce
3 tablespoons dry red wine
1 teaspoon salt
½ teaspoon pepper
½ teaspoon garlic salt
1 egg, beaten

PROCEDURE:

Preheat oven to 350°. Combine all ingredients in a large mixing bowl, using ¾ of the tomato sauce. Shape into a greased loaf pan; spoon remaining tomato sauce on top and bake 1 hour.

Increase cooking time and bake potatoes to complement meal.

Marilyn Greco

Chili

Serves 20-25

INGREDIENTS:

4 pounds ground beef
2-3 large onions, chopped
garlic to taste, minced
1-2 green peppers, seeded
  and chopped
3 16-ounce cans chili beans,
  undrained
2 27-ounce cans kidney beans,
  drained
2 28-ounce cans tomatoes,
  undrained

1 46-ounce can tomato juice
2 8-ounce cans tomato sauce
2 6-ounce cans tomato paste
2 fresh tomatoes, chopped
salt to taste
pepper to taste
chili powder to taste
2 cups water
cheddar cheese, grated

PROCEDURE:

Brown beef, onions and garlic in a large, heavy kettle or Dutch oven; drain off fat. Add green peppers, chili beans and kidney beans. Whirl canned tomatoes in blender; add them and all remaining ingredients except cheese. Bring to a boil, cover and simmer 2-3 hours. Garnish with cheese and serve.

Freezes very well. Always a crowd pleaser!

Anita Tashchian

Hungry Boys Casserole

Serves 6

INGREDIENTS:

2 pounds lean ground beef
2 tablespoons onion flakes
1 10½-ounce can cream of
  celery soup, undiluted
1 cup catsup

1 teaspoon salt
1 16-ounce can pork and beans
½ cup stuffed olives, sliced
  (optional)
biscuits (homemade or
  refrigerated)

PROCEDURE:

Preheat oven to 425°. Brown ground beef; add onion, soup, catsup, salt and olives; mix well. Add beans and simmer until heated through. Transfer to a 12″ by 8″ casserole, top with biscuits and bake 30 minutes.

An easy and popular casserole for the entire family.
Ann Poovey

Shepherd's Pie

Serves 3-4

INGREDIENTS:

1 small onion, finely chopped
butter (or margarine)
1 pound lean ground beef
3 tablespoons tomato paste
3 tablespoons beef extract

1 teaspoon garlic powder
salt to taste
pepper to taste
1 8-ounce can corn, drained
2 potatoes, cooked and mashed

PROCEDURE:

Preheat oven to 350°. Sauté onion in butter; add ground beef and brown.
Mix in tomato paste, beef extract, garlic powder, salt and pepper; simmer
a few minutes. Transfer to a casserole, top with corn, spoon on mashed
potatoes and bake 15 minutes or until heated through.

Carla Jesak

Johnny Marzetti

Serves 6-8

INGREDIENTS:

2 onions, chopped
1 green pepper, seeded and
chopped
3-4 celery stalks, chopped
3 3-ounce cans sliced mushrooms,
drained
butter (margarine or oil)
1 pound ground beef round
1 pound lean ground pork

1 16-ounce can tomatoes,
undrained, chopped
1 6-ounce can tomato paste
1 10¾-ounce can condensed
tomato soup
1 8-ounce package ¼" noodles,
cooked
¾ pound sharp cheddar cheese,
grated

PROCEDURE:

Preheat oven to 325°. Sauté onions, pepper, celery and mushrooms in butter; add meat and brown. Mix in tomatoes, tomato paste and soup; cover
and simmer slowly about 10 minutes. Combine cooked noodles with meat
mixture; add cheese, reserving some to sprinkle over top, and toss lightly
to mix. Spoon into a casserole, top with reserved cheese and bake 1 hour.

*Goes great with a green salad and crusty bread. A widely popular casserole
to make-ahead or freeze.*

Marianna Morgan

73

Treasure Hunt

Serves 6-8

INGREDIENTS:

2 pounds ground round steak
2-4 large onions, chopped
2 large green peppers, seeded and
  chopped
1 garlic clove, minced
1 16-ounce package medium-width
  noodles, cooked barley al dente
1 28-ounce can tomatoes,
  undrained, chopped
1 8-ounce can sliced mushrooms,
  drained
1 16-ounce can corn, drained

1 12-ounce can sliced black olives,
  drained
3 large frozen tamales, thawed
  cut up
5 tablespoons Worcestershire
  sauce
6 dashes cayenne pepper
salt to taste
pepper to taste
paprika to taste
1 pound cheddar cheese, grated

PROCEDURE:

Preheat oven to 350°. Brown meat lightly; add onions, peppers and garlic and sauté until done. Remove from heat; add all remaining ingredients except cheese and mix well. Transfer to a large casserole, sprinkle with cheese and bake 45 minutes to 1 hour, until hot and bubbly.

Delicious served hot or cold. Goes well with tabbouli (p. 420).
Can be made ahead.

Julia Cory Potter

Everyone's Favorite Chili Casserole

Serves 8

INGREDIENTS:

1 pound ground beef
salt to taste
pepper to taste
garlic salt to taste
1 12-ounce can corn, drained
1 12-ounce can mexicorn, drained
1 15-ounce can chili with beans
1 15-ounce can chili without beans

1 7-ounce box Creamettes
  macaroni, cooked
4 dashes Worcestershire sauce
1 15-ounce can tamales
1 pound extra sharp cheddar
  cheese, grated

74

PROCEDURE:

Preheat oven to 325°. Brown ground beef; season with salt, pepper and garlic salt. Mix in corn, mexicorn and chili; add Creamettes and Worcestershire sauce and toss to mix. Place half of the meat mixture in a greased casserole; layer on half of the tamales, sprinkle with half of the cheese; repeat. Transfer to oven and bake 45 minutes.

A family favorite popular with everyone, 2 to 72 years young. Freezes well.

Suzanne Stewart

Easy Mock Beef Stroganoff

Serves 4-6

INGREDIENTS:

1 pound ground beef round
¼ cup butter
1 large onion, chopped
2 garlic cloves, minced
2 10¾-ounce cans cream of
   chicken soup, undiluted
2 teaspoons dill weed
1 4-ounce can black olives,
   drained and chopped

1 8-ounce can water chestnuts,
   drained and diced
12-15 fresh mushrooms, sliced
1 8-ounce package noodles (or
   wild rice), cooked
½ pint sour cream at room
   temperature
fresh Parmesan cheese, grated

PROCEDURE:

Preheat oven to 300°. Sauté ground beef in butter until browned and crumbly; drain off fat. Remove meat to a casserole. Add onion, garlic, soup and dill to skillet and simmer briefly to blend flavors. Stir in olives, water chestnuts and mushrooms; simmer 2-3 minutes. Add beef and noodles (or rice), toss lightly to mix; fold in sour cream. Transfer back to casserole, sprinkle with cheese and bake 30 minutes.

If made a day ahead, assemble omitting sour cream and cheese
until ready to bake.

Joy Charney

Mexican Casserole

Serves 6

INGREDIENTS:

1 pound ground beef
1 tablespoon instant minced onion
½ teaspoon garlic salt
2 8-ounce cans tomato sauce
1 cup black olives, chopped
½ pint sour cream

½ pint small curd cottage cheese
1 4-ounce can diced green chiles, drained
1 12-16 ounce bag nacho cheese tortilla chips
2 cups Monterey jack cheese, grated

PROCEDURE:

Preheat oven to 350°. Brown ground beef and drain; add onion, garlic salt, tomato sauce and olives; simmer 5 minutes. Combine sour cream, cottage cheese and chiles in a bowl. Crush chips, reserving some whole for top of casserole. Place half of the crushed chips in bottom of well-greased 2½-quart casserole; add half of the meat mixture, then half of the sour cream mixture; sprinkle with half of the grated cheese; repeat. Bake, uncovered 30-35 minutes or until bubbly. Top with reserved chips and serve.

A great casserole. Reheats very well.

Bill Cahoone

Baked Zucchini With Beef And Cheese

Serves 6

INGREDIENTS:
1 pound ground beef
1 medium onion, chopped
1 cup instant rice, uncooked
1 teaspoon seasoned salt
1 teaspoon oregano, crushed

1½ pounds zucchini, cut in ¼" rounds
2 cups small curd cottage cheese
1 10½-ounce can cream of mushroom soup
1 pound cheddar cheese, grated

PROCEDURE:

Preheat oven to 350°. Brown ground beef in skillet; add and brown onion, rice, salt and oregano. Place half the zucchini in a greased 9" by 13" baking dish; cover with beef mixture, then spoon on cottage cheese. Add remaining zucchini, spread soup over all, sprinkle with grated cheese and bake 35 minutes.

76   *Connie Reins*

Zucchini Pizza

Serves 6

INGREDIENTS:

4 cups zucchini (about 1½ pounds)
1½ cups mozzarella cheese, shredded
1½ cups sharp cheddar cheese, shredded
2 eggs, slightly beaten
¼ teaspoon salt
¼ teaspoon garlic salt

1½ pounds lean ground beef
1 medium onion, chopped
2 8-ounce cans tomato sauce
2 teaspoons oregano leaves
1 green pepper, seeded and thinly sliced (optional)
¼ pound mushrooms, sliced
⅓ cup grated Parmesan cheese

PROCEDURE:

Preheat oven to 400°. Shred zucchini and squeeze out any moisture. Mix with ¾ cup each mozzarella and cheddar cheeses and eggs; press into a greased 10″ by 15″ jelly-roll pan and bake 10 minutes. Sprinkle salts into a skillet over medium heat and brown beef until crumbly; add onion, cook until limp; drain off fat. Stir in tomato sauce and oregano; simmer until thickened, then spoon over zucchini. Arrange green pepper and mushrooms on meat sauce; sprinkle with all remaining cheeses and bake 30 minutes or until bubbly.

Superb! A family favorite especially popular with the young.

Gleneva Belice

Wiener Schnitzel

Serves 4-6

INGREDIENTS:

4-6 veal steaks (about ⅜″ thick)
2 eggs
salt to taste
1 cup flour
1 cup bread crumbs

1 stick butter (½ cup)
1 cup oil
lemon slices (for garnish)
parsley (for garnish)

PROCEDURE:

Pat steaks dry and slash edges 5 to 6 times to prevent curling. Beat eggs with salt. Dip steaks in flour, then in eggs, then in crumbs, coating thinly but evenly all over. Heat butter and oil and saute veal until golden brown. Garnish with lemon and parsley and serve immediately.

Sensational with rice and a green salad.

Marilies Schoepflin

77

Veal Birds

Serves 6

INGREDIENTS:

3 slices bacon
¼ cup onion, chopped
⅓ cup celery, chopped
1½ cups herb-seasoned bread
  .stuffing mix
½ cup hot water
6 4-ounce veal cutlets, pounded
  flat

2 tablespoons flour
2 tablespoons butter (or
  margarine)
1 10½-ounce can beef bouillon
water
¼ cup flour
½ cup cold water

PROCEDURE:

Fry bacon until crisp; remove and crumble. Sauté onion and celery in drippings until tender but not brown. Toss together stuffing mix, bacon, onion, celery and drippings; gently mix in hot water. Place ½ cup stuffing on each cutlet, roll and secure with toothpicks. Flour rolls and brown in butter; add bouillon, cover and simmer 1 hour or until tender (or simmer in preheated 350° oven). Remove and keep warm. Add enough water to skillet liquid to make 1½ cups; bring to a boil, stir in flour blended with ½ cup cold water and heat, stirring, until thickened. Spoon over veal birds and serve.

Joyce Aftahi

Kalbsgulaš
Hungarian Veal Stew

Serves 5-6

INGREDIENTS:

4 ounces bacon, diced
1 pound onions, chopped
3-5 teaspoons paprika
salt to taste
2 teaspoons vinegar

2 pounds boneless stewing veal,
  cubed
2 cups beef (or chicken) broth
1-2 tablespoons flour
¾ cup sour cream

PROCEDURE:

Brown bacon in large skillet until crisp; add onion and saute until golden. Stir in paprika, salt, vinegar and veal; add broth, cover and simmer 1 hour or until tender. Cool slightly. Blend well flour and sour cream, stir into stew and heat, stirring, for about 1 minute or until thickened. Thin sauce with broth or thicken with flour if necessary. Serve with pasta or French bread.

Can be prepared the day ahead.

Marilies Schoepflin

Butterflied Leg Of Lamb With Herb Butter

Serves 6-8

INGREDIENTS:

HERB BUTTER
4 tablespoons butter
juice of 1 lemon
½ teaspoon dried rosemary,
  crumbled

1 teaspoon savory, crumbled
1 teaspoon instant coffee powder

1 6-pound leg of lamb, boned and
  flattened

PROCEDURE:

Prepare barbecue. Melt butter and blend in lemon juice, rosemary, savory and coffee. Place lamb, fat side down, on barbecue and grill 30 minutes, brushing frequently with herb butter. Turn lamb and grill, basting often, another 30 minutes.

Lamb may be grilled or roasted in oven. Delicious hot or cold.

Ann Poovey

Marinated Butterflied Leg Of Lamb

Serves 6-12

INGREDIENTS:

MARINADE
½ cup Dijon mustard
1 cup soy sauce

½ teaspoon (or less) salt
½ teaspoon pepper
1 leg (or half) of lamb,
  butterflied

PROCEDURE:

Combine marinade ingredients, pour over lamb, cover and refrigerate overnight. Remove from marinade; place on barbecue and grill about 45-50 minutes or to desired doneness.

Mary Eikel

79

Moussaka

Serves 12

INGREDIENTS:

MEAT SAUCE
1 cup onion, finely chopped
1½ pounds ground lamb (or ground beef chuck)
1 garlic clove, crushed
2 tablespoons butter (or margarine)
½ teaspoon oregano leaves
1 teaspoon basil leaves
½ teaspoon cinnamon
1 teaspoon salt
dash of pepper
2 8-ounce cans tomato sauce
2 20-ounce eggplants, unpared

salt
½ cup butter (or margarine), melted

CREAM SAUCE
2 tablespoons butter (or margarine)
2 tablespoons flour
½ teaspoon salt
dash of pepper
2 cups milk
2 eggs, whisked
½ cup Parmesan cheese, grated
½ cup cheddar cheese, grated
2 tablespoons dry bread crumbs

PROCEDURE:

For meat sauce, sauté onion, lamb and garlic in hot butter about 10 minutes until browned. Stir in herbs, spices and tomato sauce; bring to a boil, stirring, then reduce heat and simmer, uncovered, 30 minutes. Preheat broiler. Halve eggplants lengthwise; slice ½" thick crosswise. Place in bottom of broiler pan; salt lightly, brush with melted butter and broil 4" from heat, 4 minutes per side, or until golden.

For cream sauce, melt butter in saucepan; off heat, stir in flour, salt and pepper. Add milk gradually, heat and stir until thickened; remove from heat. Blend a little cream sauce into eggs; return mixture to saucepan and mix well. Preheat oven to 350°. Layer, overlapping slightly, half of the eggplant in bottom of 12" by 7½" baking dish; sprinkle with 2 tablespoons each grated cheeses. Stir bread crumbs into meat sauce; spoon over eggplant, sprinkle with 2 tablespoons each of the cheeses. Layer, overlapping, remaining eggplant; pour cream sauce over all; top with remaining cheeses and bake 35-40 minutes until golden brown and top is set. If desired, brown under broiler 1 minute. Cool slightly, cut in squares and serve.

Joyce Aftahi

Roast Leg Of Lamb With Vegetables

Serves 8

INGREDIENTS:

1 5-6 pound leg of lamb
2 garlic cloves, slivered
1¾ teaspoon salt
pepper to taste
1 teaspoon oregano
2 tablespoons tomato paste

1 cup dry white wine (or chicken
  broth)
16 small whole onions, peeled
4 large carrots, pared, cut in 1″
  pieces
4 cups water

PROCEDURE:

Preheat oven to 325°. Cut small slits in lamb and insert garlic. Place lamb, fat side up, in roasting pan. Season with ¾ teaspoon salt, pepper and ½ teaspoon oregano; roast 45 minutes. Mix together tomato paste, wine and remaining oregano; pour over lamb and roast 40 minutes, basting after 20 minutes. Cut a small "x" in stem-end of onions to prevent bursting. Add onions and carrots to boiling water with remaining teaspoon salt, cover and simmer 10 minutes; drain. Arrange vegetables around lamb, baste all with drippings and roast 1 hour. Remove lamb to serving platter and accompany with vegetables.

Rhonda Read

Braised Lamb Steaks

Serves 6

INGREDIENTS:

½ teaspoon salt
1 teaspoon celery seed
1 teaspoon lemon juice
2 teaspoons Dijon (or any
  prepared) mustard
rind of 2 oranges, grated
¼ cup brown sugar

¼ cup vinegar
¼ cup orange juice
1 teaspoon Worcestershire sauce
1 8-ounce can tomato sauce (or
  Italian plum tomatoes, chopped)
1 onion, thinly sliced
6 lamb steaks, ½″ thick

PROCEDURE:

Preheat oven to 350°. Combine all ingredients except lamb in a saucepan; bring to a boil, cover and simmer 10 minutes. Pour sauce over lamb in an oven-proof dish, cover and bake 1 hour or until tender. If desired, remove cover and brown under broiler 2-3 minutes.

Delicious accompanied with rice or pasta.

Connie Galluzzi

Lamb Curry

Serves 8

INGREDIENTS:

8 lamb shoulder chops
2 tablespoons peanut oil
4 large onions, sliced
3 garlic cloves, slivered
3 heaping tablespoons curry
  powder
white wine vinegar
½ cup homemade tomato sauce (or
  canned tomato purée)

soy sauce to taste
coarse salt to taste
½ teaspoon dried ginger
½ teaspoon coriander
water (as needed)
4 large white potatoes, peeled and
  quartered

PROCEDURE:

Brown lamb chops in oil until the fat is crisp; remove. Add onions and garlic and sauté slowly over low/medium heat until golden. Blend curry powder and vinegar into a paste; stir into onions. Mix in all remaining ingredients except potatoes, thinning with a little water, if necessary. Return lamb to pot, cover and simmer 30 minutes. Add potatoes and cook, covered, until tender.

Splendid served with rice and a selection of traditional accompaniments: chutney, chopped tomatoes, sliced bananas, grated coconut, chopped peanuts, chopped green pepper, chopped cucumber mixed with plain yogurt and chopped fresh dill, sliced papaya and mangoes.

Helen Mayer

Oven Kalua Pork

Serves 12

INGREDIENTS:

1 6-pound pork butt
1 tablespoon liquid smoke

2½ tablespoons Hawaiian salt (or
  very coarse rock salt)

PROCEDURE:

Preheat oven to 350°. Rub pork with liquid smoke and 1½ tablespoons salt. Wrap with foil, sealing completely; place in roasting pan and roast 5 hours. Shred pork; sprinkle with remaining salt and serve.

Easy and delicious alternative to pit-roasted Hawaiian kalua pig.

Lani H. Donohoe

Butterflied Pork Chops With Sour Cream

Serves 8-10

INGREDIENTS:

8 ½″ thick pork chops, butterflied
½ cup flour
1 teaspoon salt
pepper to taste
2 10¾-ounce cans condensed
   cream of mushroom soup

⅔ cup water
1 teaspoon ginger
½ teaspoon rosemary, crushed
2 3½-ounce cans French-fried
   onion rings
1 cup (or more) sour cream

PROCEDURE:

Preheat oven to 350°. Trim chops. Heat trimmings to yield 4 tablespoons drippings in flameproof casserole or 13″ by 9″ baking dish; remove trimmings. Dredge chops in a mixture of flour, salt and pepper and brown. Combine soup, water, ginger and rosemary; pour over chops, sprinkle with half of the onions, cover and bake 50 minutes or until tender. Sprinkle with remaining onions and bake, uncovered, 10 minutes. Remove meat to a platter. Smooth sour cream into sauce; heat through and serve with chops and fluffy rice.

Linda Goodwin

Sweet And Sour Pork

Serves 4

INGREDIENTS:

1 pound boned lean pork, cubed
1 tablespoon sherry
1 tablespoon soy sauce
½ teaspoon salt
5 tablespoons cornstarch
2 cups cooking oil

⅓ cup cold water
⅔ cup sugar
½ cup vinegar
¼ cup catsup
⅓ cup pineapple juice
1 cup pineapple chunks

PROCEDURE:

Marinate pork in mixture of sherry, soy sauce and salt 30 minutes; drain and roll in 3 tablespoons cornstarch. Deep fry in hot oil until crisp; drain, then transfer pork to warm oven. Blend remaining 2 tablespoons cornstarch with cold water. Combine sugar, vinegar, catsup and pineapple juice in a saucepan and bring to a boil; stir in cornstarch mixture and cook until thickened and translucent. Add pineapple chunks and pork, mix well and serve immediately with white rice.

Josie Kan

Argentine Ribs

Serves 4

INGREDIENTS:

¼ cup parsley flakes
¼ cup oregano leaves
2 tablespoons thyme
1 tablespoon freshly ground pepper
1 tablespoon crushed red pepper
 (or to taste)

1 rack spareribs, cut into
 individual ribs (about 4 pounds)
salt to taste
Worcestershire sauce to taste

PROCEDURE:

Prepare barbecue. Mix herbs and peppers. Place ribs on barbecue meat side up. Sprinkle with salt, brush with Worcestershire sauce, then sprinkle with half of the seasoning mix; turn ribs, repeat. Grill over low coals 10-15 minutes; turn and grill until tender.

Bernie Fipp

Barbecued Spareribs

Serves 4-6

INGREDIENTS:

4-6 pounds spareribs, cut in
 serving-size pieces
salt to taste
1 cup catsup
⅓ cup Worcestershire sauce

1 teaspoon chili powder
2 dashes Tabasco sauce
1½ cups water
1 onion, thinly sliced
1 lemon, thinly sliced

PROCEDURE:

Preheat oven to 450°. Salt ribs well, place in a shallow roasting pan and bake 30 minutes; drain off fat. Mix catsup, Worcestershire sauce, chili powder, Tabasco and water; heat through. Pour sauce over ribs, top with onion and lemon; reduce heat to 350° and bake, uncovered, 1½ hours.

Delicious served with a green salad and spoon bread (p. 371).

Phyllis Queen Healy

Ham Mousse With Mushroom Sauce

Serves 4

INGREDIENTS:

3 tablespoons butter (or
    margarine)
3 tablespoons flour
1 cup milk
3 eggs, separated
½ pound ham, finely ground

¼ teaspoon Worcestershire sauce
¼ teaspoon prepared mustard
pinch of ground cloves
mushroom sauce (recipe follows)

PROCEDURE:

Preheat oven to 350°. Make white sauce by melting butter, adding flour and cooking over low heat until it bubbles. Add milk gradually and cook until thickened. Slightly beat egg yolks. Whip whites until stiff. Pour cream sauce over egg yolks. Fold in ham, egg whites and seasonings. Bake in square dish for 30 minutes or until knife comes out clean. Cut in squares, top with mushroom sauce.

Valdene Ramrus

Mushroom Sauce

INGREDIENTS:

2 tablespoons butter
1 teaspoon onion, grated
1 cup mushrooms, sliced
2 tablespoons flour

¼ teaspoon salt
⅛ teaspoon pepper
1 cup milk

PROCEDURE:

Melt butter. Add onions and mushrooms and sauté for 5 minutes. Blend in flour and seasonings. Cook over low heat, stirring until mixture is smooth and bubbly. Remove from heat, gradually stir in milk. Bring to boil, stirring constantly. Boil 1 minute. Pour over ham mousse or ham loaf.

Valdene Ramrus

85

Santa Fe Steal

Serves 2

INGREDIENTS:

½ pound prosciutto ham
½ head red cabbage, thinly sliced

2 cups creamy, small curd cottage
  cheese
pimiento, slivered

PROCEDURE:

Cut prosciutto in very thin slices, almost shredded; stirfry over medium/high heat; do not allow to stick. Reduce heat, add cabbage, cover and simmer, stirring occasionally, until cabbage begins to soften. Serve, topped with cottage cheese and garnished with pimiento.

Easy, interesting and effective dish conceived by Santa Fe Grill, Berkeley.

Sharon Horan

Ham Loaf With Mustard Sauce

Serves 10

INGREDIENTS:

1½ pounds ground ham
½ pound ground pork
½ pound ground veal
1 tablespoon onion, minced
½ teaspoon celery salt
1 cup cornflakes, crushed
1 cup milk
2 eggs, beaten
1 cup brown sugar

cinnamon to taste

MUSTARD SAUCE
½ cup brown sugar
1 tablespoon flour
1 tablespoon dry mustard
1 egg, beaten
½ cup vinegar

PROCEDURE:

Preheat oven to 350°. Mix well all ingredients except brown sugar, cinnamon and mustard sauce and form into 2 loaves. Press 1 cup brown sugar onto baking sheet; place loaves on top, sprinkle with cinnamon and bake 1½ hours. Combine brown sugar, flour and mustard in a saucepan. Mix in egg, add vinegar and cook, stirring constantly, over low heat until thickened. Serve with ham loaves. Variation: subsitute 2 pounds ground ham and ½ ground pork for ham/pork/veal mixture.

Cindy Wise

Ham And Cheese Crepas

Serves 6-12

INGREDIENTS:

12 thin slices boiled ham
12 thick sticks Monterey jack
  cheese
12 flour tortillas

2 7-ounce cans whole green chiles,
  drained, rinsed
1 14½-ounce can tomato sauce
1 cup cheddar cheese, grated

PROCEDURE:

Preheat oven to 375°. Place ham slice and cheese stick on a flour tortilla
and roll up. Arrange seam side down in a greased baking pan; repeat, spac-
ing crepas so they do not touch. Top each with a split chile; pour tomato
sauce over all and sprinkle with grated cheese. Cover with foil and bake
30 minutes or until bubbly. Variation: substitute cooked chicken for ham.
May be assembled, frozen, then baked.

Susan J. Reisner

Mrs. C's Sausage And Spinach Pie

Serves 10

INGREDIENTS:

1 pound sweet Italian sausage
  links, chopped
6 eggs, 1 yolk reserved
2 10-ounce packages frozen,
  chopped spinach, thawed and
  well drained
1 pound mozzarella cheese,
  shredded
⅔ cup ricotta cheese

⅔ cup ricotta cheese
½ teaspoon salt
pepper to taste
⅛ teaspoon garlic powder
pie crust mix for 2 crust pie (or
  ready-made pie crusts)
1 tablespoon water

PROCEDURE:

Preheat oven to 350°. Brown sausage over medium heat until well done;
drain. Beat eggs in a large bowl; add sausage and mix in all remaining ingredients except reserved yolk, pie crust and water. Set aside. Prepare pie
crust according to package directions. Roll bottom crust into an 11″ circle
and fit into a 9″ pie pan. Spoon in sausage mixture. Roll top crust into a
10″ circle; cut a small, circular steam vent in center. Fit over filling and
trim to ½″ overhang. Roll overhang under, seal and crimp edges; cut steam
slits. Beat reserved egg yolk with water; brush crust to glaze. Decorate around
steam vent with petals cut from re-rolled pastry scraps; glaze. Bake 1¼ hours;
let stand 10 minutes before serving.

Connie McGrath

Calf's Liver Sautéed

Serves 4-6

INGREDIENTS:

1½ pounds calf's liver, cut in ¼″ strips
2 tablespoons olive oil
2 tablespoons butter
1 tablespoon onion, chopped
1½ teaspoons chives, chopped

1 teaspoon parsley, chopped
½ teaspoon thyme
1 teaspoon marjoram
½ teaspoon basil
½ teaspoon sage

PROCEDURE:

Sauté liver in olive oil in a heavy skillet, stirring, about 1 minute. Transfer with a slotted spoon to a heated serving dish and keep warm. Add butter to the skillet, stir in onion, 1 teaspoon chives, parsley, thyme, marjoram and basil and sauté until onion is limp. Return liver to skillet and stir over high heat until heated through. Transfer to serving dish, garnish with remaining chives and sage and serve immediately.

Joyce Aftahi

Calf's Liver And Avocado

Serves 6

INGREDIENTS:

4 avocadoes, thinly sliced
lemon juice
12 slices calf's liver (about 1½ pounds), cut very thinly
½ cup flour
1 teaspoon salt
½ teaspoon pepper

2 ounces butter

SAUCE
8 ounces butter
juice of 2-3 lemons
½ cup beef stock
½ teaspoon thyme

PROCEDURE:

Sprinkle avocado slices with lemon juice. Dredge liver and avocado lightly in a mixture of flour, salt and pepper; sauté quickly in butter, browning a few pieces at a time. Remove to heated platter and keep warm. Heat 8 ounces butter in same skillet until browned, stir in lemon juice, stock and thyme. Heat and stir quickly, pour over liver and avocado and serve.

Libby Clemmer

Surprisingly Good Liver

Serves 6

INGREDIENTS:

6 slices bacon
1½ pounds baby beef liver, cut in
  serving-size pieces
flour
1 large onion, sliced
1 medium green pepper, seeded
  and sliced

1 1⅜-ounce envelope dry onion
  soup mix
1 16-ounce can stewed tomatoes
seasoned salt to taste
pepper to taste

PROCEDURE:

Preheat oven to 350°. Fry bacon in a large skillet over medium heat until crisp; drain on paper towels. Pour off all but 2 tablespoons drippings. Dredge liver lightly with flour, shaking off excess, and fry in drippings just until slightly browned on both sides; add drippings as needed. Arrange liver in a 9″ by 13″ baking dish. Sauté onion and green pepper in skillet until onion is limp; spoon over liver, then sprinkle evenly with onion soup. Cover with tomatoes, season with salt and pepper and top with bacon. Cover and bake 25 minutes or until hot.

Delicious served with noodles. A surprisingly big success with non-liver lovers.

Anne Coleman

Italian Liver

Serves 4

INGREDIENTS:

½ cup fine dry bread crumbs
4 tablespoons Parmesan cheese,
  grated
½ teaspoon garlic salt
¼ teaspoon whole oregano,
  crumbled
salt to taste
pepper to taste
1 pound calf's liver, sliced

2 eggs beaten
2 tablespoons butter
2 tablespoons salad oil
4 ounces mozzarella cheese, sliced
1 8-ounce can (or more) tomato
  sauce
Parmesan cheese, grated
parsely, finely chopped

PROCEDURE:

Preheat oven to 350°. Combine crumbs, 4 tablespoons Parmesan cheese, garlic salt and oregano in a shallow pan. Salt and pepper liver lightly; dip in eggs, drain briefly; coat with crumbs and brown quickly in hot butter and oil, about 2-3 minutes; drain on paper towels. Alternate liver with mozzarella cheese in a shallow 9″ by 9″ baking dish; cover with tomato sauce, sprinkle with Parmesan cheese and parsley for color. Bake, uncovered, about 20 minutes.

Always a favorite, an outstandingly delicious way to serve liver.

Anne Coleman

89

Barbecue Sauce

INGREDIENTS:

1 large onion, sliced
2 tablespoons bacon drippings
½ cup chile sauce
¼ cup molasses

2 tablespoons prepared mustard
1 tablespoon vinegar
1 tablespoon Worcestershire sauce
4-5 drops liquid hot pepper sauce

PROCEDURE:

Sauté onion in drippings until tender. Stir in remaining ingredients and heat to blend flavors. Use as a cooking or basting sauce for any barbecued dish.

Cynthia Moyers

Marinade For Flank Steak Feast

Serves 8-10

INGREDIENTS:

MARINADE
⅔ cup corn oil
⅔ cup teriyaki sauce
½ teaspoon ginger
½ teaspoon seasoned salt
½ teaspoon pepper
2 tablespoons Worcestershire
    sauce

2 garlic cloves, crushed
2 tablespoons lemon juice
1 teaspoon brown sugar
½ teaspoon dry mustard

2 2-pound flank steaks

PROCEDURE:

Combine all marinade ingredients. Pour over steaks, pierce deeply with a fork, cover and refrigerate overnight or all day. Pierce meat and turn occasionally in marinade. Remove from marinade; place on barbecue and grill to desired doneness. Slice diagonally across the grain and serve.

An original and superb marinade.

Linda Goodwin

Marinade Par Excellence

INGREDIENTS:

¾ cup salad oil
¾ cup dry red wine
3 tablespoons red wine vinegar
1 tablespoon lemon juice
5-8 garlic cloves, chopped
⅓ cup red onion, chopped

1 teaspoon oregano
½ teaspoon thyme
1 tablespoon sugar
1 tablespoon salt
1 tablespoon pepper

PROCEDURE:

Mix together all ingredients. Use to marinate lamb and beef or to baste chicken. Mix into hamburgers for added zest. Will keep in refrigerator for 2 weeks.

Suzie Desmarais

Marinade For Lamb Shish Kebab

INGREDIENTS:

½ teaspoon sage
½ teaspoon thyme
½ teaspoon oregano
½ teaspoon pepper
½ teaspoon basil
1 teaspoon rosemary
1 bunch parsley

5-6 garlic cloves
1 teaspoon prepared mustard
½ cup catsup
2 teaspoons Worcestershire sauce
1 cup salad oil
¾ cup sauterne

PROCEDURE:

Finely chop herbs and spices in blender. Add remaining ingredients and blend. Use to marinate lamb overnight.

Mary Stolberg

Notes

4

Poultry & Game

Chicken Breast With Crème Fraîche
And Moutarde De Meaux

Serves 8

INGREDIENTS:

1 cup creme fraîche
2 tablespoons moutarde de meaux
12 chicken breasts
salt to taste

pepper to taste
lemon juice to taste
Gourmet's Tomato Sauce (recipe
 follows)

PROCEDURE:

Preheat broiler. Mix crème fraîche and moutarde de meaux. Skin, bone and fillet each breast. Wash breasts and pat dry. Two hours before cooking sprinkle with salt, pepper and lemon juice. On buttered cookie sheet place breasts with enough crème mixture to cover. Broil 5-7 minutes on lower middle shelf of oven. Breasts are done when they are springy to the touch and the crème fraîche is bubbly and brown. Line a heated plate with a layer of tomato sauce (recipe follows), add chicken .

Serve with haricots verts. (See page 207)

Lyn Heller

Gourmet's Tomato Sauce

Serves 8

INGREDIENTS:

3 tablespoons olive oil
6 pounds ripe plum tomatoes
6 bunches fresh basil
salt to taste
pepper to taste

2 tablespoons shallots, chopped
¼ cup dry white vermouth
¼ cup champagne white vinegar
3 tablespoons crème fraîche
1 cup unsalted butter

PROCEDURE:

In 4-quart saucepan, place washed, dried and quartered tomatoes in olive oil. Cook over medium heat until tomatoes begin to break down. Add 3 bunches of basil and cook until all liquid has evaporated (about 1 hour). Season to taste with salt and pepper. Reserve. Add shallots, vermouth and vinegar to saucepan. Boil. Continue to cook until mixture is reduced to 2 tablespoons. Add crème fraîche. Boil until reduced by half. Reduce heat to low. Add butter by tablespoons, whisking after each. When each is melted add next tablespoon butter. Whisk in tomato sauce. Add salt and pepper to taste. Stack the leaves of 3 bunches of basil. Cut across leaves in thin strips. Use for garnish.

For a finer texture run the tomato sauce through a medium disc of a Mouli food mill.

Regular tomatoes may be used in place of plum tomatoes, as well as 6 cups of canned tomatoes.

Lyn Heller

Chicken Charleau

Serves 4-6

INGREDIENTS:

3 whole chicken breasts, skinned
    and boned
½ teaspoon salt
¼ teaspoon pepper
1 garlic clove, crushed
¼ teaspoon oregano
2 sprigs parsley, chopped

3 tablespoons lemon juice
½ tablespoon olive oil
½ tablespoon butter
½ cup white wine (sauterne)
½ cup heavy cream
mushrooms (optional)
pimientos (optional)

PROCEDURE:

Wash chicken and pat dry. Cut into bite-size pieces. Marinate in salt, pepper, garlic, oregano, parsley and lemon juice for 1 hour. Sauté in oil and butter 5 minutes. Add wine and cream and heat. Add mushrooms and pimiento if desired.

Simple but elegant.

Laurie Marcus

French Chicken In Wine Sauce

Serves 10-12

INGREDIENTS:

6 whole chicken breasts, skinned,
    boned and halved
1 teaspoon salt (optional)
3 tablespoons flour
1 cup sour cream
1 10¾-ounce can mushroom soup

1 4-ounce can sliced mushrooms
½ cup sauterne
1 cup sliced almonds
2 small jars pimientos
paprika to taste

PROCEDURE:

Preheat oven to 325°. Place chicken in a flat baking dish and sprinkle with salt. Combine flour and half of sour cream, stirring until smooth. Add remainder of sour cream, soup, wine and mushrooms. Pour over chicken. Sprinkle with almonds, pimiento and paprika. Bake 1½ hours or until tender. Serve over rice or noodles.

Marilyn Sarlin

Poulet Aux Fines Herbes

Serves 4

INGREDIENTS:

4 chicken breasts, skinned and boned
½ cup butter
½ teaspoon oregano
½ teaspoon fines herbes
½ teaspoon marjoram
½ teaspoon fresh parsley, chopped

¼ pound Monterey jack cheese, cut in strips
½ cup flour
2 eggs, beaten with 2 tablespoons water and ½ teaspoon oil
1 cup dry bread crumbs
½ cup Chablis

PROCEDURE:

Preheat oven to 350°. Pound dull side of breasts to flatten and break down muscles. Combine butter with oregano, marjoram, fines herbes and parsley. Spread some of this mixture on each breast, cover with a strip of cheese and roll up tightly, tucking in ends when possible. Secure with toothpicks. Coat rolls with flour, dip in the egg mix, then roll in bread crumbs. Bake uncovered 20 minutes in flat dish. (Can be prepared to this point, refrigerated then completed as follows before serving). Melt remaining herb butter mixture, stir in wine and pour around chicken. Bake 20-25 minutes until brown and tender. Spoon sauce on top and serve.

Judy Rosenblatt

Chicken Vermouth

Serves 6-8

INGREDIENTS:

3 pounds chicken pieces
2½ teaspoons salt
½ teaspoon pepper
3 medium carrots, thinly sliced
3 celery ribs

1 medium onion, thinly sliced
12 garlic cloves
2 tablespoons parsley, chopped
⅓ cup dry white wine (or vermouth)
¼ cup sour cream

PROCEDURE:

Preheat oven to 375°. Wash and dry chicken parts. Sprinkle with salt and pepper. Place all ingredients except sour cream in 2-quart casserole. Cover and bake 1½ hours. Stir in sour cream. Serve over rice.

Susan Rantzow

Chicken Wellington

Serves 6

INGREDIENTS:

3 whole chicken breasts, skinned,
    boned and halved
1 tablespoon butter
1 package frozen pastry shells,
    thawed to room temperature
8 ounces cream cheese, softened

garlic salt to taste
salt to taste
pepper to taste
tarragon to taste
parsley (for garnish)

PROCEDURE:

Preheat oven to 350°. Sauté chicken in butter. Roll out pastry shells between wax paper until fairly thin. Divide cream cheese between 6 shells and spread on pastry. Sprinkle with garlic salt, salt, pepper and tarragon. Place chicken in center of shell and fold around it. Place chicken in greased pan, fold side down. Bake 25-30 minutes or until brown. Sprinkle with parsley and serve.

Can be prepared a day ahead.

Roberta Burnham

Angelo Chicken Gourmet

Serves 4

INGREDIENTS:

2 whole chicken breasts, skinned,
    boned and halved

4 bacon strips

PROCEDURE:

Wrap chicken in bacon. Secure with toothpick. Broil 10-15 minutes on each side. Serve with seasoned rice.

Sandra Angelo

Apricot Chicken Delight

Serves 6

INGREDIENTS:

¾ cup orange juice
½ cup dried apricots, snipped
¼ cup sugar
¼ teaspoon ground cloves

½ cup raisins
¼ cup water
6 chicken breasts, skinless
¼ cup sliced almonds (for garnish)

PROCEDURE:

Combine juice, apricots, sugar, cloves and water in a small saucepan. Bring to a boil, cover and simmer until apricots are tender (approximately 20-25 minutes). Arrange chicken breasts in a 12" by 7" by 1½" baking pan. Spoon apricot sauce on top. Cover and refrigerate for 12-24 hours. Preheat oven to 350°. Bake, covered, for 55 minutes or until chicken reaches desired tenderness. Garnish with sliced almonds and serve with rice.

A lovely, make-ahead company dish.

Sheryl Durkin

Bobbi's Chicken

Serves 8

INGREDIENTS:

8 chicken breasts, skinned
16 bacon slices
½ pound mushrooms
1 tablespoon butter

1 cup Swiss cheese, slivered
onion powder to taste
½ pint sour cream

PROCEDURE:

Preheat oven to 350°. Cook chicken for 30-40 minutes. Cut bacon in small pieces and fry until crispy. Sauté mushrooms in butter. Mix bacon, cheese, mushrooms, and onion powder. Pour over chicken and bake 15 minutes more. Stir in sour cream and serve.

Even tastier the next day.

Bobbi Susselman

Cashew Chicken

Serves 6

INGREDIENTS:

3 boneless chicken breasts, split
½ pound Chinese sugar peas
½ pound mushrooms
6 green onions
1 7-ounce can bamboo shoots
1 tablespoon chicken stock base
    and 1 cup water, mixed

¼ cup soy sauce
½ teaspoon sugar
2 tablespoons cornstarch
4 tablespoons salad oil
1 4-ounce package cashew nuts

PROCEDURE:

Slice chicken horizontally into ⅛" slices, then cut into 1" squares. Remove ends and strings from Chinese peas. Clean and slice mushrooms. Cut green part of onions into 1" lengths and slash both ends several times making fans. Slice the white part ¼" thick. Keep vegetables separate. Mix soy sauce, sugar and cornstarch. Heat oil in wok or electric frypan to 350°. Add chicken and cook quickly, turning until opaque. Add peas, mushrooms, stock water; cover and simmer 2 minutes. Add bamboo shoots and soy mixture and cook until sauce thickens, stirring constantly. Simmer 1 minute, uncovered. Mix in green onions and nuts.

A quick and delicious stirfry. Shrimp may be substituted for chicken.

Suzie Desmarais

Jason's Favorite Chicken

Serves 4

INGREDIENTS:

1 frying chicken, cut up
1 teaspoon Lawry's seasoned salt

1 teaspoon dill weed
1 teaspoon garlic powder

PROCEDURE:

Preheat oven to 350°. Put chicken on a rack over a broiler pan and sprinkle seasonings evenly. Bake 1½ hours.

Debbie Drogin

Chicken Curry

Serves 8-10

INGREDIENTS:

2 whole chickens, cut up
1 large onion, chopped
1 cinnamon stick
¾ teaspoon cardamon, ground
   (or 3-4 seeds)
2 garlic cloves, minced
1″ piece of ginger, minced
2½ cups chicken stock
1 raw potato, sliced
1 cup plain yogurt
1 teaspoon coriander
1 teaspoon turmeric
1 teaspoon cumin
3 teaspoons curry powder
   (or to taste)
juice of 1 lime

SUGGESTED CONDIMENTS
chutney
cashews, peanuts, chopped
egg yolk, white, chopped
miniature gherkins
crystallized ginger, minced
plumped raisins
coconut flakes
bananas, sliced
green pepper, chopped
green onion, chopped
tomato, cubed

PROCEDURE:

Bake chicken at 375° for 40 minutes. Cut into bite-size pieces. Sauté onion. Add cinnamon, and cardamon and cook until golden. Add garlic, ginger, ½ cup chicken stock, potato and simmer a few minutes. Add yogurt and cook 5 minutes stirring constantly. Add coriander, turmeric, cumin, curry, lime and cook 5 minutes. Add chicken, chicken stock and bring to boil. Cool. Reheat and cook 20 minutes. Remove cinnamon stick. Serve on rice with condiments.

Nancy Field Stork

Chicken And Vegetable Curry

INGREDIENTS:

Serves 6

3½ pounds chicken breast fillets
¾ teaspoon turmeric
3 tablespoons oil
2 medium onions, sliced
3 celery ribs, diced
2 carrots, sliced
1 medium green pepper, diced
2 teaspoons curry powder

¼ teaspoon cinnamon
¼ teaspoon ground cloves
½ teaspoon ginger
1-2 tablespoons flour
1½-2 cups chicken broth
1 bay leaf
2 medium tomatoes, chopped
salt to taste

PROCEDURE:

Rub chicken with ½ teaspoon turmeric. Brown chicken in oil and remove. Add onions, celery, carrots and green pepper. Sprinkle with remaining turmeric and curry powder. Cook 2 minutes. Add cinnamon, cloves, ginger and flour. Add broth, bay leaf and tomatoes. Stirring constantly, bring to a boil. Reduce heat. Add chicken. Cover and simmer 30 minutes. Serve with hot, fluffy rice.

Ann. R. Colby

Chutney Chicken

INGREDIENTS:

Serves 4

3 tablespoons butter
1 medium-size apple, cored and
   diced
1 teaspoon curry powder (or less)
½ teaspoon ground cinnamon
¼ teaspoon thyme
¼ teaspoon ground ginger
¼ cup Major Grey's Chutney,
   chopped

1 11-ounce can Mandarin oranges,
   reserve liquid
1 small can seedless grapes (or
   fresh grapes)
3 whole chicken breasts, skinned,
   split and boned
salt to taste
pepper to taste
paprika to taste

PROCEDURE:

Add apple, curry powder, cinnamon, thyme, ginger and chutney to 1½ tablespoons melted butter over medium heat. In separate pan cook drained Mandarin orange liquid until slightly reduced. Season chicken with salt, pepper, and paprika and place in a 9″ by 13″ pan. Dot with 1½ tablespoons butter and broil 10-12 minutes until brown. Pour apple mixture over chicken and bake uncovered 15 minutes at 350°. Top with oranges, grapes, and juice of grapes if canned. Bake 10 minutes or until chicken is tender. Serve chicken with fruits and juices poured on top, with rice.

Karen Sachs

East Indian Curried Turkey

Serves 4

INGREDIENTS:

½ cup onion, diced
½ cup celery, diced
¼ cup oil
⅓ cup flour
2 cups chicken broth
1 cup tomato juice

½ teaspoon Worcestershire sauce
1 teaspoon curry powder
salt to taste
pepper to taste
4 cups turkey, cooked and cubed

PROCEDURE:

Sauté onion and celery in oil. Add flour, blend and add broth. Cook until thick, stirring constantly. Add tomato juice, Worcestershire sauce, seasonings, and turkey. Heat and serve over rice.

Mary Stolberg

Baked Chicken Reuben

Serves 4

INGREDIENTS:

4 whole broiler-fryer chicken
 breasts, halved and boned
¼ teaspoon salt
⅛ teaspoon pepper
1 16-ounce can sauerkraut, drained
 well

4 slices (4″ by 6″) natural Swiss
 cheese
1¼ cups Thousand Island dressing
1 tablespoon parsley, chopped

PROCEDURE:

Preheat oven to 325°. Place chicken in a greased baking pan. Sprinkle with salt and pepper. Place sauerkraut over chicken and top with cheese. Pour dressing over cheese. Cover with foil and bake 1½ hours or until tender. Sprinkle with parsley and serve.

Anne Coleman

Buttermilk Pecan Chicken

Serves 8

INGREDIENTS:

1 cup buttermilk
1 egg, slightly beaten
1 cup flour
1 cup ground pecans
¼ cup sesame seeds
1 tablespoon salt
1 tablespoon paprika

⅛ teaspoon pepper
2 (2½-3½-pound) fryer chickens, cut up
½ cup corn oil (butter or margarine, melted)
¼ cup pecan halves

PROCEDURE:

Preheat oven to 350°. Mix buttermilk with egg. Stir together flour, ground pecans, sesame seeds, salt, pepper and paprika. Dip chicken in buttermilk mixture, then in flour mixture. Place oil in large shallow roasting pan. Add chicken, skin side down, then turn pieces to coat both sides. Place pecan halves on each piece of chicken. Bake 1-1¼ hours or until tender and golden brown.

A real award winner!

Patricia and Dick Carlson

Chicken And Noodle Casserole

Serves 8

INGREDIENTS:

2½-3 pound fryer chicken
1 12-ounce package extra wide egg noodles
2 tablespoons fat (skimmed from chicken broth)
2 tablespoons flour
4 cups chicken stock

½ lemon, squeezed
salt to taste
pepper to taste
1 cup pimiento-stuffed olives, halved
½ cup American cheese, grated

PROCEDURE:

Boil chicken until tender. Cool and cut into bite-size pieces. Cook noodles. Preheat oven to 350°. Melt chicken fat and add flour, browning slowly. Gradually add chicken stock, lemon juice, salt and pepper. Add olives and cook until thickened. Alternate layers in 3-quart casserole starting with half the noodles, ⅓ sauce, chicken, ⅓ sauce, other half of noodles, and remaining sauce. Bake 30 minutes. Add cheese and bake until melted.

Alliene Vale

Chicken And Rice Casserole

Serves 6-8

INGREDIENTS:

1 can cream of chicken soup
1 can cream of celery soup
1 can cream of mushroom soup
¼ cup margarine, melted
¼ cup French dressing
⅓ cup milk

1¼ cups rice, uncooked (not instant)
6-8 chicken breasts, boned and halved
3 ounces Parmesan cheese, grated
2½ ounces sliced almonds

PROCEDURE:

Preheat oven to 275°. Mix all 6 liquid ingredients. Pour half of mixture into 9" by 13" greased pan. Spread half of rice over mixture. Cover with chicken, then with remaining rice. Top with remaining liquid. Sprinkle Parmesan cheese on top and bake 2½ hours. During last ½ hour, cover with almonds.

Great the next day.

Dorothy Dickinson

Potato Chip Chicken

Serves 6

INGREDIENTS:

4 cups cooked chicken, in bite-size pieces
4 hard boiled eggs, chopped
2 cups celery, chopped
1 5-ounce can water chestnuts, sliced
¾ cup mayonnaise

1 10¾-ounce can cream of chicken soup plus one can milk
2 tablespoons lemon juice
1 teaspoon salt (optional)
1½ cups potato chips, crushed
1 cup sharp cheddar cheese, grated

PROCEDURE:

Combine all ingredients except chips and cheese. Place in large 1½" deep rectangular dish. Top with cheese and chips. Refrigerate overnight. Bake at 350° for 45 minutes or until lightly browned.

Good for a brunch, too.

Minda Sarlin

Honey-Baked Chicken

Serves 4

INGREDIENTS:

3 pounds chicken
3 tablespoons onion, finely
   chopped
2 tablespoons honey
2 tablespoons dark soy sauce

1 tablespoon fresh ginger, minced
1 teaspoon garlic, minced
¼ cup green onion, (green part
   only) thinly sliced

PROCEDURE:

Pour onion, honey, soy sauce, ginger and garlic mixture over chicken in 9″ by 13″ pan. Marinate 1-4 hours in refrigerator, turning pieces once. Bake 30 minutes at 400°. Turn pieces over and sprinkle with green onions. Bake 15-20 minutes more, or until tender. Serve at once.

Also good cold.

Gloria Dunne

Oyster Sauce Chicken

Serves 3-4

INGREDIENTS:

6 chicken thighs
2 9-ounce bottles Dynasty oyster-
   flavored sauce

9 ounces water
green onion, diced

PROCEDURE:

Brown chicken in electric skillet or frying pan. Mix oyster sauce and water in saucepan and bring to boil over low to medium heat. Add sauce mix to browned chicken and simmer covered for 30 minutes. Add green onions just before serving. Great with steamed rice.

Bette M. Gerstacker

Beanthread Noodle Chicken And Vegetables

INGREDIENTS:

Serves 6-8

1 8-ounce package beanthread
   noodles
8 chicken thighs (or 2 whole
   chicken breasts)
1 medium onion, sliced
¼ cup oil

4 large carrots, sliced matchstick
   size
½ head medium cabbage
salt to taste
3 tablespoons soy sauce, plus some
   for topping

PROCEDURE:

Soak beanthread noodles in warm water just until soft enough to cut with scissors into 4″ lengths. Drain and set aside. Boil chicken in 2 quarts of water until tender, about 20 minutes. Save broth. When chicken is cool remove skin and bones. Cut into bite-size pieces. Heat oil in wok and sauté onion. Add carrots and cabbage and barely cook, stirring constantly. Remove and set aside. Add broth to pan with noodles and soy sauce. Cook until noodles are soft and all liquid is absorbed, about 15-20 minutes. Toss vegetables and chicken with noodles. Add more soy sauce to taste.

Beef, pork or shrimp work well, too!

Emma Van Campen

Chicken With Chow Mein Noodles

INGREDIENTS:

Serves 6

6 chicken breasts, skinned, boned
   and halved
4 tablespoons butter
1 tablespoon oil
3 tablespoons flour
1 cup chicken broth
1 cup light cream
½ cup sharp cheddar cheese, grated
½ teaspoon salt

pinch of rosemary
basil to taste
dash of hot pepper sauce
½ pound mushrooms, sliced
salt to taste
pepper to taste
½ teaspoon slivered almonds,
   toasted
3-ounce can chow mein noodles

PROCEDURE:

Preheat oven to 350°. Cook chicken breasts in 1 tablespoon butter and oil. Melt 2 tablespoons butter and blend in 3 tablespoons flour. Stir in chicken broth and cream until thickened. Add cheese, salt, rosemary, basil, and hot pepper sauce. Saute mushrooms in 1 tablespoon butter and salt and pepper. Lay chicken in shallow pan and sprinkle with mushrooms. Cover with sauce. Bake covered 25 minutes. Just before serving, sprinkle almonds on top and bake a few minutes more. Serve over noodles.

Goes nicely with fresh spinach and orange salad.

Linda Goodwin

106

Chicken With Hoisin Sauce

Serves 4

INGREDIENTS:

1½ pounds chicken breasts in bite-
   size pieces
1 tablespoon cornstarch
1 teaspoon rice wine (or sherry)
1 tablespoon soy sauce
¼ cup peanut oil
1 medium green pepper, seeded
   and cut in bite-size pieces

8 water chestnuts, chopped
¼ pound mushrooms, chopped
½ teaspoon salt
2 tablespoons hoisin sauce
¼ cup cashews (or almonds)

PROCEDURE:

Coat chicken with cornstarch. Add soy sauce and wine and toss again.
Marinate less than 30 minutes. Set wok over high heat for 30 seconds, add
1 tablespoon oil. Coat wok and heat for 30 seconds more. (Turn down if oil
starts to smoke). Add green pepper, chestnuts, mushrooms, and salt. Stir fry
2-3 minutes. Remove with slotted spoon. Add 3 tablespoons oil. Heat
almost to smoking. Cook chicken 2-3 minutes or until white and firm. Add
hoisin sauce, vegetables and cook 1 minute. Add nuts. Serve at once with
sticky white rice.

Judy Rosenblatt

Curry Crumb Chicken

Serves 6

INGREDIENTS:

1 cup mayonnaise
½ teaspoon curry powder

12 chicken portions
seasoned bread crumbs

PROCEDURE:

Preheat oven to 350°. Combine mayonnaise and curry powder. Spread
mixture over chicken. Dip pieces in bread crumbs. Line baking sheet with
foil and place chicken pieces skin side up on sheet. Bake 1 hour. No turning
necessary.

Denise Selati

Ginger Chicken

Serves 6

INGREDIENTS:

6 whole chicken breasts, skinned
   and boned
¾ cup soy sauce
½ cup honey

4 garlic cloves, minced
2 tablespoons ginger
¼ cup lemon juice
vegetables (of your choice)

PROCEDURE:

Cut chicken into 2″ or 3″ squares. Mix soy sauce, honey, garlic, ginger, lemon juice and marinate chicken 3-4 hours. Skewer and barbeque chicken and vegetables of your choice (mushrooms, onions, pineapple, green pepper) for 20-30 minutes. Baste while cooking. Serve with rice.

Phyllis Queen Healy

Jade Empress Chicken

Serves 4

INGREDIENTS:

4 boneless chicken breasts, skinned
3 tablespoons oil
2 cups fresh mushrooms, sliced
2 cups celery, sliced
1 green pepper, cut bite-size
½ cup green onions, sliced

1 13¼-ounce can pineapple tidbits
⅓ cup dry sherry
¼ cup soy sauce
1 teaspoon garlic salt
½ teaspoon ground ginger
2 tablespoons cornstarch

PROCEDURE:

Cut chicken into bite-size pieces. Heat oil in wok. Add chicken, stirring constantly until creamy white. Add mushrooms, celery, green pepper and onions and sauté until crisp tender. Drain pineapple and reserve syrup. Combine syrup, sherry, soy sauce, garlic salt, ginger and cornstarch and mix well. Add sauce to chicken and vegetables, stirring lightly until thickened. Add pineapple and mix gently. Accommpany with rice.

108
Judie Dresser

Chicken And Broccoli

Serves 6

INGREDIENTS:

2 bunches fresh broccoli
4 whole chicken breasts, cooked
   and boned
2 cans cream of chicken soup
1 cup mayonnaise
4 tablespoons lemon juice

1 teaspoon curry powder
Pam
1 cup cheddar cheese, grated
½ cup crushed corn flakes
   (optional)
¼ cup slivered almonds (optional)

PROCEDURE:

Preheat oven to 350°. Steam broccoli until half-cooked. Combine soup, mayonnaise, lemon and curry. Spray a 9″ by 13″ pan with Pam. Layer broccoli, chicken and sauce in pan. Top with cheese. Sprinkle with corn flakes and/or almonds if desired. Bake 30 minutes.

Always a pleasing company dish.

Janis Butcher
Jane Smith

Chicken Broccoli Quiche

Serves 4

INGREDIENTS:

1 10-ounce package frozen broccoli
   (or 1 pound fresh)
1 whole chicken breast, skinned
   and boned
1 cup Gruyère cheese, grated
1 9″ pastry shell, partially baked

3 eggs
1 cup heavy cream
2 tablespoons lemon juice, fresh
1 teaspoon salt
dash of pepper
green onions, minced for topping

PROCEDURE:

Cook broccoli until crisp tender. Cook chicken and cut into bite-size pieces. Preheat oven to 375°. Partially bake pastry shell. Layer shell with broccoli, chicken, and then cheese. Beat eggs, cream, lemon juice, salt and pepper until mixed, but not frothy. Pour over layers. Bake 35-40 minutes or until center is set and top is golden. Garnish with onions.

This popular and hearty quiche can be prepared in advance and refrigerated. We enjoy it with a fresh spinach salad, warm sourdough and Strawberries Romanov for dessert.

Lyda Girton Goldsmith

109

Chicken Raisin Casserole

Serves 4-6

INGREDIENTS:

3 pounds chicken, cut up
¼ cup butter
2 tablespoons olive oil
1 onion, chopped
1 garlic clove, pressed
1 green pepper, chopped
1½-2 tablespoons flour

½ cup white wine
½ cup chicken broth
2 large tomatoes, chopped
1 cup golden raisins
½ teaspoon salt
½ teaspoon ground pepper
½ teaspoon basil

PROCEDURE:

Preheat oven to 300°. Brown chicken in butter and oil and place in large greased casserole with cover. Sauté onion, green pepper and garlic in remaining oil for about 3 minutes. Stir in flour. Add wine, chicken broth, tomatoes and raisins. Simmer several minutes, then pour over chicken. Salt and pepper to taste. Bake 1 hour covered or until chicken is tender. Sprinkle with basil during last 10 minutes of cooking. Serve with wild rice.

Karen Stewart

Lemon Chicken In Wine With Mushrooms

Serves 4

INGREDIENTS:

½ pound fresh mushrooms, sliced
4 tablespoons butter
2 fresh lemons
¼ cup flour
paprika to taste
salt to taste

pepper to taste
1 ¼ pound boneless chicken breasts, skinned
3 tablespoons olive oil
½ cup dry white wine (or vermouth)

PROCEDURE:

Sauté mushrooms in 1 tablespoon butter over high heat. Remove from pan and set aside. Cut 1 lemon in half and the other in slices; set aside. Mix salt, pepper and paprika into flour. Coat each breast with flour mixture and sauté in 3 tablespoons butter and olive oil over medium-high heat for 3 minutes each side, or until lightly browned. Squeeze juice from lemon halves over cooked chicken, then add wine. Heat 1 minute and remove to serving platter. Add mushrooms to pan and heat. Arrange lemon slices on breasts. Pour mushrooms and juices over chicken. Serve with rice.

Looks and tastes great!

Linda Clark

Lime-Cucumber-Dill Chicken

Serves 6

INGREDIENTS:

6 boneless chicken breasts, skinned
salt to taste
pepper to taste
juice of 1 lime

1 teaspoon dill weed
1 green pepper, diced
1 8-ounce bottle creamy cucumber
   dressing

PROCEDURE:

Preheat oven to 350°. Season chicken with salt and pepper. Place in a 13″ by 9″ dish. Sprinkle lime juice and dill weed over chicken. Bake 30 minutes. Sprinkle green pepper over chicken and spread dressing on top. Bake another 15 minutes. Serve hot with rice.

Joan Schultz

Rolled Baked Chicken

Serves 4

INGREDIENTS:

3 whole chicken breasts, skinned,
   boned and halved
½ teaspoon salt
½ teaspoon pepper
½ teaspoon garlic salt
1 3-ounce can chopped mushrooms

4 tablespoons butter, melted
1 tablespoon lemon juice
½ bag Pepperidge Farm bread
   crumbs
1 pint heavy cream
10 pats of butter

PROCEDURE:

Marinate chicken in salt, pepper and garlic salt 24 hours. Preheat oven to 350°. Butter dish. Mix mushrooms, melted butter, lemon juice, and bread crumbs. Reserve 4 tablespoons of bread crumbs for topping. Cover chicken with 1 teaspoon cream and mushroom mixture. Roll and fasten with toothpick. Cover with remaining cream and 6 pats of butter. Sprinkle bread crumbs on top, dot with 4 pats of butter. Bake 1 hour.

Freezes well. We enjoy this dish often with rice pilaf
and a mixed greens salad.

Jan Friedman

Roast Chicken Stuffed With Grapes

Serves 4-6

INGREDIENTS:

1 roasting chicken, 4-5 pounds
salt to taste
fresh-ground black pepper to taste
½ tablespoon butter
1 Spanish onion, finely chopped
4 garlic cloves, finely chopped
4 slices dry bread, in bite-size
    pieces

4-6 ounces white seedless grapes
6 tablespoons butter, melted
parsley, finely chopped (to taste)
¼ teaspoon dried sage
butter
dry white wine

PROCEDURE:

Preheat oven to 325°. Rub inside cavity of chicken with salt and pepper. Prepare stuffing by sautéing onion and garlic in ½ tablespoon butter. To the onion/garlic mix add the bread, grapes, 6 tablespoons melted butter, parsley, sage, salt and pepper to taste. Stuff chicken, skewering the opening. Truss the chicken and rub with butter, salt and pepper. Bake 1½-2 hours, basting with wine.

Eva Sonnenberg Lewin

Chicken Breast Olé

Serves 4-6

INGREDIENTS:

1 4-ounce can diced chiles
1 2¼-ounce can chopped black
    olives
¾ cup cheddar cheese, grated
¾ cup Monterey jack cheese,
    grated
3 tablespoons onion, chopped

3 chicken breasts, halved, boned
    and flattened
⅓ cup margarine (or butter), melted
¼ teaspoon chile powder
¼ teaspoon cumin
1 cup tortilla chips, crushed

PROCEDURE:

Preheat oven to 375°. Drain chiles and olives and combine with cheeses and onion. Down the center of each breast place some of this mixture. Roll chicken around filling, folding in ends, securing with toothpicks. Combine butter with chile powder and cumin. Coat chicken with butter mixture and roll in tortilla chips. Arrange chicken, seam side down, in shallow greased casserole. Bake 35 minutes. Serve with sour cream and taco sauce.

112   *Linda Hull*

Chicken Enchiladas

Serves 4

INGREDIENTS:

3 chicken breasts, cooked
3 cans cream of chicken soup
1 pint sour cream
1 4-ounce can diced green chiles

1 pound cheese, grated (cheddar or Monterey jack)
1 2.2-ounce can sliced olives
12 flour tortillas, regular or burrito size

PROCEDURE:

Preheat oven to 325°. Cut chicken into bite-size pieces and combine with 1 can soup, sour cream, chiles, olives, and ¼ of cheese. Stuff tortillas. Place in greased baking dish, seam-side down. Cover with 2 cans soup and remaining cheese. Bake 30 minutes.

Freezes very well.

Linda Goodwin

Chicken Enchilada Casserole

Serves 6

INGREDIENTS:

1 cup onion, chopped
½ cup green pepper, chopped
2 tablespoons butter
2 cups cooked chicken, chopped bite-size
1 4-ounce can green chile peppers
3 tablespoons butter
¼ cup flour

1 teaspoon ground coriander seed
¾ teaspoon salt
2½ cups chicken broth
1 cup sour cream
1½ cups Monterey jack cheese, shredded
12 6"-tortillas

PROCEDURE:

Preheat oven to 350°. Sauté onion and green pepper in 2 tablespoons butter. Add to chicken and chile peppers in bowl. Melt 3 tablespoons butter and blend in flour, coriander and salt. Add chicken broth and stir until thickened. Remove from heat and stir in sour cream and ½ cup cheese. Stir ½ cup of sauce into chicken mixture. Dip each tortilla into remaining sauce to soften. Fill each tortilla with ¼ cup of chicken mixture. Roll up. Arrange rolls in 9" by 13" pan and pour remaining sauce over tortillas. Sprinkle with remaining cheese. Bake 25-30 minutes or until bubbly.

Terri Zelt Albritton

Chicken And Tortilla Gratin

Serves 4-6

INGREDIENTS:

4 chicken breasts, cooked and
   boned
1 can cream of chicken soup
1 can cream of celery soup

3 tablespoons onions, chopped
2 tablespoons chiles, finely
   chopped (optional)
8-10 corn tortillas, cut in quarters

PROCEDURE:

Preheat oven to 350°. Shred chicken into bite-size pieces. Mix both soups, onions, and chiles. Alternate layers in a greased casserole of soup mixture, tortilla pieces, and chicken ending with cheese on top. Bake 1-1½ hours.

Coryna Phillips

Chicken Cacciatore

Serves 4-6

INGREDIENTS:

2 2-pound fryers
½ cup flour
½ teaspoon salt
¼ teaspoon pepper
⅓ cup olive oil
2 garlic cloves, chopped
1 medium onion, chopped

1 green pepper, seeded and diced
1 cup canned tomatoes
½ teaspoon oregano
½ cup sherry (or white wine)
1 3-ounce can sliced mushrooms
salt to taste
pepper to taste

PROCEDURE:

Cut fryers into serving pieces and coat with flour, salt and pepper mixture. Add chicken to heated oil and brown on both sides. Add garlic, onion, pepper, tomatoes, oregano and sherry and simmer 30 minutes. Add mushrooms and salt and pepper if needed. Simmer 10 minutes more. Serve over plain spaghetti.

Anne Coleman

Chicken Parmigiana

Serves 6

INGREDIENTS:

6 boneless chicken breasts, skinned
    and halved
1 cup Parmesan cheese, grated
2 cups seasoned bread crumbs
2 eggs slightly beaten with 2
    tablespoons water

1 jar spaghetti sauce
1 pound mozzarella cheese, thinly
    sliced
2 tablespoons oil
2 tablespoons butter

PROCEDURE:

Pound chicken very flat. Mix bread crumbs with ½ cup Parmesan cheese.
Dip chicken in egg/water mixture and coat with crumbs. Refrigerate at
least 10 minutes. Add chicken to oil and melted butter and brown. Preheat
oven to 350°. Pour half of spaghetti sauce into shallow baking dish.
Arrange alternately, chicken and mozzarella cheese. Cover with other half
of sauce. Top with remaining mozzarella and Parmesan. Bake 20 minutes
or until sauce bubbles and cheese melts.

A lovely company dish to prepare, freeze and bake just before serving.

Estelle Graff

Chicken Romano

Serves 4-6

INGREDIENTS:

3 whole chicken breasts, halved
3 tablespoons flour, seasoned to
    taste
¼ cup oil
¼ cup onions, minced
2 cups tomato juice
2 tablespoons Romano cheese
1 tablespoon sugar

½ teaspoon salt
½ teaspoon garlic salt
½ teaspoon oregano
¼ teaspoon basil
1 teaspoon vinegar
1 3-ounce can mushrooms
1 tablespoon parsley
1 cup cheddar cheese, grated

PROCEDURE:

Shake chicken in flour and fry in oil. Remove chicken. Sauté onion, then
add remaining ingredients except cheese. Add chicken and cook 45 minutes
over low flame. Top with cheese.

Jan Friedman

Chicken Tetrazzini

Serves 6

INGREDIENTS:

¼ cup butter
¼ cup flour
1 teaspoon salt
¼ teaspoon white pepper
⅛ teaspoon nutmeg
2 cups chicken broth
1 cup light cream
½ cup sherry

½ pound egg noodles, cooked
½ pound mushrooms, sautéed
2½ cups chicken, cooked and sliced
  to match-stick size
¼ cup fresh Parmesan cheese,
  grated
paprika to taste

PROCEDURE:

Preheat oven to 375°. Melt butter, blend in flour, salt, pepper and nutmeg. Gradually stir in chicken broth. Cook over low heat, stirring constantly until thickened. Add cream and sherry and heat just to boiling. Combine half of sauce, noodles, and half of mushrooms. Place in greased pan, making a hole in the center. Place chicken, remaining sauce and mushrooms in center. Sprinkle on cheese and paprika. Bake 20-25 minutes or until top is brown and sauce bubbles.

May be prepared and refrigerated a day ahead, or frozen.

Nancy Bixby

Parmesan Chicken Breasts

Serves 4

INGREDIENTS:

¼ cup Italian salad dressing
4 chicken breasts, skinned and
  boned
1 egg, slightly beaten
2 tablespoons water
½ cup Parmesan cheese, grated

½ cup seasoned bread crumbs
2 tablespoons snipped parsley
½ teaspoon salt
½ teaspoon paprika
⅛ teaspoon pepper

PROCEDURE:

Pour salad dressing into square baking dish. Add chicken, turning to coat on all sides. Cover and refrigerate 4 hours (or overnight) turning pieces occasionally to recoat. Preheat oven to 350°. Drain chicken, reserving dressing. Combine egg and water. Combine cheese, bread crumbs, parsley, salt, paprika and pepper in a plastic bag. Dip chicken in egg mixture, then shake in crumb mixture. Return chicken to baking dish, spooning on remaining dressing. Bake 45 minutes.

Patti Hall

Elegant Chicken Livers

Serves 4-6

INGREDIENTS:

12 chicken livers, cut bite-size
6 bacon slices, cut bite-size
½ pound lean ground beef, pressed
   into miniature meatballs
4 tablespoons onion, chopped
3 tablespoons fresh parsley,
   chopped

½ pound fresh mushrooms, sliced
1 tablespoon Italian herb seasoning
1 teaspoon salt
fresh ground pepper to taste
3 teaspoons tomato paste
6 tablespoons heavy cream

PROCEDURE:

In a large teflon skillet fry livers, bacon, meatballs, onion, parsley, mushrooms, and seasonings until meat is no longer pink. Stir in tomato paste and cream and cook until hot.

Serve with garlic bread and a tossed green salad.

Joyce Aftahi

Rabbit In Cream

Serves 4

INGREDIENTS:

1 rabbit
salt to taste
pepper to taste
1 tablespoon peanut oil
2 tablespoons butter
3 tablespoons cognac
6 shallots, minced

½ cup dry white wine
1 bay leaf
½ teaspoon thyme (or 1 tablespoon
   fresh thyme)
1 cup crème fraîche (or heavy
   cream)

PROCEDURE:

Cut rabbit into serving pieces for frying. Season with salt and pepper and sauté in the oil and butter over fairly high heat until golden on all sides. Remove from pan and keep warm. Add cognac to pan and flame. Add shallots and cook until golden. Add rabbit and its juices, wine, bay leaf and thyme. Cover and simmer for 30 minutes, or until pieces are tender. Place meat in hot deep serving dish. Stir crème fraîche into pan juices. Discard bay leaf. Bring to boil and cook until sauce is slightly reduced. Check seasoning. Coat rabbit pieces with sauce and serve immediately. Good with buttered noodles.

As popular on European tables as chicken in the States!

Janine Ryder

117

Roast Turkey

Serves 10-12

INGREDIENTS:

1 12-20 pound turkey
2 large carrots, sliced lengthwise
3 celery sticks, sliced lengthwise
3 cups tomato juice
1 cup sherry

1 tablespoon paprika
1½ tablespoons salt
½ teaspoon black pepper, freshly
   ground
3 cups water

PROCEDURE:

Preheat oven to 375°. Stuff turkey with carrots and celery and place in roasting pan. Combine remaining ingredients and pour over turkey. Bake 3-4 hours, turning turkey every half hour. The skin will be crisp.

Absolutely fail proof!

Lee Lichter

Turkey Tetrazzini

Serves 4-6

INGREDIENTS:

4-6 tablespoons butter
1 medium onion, chopped
8 ounces mushrooms, sliced
⅓ cup flour
1 teaspoon salt
½ teaspoon pepper
2 cups milk
1 tablespoon sherry

1 tablespoon lemon juice
½ cup pitted black olives, sliced
½ cup Swiss cheese, shredded
1½ cups cooked turkey, shredded
dash of nutmeg
8 ounces thin spaghetti, cooked
   and drained
Parmesan cheese, freshly grated

PROCEDURE:

Preheat oven to 350°. Sauté onions in butter. Add mushrooms, stirring constantly for about 5 minutes. Remove from pan. Add flour, salt and pepper to pan. Add milk in a slow, steady stream and cook, stirring constantly until thick and smooth. Blend in sherry and lemon juice. Blend in olives and Swiss cheese. Add onions, mushrooms, turkey and nutmeg. Add spaghetti and pour into a 2-quart casserole. Top with Parmesan cheese and bake for 30 minutes.

A natural for leftover turkey, but also good with crab, shrimp or tuna. Does not freeze.

Brooke Peterson

5

Seafood

Ceviche Maruca

Serves 8-10

INGREDIENTS:

5 cups firm uncooked white fish
    fillets, diced
1½ cups lemon juice
1 cup catsup
4 tablespoons olive oil
1 teaspoon ground oregano
1 teaspoon ground black pepper

½ teaspoon Tabasco sauce
    (optional)
½ cup orange juice
2 cups fresh tomatoes, diced
1 cup onions, finely chopped
salt to taste

PROCEDURE:

Marinate fish in lemon juice for at least 40 minutes. Drain and rinse in cold water. Combine remaining ingredients in attractive serving bowl. Add fish. Mix and refrigerate for several hours. Serve with crackers and slices of avocado or as a first course.

Can be prepared ahead. Keep refrigerated.

Doryna Phillips

Easy Mexican Style Fish

Serves 6

INGREDIENTS:

2-3 pounds firm fleshed white fish
cooking oil
2 7-ounce cans green chile salsa
½ pound cheddar cheese, grated
½ pound Monterey jack cheese,
    grated

½ pint sour cream
3-4 green onions, sliced (include
    some tops)

PROCEDURE:

Preheat oven to 375°. Oil a baking dish large enough to arrange fillets in a single layer. Cover bottom of dish with small amount of salsa. Arrange fish in baking dish and cover each fillet with equal amounts of both cheeses. Spoon remaining salsa over cheeses. Bake for 20-25 minutes or until cooked through and bubbly. Serve garnished with sour cream and green onions.

A quick and simple family favorite.

Helen Froeb

119

Fillets Of Fish Thermidor

Serves 6

INGREDIENTS:

water
salt
3 pounds firm flesh white fish, in
    large fillets
5 tablespoons butter
4 tablespoons flour

3 cups milk
1 cup beer
4 tablespoons green onions,
    chopped
1 pound mushrooms, chopped
1 pound cheddar cheese, grated

PROCEDURE:

Poach fillets. Bring enough water to cover fish to a boil in a large pan. Add salt and fish. Simmer over low heat until cooked through, about 10 minutes. Do not overcook. Lift from water and put in ovenproof platter. Preheat oven to 375°. Melt 4 tablespoons butter in a saucepan over low heat. Stir in flour and blend well. Slowly add milk and beer stirring constantly, raising heat to medium, until thickened and smooth. In another pan brown onions and mushrooms in remaining tablespoon of butter. Add to sauce and pour over fish. Sprinkle cheese over all. Bake for 10 minutes or until heated through and bubbly.

An elegant company dish.

Helen Mayer

Barbequed Fish In Tarragon Butter

Serves 4

INGREDIENTS:

¾ cup butter (or margarine)
¼ cup onions, finely chopped
1 large garlic clove, minced
2 tablespoons lemon juice
1 teaspoon Beau Monde seasoning
¾ teaspoon dried tarragon,
    crumbled

½ teaspoon salt
¼ teaspoon pepper
4 fish fillets (halibut, sea bass,
    snapper, cod)
lemon slices (for garnish)
green onion (for garnish)

PROCEDURE:

Prepare coals. Melt butter in a medium saucepan over medium heat. Add onions and garlic and sauté gently about 2 minutes or until transparent. Stir in lemon juice, Beau Monde, tarragon, salt and pepper. Blend well. Place each fillet on a sheet of foil large enough to form a packet and spoon ¼ of butter mixture over each. Wrap foil around each fillet and seal edges well. Place foil packets about 4" from the coals. Grill about 20-30 minutes or until fish flakes easily when tested with a fork. Remove to a serving platter and garnish with green onions and lemon slices. Pour butter sauce from foil over each.

Brenda Kerr

Spicy Broiled Halibut

Serves 4

INGREDIENTS:

2 pounds halibut (in 4 fillets)
2 tablespoons lemon juice
6 tablespoons olive oil
1 garlic clove, minced
¼ teaspoon pepper

¼ teaspoon paprika
1 tablespoon parsley, finely
   chopped
Worcestershire sauce (optional)
walnuts (optional)

PROCEDURE:

Lay fish in single layer in shallow baking pan. Combine lemon juice, oil, garlic, pepper, paprika and parsley. Blend well and pour over halibut. Let sit 10-15 minutes. Preheat broiler and position rack 10"-12" from heat. Broil halibut 6-8 minutes per side or until fish flakes easily with a fork. After turning you can add a dash of Worcestershire and a sprinkling of chopped blanched walnuts to the top of each fillet. Remove fish to serving platter. Spoon pan juices over fillets.

This is also good on the barbeque.

Rosario Reyes Kurtz

Swordfish With Rosemary

Serves 6

INGREDIENTS:

3 pounds swordfish steaks,
  trimmed and cut into 6 serving-
  size pieces
¼ teaspoon salt
dash of pepper
2 cups flour
1 teaspoon ground rosemary

2 eggs
3 tablespoons butter
3 tablespoons oil
¼-½ cup sherry
chopped parsley (for garnish)
lemon wedges (for garnish)

PROCEDURE:

Rinse and dry steaks. Mix flour, salt, pepper and rosemary. Beat eggs in a shallow dish. In a large skillet, melt butter and oil over medium heat. Have it hot but not smoking. Dip each steak into egg, coat well, then dredge in seasoned flour. Coat evenly. Cook in hot oil and batter until golden brown on one side (7-8 minutes). Turn and brown well on the other side. (For 1½″ swordfish steaks the total time should be 15 minutes). Remove steaks to a warm platter and keep warm. Add sherry to the pan and swirl in more butter (optional). Heat, scraping up brown bits from bottom. Pour over swordfish. Garnish with chopped parsley and lemon wedges.

Brooke Peterson

Fast And Easy Fish Florentine

Serves 2

INGREDIENTS:

1 bunch fresh spinach, washed,
  well-drained and stemmed
1 pound sole (or flounder)

salt to taste
pepper to taste
lemon wedges

PROCEDURE:

Cook spinach in a covered pan over medium heat. Use only the water left on leaves. When wilted and tender, after 5-10 minutes, place fish on top of spinach. Cover and cook over medium heat for 8-10 minutes. Salt and pepper to taste. Serve with lemon wedges.

This is a fast, nutritious, and low calorie meal.

Fletcher Bingham

Swordfish Kabobs

Serves 6

INGREDIENTS:

2 pounds swordfish steaks, cut into
    ¾"-1" pieces
½ pound butter, melted
2 tablespoons olive oil
salt to taste

pepper to taste
juice of 1 lemon
bay leaves
6 skewers

PROCEDURE:

Combine butter, oil, salt and pepper in a large bowl. Add swordfish and marinate 1 hour. Skewer the pieces of fish with a bay leaf between each piece. These can be broiled 10"-12" from heat, turning after 5 minutes and cooked 5-6 minutes more) or barbecued over charcoal. (Cook 5 minutes over medium coals, turn and cook 5 more minutes or until done). Squeeze lemon juice over fish before serving.

Great with a good soup and crisp salad.

Ayse Underhill

Poached Salmon

Serves 6

INGREDIENTS:

water
For every quart of water:
3 tablespoons white wine vinegar
1 tablespoon salt
7 peppercorns
5 whole allspice

1 bay leaf
1 whole onion, cleaned
1 carrot, scraped
3 pounds salmon
5 sprigs fresh dill

PROCEDURE:

Put enough water to cover fish in a kettle and add correct amounts of vinegar, salt, peppercorns, allspice, bay leaf, onion and carrot. Cover and bring to a boil. Boil gently for 15 minutes. Strain. Add fish and dill. Leave uncovered and bring to boil. Skim off any scum. Cover and simmer 8 minutes per pound. If serving hot, remove fish carefully to a warmed serving platter, garnish with fresh dill and serve immediately. If serving cold, let cool in liquid and remove just before serving.

Try poaching trout the same way.

Helen Mayer

123

Salmon Roll

Serves 10

INGREDIENTS:

4 tablespoons butter
½ cup flour
pinch of salt
2 cups milk
4 egg yolks
1 teaspoon sugar

4 egg whites, stiffly beaten
7 ounces canned salmon
1 tablespoon onion, minced
4 tablespoons sour cream
dash of paprika

PROCEDURE:

Preheat oven to 325°. Oil a 10″ by 15″ jelly roll pan. Line with wax paper and oil paper. Dust lightly with flour. Melt butter in a double boiler over moderate heat. Add flour and salt and blend well. Add milk slowly in a steady stream, stirring constantly until smooth and thickened. Remove from heat and blend in egg yolks and sugar. Stir until smooth over medium heat. Remove again from heat and fold in egg whites. Spread batter evenly in prepared pan. Bake for 40 minutes. Meanwhile prepare filling. Drain and flake salmon. Combine with onion, sour cream and paprika. Use more sour cream if needed for smooth spreading consistency. Remove roll from pan after baking, placing on a clean cloth. Spread with filling and roll immediately. To serve cut in 1″ slices and place on individual plates with sour cream and chives.

Try this elegant dish as an appetizer filling it with 2 ounces caviar spread first, then a layer of sour cream followed by a layer of sliced green onions.

Ann Lipschitz

Salmon Loaf

Serves 4-6

INGREDIENTS:

1 15-ounce can salmon
⅓ cup milk
¾ cup soft bread crumbs
2 eggs
2 tablespoons onion, minced

1 tablespoon lemon juice
1 tablespoon parsley, minced
¼ teaspoon salt
dash of pepper

PROCEDURE:

Preheat oven to 350°. Drain salmon, reserving liquid, and flake. Pour milk over bread crumbs and let stand 5 minutes. Add salmon, its liquid, and remaining ingredients. Blend well. Spoon into an oiled loaf pan. Bake 40-50 minutes or until firm. Unmold. Garnish with chopped parsley. Can be served with a white sauce.

Jean Mitchell

Salmon Quiche

Serves 6

INGREDIENTS:

CRUST
1 cup whole wheat flour
⅔ cup sharp cheddar cheese,
   shredded
¼ cup almonds, chopped
½ teaspoon salt
¼ teaspoon paprika
6 tablespoons cooking oil

FILLING
1 15-ounce can salmon
3 eggs, beaten
1 cup sour cream
½ cup sharp cheddar cheese,
   shredded
1 tablespoon onion, grated
¼ teaspoon dried dillweed
3 drops hot pepper sauce

PROCEDURE:

Preheat oven to 400°. Combine flour, ⅔ cup cheese, almonds, salt and paprika. Stir in oil. Mix well. Set aside ⅓ of the dough. Press remaining dough into bottom and up sides of a 9″ pie plate. Bake 10 minutes. (Crust can be prepared and refrigerated in advance). Drain and flake salmon, reserving liquid. Add enough water to liquid to make ½ cup. Remove bones and skin from salmon. Blend together eggs, sour cream, and salmon liquid. Stir in salmon, cheese, onion, dillweed, and pepper sauce. Pour filling into baked crust. Sprinkle with reserved crust mixture. Lower oven to 325°. Bake 45 minutes or until firm in center.

Lucy Smith

125

Cold Salmon With Herb Mayonnaise

Serves 6

INGREDIENTS:

4 quarts water
2 medium onions, quartered
2 carrots, cut in large pieces
1 teaspoon salt
1 bay leaf
3 parsley sprigs
6 peppercorns
1 sprig fresh thyme (or ½ teaspoon dried)
3 tablespoons lemon juice
½ cup dry white wine
2 pounds whole salmon

GARNISHES
lettuce leaves, parsley sprigs, hard boiled eggs, tomatoes, olives, lemon slices
MAYONNAISE
1 egg
juice of ½ lemon
½ teaspoon salt
1 tablespoon mustard
1 cup oil
3 tablespoons parsley, minced
watercress (or any fresh herb)
2 gherkins, minced

PROCEDURE:

Prepare poaching liquid in a fish poacher or large kettle. (The solid ingredients may be wrapped in cheesecloth. For easier handling the fish may also be wrapped in cheesecloth and tied with a string for easy removal). Bring the poaching liquid to a boil and simmer 30 minutes. Lower fish into poaching liquid. Simmer 8 minutes per pound of fish or until it flakes easily with a fork. Remove salmon and transfer to an oval or special fish serving platter. Peel off skin and decorate with lettuce, tomatoes, parsley, eggs and olives if desired. Pass with mayonnaise. Mayonnaise: blend egg, lemon juice, salt, mustard, herbs and gherkins well. Slowly add oil beating until thickened. This can be done in a blender, with a mixer, or in a food processor. Correct seasoning.

Salmon can be served warm with hollandaise sauce or prepared and served cold the next day. Keep in refrigerator.

Janine Ryder

126

Shrimp Steamed In Beer

Serves 6-8

INGREDIENTS:

2½ pounds large shrimp (10-12 per pound), shell on
24 ounces beer
2 garlic cloves, whole
1 teaspoon fresh thyme
1 bay leaf
1 teaspoon celery seed
2 tablespoons fresh parsley, chopped
generous pinch of cayenne pepper
juice of 1 lemon

ORIENTAL SAUCE
½ cup unseasoned rice vinegar
3 egg yolks
2 cups peanut oil
6 drops sesame oil
1 piece fresh ginger (size of small garlic clove)
salt to taste
pepper to taste
1 bunch chives, chopped

PROCEDURE:

Wash shrimp. Remove thyme leaves from stems. Combine beer, garlic, parsley, thyme, bay leaf, celery seed, cayenne pepper and lemon juice in a saucepan. Bring to a boil. Add shrimp and cook 5 minutes. Do not overcook.(Cooking time will be less for smaller shrimp).Remove shrimp, let cool, then peel and devein. Refrigerate. Prepare oriental sauce. In a mixing bowl, combine well egg yolks and rice vinegar. Beat in peanut oil in small amounts. Incorporate well after each addition, beating constantly. As oil is emulsified sauce will thicken into a heavy cream. Mash then mince fine fresh ginger. Add to sauce. Add salt and pepper to taste. (This sauce can be made with a mixer or a food processor if desired). One half hour before serving shrimp marinate in half the oriental sauce. Serve as a first course with remaining sauce and chopped chives as garnish.

Lyn Heller

127

Savory Stuffed Shrimp

Serves 4

INGREDIENTS:

1½ pounds jumbo shrimp, shell on
½ cup seasoned bread crumbs
¼ cup grated Parmesan cheese
½ cup butter, melted

1 garlic clove, minced
1 tablespoon fresh parsley, minced
2 tablespoons lemon juice

PROCEDURE:

In a large kettle or Dutch oven bring about 3 quarts of salted water to a rolling boil. Add shrimp and return water to a boil. When shrimp curl and turn pink, drain in a colander and rinse with cold water. (They cook very quickly after water returns to a boil). When cooled peel and devein leaving tails on. Butterfly shrimp by making a deep slit along back and pressing shrimp open. Mix remaining ingredients well and fill cavities in shrimp. Preheat broiler and place shrimp on an oiled, shallow baking pan. Set shrimp about 10″ from heat and broil until bread crumbs are golden, about 2-3 minutes.

This dish also makes a great appetizer or first course.

Betsy Grasso

Shrimp Scampi

Serves 4

INGREDIENTS:

20 jumbo shrimp
½ cup olive oil
2 teaspoons garlic, minced
2 tablespoons parsley, finely
    chopped
⅛ teaspoon crushed red pepper
    flakes

½ teaspoon dried crushed oregano
2 tablespoons fine fresh bread
    crumbs
salt to taste
pepper to taste

PROCEDURE:

Peel and devein shrimp leaving last tail segment intact. Preheat broiler. Add remaining ingredients to shrimp and toss to coat evenly. (This can be done several hours in advance. Refrigerate shrimp until ready to broil). Line a baking pan with foil and arrange shrimp on top. Place under broiler about 3″-4″ from heat source. Broil 5-6 minutes. It is not necessary to turn the shrimp. Baste shrimp and serve.

Ellen Sims

Shrimp And Wild Rice

Serves 6

INGREDIENTS:

1½ pounds medium shrimp, peeled, deveined and cooked
1 cup wild rice
½ cup onions, diced
2 cups celery, diced
3 tablespoons butter

½ pound fresh mushrooms, sliced
1 bell pepper, diced
2 cans cream of mushroom soup
1 small can water chestnuts, drained and sliced
1 cup slivered almonds

PROCEDURE:

Cook wild rice according to directions. Preheat oven to 350°. Melt butter in a medium skillet over medium heat. Sauté onions and celery stirring occasionally. Cook until softened, about 3-4 minutes. Add mushrooms and peppers and continue to sauté until vegetables are softened and cooked through, about 5 minutes. Mix vegetables with cooked rice, shrimp, soup and water chestnuts. Turn into an ovenproof serving dish. Bake for 30 minutes. Brown almonds and sprinkle on top. Bake 10 minutes more.

This dish freezes well. It can be prepared a day ahead and kept refrigerated.

Carolyn Colwell

Sweet And Pungent Shrimp

Serves 4

INGREDIENTS:

¼ cup brown sugar
2 tablespoons cornstarch
½ teaspoon salt
¼ cup vinegar
1 tablespoon soy sauce
¼ teaspoon ground ginger

2½ cups canned pineapple chunks
    (in juice)
1 large green pepper, chopped
2 small onions, sliced in rings
1 pound large shrimp, peeled,
    deveined and cooked

PROCEDURE:

Mix sugar, cornstarch and salt in a saucepan over low heat. Add vinegar, soy sauce, ginger and juice from pineapple chunks. Heat gently and stir constantly until slightly thickened. In a separate pan, over medium heat, sauté green pepper and onion and add to sweet and pungent sauce. Add pineapple chunks and simmer 2 minutes more. Add shrimp, bring sauce to boil and serve immediately over hot rice.

Karen Michelson

Shrimp Marinara With Linguini

Serves 4

INGREDIENTS:

1 onion, finely chopped
2 garlic cloves, minced
2 tablespoons olive oil
1 16-ounce can Italian plum
    tomatoes, drained, seeded and
    chopped
salt to taste
pepper to taste
¼ teaspoon dried oregano
½ teaspoon dried basil

¼ pound fresh mushrooms, sliced
2 tablespoons fresh parsley,
    chopped
1½ pounds medium uncooked
    shrimp, peeled and deveined
1-3 pats butter (optional)
12 ounces linguini, cooked and
    drained
Parmesan cheese, grated

PROCEDURE:

In a medium skillet, sauté onions and garlic in olive oil for 2-3 minutes. Add tomatoes and spices. Simmer, partially covered, 25 minutes stirring occasionally. Add mushrooms and cook stirring until soft, about 3 minutes. Add shrimp and parsley. Cook and stir until shrimp is pink and cooked through. Do not overcook. Swirl in 1-2 pats of butter if desired. Mix with freshly cooked and drained linguini. Garnish with grated Parmesan. Serve immediately.

Brooke Peterson

Baked Shrimp And Artichokes

Serves 4

INGREDIENTS:

1 10-ounce package frozen
   artichoke hearts, cooked
1 pound medium shrimp, peeled,
   deveined and cooked
¼ pound fresh mushrooms, sliced
5 tablespoons butter
3 tablespoons flour

1½ cups milk
¼ cup sherry
1 teaspoon Worcestershire sauce
salt to taste
pepper to taste
¼ cup Parmesan cheese, grated
2 tablespoons parsley, chopped

PROCEDURE:

Preheat oven to 375°. Sauté mushrooms in 2 tablespoons of butter in a saucepan over medium heat. Set aside. Melt remaining butter in a saucepan over medium heat and blend in flour. Stir and cook about 1 minute. Add milk in a steady stream stirring constantly until smooth and thickened. Add sherry and Worcestershire sauce and heat through. Salt and pepper to taste. Place artichokes in a 2-quart ovenproof serving dish. Put shrimp on top of artichokes and mushrooms over shrimp. Pour cream sauce over all. Sprinkle top with Parmesan cheese. Bake 20 minutes or until heated through. Garnish with chopped parsley and serve.

Edmarie Riley

Baked Shrimp With Asparagus

Serves 4

INGREDIENTS:

2 packages frozen asparagus spears
¼ cup butter
¼ cup flour
1 cup milk
½ cup cream
½ cup white wine
1 teaspoon salt

⅛ teaspoon pepper
1 pound shrimp, peeled, deveined
  and cooked
1 egg yolk, beaten
½ cup Parmesan cheese, grated
buttered bread crumbs

PROCEDURE:

Cook asparagus according to package directions until tender crisp. Drain and set aside. Preheat oven to 350°. Melt butter in a saucepan over medium heat. Add flour and blend well. Gradually add milk stirring constantly until smooth and thickened. Add salt, pepper, cream and wine. Heat through stirring constantly. Turn off heat, rapidly stir in egg yolk, shrimp and cheese. Arrange asparagus and shrimp sauce in a buttered 2-3 quart casserole. Layer sauce and asparagus beginning and ending with sauce. Top with crumbs. Bake 30 minutes.

Jeannie Riley

Shrimp Dijonaise

Serves 4-6

INGREDIENTS:

5 tablespoons butter
4 tablespoons flour
2 cups milk
salt to taste
pepper to taste
3 tablespoons shallots, minced
½ cup white wine
¼ cup parsley, chopped

⅛ teaspoon cayenne pepper
1 tablespoon Dijon mustard
1 egg yolk
½ cup Parmesan cheese, grated
cooked rice for 4-6 people
1½ pounds small shrimp (frozen or
  canned)

132

PROCEDURE:

In a medium saucepan, over medium heat, melt 3 tablespoons butter and stir in flour. Cook and blend well about 30 seconds. Add milk slowly in a steady stream stirring constantly. Continue to cook and stir until smooth and thickened. Add salt and pepper to taste. Melt remaining butter in another pan over medium heat and cook shallots until softened. Add wine, parsley and white sauce. Cook and stir until heated through. Preheat oven to 400°. Add cayenne and mustard to sauce and heat through. Remove from heat. Beat egg yolk and stir rapidly into sauce. In an ovenproof serving dish put shrimp on top of cooked rice. Pour sauce over shrimp. Sprinkle grated Parmesan on top. Bake 10-15 minutes or until heated through.

Quick and easy company dinner.

Sally Peters Davidson

Louisiana Style Beer Shrimp

Serves 4

INGREDIENTS:

2 12-ounce cans of beer
2 sprigs celery tops
1 bay leaf
½ teaspoon Worcestershire sauce
½ teaspoon dried oregano, crumbled
¼ lemon with peel (squeeze juice in beer)

½ teaspoon salt
1 small onion, sliced
16-20 large shrimp, uncooked, shell on
1 cup butter, melted

PROCEDURE:

Combine all ingredients and marinate for at least 15 minutes. If longer refrigerate. Put mixture in a pot and bring to a boil. Simmer 3-5 minutes or until shrimp are cooked. Do not overcook. Serve in marinade, warm or chilled, with melted butter for dipping.

This is a messy dish but lots of fun. Serve with big napkins and an extra dish for shells.

Connie Engelhardt

Szechwan Shrimp

Serves 4

INGREDIENTS:

1 pound large shrimp, peeled and
  deveined
2 tablespoons oil
¼ cup green onions, sliced
⅜ teaspoon ground ginger
3 garlic cloves, minced
2 tablespoons dry sherry
2 tablespoons soy sauce

2 teaspoons sugar
½ teaspoon salt
2 tablespoons catsup
2 tablespoons salsa picante
1 teaspoon red pepper, crushed
dash of Tabasco sauce
hot cooked rice

PROCEDURE:

Heat oil in skillet or wok. Add shrimp, onion, garlic and ginger. Stir fry
until shrimp are pink. Add sherry, soy sauce, sugar and salt. Stir in catsup,
salsa, pepper flakes and Tabasco. Serve piping hot over rice.

Mike Gentry

Tasty Crab Casserole

Serves 6

INGREDIENTS:

1 8-ounce package stuffing mix
6 ounces crabmeat (not canned)
2 cups small shrimp
1 medium onion, chopped
1 green pepper, chopped (optional)
2 cups celery, diced
1 4-ounce can water chestnuts,
  sliced

1 cup mayonnaise
1 4-ounce can mushrooms, drained
1 teaspoon salt
2 teaspoons Worcestershire sauce
dash of paprika
1 3-ounce package slivered
  almonds
1 cup cheddar cheese, grated

PROCEDURE:

Preheat oven to 350°. Prepare stuffing mix according to package directions. Lightly grease a shallow 2-quart baking/serving dish and line bottom with half the stuffing. Combine remaining ingredients except cheese. Add to casserole and top with remaining stuffing. Sprinkle with cheese. Bake 1 hour.

Light and tasty!

Linda Smith

Elegant Crab And Artichokes

Serves 4

INGREDIENTS:

3 tablespoons flour
3 tablespoons butter
1 cup milk
½ cup white wine (or chicken broth)
½ cup Swiss cheese, grated
2 teaspoons Worcestershire sauce
salt to taste

pepper to taste
2 9-ounce packages frozen artichoke hearts, cooked
4 hard boiled eggs, sliced
¾ pound crab meat (canned or frozen)
2 tablespoons Parmesan cheese, grated

PROCEDURE:

Preheat oven to 350°. In a medium saucepan, over medium heat, melt butter and blend in flour. Stir and cook about 1 minute. Add milk in a steady stream stirring constantly until smooth and thickened. Add wine or broth, salt and pepper, and Worcestershire sauce. Butter a 2-quart baking/serving dish or individual ramekins. Layer cream sauce, artichoke hearts, crab, eggs and cheese in prepared dish or ramekins. Begin and end with sauce. Top with grated Parmesan. Bake 30 minutes.

Libby Clemmer

135

King Krab Krunch

Serves 4

INGREDIENTS:

1 pound King crabmeat (frozen)
1 8¾-ounce can crushed pineapple
3 tablespoons butter
½ cup celery, thinly sliced
1 tablespoon cornstarch

1 cup chicken broth
½ cup slivered almonds, blanched
 and toasted
1 tablespoon lemon juice
1 can chow mein noodles

PROCEDURE:

Thaw, drain and rinse frozen crabmeat. Drain pineapple, reserving liquid. Melt butter in a medium skillet over medium heat. Add crab, celery and pineapple. Simmer 5 minutes stirring frequently. Dissolve cornstarch into pineapple juice. Stir into crab mixture. Add chicken broth, raise heat to medium and cook, stirring constantly, until heated through and thickened. Add lemon juice and almonds. Serve over noodles.

Quick, easy and very tasty.

E. Bernice Stetl

Crab And Pasta

Serves 4

INGREDIENTS:

1 pound crabmeat (not canned)
2 tablespoons olive oil
½ cup butter
4 garlic cloves, minced
1 bunch green onions, sliced
2 medium tomatoes, chopped
½ cup parsley, chopped

½ teaspoon Italian seasoning
2 tablespoons lemon juice
½ teaspoon salt
12 ounces pasta (preferably
 spaghetti, linguini or fettucini)
Parmesan cheese, grated

PROCEDURE:

In a large skillet melt butter and oil over medium heat. Add and sauté garlic 2-3 minutes. Add remaining ingredients and heat gently 8-10 minutes. Meanwhile cook pasta to taste. Drain. Toss with crab mixture. Garnish with grated Parmesan.

Melody Gentry

Crab Imperial

Serves 6

INGREDIENTS:

1 tablespoon green pepper, chopped
1 teaspsoon onion, chopped
4 tablespoons butter
¼ cup all purpose flour
½ teaspoon salt
½ teaspoon dry mustard

dash of ground mace
1½ cups milk
2 teaspoons lemon juice
¼ teaspoon Worcestershire sauce
2 eggs, beaten
2 7½-ounce cans crabmeat, drained and flaked

PROCEDURE:

Preheat oven to 350°. In a medium saucepan, over medium heat, melt butter and sauté pepper and onions until tender but not browned. Stir in flour and blend well. Add salt, mustard and mace. Cook, stirring, about 2 minutes. Add milk in a steady stream and stir until smooth and thickened. Add lemon juice and Worcestershire sauce. Remove from heat and stir in beaten eggs. Fold in crabmeat. Spoon into 6 individual baking dishes. Bake 20 minutes. Can garnish with slivered almonds.

An elegant entrée for a dinner party.

Debbie Greenfield

137

Scallops Mexicana

Serves 6

INGREDIENTS:

2 pounds scallops, washed
2 teaspoons garlic powder
4 tablespoons salad oil
½ cup celery, sliced
4 bell peppers, cut in medium
    chunks
1 bunch green onions, sliced with
    some tops
1 pound fresh mushrooms, sliced

⅓ cup sauterne
3 teaspoons dried oregano
3 bay leaves
dash of Tabasco sauce
1 8-ounce can tomato sauce
1 bunch fresh cilantro, chopped
4 tablespoons parsley, chopped
hot cooked rice for 6

PROCEDURE:

Sprinkle scallops on both sides with garlic powder. Heat oil in a large skillet over high heat or in an electric skillet set to 400°. Add celery and green pepper and cook and stir for 2-3 minutes or unitl softened. Add green onions and sauté another 2 minutes. Add mushrooms and wine and heat through. Add scallops, spices, and tomato sauce. heat and stir until scallops are done and vegetables are tender crisp. Serve over rice.

Beatriz Mort

Seafood En Bouchees Brunch

Serves 6

INGREDIENTS:

6 frozen pastry shells
1 10¾-ounce can cream of shrimp
    soup
1 10¾-ounce can cream of celery
    soup
1 7½-ounce can crab, drained

1 7½-ounce can shrimp, drained
¼ cup dry sherry (or white wine)
¼ teaspoon paprika
6 peach halves (fresh or canned)
chutney (for garnish)

PROCEDURE:

Bake pastry shells according to package directions. Combine first six ingredients and heat through. Stuff pastry shells. Accompany each with a peach half with a dot of chutney in center.

Mabel Erickson

Easy Seafood Curry

Serves 6-8

INGREDIENTS:

¼ cup olive oil (or butter)
1 garlic clove, minced
1 cup onions, chopped
2 tablespoons fresh ginger, chopped
¼ cup flour
2 tablespoons curry powder (or to taste)
1 quart rich milk
salt to taste
pepper to taste
¾ pound medium shrimp, peeled, deveined and cooked
1 pound crabmeat (or lobster)
¾ pound poached scallops

¾ cup heavy cream
hot cooked rice for 6-8, combined with ⅓ cup currants and ⅓ cup shelled pistachios
SAMBALS
chutney, mild and hot
chopped peanuts or cashews
light and dark raisins plumped in rum
toasted salted coconut
chopped green onions
toasted sesame seeds
pineapple chunks
mandarin orange sections
banana chips

PROCEDURE:

Heat oil or butter in a large skillet. Add onions, garlic and ginger and cook over low heat until onions are translucent. Combine flour and curry powder and blend well. Add to onions and cook slowly for about 5 minutes, stirring constantly. Add milk slowly, stirring constantly, until smooth and slightly thickened. Simmer over very low heat 20 minutes. Pour curry mixture through a strainer. (At this point the curry mixture can be refrigerated, covered with plastic wrap). When ready to serve, add the heavy cream, shrimp, scallops and crab or lobster. Slowly heat through and add salt to taste. Serve with rice and sambals.

This recipe doubles and triples very well to make good buffet fare.

Suzie Desmarais

139

Seafood Lasagne

Serves 12

INGREDIENTS:

8 lasagne noodles
1 cup onions, chopped
2 tablespoons butter
1 8-ounce package cream cheese, softened
1½ cups cream style cottage cheese
1 egg, beaten
2 teaspoons dried basil, crushed
salt to taste
pepper to taste

2 cans condensed cream of mushroom soup
⅓ cup milk
⅓ cup dry white wine
1 pound cooked medium shrimp, peeled and halved
1 7½-ounce can crabmeat, drained and flaked
¼ cup Parmesan cheese, grated
½ cup sharp American cheese, shredded

PROCEDURE:

Cook lasagne noodles according to package directions and drain. Preheat oven to 350°. Melt butter in medium skillet over medium heat and sauté onions until tender. Blend in cream cheese, cottage cheese, egg, basil, salt and pepper. Set aside. Combine soup, milk, wine and shrimp. In a 13″ by 9″ by 2″ greased baking dish, arrange 4 noodles. Spread half of cottage cheese mixture on top of noodles and half the seafood mixture on top of cottage cheese layer. Repeat layers and top with Parmesan cheese. Bake uncovered 45 minutes. Top with American cheese and bake 2-3 minutes more. Let stand 15 minutes before serving.

Deborah Baronofsky

Seafood Stuffed Eggplant Creole

Serves 4

INGREDIENTS:

2 large eggplants
3 tablespoons butter
4 tablespoons green onions, chopped
2 tablespoons fresh parsley, chopped
¼ cup fresh mushrooms, chopped
4 tablespoons celery, finely chopped

1 cup crabmeat
1 cup medium-sized shrimp, peeled, deveined and cooked
toasted bread crumbs
salt to taste
pepper to taste
Parmesan cheese, grated

140

PROCEDURE:

Preheat oven to 350°. Cut each eggplant in half and scoop out pulp leaving ¼" thick shell. Chop pulp. Melt butter in a skillet and sauté onions, parsley, celery and mushrooms for 1-2 minutes. Add eggplant pulp and simmer until the eggplant is tender. Blend these ingredients together well. Add shrimp and crab and enough of the bread crumbs to firm mixture for stuffing eggplant shells. Add salt and pepper to taste and heat through. Stuff eggplant shells with seafood mixture. Sprinkle tops with additional bread crumbs and Parmesan cheese. Place stuffed eggplants in a baking pan with a small amount of water. Bake 20-30 minutes or until thoroughly heated and shells are softened

Freezes well, can be prepared a day ahead and refrigerated until baking time.

Hosh Abramson

Norfolk Tuna Noodle Bake

Serves 6-8

INGREDIENTS:

12 ounces wide egg noodles
½ cup fresh parsley, chopped
1 cup small curd cottage cheese
1 cup sour cream
1 7½-ounce can tuna, drained and flaked
1 4-ounce can sliced mushrooms, drained

1 teaspoon Worcestershire sauce
dash of Tabasco sauce
3 green onions, sliced with some tops
1 cup Monterey jack cheese, grated
1 teaspoon paprika

PROCEDURE:

Cook noodles in boiling, salted water with a little cooking oil added. Drain. Preheat oven to 350°. Combine all other ingredients except cheese and paprika. Mix in noodles. Put in a greased shallow baking/serving dish. Sprinkle top with grated cheese then paprika. Bake uncovered 30-40 minutes.

A real family favorite. Great side dish without the tuna.

Harriet Campbell

141

Tuna Hash

Serves 6

INGREDIENTS:

¼ cup olive oil
½ green pepper, chopped
1 medium onion, chopped
2 6½-ounce cans tuna, drained and
 flaked
¾ cup tomato sauce

¼ cup sherry
½ cup pimiento-stuffed olives,
 halved
3 hard boiled eggs, chopped
½ teaspoon salt (optional)

PROCEDURE:

Sauté pepper and onion in hot oil. Add tuna, tomato sauce and sherry. Simmer 10 minutes. Stir in olives and eggs. Season with salt if desired. Stir and cook 3-5 minutes more. Serve over white rice.

Kids love this! A new twist to tuna.

Gloria Andújar

Berwyn's Barbequed Marinated Albacore

Serves 10-14

INGREDIENTS:

1 cup Durkee's salad dressing
3 cups mayonnaise
1 cup bottled Italian dressing
1 red onion, chopped
2 tablespoons Worcestershire sauce
1 tablespoon sherry
1 tablespoon dried tarragon

juice of 1 lemon
salt to taste
pepper to taste
paprika to taste
1 albacore fillet cut in half (about
 10 pounds)

PROCEDURE:

Combine all ingredients except fish. Marinate fish for at least ½ hour or up to 24 hours in refrigerator. Barbeque over medium coals turning frequently. Baste with marinade during entire cooking time.

Also good with chicken!

142

David Burton

Gratin Of Baked Clams

Serves 12

INGREDIENTS:

3 dozen clams
1 teaspoon powdered mace
1 teaspoon powdered nutmeg

2½-3 cups bread crumbs
butter

PROCEDURE:

Take clams out of shells. Wash clams. Leave whole or mince. Wash shells. Preheat oven to 375°. Butter a baking dish large enough for clams. Toss clams in mace and nutmeg. Spread bottom of baking dish with bread crumbs. Scatter some small bits of butter over crumbs. Layer clams, minced or whole, then another layer of crumbs and small pieces of butter. Bake 15 minutes or until heated through. Have ready a serving dish with shells. Fill shells with baked mixture. Serve piping hot.

Francine LaMeire

Bill Mitchell's Oyster Stew

Serves 8-12

INGREDIENTS:

¼ pound butter
2 pints fresh eastern oysters
2 heaping tablespoons fresh basil, chopped
½ teaspoon celery salt
fresh dill, chopped

Tabasco sauce to taste
salt to taste
pepper to taste
2 cups sherry
2 quarts cream

PROCEDURE:

Melt butter in a deep skillet over medium heat. Add oysters. Sprinkle with basil and simmer until edges curl. Add celery salt, 1 teaspoon dill, salt and pepper. Simmer 15 minutes. Add 1 cup sherry and simmer another 10 minutes. Meanwhile scald cream in a deep pan. Add 1 cup sherry and oysters. Simmer 10-15 minutes. Serve garnished with fresh chopped dill.

Bill Mitchell

143

Notes

6

Pasta, Cheese, Eggs & Rice

Noodle Spinach Ring

Serves 8

INGREDIENTS:

1 8-ounce package broad noodles
1 10-ounce package chopped
  spinach, defrosted
1 onion, chopped

½ cup margarine
3 eggs, lightly beaten
1 cup sour cream
1 teaspoon salt

PROCEDURE:

Cook noodles. Drain. Preheat oven to 350°. Mix noodles with spinach. Sauté onion in margarine. Mix onions with noodle/spinach mixture. Fold in eggs, sour cream and salt until well blended. Pour into greased 8-cup ring mold. Place mold into pan of hot water. Bake for 45-50 minutes. Unmold on heated platter.

Jane Shore

Florentine Noodles

Serves 6

INGREDIENTS:

4 tablespoons butter
½ cup olive oil
2 garlic cloves, minced
1 large onion, sliced
1 10-ounce package frozen
  chopped spinach, thawed

1 teaspoon basil
½ teaspoon salt
½ cup Parmesan cheese, grated
1 pound spinach noodles, cooked
  and drained

PROCEDURE:

Melt butter in oil. Add garlic, onion and spinach. Cover, cook over medium heat for 10 minutes. Add basil and salt. Cook 5 minutes, covered. Combine with cheese and noodles. Top with additional Parmesan if desired.

Judith Rosenberg

Turkish Spaghetti

Serves 10

INGREDIENTS:

1 pound spaghetti, cooked and
    drained
4 large tomatoes, peeled and diced
    into ½″ cubes

¼ cup butter
salt to taste

PROCEDURE:

While spaghetti cooks, place tomatoes in sauce pan with butter and salt. Simmer over medium heat about 20 minutes. Pour over cooked spaghetti. Stir and serve at once.

Ayse Underhill

Dill Weed Casserole

Serves 6

INGREDIENTS:

1 8-ounce package small shell
    noodles
1½ teaspoons dill weed
2 tablespoons margarine
½ cup onion, minced
1 garlic clove
1 pound ground round

1 tablespoon flour
½ cup beef bouillon
1 8-ounce can tomato sauce
¼ cup red wine
½ teaspoon pepper
1 can cream of mushroom soup

PROCEDURE:

Preheat oven to 350°. Cook noodles. Drain and sprinkle with dill weed. Sauté onion and garlic in margarine for 5 minutes. Add beef. Cook until browned. Drain. Add flour, bouillon, tomato sauce, red wine, salt and pepper. Simmer for 10 minutes. Remove from heat. Add noodles and cream of mushroom soup. Pour into greased 2-quart casserole. Bake uncovered for 25 minutes.

Marsha Neffeler

Pasta Primavera

Serves 8-10

INGREDIENTS:

1 bunch broccoli cut into florets
　　with 1″ stem
1 zucchini squash, sliced
1 yellow squash, sliced
2 carrots, cut in 2″ strips
10 tablespoons butter
½ tablespoon parsley, chopped
½ cup basil, chopped

nutmeg to taste
salt to taste
pepper to taste
1 cup fresh mushrooms
1 pound taglierini (ribbon
　　macaroni)
1 cup heavy cream
½ cup fresh Parmesan cheese

PROCEDURE:

Steam vegetables al dente. Drain and rinse under cold water. In saucepan, melt 8½ tablespoons butter. Add parsley, basil, spices and mushrooms. Cook 5 minutes. Add steamed vegetables and cook additional 5 minutes. Boil taglierini. Drain. Melt remaining butter and toss pasta in it. Add vegetable mixture and cream. Stir well. Mix with ½ cup Parmesan cheese. Top with additional Parmesan cheese and ground pepper.

This is always popular as a main course or as an accompaniment to chicken or fish.

Nancy Gordon

Pasta With Broccoli

Serves 4

INGREDIENTS:

2 large bunches broccoli, chopped
1 16-ounce package curly macaroni
¾ cup cream (or ½ cup whole milk)

¾ cup Parmesan cheese
salt to taste
pepper to taste
fresh parsley (for garnish)

PROCEDURE:

Cook broccoli until tender. Drain, mash and set aside. Boil macaroni for 2 minutes less than package directions. Drain and return to pot. Add cream, Parmesan, broccoli, salt and pepper. Cook over high heat for 2 minutes, stirring constantly. Sprinkle with additional Parmesan. Garnish with parsley.

Susan K. Liguori

Spinach Lasagne

Serves 6-8

INGREDIENTS:

1 medium onion, chopped
2 garlic cloves, minced
2 tablespoons olive oil
1 28-ounce can tomatoes
1 6-ounce can tomato paste
¼ cup parsley, minced
½ teaspoon oregano
1 bay leaf
8 ounces lasagne noodles

1 10-ounce package frozen
  chopped spinach, cooked and
  drained
1 pound ricotta cheese
1 egg
¾ cup fresh Parmesan, grated
1 teaspoon salt
¼ teaspoon pepper
8 ounces mozzarella cheese, grated

PROCEDURE:

Preheat oven to 350°. Sauté onion and garlic in oil until brown. Stir in tomatoes, paste, parsley, oregano and bay leaf. Simmer uncovered for 20 minutes. Cook noodles and drain. Combine spinach, ricotta, egg, ¼ cup Parmesan, salt and pepper. Spoon ⅓ tomato sauce in 13″ by 9″ baking dish. Cover with ⅓ lasagne noodles, ½ spinach/ricotta filling, ½ mozzarella and ¼ cup Parmesan. Repeat layers, using ½ remaining sauce, noodles and all remaining filling. Top with single layer of noodles, sauce, Parmesan and mozzarella. Bake 45 minutes. Let stand a few minutes before cutting into squares. Freezes well.

Margie Edwards

Valerie And Brandon's Favorite Lasagne

INGREDIENTS:

Serves 6

1 pound ground round
2 8-ounce cans tomato sauce
½ teaspoon oregano
salt to taste
9 cooked lasagne noodles, boiled
  and drained
1 cup cottage cheese

1 8-ounce package cream cheese
⅛ teaspoon pepper
3 green onions, chopped
¾ cup sour cream
½ pound mozzarella cheese, thinly
  sliced

PROCEDURE:

Preheat oven to 350°. Brown and crumble meat. Drain. Add tomato sauce, oregano and salt to taste. Heat. Combine cottage cheese, cream cheese, pepper, onions and sour cream. Sparingly cover the bottom of a 9" by 9" baking dish with tomato sauce and line with a layer of noodles/mozzarella/meat sauce. Top with second layer of noodles/cheese/meat sauce mixture. Bake for 30 minutes.

Serve with a fresh green salad and crusty bread. Freezes well or can be baked, refrigerated and reheated.

Karen Kessler

Mexican Lasagne

Serves 6

INGREDIENTS:

1½ pounds lean ground beef
1 medium onion, chopped
1 garlic clove, minced
1 16-ounce can tomatoes
1 10-ounce can red chile sauce
1 4-ounce can ripe olives, chopped
1 teaspoon salt
¼ teaspoon pepper

¼ cup oil
12 corn tortillas
1 pound ricotta cheese
2 eggs, lightly beaten
¾ pound Monterey jack cheese, shredded
tortilla chips
1 cup cheddar cheese, shredded

PROCEDURE:

Preheat oven to 350°. In large skillet brown meat, onion and garlic. Discard fat. Stir in tomatoes, chile sauce, olives, salt and pepper. Simmer for 20 minutes stirring occasionally. Heat oil in small skillet and add tortillas one at a time to soften. Drain on paper towels. Mix ricotta with eggs. Spread ⅓ of the meat mixture in a 9" by 13" baking dish. Top with half the ricotta mixture and half the jack cheese. Add a layer of tortillas, cut in half. Repeat layers reserving ⅓ of the meat sauce for the top. Cover with tortilla chips and cheddar cheese. Bake for 30 minutes. Let stand for 5-10 minutes. Garnish with sour cream, cherry tomatoes, avocado slices and ripe olives. Pass your favorite Mexican salsa at the table.

Gleneva Belice
Judy Rosenblatt

149

Manicotti Alla Romana

Serves 6

INGREDIENTS:

12 manicotti shells, cooked and
   drained
¼ cup butter
¼ onion, chopped
1 garlic clove, crushed
1 pound ground beef
1 package frozen spinach, thawed
   and drained
½ cup cottage cheese
2 eggs, beaten
1 teaspoon salt

SAUCE
¼ cup butter
¼ cup flour
1½ teaspoon chicken stock
1½ cups milk
¼ cup parsley, chopped
1 15-ounce jar spaghetti sauce with
   mushrooms
2 teaspoons basil leaves, crushed
½ cup Parmesan cheese

PROCEDURE:

Preheat oven to 350°. Sauté onion and garlic in butter. Add meat and
brown. Remove from heat. Stir in spinach, cottage cheese, eggs and salt.
Stuff manicotti shells with the mixture and arrange in baking dish. To
prepare sauce, melt butter, blend in flour and chicken stock. Remove from
heat. Stir in milk. Heat 1 minute until thickened. Stir in parsley. Pour over
manicotti. Combine spaghetti sauce and basil. Pour over white sauce and
sprinkle with Parmesan. Bake for 30 minutes.

May be made ahead.

Cherry Lee

Linguini With Clam Sauce

Serves 4

INGREDIENTS:

1 pound linguini noodles, cooked
   and drained
1 medium onion, chopped
1 garlic clove, minced
3 tablespoons margarine

3 tablespoons flour
3 6½-ounce cans clams
½ teaspoon salt
½ teaspoon basil
⅛ teaspoon pepper

150

PROCEDURE:

Sauté onion and garlic in margarine until onion becomes transparent. Blend in flour. Add clams with juice, salt, basil and pepper. Bring to a boil, reduce heat, cover and simmer for 5 minutes. Serve over linguini.

Kathy Burns

Inside-Out Ravioli

Serves 6-8

INGREDIENTS:

1 pound ground beef
1 medium onion, chopped
1 garlic clove, minced
1 tablespoon salad oil
1 10-ounce package frozen chopped spinach
1 16-ounce jar spaghetti sauce with mushrooms
1 8-ounce can tomato sauce
1 6-ounce can tomato paste

½ teaspoon salt
dash of pepper
1 7-ounce package shell (or elbow) macaroni, cooked and drained
4 ounces American cheese, shredded
½ cup bread crumbs, softened
2 eggs, well-beaten
¼ cup salad oil

PROCEDURE:

Preheat oven to 350°. Brown meat, onion and garlic in 1 tablespoon of oil. Cook spinach, drain and reserve liquid. Add sufficient water to make 1 cup. Stir liquid with spaghetti sauce, tomato sauce, paste, salt and pepper into meat mixture. Simmer 10 minutes. Combine spinach with noodles, cheese, bread crumbs, eggs and ¼ cup oil. Spread in a 9″ by 13″ casserole dish. Top with meat sauce. Bake for 30 minutes. Let stand 10 minutes before serving.

Joyce Aftahi

151

Pasta Shells Stuffed With Salmon

Serves 4-6

INGREDIENTS:

1 package jumbo pasta shells
1 bay leaf
1 garlic clove
2 tablespoons olive oil
1 16-ounce can Red Sock Eye
  salmon

3 green onions, chopped
3 celery stalks, chopped
4 ounces capers
4 ounces black olives, chopped
mayonnaise, enough for smooth
  consistency

PROCEDURE:

Cook shells according to directions, but add bay leaf, garlic and oil to boiling water. Drain and cool. Process the salmon in food processor (5 times) or blender. Transfer to bowl. Add remaining ingredients. Mix to blend well. Stuff shells with salmon mixture.

Enjoy with salad or sweet pickles and a favorite vegetable.

Rosario Reyes Kurtz

Spaghetti Sauce

Serves 6-8

INGREDIENTS:

3 pounds ground beef
½ pound cooked bacon, diced
2 6-ounce cans tomato paste
2 8-ounce cans tomato sauce
1 10¾-ounce can beef broth

1 teaspoon garlic powder
1 teaspoon basil
1 teaspoon Italian seasoning
1 teaspoon sugar

PROCEDURE:

Brown beef and drain. Add bacon. Stir in paste, sauce and broth. Stir well. Add remaining seasonings. Simmer slowly all day.

Phyllis Queen Healy

Italian Spaghetti Sauce

INGREDIENTS: Serves 6-8

2 16-ounce cans Italian packed
   tomatoes
2 pork chops, trimmed (or 3 sweet
   Italian sausages)
3 tablespoons olive oil
1¼ teaspoon tomato paste
2 onions, finely chopped
2 garlic cloves

½ teaspoon oregano
1 teaspoon salt
½ teaspoon pepper
1 tablespoon parsley
½ teaspoon fennel, finely mashed
¼ teaspoon Accent
1 teaspoon sugar

PROCEDURE:

Strain tomatoes. Sauté pork chops or sausage in olive oil. Add tomato paste with onions and garlic. Brown these. Raise heat. Add tomatoes and stir. Add oregano, salt, pepper, parsley, fennel, Accent and sugar. Boil vigorously 3-5 minutes. Reduce heat. Simmer uncovered. Stir occasionally for 1-2 hours. Add ½ cup water if necessary. Skim excess grease from top.

Jonnie Soper

Spicy Spaghetti Sauce

Serves 6

INGREDIENTS:

2 pounds hot Italian sausages
2-4 tablespoons olive oil
2 large onions, sliced
2 large green peppers, sliced
3 celery stalks, diced

2 garlic cloves, minced
1 12-ounce can tomato paste
2 16-ounce can tomatoes
½ teaspoon dried oregano
1 bay leaf

PROCEDURE:

Slice half the sausage into bite-size pieces. Brown in olive oil. Set aside. Add more oil if needed and brown rest of sausages, whole (prick to avoid bursting). Set aside. Sauté onion, pepper, celery and garlic. Add meat, paste, and tomatoes. Use juice of tomatoes to rinse paste can. Add oregano. Cover and simmer 1 hour. Add bay leaf last few minutes. Add water if desired for thinner sauce.

Best if made ahead and aged. Look for quality sausage for truly flavorful results.

Billy Simms   153

Mozzarella Marinara

Serves 4

INGREDIENTS:

1 piece whole milk mozzarella
  cheese, 2″ by 3″ by 5″
flour
2 jumbo eggs
2 tablespoons olive oil

⅛ teaspoon salt
unseasoned bread crumbs
2 basil sprigs, leaves only
vegetable oil
marinara sauce (recipe follows)

PROCEDURE:

Cut the mozzarella into 8 fingers, approximately 1″ by 3″ by 1¼″. Place flour in plastic bag. In a pie plate, whisk eggs, olive oil and salt. Place bread crumbs in another pie plate. Flour the mozzarella, coat it with egg mixture and then bread crumbs. Coat the breaded cheese, once again with the egg mixture and then bread crumbs. Refrigerate at least 4 hours. Slice basil leaves in strips. On medium high, heat 1″ of vegetable oil in a 12″ fry pan. Add mozzarella in a single layer. Cook 5 minutes per side, turning once. Remove cheese from pan if it begins to ooze. Drain on paper towels on heated platter. Line individual heated serving plates with marinara sauce. Center 1 piece of mozzarella on the plate. Garnish with basil. Serve with buttered French beans.

Marinara Sauce

Serves 4-6

INGREDIENTS:

¼ cup butter
¼ cup olive oil
3 garlic cloves
1 bunch parsley, leaves only
6 pounds fresh plum tomatoes (or
  2 28-ounce cans chopped plum
  tomatoes in purée)

2 basil sprigs
2 heaping tablespoons tomato
  paste
1 2-ounce can flat anchovy fillets
freshly ground black pepper to
  taste

PROCEDURE:

Place butter and oil in saucepan. Heat to melt. Mince garlic and parsley together. Sauté for 5 minutes. Peel, seed and chop fresh tomatoes. Add tomatoes and basil to the saucepan. Cook tomato sauce on low heat until all excess water has evaporated and sauce has turned dark red. Place tomato paste and anchovies in Cuisinart or blender. Process until anchovies are puréed. Add tomato paste/anchovy mixture to the tomato sauce, whisking until well blended. Season with freshly ground black pepper to taste.

Lyn Heller

154

Fresh Pesto

Yields 2 cups

INGREDIENTS:

3 cups basil leaves, finely chopped
1 cup parsley, finely chopped
1 cup olive oil
½ cup Parmesan cheese

1 teaspoon salt
½ teaspoon pepper
3 garlic cloves, minced
½ cup pine nuts

PROCEDURE:

Mix well. Beat until smooth. Serve with your favorite pasta lightly tossed in butter.

Freezes well.

Sally Peters Davidson

Noodle Pudding

Serves 8-10

INGREDIENTS:

½ pound medium noodles, cooked
   and drained
1 pound cottage cheese
¼ pound butter, melted
½ pint sour cream
3 eggs
½ cup sugar

½ teaspoon salt
1 teaspoon vanilla extract
2 cups milk
¼ cup cornflake crumbs
1 tablespoon brown sugar
dash of cinnamon

PROCEDURE:

Combine cottage cheese, butter and sour cream. Add to cooked noodles. Mix eggs, sugar, salt, vanilla and milk. Place noodle mixture in buttered 3-quart baking dish. Pour egg mixture on top. Cover with foil and refrigerate overnight. Before baking top with mixture of cornflake crumbs, brown sugar and cinnamon. Bake at 325° for 2 hours. Serve at room temperature.

Can be prepared at least two days ahead!

Jane Shore

155

Kugel

Serves 12

INGREDIENTS:

1 1-pound package broad noodles,
    cooked and drained
1 10-ounce can condensed milk,
    add water to make 1 quart
1 cup sugar
6 eggs
1 stick butter, melted

1 16-ounce creamed cottage cheese
1 16-ounce can crushed pineapple,
    drained
1 teaspoon vanilla extract
3 ounces raisins
cinnamon to taste

PROCEDURE:

Preheat oven to 350°. Combine all ingredients in one large bowl. Spread evenly in 16″ by 10″ greased pan. Bake uncovered for 1 hour or until top browns.

A favorite of adults and kids alike, this dish may accompany any meat course or be served alone.

Rae Selevan

Cheese Grits Special

Serves 6-8

INGREDIENTS:

1 cup grits
4 cups water
1 teaspoon salt
1 stick butter

¼ pound Velveeta cheese
¼ pound sharp cheddar cheese
3 eggs lightly beaten
⅓ cup milk

PROCEDURE:

Preheat oven to 350°. Cook grits in salted water until done. Add butter, cheese, eggs and milk. Stir until melted. Place in 1½-quart casserole. Bake for 1 hour.

Lovely for dinner with Country Ham and a fresh green vegetable.

Kiki Henry

Ham And Cheese Soufflé

Serves 8-10

INGREDIENTS:

16 slices white bread, cut off crusts and cube
1 pound cubed ham
1 pound sharp cheddar, grated
1½ cups Swiss cheese, cubed
6 eggs

3 cups milk
½ teaspoon onion salt
½ teaspoon dry mustard
3 cups crushed cornflakes
½ cup butter, melted

PROCEDURE:

Grease a 9″ by 13″ glass baking dish. Spread half bread cubes in dish. Add ham and both cheeses. Cover with remaining bread cubes. Mix eggs, milk, onion salt and mustard. Pour evenly over bread cubes. Refrigerate overnight. Combine cornflakes and butter for topping. Bake at 375° for 40 minutes. Let stand 10 minutes before cutting.

Joyce Aftahi

Mock Cheese Soufflé

Serves 8

INGREDIENTS:

6 eggs, beaten
1 cup milk
1 pound Monterey jack cheese, cut in chunks
3 ounces cream cheese, cut in chunks

8 ounces cottage cheese
¼ pound butter, melted
½ cup flour
1 teaspoon baking powder

PROCEDURE:

Preheat oven to 350°. Combine eggs and milk. Cut in jack cheese, cream cheese and cottage cheese. Stir in melted butter. Add flour and baking powder. Pour into greased 12″ by 8″ pan. Bake for 1 hour. This will rise and then fall when removed from oven.

A versatile dish, this recipe may be served as a main dish for brunch, lunch or dinner. Also good, hot or cold, as an appetizer when cut into small squares. Try adding chopped chiles or artichokes for variety.

Laurie Marcus

Cheddar Cheese Soufflé

Serves 6

INGREDIENTS:

6 eggs
½ cup heavy cream
¼ cup Parmesan cheese, grated
½ teaspoon prepared mustard
½ teaspoon salt

¼ teaspoon pepper
½ pound sharp cheddar cheese
11 ounces cream cheese
1 tablespoon butter

PROCEDURE:

Preheat oven to 375°. In blender place eggs, cream, cheese, mustard, salt and pepper. Blend until smooth. With blender running, add pieces of cheddar cheese to mixture, followed by pieces of cream cheese. Continue until all cheese is used. Blend at high speed for 5-10 seconds. Smear butter in 6-cup soufflé dish or individual 1 cup baking dishes. Pour in batter. Bake 45 minutes (or 20 minutes if using small dishes). Top should be nicely browned and when the dish is jiggled, the center should move a little. For a firmer soufflé bake until completely set (45-50 minutes) and surface has cracked. Serve immediately or turn off oven and open door a crack to prevent overbaking. To prepare in advance, assemble the soufflé, pour into dish, cover and refrigerate. Allow additional 5-10 minutes of baking time.

Joan Shultz

Enchiladas

Serves 4

INGREDIENTS:

¼ cup shortening
2 10-ounce cans chile sauce
1 8-ounce can tomato sauce
3 garlic cloves, minced
flour

1 pound Tillamook cheese, grated
2 4½-ounce cans olives, minced
1 medium onion, minced
1 dozen corn tortillas
½ head lettuce, shredded

PROCEDURE:

Preheat oven to 350°. Melt shortening in saucepan. Add chile sauce, tomato sauce and garlic. Stir adding small amount of flour as needed to thicken. Combine cheese, olives and onions. Deep fry tortillas or run through oil in frying pan to soften. Dip tortillas in chile sauce. Fill with cheese mixture and roll. Cook covered for 20 minutes. Top with shredded lettuce.

Diane Bliss

Enchilada Sauce

Serves 4-6

INGREDIENTS:

2 tablespoons shortening
2 tablespoons flour
2 cups water
3-4 tablespoons chile powder

¾ teaspoon salt
½ teaspoon garlic salt
pinch of oregano
pinch of cumin

PROCEDURE:

Heat shortening in saucepan over medium heat. Stir in flour. Cook and stir about 1 minute. Slowly stir in water alternating with seasonings. Stir constantly. Bring to boil. Simmer 10 minutes. Makes sauce for 12 enchiladas.

Marilyn Greco

Salsa Darla

Serves 4-6

INGREDIENTS:

1 28-ounce can tomatoes
1 4½-ounce can green chiles, diced, with seeds
1 medium onion, minced
2 tablespoons vinegar

garlic salt to taste
oregano to taste
pepper to taste
1 tablespoon oil

PROCEDURE:

Combine all ingredients in bowl. Mix well. Let marinate for 24 hours. For a variation drain excess juice and add minced cilantro (coriander) or add a jar of Salsa Victoria for an even hotter taste.

Darla Cox

159

Kiki's Easy Quiche

Serves 4-6

INGREDIENTS:

1 8" pie crust, frozen or
   homemade
6 ounces cheddar and Gruyère
   cheese, grated

3 eggs
1½ cups cream
dash of cayenne pepper
dash of nutmeg

PROCEDURE:

Preheat oven to 350°. Sprinkle grated cheese over bottom of pie crust. Mix eggs with cream. Add spices. Pour over cheese. Bake 40 minutes.

Kiki Henry

No-Crust Spinach Quiche

Serves 4-6

INGREDIENTS:

1 10-ounce package frozen
   chopped spinach
1 cup cottage cheese
¼ pound cheddar cheese
½ medium onion, sliced
1 tablespoon oil

1 teaspoon basil leaves
¼ teaspoon garlic powder
pinch of cayenne pepper
4 eggs
⅓ cup milk

PROCEDURE:

Preheat oven to 325°. Thaw spinach. Drain well. Set aside. In blender or food processor blend cheeses, onions, oil, seasonings, eggs and milk until smooth. Pour in bowl with spinach and blend. Grease 9" pie plate. Pour in mixture. Bake for 35-45 minutes or until knife inserted in center comes out clean. Let stand 10 minutes before cutting.

Linda Sweedler

160

Green Chile Quiche

Serves 6-8

INGREDIENTS:

2 4½-ounce cans green chiles
1 pound Monterey jack cheese,
   cubed or shredded
¼ pound cheddar cheese, cubed or
   shredded

5 eggs, beaten
½ cup milk
½ teaspoon dry mustard (optional)
¼ cup flour
1 teaspoon baking powder

PROCEDURE:

Preheat oven to 400°. Combine chiles and cheeses. Place in greased 9" by 13" baking dish. Mix eggs, milk, mustard, flour and baking powder. Pour over cheese mixture. Bake for 15 minutes followed by 20 minutes at 300°.

Good as a main dish and appetizer, too!

Jackie Hassler

Cheese And Tomato Quiche

Serves 4-6

INGREDIENTS:

1 9" unbaked pie crust
½ pound Edam or Gruyère cheese,
   shredded
3 tomatoes, peeled, chopped and
   drained
3 tablespoons minced onion,
   soaked in 3 tablespoons hot
   water

salt to taste
pepper to taste
1 teaspoon basil
2 eggs
¾ cup milk
2 tablespoons Parmesan cheese

PROCEDURE:

Preheat oven to 350°. Sprinkle shredded cheese over uncooked pie shell. Layer tomatoes over cheese, add onions. Sprinkle with salt, pepper and basil. Mix eggs and milk. Pour into pie shell. Sprinkle Parmesan cheese on top. Bake 60 minutes or until set in middle.

Easy, fast and always popular. Can be frozen or made ahead and reheated.

Susan Plazak

Quiche Lorraine

Serves 6

INGREDIENTS:

pastry for 9" pie crust
4 bacon strips
1 onion, thinly sliced
1 cup Gruyère or Swiss cheese,
    grated
¼ cup Parmesan cheese, grated

4 eggs, lightly beaten
2 cups cream (or 1 cup milk &
    1 cup cream)
¼ teaspoon nutmeg
½ teaspoon salt
¼ teaspoon white pepper

PROCEDURE:

Preheat oven to 450°. Line pie pan with pastry and bake 5 minutes. Cook bacon until crisp. Remove from skillet. Drain all but 1 tablespoon of fat. Sauté onion until transparent. Crumble bacon. Sprinkle bacon, onion and cheeses over partly cooked shell. Combine eggs, cream, nutmeg, salt and pepper and pour over onion/cheese mixture. Bake pie for 15 minutes, reduce oven temperature to 350° and bake until knife comes out clean which is about 10-20 minutes longer. (May be made ahead with cheese mixture in the pastry, then refrigerated. Before baking, warm to room temperature, add egg mixture and bake).

Sherry Cook

Baked Fondue

Serves 4

INGREDIENTS:

12 slices quality white bread
softened butter
2 cups Gruyère cheese, grated
3 large eggs, lightly beaten

2 cups milk
1 teaspoon salt
pinch of paprika (or cayenne)

PROCEDURE:

Trim crusts from bread. Spread one side with softened butter. Place 4 slices of bread in ungreased 8" or 9" square glass baking dish, buttered side up. Sprinkle ⅓ cheese over bread. Layer 4 more slices of bread on top. Sprinkle with ⅓ cheese. Repeat with remaining bread and cheese. Combine eggs, milk and salt. Pour mixture over bread and cheese. Sprinkle with paprika or cayenne. Cover with plastic wrap. Refrigerate overnight or not less than 8 hours. Bake uncovered at 350° for 50 minutes. Serve immediately.

Ann Wheelock

Traditional Cheese Fondue

Serves 4

INGREDIENTS:

1 garlic clove
1½ cups dry white wine
1 teaspoon lemon juice
4 cups Emmenthaler cheese, grated
4 cups Gruyère cheese, grated
1 tablespoon cornstarch

3 tablespoons Kirsch
white pepper to taste
nutmeg to taste
paprika to taste
crusty French bread, in 1″ cubes

PROCEDURE:

Rub the inside of fondue pot with garlic clove. Heat wine with lemon juice slightly. Add cheese gradually, stir continuously in figure 8 motion. Blend cornstarch and Kirsch. Add to mixture when bubbling. Cook 2-3 minutes. Season to taste. Dip in bread.

This is the traditional Swiss Fondue from the Neuchatel region. It is served with gherkins and pickled onions, followed by a green salad. The Swiss suggest white wine or tea with this dish.

Madelyn Sheets

Classic Cheese Strata

Serves 4

INGREDIENTS:

4 slices Monterey jack cheese
4 slices Kraft "Old English" cheese
4 eggs, beaten
8 slices white bread, crusts
    removed

2 cups milk
2 tablespoons instant onion
1 teaspoon dry mustard
½ teaspoon salt

PROCEDURE:

Cover surface of 8″ square baking dish with bread. Top bread with 4 slices of jack cheese. Cover jack cheese with Old English slices. Top with layer of trimmed bread. Combine eggs, milk, instant onion, dry mustard and salt. Mix well. Pour over bread. Let mixture blend into bread. Let stand for 15 minutes. Bake at 325° for 45 minutes or until puffy and brown. Let stand for 5 minutes before cutting. Recipe may be doubled to serve 8. Strata may be prepared ahead but pour the liquid mixture on the bread right before baking.

Delicious for brunch served with ham or fruit and garnished with parsley.

Judy Backhaus

Cheese And Egg Casserole

Serves 12

INGREDIENTS:

1 loaf white sandwich bread
1 pound mild cheddar cheese, grated
8 eggs
1 pint milk

1 pint half and half
1 teaspoon salt
dash of pepper
dash of paprika

PROCEDURE:

Prepare recipe 24 hours before serving. Grease 9″ by 13″ casserole dish. Trim crusts off bread. Cube bread. Combine and mix eggs, milk, half and half, salt and pepper. Spread half the cubed bread in casserole. Spread half the cheese over bread. Cover cheese with remaining bread and top with remaining cheese. Slowly pour egg mixture over this. Top with paprika. Cover and refrigerate overnight. Remove 1 hour before baking. Bake 1 hour at 350°. Serve within ½ hour.

Good for breakfast, brunch, lunch or dinner!

Olivia Chier

Egg, Artichoke And Spinach Stacks

Serves 12

INGREDIENTS:

½ cup butter
1 medium onion, chopped
¾ cup mushrooms, sliced
½ cup flour
½ teaspoon ground nutmeg
½ teaspoon white pepper
4 chicken bouillon cubes, dissolved in 3 cups water

1 cup whipping cream
6 English muffins
2 10-ounce packages frozen spinach
12 canned artichoke bottoms
12 eggs

PROCEDURE:

Sauté onion and mushrooms in butter. Stir in flour, seasonings, broth and cream. Mix well, stirring until mixture boils and thickens. Remove from heat. (Cover and chill at this point if made ahead). About 30 minutes before serving, toast 6 English muffins. Keep warm. Cook spinach. Drain well. In a 3-quart pan, mix spinach with 1½ cups of mushroom sauce. Heat and stir. Spread on serving plate. Top with 12 canned artichoke bottoms. Cover with foil. Keep warm. Poach eggs. Place 1 on each artichoke. Reheat remaining sauce (add milk if needed to thin). Drizzle some over tops of eggs. Spoon egg mixture on muffin for a lovely brunch! Pass extra sauce and muffins.

A bit time consuming, but well worth the effort.

Janine Ryder

Baked Eggs And Mushrooms

Serves 4

INGREDIENTS:

4 tablespoons butter
½ pound mushrooms
⅓ cup chopped onion
¼ cup flour
¼ cup chicken broth
¼ cup whipping cream

salt to taste
pepper to taste
6 eggs
6 bacon slices
3 English muffins
chopped parsley (for garnish)

PROCEDURE:

Preheat oven to 350°. Melt 2 tablespoons butter. Sauté mushrooms and onions. Stir in flour, broth and cream gradually until thickened. Add salt and pepper. Pour sauce in shallow 2-quart baking dish. Break eggs over sauce. Top eggs with remaining butter and sprinkle with cheese. Bake uncovered for 15 minutes. Fry bacon. Crumble on toasted English muffin. Top with egg recipe. Garnish with parsley.

Nancy Pausic

Brunch Eggs Olé

Serves 6-8

INGREDIENTS:

8 slices white bread, not too fresh
½ cup butter, softened
2 cups sharp cheddar cheese,
  grated
1 4-ounce can green chiles, diced
½ cup green onions, sliced
8 slices cooked Canadian bacon,
  shredded (sautéed mushrooms
  or dried beef also work)

8 eggs, beaten
2½ cups milk
½ cup half and half
½ teaspoon salt
cayenne pepper to taste
dry mustard to taste

PROCEDURE:

Trim crusts off bread. Butter bread on both sides. Cut into cubes. Grease 9″ by 13″ casserole. Spread bread cubes on bottom and sprinkle cheese, chiles, green onions and bacon over top. Beat eggs, milk, and half and half together with spices. Pour over mixture in casserole. Refrigerate overnight. Bake 45 minutes, uncovered at 325°.

Juices, a fresh fruit salad and breakfast pastries are all you need to turn this into a special brunch.

Alma Hertweck

Tiered Omelet Ranchero

Serves 4-6

INGREDIENTS:

8 eggs
2 tablespoons milk
¾ teaspoon salt
½ teaspoon pepper
2 teaspoons butter
½ cup sour cream

1 large avocado, sliced
1¼ cups sharp cheddar cheese,
  shredded
1 jar salsa
black olives (for garnish)
chopped tomatoes (for garnish)

PROCEDURE:

Beat eggs, milk, salt and pepper. Heat butter in 6"-8" skillet. Pour ½ cup egg mixture into pan and tilt to cover pan bottom. As mixture begins to set, use a spatula to lift omelet so uncooked egg flows underneath. Cook until eggs are set and bottom is lightly brown. Invert omelet onto wax paper. Repeat 3 more times. To assemble, spread first omelet with salsa. Place second omelet over this and spread with ¼ cup sour cream and avocado slices (save about 4 slices for top). Layer with third omelet and sprinkle ¾ cup of cheese over it. Place fourth omelet over this and sprinkle remaining salsa, cheese, sour cream and avocado. Garnish with black olives and chopped tomatoes. Heat in warm oven to melt cheese. Can be made ahead and reheated in microwave or warm oven.

A different and delicious brunch dish!

Kristie Jones

Hearty Baked Eggs

Serves 4

INGREDIENTS:

2 tablespoons olive oil
1 onion, finely chopped
2 garlic cloves, minced
6 plum tomatoes (canned will work), coarsley chopped
salt to taste
pepper to taste
½ pound ham, cubed
8 eggs
12 steamed asparagus spears
8 tablespoons cooked peas
1 jar pimiento strips

PROCEDURE:

Preheat oven to 450°. In hot oil, sauté onion with garlic. Add the tomatoes, salt and pepper. Cover and simmer for 10 minutes. Pour tomato sauce into 4, 6" ovenproof ramekins. Break 2 eggs into each dish, over sauce. Arrange the cubed ham, asparagus, peas and pimento strips around the eggs. Sprinkle with salt and fresh pepper to taste. (Chopped parsley may be added as well). Cook for approximately 6 minutes or until the whites are set.

Serve with crusty bread for brunch or with white rice for a light supper.

Gloria Andújar

Spinach Frittata

Serves 4

INGREDIENTS:

1 onion, thinly sliced
2 garlic cloves, minced
4 tablespoons olive oil
2 10-ounce packages frozen
   spinach, cooked and drained

1 teaspoon salt
½ teaspoon black pepper
¼ teaspoon nutmeg
8 eggs, beaten
½ cup Parmesan cheese, grated

PROCEDURE:

Sauté onion and garlic in olive oil until wilted. Heat spinach through, blending with onion and garlic. Add spices. Pour eggs over vegetables. Cook over medium heat. When eggs are set, invert pan onto a hot plate. Slide the omelet back into pan. Sprinkle with cheese. Cook until set on reverse side. Slide onto a hot platter. Serve cut in wedges.

Good with Canadian bacon and fresh muffins.

Valdene Ramrus

Garden Frittata Parmesan

Serves 6

INGREDIENTS:

1½ cups fresh broccoli, cut into
   bite-size pieces, (or 1 10-ounce
   package frozen broccoli)
1 cup carrots, thinly sliced
6 eggs, beaten
¼ teaspoon salt
dash of pepper

1 cup cottage cheese
1 cup fresh mushrooms, sliced
2 tablespoons butter (or margarine)
6 thin tomato slices (for garnish)
grated Parmesan cheese (for
   garnish)

PROCEDURE:

Preheat broiler. Steam broccoli with carrots. In a medium bowl, combine eggs, salt and pepper. Beat in cottage cheese. Stir in steamed vegetables and mushrooms. In a 10″ oven-proof skillet or omelet pan melt the butter. Pour in egg mixture, cook over medium heat lifting edges to allow uncooked portion to flow underneath until top is almost set and bottom is lightly browned. Place skillet under broiler 5″ from heat for 1-2 minutes. Top with tomato slices. Sprinkle with Parmesan cheese; broil about 1 minute longer.

Also good cold.

Joyce Aftahi

Everything Omelet For One

Serves 1

INGREDIENTS:

¼ cup zucchini, chopped
¼ cup onion, chopped
2 tablespoons butter
3 eggs, beaten
1 tablespoon milk

salt to taste
pepper to taste
1 cup combination white cheeses,
    grated (mozzarella, jack, Swiss)
3 tablespoons salsa

PROCEDURE:

Sauté vegetables in butter. Combine eggs with milk. Add to vegetables in pan. Cook slowly over low heat until surface becomes set. Sprinkle cheeses, salt and pepper over top. Cover. Cook approximately 7 minutes over low heat. Fold omelet in half. Smother with hot salsa.

Laura Galinson

Swiss Eggs For Two

Serves 2

INGREDIENTS:

2 hard boiled eggs
1 cup white sauce
1 tablespoon Worcestershire sauce
4 tablespoons shredded cheese
salt to taste

pepper to taste
2 English muffins
4 strips bacon (or ham), cooked
    and crumbled

PROCEDURE:

Shell eggs. Cut up the whites. Crumble the yolks. Set aside. Add cut up whites, Worcestershire sauce, cheese, salt and pepper to the white sauce. Toast English muffins. Sprinkle with bacon and cover with cream sauce. Top with crumbled yolks.

Jules Brennan

Presnac

Serves 6-8

INGREDIENTS:

6 eggs, beaten
1 cup milk
2 teaspoons sugar
1 teaspoon salt
1 pound Monterey jack cheese

8 ounces cottage cheese
4 ounces cream cheese
¾ stick butter
1 teaspoon baking powder
½ cup flour

PROCEDURE:

Preheat oven to 350°. Place eggs, milk, sugar and salt in bowl. Cube the jack cheese. Combine with cottage and cream cheese. Cut in the butter. Add this to the egg mixture. Add baking powder and flour to this. Mix gently. Grease a 9″ by 13″ casserole dish. Pour in the mixture. Bake for 40 minutes.

Delicious with a green or fruit salad.

Carol Hinrichs

Tea Eggs

Serves 20

INGREDIENTS:

20 eggs
10 cups water
1½ teaspoons salt
½ cup red tea leaves

2 star anise
1 tablespoon cinnamon
10 cups water

PROCEDURE:

Place eggs in water in a large pot. Boil. Lower heat and simmer for 10 minutes. Remove eggs. Lightly tap eggs so that shells crack. Combine salt, tea leaves, star anise, cinnamon and water. Boil. Add the hard boiled eggs (with shells) and simmer over low heat for 1 hour. Drain and serve hot or cold.

Festive picnic treat.

Candice Woo

Rice Casserole

Serves 6

INGREDIENTS:

1½ cups uncooked rice (Uncle
   Ben's converted)
1 stick margarine, melted
1 10¾-ounce can onion soup

1 10¾-ounce can beef consomme
1 1¾-ounce can mushrooms, broth
   included

PROCEDURE:

Preheat oven to 350°. Add 1½ cups uncooked rice to melted margarine. Mix with remaining ingredients. Cover and bake 1 hour.

Carol Vadnais

White Rice Browned

Serves 8

INGREDIENTS:

½ cup butter
2 cups uncooked white rice
2½ teaspoons salt
¼ teaspoon pepper

2 cans beef consommé
2 cups water
½ cup blanched almonds, chopped

PROCEDURE:

Preheat oven to 300°. Melt butter in large frying pan. Add rice. Cook over very low heat stirring often until rice is golden brown. Place in 2-quart, high casserole. Sprinkle on seasonings. This may be done ahead. When ready to bake, add consommé, water and nuts. Mix gently. Cover and bake for 1 hour and 15 minutes. Do not stir.

Janet Selevan

Spiced Rice

Serves 6

INGREDIENTS:

¼-½ cup butter
½ cup pine nuts
2 cups brown rice, cooked
1 cup garbanzo beans

1 teaspoon salt
¼ cup raisins
1-2 tablespoons angostura bitters

PROCEDURE:

Sauté nuts in butter until golden. Combine rice, beans, salt and raisins. Add to nuts. Add bitters to taste. Add more butter as needed. Heat through.

Also excellent as stuffing for cornish game hens.

Melody Gentry

Chile Cheese Rice

Serves 4-6

INGREDIENTS:

1½ cups brown rice, cooked
1-1½ cups sour cream
¼ cup canned green chiles, diced
salt to taste
½ cup olives, (black or green) sliced

1 cup sharp cheddar (or jack) cheese, grated
½ cup grated cheddar cheese (for garnish)

PROCEDURE:

Preheat oven to 325°. Combine all ingredients. Place in casserole dish. Top with ½ cup cheddar cheese. Bake for 15 minutes.

Nancy Walter

Rice Monterey

Serves 4-6

INGREDIENTS:

¾ cup long grain white rice
2 tablespoons onion, minced
1 cup sour cream
½ cup mayonnaise
1 tablespoon lemon juice
½ cup black olives, sliced
¼ cup fresh parsley, chopped

¼ teaspoon pepper
½ pound fresh crab (or 7-ounce
   can)
½ pound fresh shrimp
¼ cup bread crumbs
1 ounce sharp cheddar cheese,
   grated

PROCEDURE:

Preheat oven to 350°. Cook rice as directed on box. Cool slightly. Mix with all other ingredients except bread crumbs and cheese. Place in greased 1½-quart casserole. Top with bread crumbs and grated cheddar cheese. Cover and bake for 30 minutes. Uncover last 10 minutes to crisp.

Can be made ahead. Goes well with salad and bread.

Lisa R. Wright

Oriental Rice Casserole

Serves 8

INGREDIENTS:

⅔ cup fresh mushrooms
1 cup onion, chopped
1 cup celery, chopped
4 tablespoons butter
¾ cup wild rice
¾ cup long grain rice

¼ cup soy sauce
1 5-ounce can water chestnuts,
   drained and sliced
⅓ cup slivered almonds, toasted
3½ cups chicken broth

PROCEDURE:

Preheat oven to 350°. Sauté mushrooms, onion and celery in butter. Combine with all other ingredients and bake in a lightly greased 2-quart casserole until liquid is absorbed, about 1 hour.

Michelle Benson

Curried Rice

Serves 6-8

INGREDIENTS:

1 cup long grain rice
2 beef bouillon cubes
1 tablespoon onion, minced
1 tablespoon butter
2 teaspoons curry powder

1 teaspoon salt
¼ teaspoon garlic powder (or 1 garlic clove, crushed)
¼ teaspoon pepper
2 cups water

PROCEDURE:

Mix all ingredients in a saucepan over high heat. When it begins to boil, reduce heat and cover with a tightly fitted lid. Simmer for 15 minutes.

Catherine vanSonnenberg

Rice Ring Indienne

Serves 8

INGREDIENTS:

½ cup butter, melted
1 large onion, minced
1 garlic clove, minced
⅔ cup slivered almonds, toasted
½ cup raisins, soaked in sherry
¼ cup chutney, finely chopped
2 teaspoons turmeric

¾ teaspoons nutmeg
2 cups long grain converted rice
4 cups chicken stock
chopped scallions (for garnish)
chopped egg yolks (for garnish)
mint sprigs (for garnish)

PROCEDURE:

Grease 1½-quart ring mold. Sauté onion and garlic in butter. Mix in nuts, drained raisins, turmeric and nutmeg. Combine rice and stock in large saucepan. Cover and bring to boil over high heat. Reduce heat. Simmer covered for 20-25 minutes until liquid is gone and rice is tender. Add sautéed mixture and blend well with fork. Pour into prepared mold. Set in larger pan of hot water. Cover loosely with foil. Let stand at room temperature until ready to serve. Unmold onto platter, garnish with green onions, small mounds of egg yolk and mint sprigs.

Karen Sachs

Fried Rice

Serves 6

INGREDIENTS:

2 tablespoons peanut oil
¼ cup green onion, diced
4 cups cooked white rice, cold
2 tablespoons soy sauce
½ teaspoon salt
½ teaspoon sugar

1 teaspoon dry sherry (or sake)
2 eggs, beaten
1½ cups cooked pork (or chicken) diced
1 cup frozen peas, thawed

PROCEDURE:

Heat oil. Cook onion and rice stirring constantly for about 5 minutes. Add soy sauce, salt, sugar and sherry. Mix well. Make a well in center of rice and add eggs. Cook until eggs begin to set, then blend into rice mixture. Add meat and peas, cooking until heated through.

Amber Coburn

Company Wild Rice Casserole

Serves 4-6

INGREDIENTS:

½ pound pork, cubed
½ pound round steak, cubed
½ pound mushrooms, sliced
1 onion, diced
¼ cup butter (or margarine)
salt to taste
pepper to taste

1 can cream of mushroom soup
¼ cup water
¼ cup soy sauce
2 cups celery, diced
½ cup brown rice, cooked
½ cup wild rice, prepared as directed

PROCEDURE:

Preheat oven to 350°. Brown meat, mushrooms and onion in butter. Season with salt and pepper. Combine soup, water and soy sauce. Mix well. Combine remaining ingredients in 3-quart casserole. Cover and bake for 1 hour and 45 minutes.

Anne Coleman

Mother Mitchell's Rice Fritters

Serves 2

INGREDIENTS:

cooking oil
1 cup pancake mix
¾ cup whole milk
1 egg

1 cup cooked Minute Rice
butter
maple syrup

PROCEDURE:

Heat 1″ of cooking oil in a deep skillet until it is sizzling. Combine pancake mix, milk and egg. Add rice. Scoop mixture into skillet forming 3″ fritters. Cook until golden brown on both sides. Serve with butter and maple syrup.

Bill Mitchell

7

Salads

Cranberry-Raspberry Mold

Serves 12

INGREDIENTS:

1 3-ounce package raspberry Jello
1 3-ounce package lemon Jello
1½ cups boiling water
1 10-ounce package frozen
    raspberries

1 16-ounce can jellied cranberry-
    raspberry sauce
1 7-ounce can lemon-lime
    carbonated beverage
¼ cup nuts, chopped

PROCEDURE:

Dissolve gelatins in boiling water. Stir in frozen raspberries, breaking up large pieces. Add cranberry sauce, blend well. Chill until partially set. Pour in lemon-lime beverage, stirring gently. Add nuts. Pour into 6-cup mold. Chill 5-6 hours or overnight.

> *Great with turkey and pork. Also heavenly as a dessert garnished with whipped cream.*

> *Lucy Smith*

Frozen Cranberry Salad

Serves 8

INGREDIENTS:

1 16-ounce can cranberry sauce
2 tablespoons lemon juice
1 3-ounce cream cheese, softened
⅓ cup powdered sugar

¼ cup mayonnaise
¾ cup pecans, chopped
1 cup whipped cream

PROCEDURE:

Mash cranberry sauce. Add lemon juice and blend. Pour into 4-cup mold. Soften cream cheese. Gently blend sugar, mayonnaise, pecans and whipped cream into cream cheese. Spoon over cranberries and freeze.

> *Carol Vadnais*

Ribbon Salad

Serves 10-12

INGREDIENTS:

1 3-ounce package cherry Jello
1¾ cups boiling water
1 3-ounce package lemon Jello
1 cup boiling water
½ cup sour cream

½ cup mayonnaise
¼ cup chopped pecans
1 3-ounce package lime Jello
1 cup boiling water
1 8½-ounce can crushed pineapple

PROCEDURE:

First layer: dissolve cherry Jello in 1¾ cups boiling water. Pour into Jello mold. Refrigerate until set. Second layer: dissolve lemon Jello in 1 cup boiling water. Add sour cream, mayonnaise and nuts. Refrigerate until slightly set. Pour over cherry layer. Refrigerate until completely set. Third layer: dissolve lime Jello in scant cup boiling water. Add undrained pineapple. Refrigerate until slightly set. Pour over lemon layer. Refrigerate until set. Serve.

This salad looks and tastes wonderful with a holiday turkey.

Valdene Ramrus

Pear Jello Mold

Serves 8-10

INGREDIENTS:

1 6-ounce package red Jello, any
    flavor
1 16-ounce can pears, reserve
    liquid

1 8-ounce package cream cheese
½ pint heavy cream, whipped

PROCEDURE:

Boil pear juice. Dissolve Jello in pear juice. In a blender combine pears and cream cheese. Add the Jello to the cream cheese mixture. Gently fold in whipped cream. Pour into mold and refrigerate.

Bobbi Susselman

Ribbon Delight

Serves 12

INGREDIENTS:

5 3-ounce packages Jello (lime,
   lemon, orange, strawberry and
   blackberry)
5 cups boiling water
1 cup sugar

2 cups milk
2 envelopes Knox gelatine
2 cups sour cream
2 teaspoons vanilla extract

PROCEDURE:

Lightly grease 13" by 9" by 2" glass dish. Dissolve lime Jello in 1 cup
boiling water. Pour into greased dish. Set until firm. Bring 2 cups of milk to
a boil. Add 1 cup sugar. Dissolve 2 envelopes of plain gelatine in ½ cup cold
water. Add it to the milk mixture. Stir thoroughly. Cool. Add 2 cups sour
cream and 2 teaspoons vanilla. Blend using mixer. Set aside. Pour exactly
1¼ cups milk mixture on top of firm lime Jello. Let set. Dissolve orange
Jello in 1 cup boiling water. Pour on top of milk mixture. Let set. Pour 1¼
cups milk mixture on top of orange Jello. Let set. Repeat this procedure
with the lemon, strawberry then blackberry Jello. Be careful to use exactly
1¼ cups of milk mixture or you will run out. Allow approximately 2 hours
to prepare.

Edna Phillips

Peach-Pineapple Mold

Serves 8-10

INGREDIENTS:

1 6-ounce package orange Jello
1 8-ounce can pineapple chunks
1 11-ounce can Mandarin oranges

1 16-ounce can peaches
½ pint sour cream (or plain yogurt)
fresh strawberries (optional)

PROCEDURE:

Boil juice from 3 cans of fruit. Dissolve Jello in juice. Add fruit and sour
cream. Stir gently, pour into mold. Let set. Salad may be made up to 3 days
ahead.

Bobbi Susselman

White Salad

Serves 8-10

INGREDIENTS:

2 tablespoons Knox gelatine
½ cup pineapple juice
¼ cup confectioners sugar
1 cup white cherry juice
½ cup slivered blanched almonds

1 cup crushed pineapple
1 cup white pitted cherries
¾ cup mayonnaise
1 cup heavy cream, whipped
pinch of salt

PROCEDURE:

Dissolve gelatine in pineapple juice over double boiler. Add sugar and cherry juice. Cool slightly. Add nuts, fruit, mayonnaise, whipped cream and pinch of salt. Mix well, pour into 11″ by 7″ by 1½″ Pyrex dish. Chill until set.

Megan Hooker

Spiced Peach Salad

Serves 8-10

INGREDIENTS:

1 3-ounce package lemon gelatin
1 envelope unflavored gelatine
1 1-pound 13-ounce can spiced peaches
1 16-ounce can pineapple tidbits (or chunks)

5 sweet gherkin pickles, sliced very thin
½ cup pimiento-stuffed olives, sliced very thin
1 cup pecans, broken (not chopped or sliced)

PROCEDURE:

Reserve peach and pineapple juice. Add enough water to make 2¼ cups liquid. Heat to boiling and pour over unflavored gelatine which has been soaked in ½ cup cold water. Add lemon gelatin to hot syrup. Stir until dissolved. Let cool to consistency of egg whites. Add chopped peaches, pineapple, sliced olives, pickles and broken pecan meats. Pour into lightly greased quart mold or individual molds. Refrigerate until firm.

Nice complement to ham or turkey.

Alliene Vale

Mango Mold Salad

Serves 10-12

INGREDIENTS:

SALAD	DRESSING
3 3-ounce packages lemon Jello	2 tablespoons lemon juice
3 cups boiling liquid (2 cups water, 1 cup juice from fruit)	½ cup oil
1 8-ounce package cream cheese	1 garlic clove
1 29-ounce can mangoes (or peaches)	½ teaspoon salt
strawberries (for garnish)	⅛ teaspoon pepper
	½ teaspoon Worcestershire sauce
	1 egg

PROCEDURE:

Dissolve Jello in boiling liquid. Set aside to cool in ring mold. Combine mangoes and cream cheese in blender until creamy. Add to Jello and chill. Prepare salad dressing by mixing in blender all dressing ingredients. Serve salad with dressing and garnish with fresh strawberries.

Dressing is also wonderful on green salads.

Laurene Izner Ramenofsky

Rice Salad

Serves 8

INGREDIENTS:

1 6-ounce box Uncle Ben's Original Long Grain Wild Rice	1 8-ounce bottle Hollywood Italian dressing
1 box cherry tomatoes	1 6-ounce can olives
1 box frozen peas, thawed	2 carrots, diced
6 green onions, diced	1 6-ounce jar artichoke hearts

PROCEDURE:

Cook rice as directed for firm rice. Cool. Combine rice, tomatoes, onions, olives, carrots, artichokes and dressing. Add peas right before serving. Serve cold.

Great for picnics!

Jackie Hassler

Artichoke-Rice Salad

Serves 6-8

INGREDIENTS:

5 cups stock (3 bouillon cubes, 5 cups water)
2 cups rice, uncooked
3 6-ounce jars marinated artichoke hearts, quartered, reserve liquid
5 green onions, chopped
1 4-ounce jar olives
1 green pepper, diced

3 celery stalks, diced
¼ cup parsley, chopped
2 cups mayonnaise (or 1 cup mayonnaise and ½ cup sour cream)
1 teaspoon curry powder
salt to taste
pepper to taste

PROCEDURE:

Boil stock and stir in rice, lower heat and simmer until done. Drain and cool. Add quartered artichoke hearts, onions, olives, green pepper, celery and parsley to rice. Blend well. Prepare a dressing by whisking mayonnaise and curry with enough artichoke marinade to make a creamy yet not liquid dressing. Toss dressing into rice mixture. Salt and pepper to taste. Refrigerate overnight.

Lois Kline

Chicken-Rice Salad

Serves 8

INGREDIENTS:

1 package Rice-a-Roni, chicken flavored
2½ cups water
4 cups chicken, cooked and cut in bite-size pieces
1 5-ounce can water chestnuts, drained, sliced
1 6-ounce jar marinated artichoke hearts, quartered

5 green onions, thinly sliced
3 large celery stalks, sliced
½ green bell pepper, chopped
1 cup mayonnaise
1¾ tablespoons soy sauce
1¾ teaspoon curry powder

PROCEDURE:

Cook Rice-a-Roni according to directions using the 2½ cups water. Let rice cool. Mix all ingredients together.

This salad can be made 24 hours ahead and will last up to 6 days.

182   *Karen Stewart*

Vegetable Pesto Pasta Salad

Serves 10-12

INGREDIENTS:

1 pound fusilli, rotelle or shell
    pasta
1 tablespoon olive oil
3 large red bell peppers
3 large green bell peppers
2-3 tablespoons vegetable oil
4 garlic cloves, minced
salt to taste
pepper to taste
1 6-ounce can pitted black olives,
    drained
olive oil

1 tablespoon fresh oregano (or 1
    teaspoon dried)
1 bunch green onions, chopped,
    including greens
1 medium bunch broccoli
1 cup Chinese pea pods
½ recipe Basil Pesto Sauce (recipe
    follows)
1 tablespoon each of fresh herbs
    — oregano, rosemary,
    marjoram and basil
⅓ cup Italian parsley
2-3 tablespoons red wine vinegar

PROCEDURE:

Cook pasta al dente. Dry carefully in large towel. Place pasta in large bowl, toss gently with a little olive oil. Cover and cool to room temperature. Oil peppers lightly with vegetable oil. Place over open flame or under broiler. Turn often and char all sides. Drop peppers in plastic bag. Cover with towel and allow to set for 10 minutes. Remove from bag. Under running water gently rub off skin. Remove seeds and cut into strips ¼" by 2". Toss with ½ teaspoon salt, 2 garlic cloves and 3-4 tablespoons olive oil. Set aside. Toss olives with 1 tablespoon olive oil, 2 garlic cloves and 1 tablespoon oregano. Set aside. Remove stems from broccoli. Blanch for 1 minute. Cool quickly under cool water. Dry, toss with olive oil and salt. Repeat process with pea pods. To assemble salad combine pasta with Pesto Sauce. Add peppers, olives, green onions, vegetables and herbs. Blend in half of parsley. Sprinkle with 2-3 tablespoons red wine vinegar. Garnish with remaining parsley. Serve at room temperature.

This salad can be varied with seasonal vegetables as well as adding cooked chicken, ham, turkey, beef or fish.

Fran Jenkins

Basil Pesto Sauce

INGREDIENTS:

4 cups basil leaves
2 garlic cloves
½ cup pine nuts
1 teaspoon salt

½ cup olive oil
½ cup freshly grated Parmesan
   cheese
3 tablespoons butter, softened

PROCEDURE:

Combine basil, pine nuts, garlic and salt in food processor. Mix with quick on/off motion. Slowly add olive oil through feed tube. If not using food processor, a mortar and pestle may be used. When ingredients are evenly blended, pour into bowl and beat in cheese by hand. Gradually incorporate the softened butter.

Serve with pasta salad or as sauce for fresh hot pasta.

Fran Jenkins

Italian Pasta Salad

Serves 4-6

INGREDIENTS:

8 ounces shell macaroni
½ cup olive oil
⅓ cup white wine vinegar
1 tablespoon dried sweet basil
1 garlic clove, minced
⅓ cup grated Parmesan cheese

salt to taste
pepper to taste
2 tablespoons parsley, chopped
1 large green pepper, diced
1-2 large tomatoes, chopped

PROCEDURE:

Cook macaroni in boiling, salted water until firm. Drain, rinse under cold water. Set aside. Stir together oil, vinegar, basil, garlic and Parmesan cheese in large salad bowl. Add macaroni. Season to taste with salt and pepper. Cover and refrigerate at least 4 hours. Just before serving add parsley, bell peppers and tomatoes. Toss lightly and garnish with additional Parmesan cheese.

Great for picnics or a pot luck, no refrigeration needed. Try cubed hard salami or baby shrimp for a heartier salad.

Linda Clark

Mango Curried Pasta Salad

Serves 6-8

INGREDIENTS:

1 8½-ounce jar mango chutney
1½ cups mayonnaise
1½ tablespoons curry powder
½ pound pasta, spiral curls or
   shells, cooked al dente

1 medium chicken, cooked, cut in
   bite-size pieces
3 cups fresh broccoli florets,
   blanched

PROCEDURE:

Chop chutney in blender or food processor 15-20 seconds, using on/off switch. Combine mayonnaise and curry powder in small bowl. Stir in chutney. Cover and chill about 1 hour. Combine pasta, chicken and broccoli. Toss with mango chutney mayonnaise. Chill until ready to serve.

Connie Galluzzi

Tuna Pasta Salad

Serves 4

INGREDIENTS:

1 6-ounce jar marinated artichoke
   hearts
1 6-ounce jar marinated
   mushrooms
1 7-ounce jar roasted red peppers
1 12½-ounce can tuna
2 tablespoons parsley flakes
1 teaspoon dry basil

1 teaspoon dry oregano
1 teaspoon dry thyme
2 tablespoons lemon juice (or
   vinegar)
4 tablespoons salad oil (or virgin
   olive oil)
1 8-ounce package pasta twists

PROCEDURE:

Drain and reserve liquid from artichoke hearts, mushrooms, peppers and tuna. Cut artichoke hearts in half. Cut roasted peppers into strips. Put artichokes, peppers, mushrooms and tuna in a large mixing bowl. To liquid add herbs, lemon juice and oil. Pour over tuna/vegetable mixture. Cook pasta al dente. Drain, add to tuna mixture. Toss well. Chill for 6 hours or overnight. Arrange on top of lettuce and garnish with carrot curls.

Keep all the ingredients as staples on your pantry shelf and toss together on the eve of a busy day.

Betsy Grasso

185

Pasta Salad

Serves 12

INGREDIENTS:

1 16-ounce package small pasta
  shells
1 4-ounce jar pimientos, chopped
1 6-ounce can olives, sliced
1½ cups fresh (or frozen) peas,
  cooked
1 4-ounce can mushrooms, drained
2 cups baby shrimp, cooked
½ cup grated Parmesan cheese

VINAIGRETTE DRESSING

1 cup salad oil
6 tablespoons wine vinegar
2 tablespoons Dijon mustard
1 teaspoon basil
1 teaspoon oregano
1 teaspoon onion salt
1 teaspoon garlic salt
salt to taste
pepper to taste

PROCEDURE:

Cook pasta shells as directed. Rinse, drain and add remaining ingredients.
Mix all dressing ingredients well. Toss with salad. Refrigerate several hours
or overnight before serving.

Di Ann Hjermstad

Oriental Crab Salad

Serves 4-6

INGREDIENTS:

1 pound crab meat
1 10-ounce package frozen peas,
  barely cooked, drained
1 cup celery, chopped
1 small onion, minced
¾ cup mayonnaise

1 tablespoon lemon juice
¼ teaspoon curry
1 teaspoon soy sauce
⅛ teaspoon garlic salt
1 5-ounce can chow mein noodles
½ cup slivered almonds, toasted

PROCEDURE:

Mix crab, peas, celery and onion. Chill overnight. Blend mayonnaise,
lemon juice, curry, soy sauce and garlic. Toss crab mixture, dressing and
noodles together. Top with slivered almonds. Serve with French bread or
stuffed artichokes, tomatoes or avocadoes.

Susie Armstrong

Crab Salad

Serves 6

INGREDIENTS:

1 pound crab meat, cooked
1 10-ounce package frozen English
   peas
5 green onions, chopped

6 ounces sour cream
¼-½ cup cooked bacon, minced
1 avocado, sliced

PROCEDURE:

Mix all ingredients and serve with sliced avocado.

Nancy Bolton

Sugar Pea Salad With Shrimp Or Chicken

Serves 8

INGREDIENTS:

1½ pounds Chinese sugar peas,
   washed, strings pulled
1 bunch scallions, chopped
1 pound shrimp, cooked (use size
   larger than bay shrimp) or 4
   chicken breasts, boned, skinned
   and cut in 1″ pieces

1 bottle Girard's Champagne
   Dressing
2 tablespoons sesame oil
½ cup cashew nuts
1 bottle Bob's California-style
   dressing

PROCEDURE:

For shrimp: marinate shrimp in Girard's Champagne Dressing for 4 hours.
Combine shrimp, sugar peas and scallions. Toss with Bob's California-style
dressing. Serve. For chicken: quickly stirfry chicken pieces in 2 tablespoons
of sesame oil. Let cool, add to the sugar peas, scallions and cashew nuts.
Toss with Bob's California-style dressing. Serve.

*A tasty luncheon salad with warm, crunchy bread. Also marvelous as a first
course on a bed of butter lettuce!*

Suzie Desmarais

187

Avocado And Shrimp Salad

Serves 6

INGREDIENTS:

3 tablespoons olive oil
2 tablespoons French white wine
   vinegar
1 teaspoon Dijon mustard
1 pound fresh shrimp, cooked,
   shelled, deveined and cubed
1 cup mayonnaise
2 tablespoons chile sauce
1 large garlic clove, crushed

dash of hot pepper sauce
salt to taste
freshly ground pepper to taste
1 ripe avocado, cubed
juice of ½ lemon
2 tablespoons dill, finely minced
2 tablespoons chives, finely minced
dill sprigs, lemon wedges and
   avocado slices (for garnish)

PROCEDURE:

Whisk together olive oil, vinegar, and Dijon mustard. Add shrimp, toss
thoroughly, cover and marinate. Blend mayonnaise, chile sauce, garlic, hot
pepper sauce, salt and pepper until smooth. Set aside. Sprinkle lemon juice
over cubed avocado. Set aside. Drain shrimp. Add cubed avocado, dill and
chives. Gently fold in enough mayonnaise mixture to coat lightly. Cover
and chill until ready to serve. Divide salad among chilled plates and garnish
with dill sprigs, lemon wedges and avocado slices.

Grace Bowman

Taos Salad

Serves 4-6

INGREDIENTS:

2 cups lettuce, shredded
1 1-pound can kidney beans,
   drained
1 tablespoon green chiles, chopped
2 medium tomatoes, chopped and
   drained
½ cup sliced ripe olives
1 large avocado, mashed
½ cup dairy sour cream

2 tablespoons Italian dressing
1 tablespoon onion, minced
¾ teaspoon chili powder
¼ teaspoon salt
dash of pepper
1 cup sharp cheddar cheese,
   shredded
1 cup corn chips, coarsely crushed
½ cup whole pitted olives

PROCEDURE:

Combine lettuce, beans, chiles, tomatoes and sliced olives in large bowl. Blend avocado, sour cream, salad dressing, onion and seasoning; mix well and chill. Season salad with additional salt and pepper; toss lightly with avocado dressing. Top with cheese and corn chips. Garnish with whole pitted olives.

Always devoured with compliments.

Cherry Lee

Mandarin Salad

Serves 4-6

INGREDIENTS:

SALAD	DRESSING
1⅓ tablespoons sugar	½ teaspoon salt
¼ cup sliced almonds	2 tablespoons sugar
¼ head romaine lettuce	2 tablespoons vinegar
¼ head butter lettuce	¼ cup salad oil
1 cup celery, chopped	dash of pepper
2 green onions, chopped with tops	dash of Tabasco sauce
1 tablespoon parsley, chopped	
1 11-ounce can Mandarin oranges, drained	

PROCEDURE:

Mix all dressing ingredients, refrigerate overnight. Melt 1⅓ tablespoons sugar in skillet by turning temperature on high. Continue stirring until sugar melts. Turn temperature down so sugar doesn't burn. Add ¼ cup sliced almonds, continue stirring until sugar. Set aside. Toss salad mixings with salad dressing. Sprinkle sugar coated almonds on top and serve.

Sheryl Durkin

Leon Salad

Serves 6

INGREDIENTS:

1 head iceberg lettuce, finely
    chopped
1 head romaine lettuce, finely
    chopped
¼ pound Italian salami, chopped
¼ pound mozzarella cheese,
    chopped
1 15-ounce can garbanzo beans,
    drained

LEON DRESSING
2 tablespoons wine vinegar
1 teaspoon dry mustard
¼ cup oil
½ teaspoon salt
½ teaspoon pepper
¼ cup grated Parmesan cheese

PROCEDURE:

Mix dry mustard in wine vinegar, then add oil. Blend remaining dressing ingredients. Combine lettuces, salami, cheese and beans in bowl. Toss with dressing and serve.

A lovely meal accompanied by warm bread and a light wine.

Estelle Graff

Caesar Salad

Serves 6

INGREDIENTS:

1 head romaine lettuce
1 teaspoon garlic, minced
2 tablespoons Dijon mustard
2 tablespoons Moutarde de Meaux
4 tablespoons bacon, cooked and
    crumbled
4 tablespoons olive oil

4 tablespoons lemon juice
½-¾ cup Parmesan cheese
1 egg, raw
CROUTONS
¼ teaspoon garlic, minced
½ cup olive oil
4-6 slices sourdough bread, cubed

PROCEDURE:

Wash romaine, tear into bite-size pieces and dry. In wooden bowl, place garlic and mustards. Add romaine in small batches, toss after each addition. Add remaining ingredients, tossing after each addition. Croutons: add garlic to frying pan. Pour in olive oil, heat. Add bread cubes and sauté until golden brown. Just before serving add croutons and toss.

Dale Karen Kolins

Sunshine Salad

Serves 6-8

INGREDIENTS:

SALAD
½ bunch red leaf lettuce
½ bunch chicory (curly endive)
1 bunch watercress
2 large oranges, peeled and
    sectioned
1 large grapefruit, peeled and
    sectioned
1 large onion, sliced in rings
1 avocado, sliced

POPPY SEED DRESSING
½ cup sugar
¾ teaspoon dry mustard
¾ teaspoon salt
¼ cup vinegar
1 tablespoon onion juice
¾ cup oil
1 tablespoon poppy seeds

PROCEDURE:

Tear greens into bowl. Add fruits and onion. Toss. Dress with 4 tablespoons dressing. Serve remaining dressing on side.

Susan Rantzow

Cobb Salad

Serves 4

INGREDIENTS:

SALAD
4 chicken breasts, cooked and
    diced
2 heads Boston lettuce, in bite-size
    pieces
1 large tomato, peeled and
    chopped
1 large avocado, diced
4 green onions, chopped
1 tablespoon dill weed
¼ pound Gorgonzola cheese,
    crumbled
4 bacon strips, cooked and
    crumbled

DRESSING
⅔ cup salad oil
¼ cup wine vinegar
2 tablespoons white wine
2 teaspoons low salt soy sauce
1 teaspoon sugar
1 teaspoon dry mustard
½ teaspoon salt substitute
½ garlic clove, minced
1 teaspoon pepper
¾ teaspoon curry powder
¼ cup mayonnaise

PROCEDURE:

Blend all dressing ingredients. Set aside. Toss salad ingredients in large bowl. Add dressing, serve.

Norma M. James

Best Ever Spinach Salad

Serves 6

INGREDIENTS:

2 bunches fresh spinach
1 pound bacon, cooked and cut in
   1" by 1¼" pieces
4 hard boiled eggs, chopped
½ pound fresh mushrooms, sliced
½ cup fresh Parmesan (or Romano)
   cheese, grated
¼ cup pine nuts, (optional)

DRESSING
½ cup Wesson oil
¼ cup red wine vinegar
1 teaspoon onion powder
1 teaspoon salt
½ teaspoon dry mustard
½ teaspoon freshly ground pepper
1 garlic clove, slightly crushed

PROCEDURE:

Prepare salad dressing by blending all ingredients. Allow to rest so flavors blend. Clean spinach by gently washing and removing all stems. Pat dry then tear into bite-size pieces. Place in large bowl. Put bacon, eggs, mushrooms, cheese and pine nuts on top of spinach. Remove garlic clove from dressing. Blend dressing thoroughly and pour over salad. Toss and serve.

This salad makes a wonderful main course for a light meal.

Olivia Chier

Fresh Spinach Salad

Serves 6

INGREDIENTS:

3 bunches fresh spinach, washed,
   stems removed and in bite-size
   pieces
½ cup green onions, chopped, tops
   included
¼ pound Roquefort cheese

FRENCH DRESSING
⅓ cup tarragon vinegar
¼ cup olive oil
¾ teaspoon ground pepper
½ teaspoon dry mustard
juice of ½ lemon

PROCEDURE:

Mix French Dressing. Toss lightly with spinach, onions and crumbled Roquefort cheese. Serve.

Stephanie Page

Salade Aux Noix

Serves 2

INGREDIENTS:

combination lettuces
   (any except iceberg)
½ cup walnut pieces
¼ cup feta cheese, crumbled

VINAIGRETTE

3 tablespoons olive oil
1 tablespoon tarragon vinegar
½ teaspoon Dijon mustard
1 tespoon Moutarde de Meaux
½ garlic clove, finely chopped

PROCEDURE:

Tear lettuces into bite-size pieces. Rinse and dry until crisp. Combine all dressing ingredients in a wooden bowl. Just before serving toss in lettuces, walnuts and cheese. Double or triple recipe as needed.

A simple and elegant complement to almost any entrée.

Judy Rosenblatt

Tiki Tuna Salad

Serves 4-6

INGREDIENTS:

1 head romaine lettuce in bite-size
   pieces
1 8½-ounce can Mandarin oranges,
   drained
1 8½-ounce can pineapple chunks,
   drained
2 6½-ounce cans solid white tuna
½ cup celery, chopped
½ cup water chestnuts, sliced
¼ cup green onions, sliced

DRESSING

½ cup mayonnaise
2 tablespoons soy sauce
½ teaspooon salt

PROCEDURE:

Put lettuce in large salad bowl. Combine tuna, oranges, pineapple, celery, water chestnuts and onions with lettuce. Mix the dressing ingredients together, pour over salad. Toss gently.

Judie Dresser

193

Chicken Salad

Serves 8-10

INGREDIENTS:

6 cups chicken, cooked and cubed
1 8-ounce bottle creamy French
  DRESSING
1 cup celery, chopped
2 hard boiled eggs, grated

1 4-ounce jar button mushrooms
1 3½-ounce jar capers (optional)
⅓ cup mayonnaise
⅓ cup sour cream
¼ cup almonds, toasted

PROCEDURE:

Marinate chicken in French dressing overnight. Next day, stir chicken then toss in celery, eggs, mushrooms and capers. Mix together mayonnaise and sour cream. The amount you add to salad depends on how dry/moist you want your salad to be. Place in serving dish. Sprinkle toasted almonds over top.

Laurie Marcus

Oriental Chicken Salad

Serves 10

INGREDIENTS:

6 cups romaine lettuce
¼ pound bean sprouts
1 8-ounce can water chestnuts,
  drained and chopped
½ cup green onions, sliced
4 cups chicken, cooked and
  shredded
2 boxes frozen pea pods, thawed
  and drained

¼ cup cashew nuts, toasted
mint leaves (optional)
Mandarin oranges (optional)
  DRESSING
2 cups margarine
2 teaspoons curry powder
1 tablespoon sugar
½ teaspoon ground ginger

PROCEDURE:

Layer ingredients as follows: lettuce, bean sprouts, water chestnuts, green onions, chicken and peas. Mix together margarine, curry, sugar and ginger. Frost salad with dressing. Just before serving, garnish with toasted cashew nuts. Mint leaves and Mandarin orange slices add a colorful touch.

Carol Vadnais

Hot Chicken Salad

Serves 8

INGREDIENTS:

2 cups chicken, cooked and cubed
2 cups celery, thinly sliced
1 cup croutons
½ cup slivered almonds, toasted
2 teaspoons onion, grated
½ teaspoon salt
1 cup mayonnaise
2 tablespoons lemon juice

1 box frozen peas, thawed
1 8-ounce can water chestnuts, sliced
1 4-ounce can mushrooms, sliced
1 4-ounce jar red pimientos
1 cup potato chips, crushed
sprinkle of Parmesan cheese

PROCEDURE:

Preheat oven to 450°. Mix all ingredients, except potato chips and Parmesan cheese. Pour into baking dish, cover with potato chips and sprinkle of Parmesan cheese. Bake for 20-30 minutes.

Bettye Ulevitch

Hot Chicken Delight

Serves 8

INGREDIENTS:

2 cups chicken, cooked and diced
1-2 cups celery chopped
½ cup blanched almonds
1 tablespoon onion, minced
½ teaspoon salt
2 tablespoons lemon juice
2 cups potato chips, crushed

½ cup cheddar cheese, grated
MEDIUM WHITE SAUCE
2 tablespoons butter
2 tablespoons flour
1 cup chicken stock (or milk)
½ cup mayonnaise

PROCEDURE:

Preheat oven to 350°. Combine chicken, celery, almonds, onions, salt and lemon juice. Set aside. Make a white sauce by melting butter, adding flour and stirring thoroughly. Gradually add stock or milk. Stir constantly until thick. Add mayonnaise. Combine white sauce and chicken mixture. Pour in shallow 8″ by 10″ pan. Bake for 20 minutes. Serve immediately.

Orpha Keye

Hot Chicken Salad Casserole

Serves 6-8

INGREDIENTS:

3 cups chicken, cooked and cubed
1⅓ cup celery, diced
¾ cup slivered almonds, toasted
4 tablespoons lemon juice
½ cup green pepper, chopped
½ teaspoon salt
1⅓ cup mayonnaise

¾ cup milk
¼ cup pimiento, chopped
1 3½-ounce can French fried onions
¼ teaspoon poultry seasoning
½ teaspoon paprika

PROCEDURE:

Preheat oven to 350°. Combine all ingredients except ½ can of onions and paprika. Pour into casserole. Bake covered for 30 minutes. Remove cover, add remaining onions and sprinkle with paprika. Continue to bake 5 minutes. Serve as is or over rice.

Martha Shea

Chicken Salad Deluxe

Serves 8

INGREDIENTS:

4 cups chicken
¼ cup white wine
1 celery stalk
1 carrot
1 onion
1 piece ginger
1½ cups celery, chopped
3 green onions, sliced

1 5-ounce can water chestnuts, drained and sliced
2 medium pieces candied ginger, finely chopped
1 teaspoon salt
1 cup mayonnaise
½ cup whipping cream, whipped
½ cup slivered almonds, toasted

PROCEDURE:

Cook chicken in a stock of water, wine, celery, carrot, onion and piece of ginger. Let chicken cool in liquid overnight before cubing. Mix chicken, celery, onion, water chestnuts, ginger and salt. Fold mayonnaise into whipped cream. Mix with chicken. Chill 1 hour before serving. Garnish with slivered almonds.

Julie Teel Regan

Cucumber Salad Oriental

Serves 4-6

INGREDIENTS:

1 large cucumber, peeled and
    shredded
½ chicken breast, cooked and
    shredded
1 slice of ham, cooked and
    shredded
1½ cups vermicelli sheet

2 tablespoons sesame paste
2 tablespoons soy sauce
1 teaspoon sugar
1 teaspoon sesame oil
½ teaspoon garlic, chopped
½ teaspoon scallion, chopped
1 tablespoon hot pepper oil

PROCEDURE:

Set aside cucumber, chicken and ham. Break vermicelli sheet into strips,
blanch in boiling water. Drain and place on center of plate. Arrange
cucumber and meats over vermicelli. Mix remaining ingredients and pour
over meats. Serve.

Dolly Woo

Cucumber Salad

Serves 6

INGREDIENTS:

1 3-ounce package lemon (or lime)
    Jello
½ cup boiling water
1 large cucumber, finely chopped
½ cup mayonnaise

1 tablespoon onion, finely chopped
¼ teaspoon salt
1 cup cottage cheese
¼ cup olives, sliced
1 tablespoon vinegar

PROCEDURE:

Dissolve Jello in bowl with boiling water. Add all remaining ingredients.
Mix well. Pour into 1-quart mold and set in refrigerator.

Gloria Márquez Sterling

197

Oriental Salad

Serves 8

INGREDIENTS:

3 ounces slivered almonds, toasted
3 tablespoons toasted sesame seeds
1 small head cabbage, shredded
4 green onions, sliced diagonally
1 3-ounce package quick-cooking
   "Nissin Ramen" (Japanese
   noodles)

DRESSING
¼ cup sesame oil
¼ cup vegetable oil
4 tablespoons rice vinegar
2 tablespoons sugar
½ teaspoon black pepper
½ teaspoon MSG

PROCEDURE:

Combine cabbage and onions. Crumble uncooked "Nissin Ramen." Mix together. Place all dressing ingredients in shaker jar and blend thoroughly. Add dressing to salad ingredients just before serving.

Also wonderful with shredded chicken or shrimp.

Susan Fox

Cole Slaw

Serves 8

INGREDIENTS:

3 tablespoons wine vinegar
2 tablespoons sugar
3 tablespoons mayonnaise
2½ tablespoons salad oil
1 tablespoon dried minced onion

1½ pound cabbage, shredded
2-3 carrots, shredded
salt to taste
pepper to taste

PROCEDURE:

Mix vinegar, sugar, mayonnaise, oil and onion. Add to cabbage and carrots. Salt and pepper to taste. Refrigerate.

Also delicious the second day.

Mara Lawrence

Sauerkraut Salad

Serves 12

INGREDIENTS:

1 28-ounce can sauerkraut
1 red onion, chopped
1 4-ounce jar pimientos
1 bell pepper, chopped

DRESSING
½ cup vinegar
½ cup oil
1 cup sugar

PROCEDURE:

Combine all salad ingredients. Set aside. Boil dressing. Pour over salad. Refrigerate overnight.

Leftovers make wonderful "kraut dogs."

Connie and Jennifer Reins

Leek Salad

Serves 4

INGREDIENTS:

5 small leeks
4 ounces crab meat
4 ounces shrimp
DRESSING
3 tablespoons Dessauxfils wine
    vinegar

5-6 tablespoons olive oil
salt to taste
pepper to taste
pinch of thyme
pinch of basil

PROCEDURE:

Early in the day make the dressing by combining all ingredients and mixing well. Parboil the leeks in salted water, refresh them in cold water. Cool and drain well. Cut into 1″ diagonal pieces. Toss leeks with dressing then add crab and shrimp. Serve in lettuce cups.

Sally Peters Davidson

199

Mâche And Endive Salad

Serves 8

INGREDIENTS:

1 pound mâche
4 heads of endive
1 log of Belgium chévre cheese,
   coated with ashes

8 sun dried tomatoes
1 recipe of Three Mustard
   Vinaigrette (recipe follows)

PROCEDURE:

Fill the sink with cold water. Add the mâche. Bunch-by-bunch break off the stems, being careful not to bruise the leaves. Drain on paper towels in single layer. Roll the mâche inside paper towels loosely and refrigerate until serving time. Remove the whole endive leaves from each head. Wash gently in cold water and drain on paper towels in a single layer. Roll loosely and refrigerate. Slice the chévre into ½" thick rounds. You will need 8. Drain and slice the sun dried tomatoes in half, lengthwise. When you are ready to serve, toss the mâche with enough dressing to coat lightly. Arrange the mâche on 3 endive leaves. Place the cheese at the base of the plate. Garnish with sun dried tomatoes.

Lyn Heller

Three-Mustard Vinaigrette

Serves 8

INGREDIENTS:

½ cup raspberry vinegar
2 cups tasteless vegetable oil
1 teaspoon sweet, hot mustard
   (Mendocino, Napa Sweet, or
   Arizona Champagne)

1 tablespoon Dijon mustard
2 teaspoons grainy honey mustard
   (Crabtree and Evelyn)
½ teaspoons salt
pepper to taste

PROCEDURE:

Add all ingredients to the food processor, process until well blended. Taste for additional salt and pepper.

Lyn Heller

Old German Salad

Serves 6

INGREDIENTS:

1 15-ounce can French style beans   1 large red onion, sliced very fine
1 15-ounce can French style beets   1 cup mayonnaise

PROCEDURE:

Mix all ingredients together. Serve chilled.

Mrs. Lester G. Heilman

Breezy Cottage Cheese Salad

Serves 8

INGREDIENTS:

1 17-ounce can apricot halves,   1 tablespoon lemon juice
   chopped   ½ cup mayonnaise
1 3-ounce package apricot Jello   1½ cups cottage cheese
1 cup boiling water

PROCEDURE:

Drain apricots reserving liquid. Dissolve Jello in boiling water. Add ½ cup reserved liquid and lemon juice. Beat in mayonnaise and cottage cheese. Chill until slightly thickened. Fold in apricots. Pour into mold. Chill until firm, about 3 hours. Garnish as desired.

Dorthy Hunt

Hearts Of Palm

Serves 6

INGREDIENTS:

2 7½-ounce cans hearts of palm
½ cup vegetable oil
½ cup cream
1½ tablespoons catsup
1 tablespoon vinegar

salt to taste
pepper to taste
watercress (for garnish)
lettuce leaves (for garnish)

PROCEDURE:

Rinse hearts of palm under cold water, pat dry and halve or quarter them lengthwise. Thoroughly mix the oil, cream, catsup, vinegar, salt and pepper in blender or food processor for 10 seconds. Scrape sides, run additional 5 seconds and adjust seasonings as needed. Refrigerate. Arrange hearts of palm on lettuce leaves. Decorate with watercress. Spoon some dressing on each plate and pass the remainder.

Janine Ryder

Cucumber And Sour Cream Dressing

INGREDIENTS:

1 cup sour cream
½ cup cucumber, peeled, seeded
    and shredded
1 teaspoon onion, grated

½ teaspoon salt
1 teaspoon fresh dill (½ teaspoon
    dried)

PROCEDURE:

Mix all ingredients together. Refrigerate at least 1-2 hours. Serve over hearts of palm or other prepared vegetables.

Wonderful as a vegetable dip!

Elizabeth Jablecki

French Dressing

INGREDIENTS:

6 tablespoons oil
2 tablespoons lemon juice
4 green onions, finely chopped

1 teaspoon Dijon mustard
salt to taste
pepper to taste

PROCEDURE:

Whisk all ingredients together until thick. Use over any greens.

Helen Mayer

Celery Seed Salad Dressing

Yields 1¼ cups

INGREDIENTS:

1 teaspoon celery seed (or poppy)
½ cup honey
1 teaspoon dry mustard
¼ cup vinegar

¼ teaspoon dry onions
1 cup salad oil
salt to taste

PROCEDURE:

Put all ingredients in blender except salad oil. Mix then pour oil in slowly. Mix again. Refrigerate.

Especially good on avocado and fruit salads.

Helen Russell

Homemade Mayonnaise

INGREDIENTS:

1 egg yolk
1 teaspoon salt

juice of 1 lemon
3 cups vegetable oil

PROCEDURE:

Beat egg yolk at medium speed, add salt and ½ of the lemon juice. Add ½ of the oil, a teaspoon at a time. Beat well after each addition. Add remainder of lemon juice and oil, a teaspoon at a time. Refrigerate in jars or plastic containers. Do not stir.

Delicious with everything ... sliced tomatoes, cold chicken, shrimp, etc.

Kiki Henry

203

Blue Cheese Dressing

INGREDIENTS:

1 package Hidden Valley Ranch
  Salad Dressing "Add
  Buttermilk"
1 cup sour cream

1 cup mayonnaise
juice of 1 large lime
1 1-ounce wedge blue cheese

PROCEDURE:

Blend lemon juice and blue cheese in blender or Cuisinart until smooth.
Add remaining ingredients, mix until creamy. Refrigerate.

Nita Young

Kay's Blue Cheese Dressing

INGREDIENTS:

1 pint mayonnaise
1 pint sour cream
2 teaspoons garlic salt
1 teaspoon Accent
1 teaspoon prepared mustard

1 teaspoon paprika
4 tablespoons vinegar (or lemon
  juice)
2 3-ounce wedges blue cheese

PROCEDURE:

Combine all ingredients except blue cheese. Blend thoroughly. Add blue
cheese. Store in covered jars.

Margi Bingham

Sweet Mustard

INGREDIENTS:

4 2-ounce cans Colman's dry
   mustard
3 cups malt vinegar

9 large eggs, beaten
3 cups sugar

PROCEDURE:

Mix dry mustard and malt vinegar. Soak overnight. Heat mixture over medium heat. Stir in sugar. Remove from heat, let cool completely. Stir in eggs. Heat until bubbly. Do not let mixture stick or burn. Put in jars. Refrigerate up to 1 year.

Mary Newberry

Spicy Mustard Sauce

INGREDIENTS:

1 18-ounce jar apple jelly
1 18-ounce jar pineapple-apricot
   jam
1½ teaspoons coarse pepper

1 2-ounce can Colman's dry
   mustard
3 tablespoons horseradish

PROCEDURE:

Combine all ingredients. Blend at medium speed for 1 minute. Store in jars. Refrigerate.

Marvelous complement to ham or pork.

Sally Peters Davidson

Notes

8

Vegetables
& Accompaniments

Barley Casserole

Serves 6

INGREDIENTS:

1 cup pearl barley, rinsed and
 drained
½ cup pine nuts
3 tablespoons butter
1 medium onion, chopped
8 medium mushrooms, sliced

¼ cup green onions, sliced
¼ teaspoon salt
¼ teaspoon pepper
3 cups chicken (or beef) broth
1 tablespoon parsley, chopped

PROCEDURE:

Preheat oven to 375°. Melt 1 tablespoon butter. Sauté pine nuts in butter until golden. Remove from skillet and set aside. Melt 2 tablespoons butter in skillet. Sauté onion, mushrooms and barley in butter until lightly browned. Stir in nuts, green onion, salt and pepper. Slowly add broth and mix thoroughly. Spoon into 1½-quart casserole. Bake uncovered for 1 hour and 15 minutes. Garnish with chopped parsley.

This has a wonderful chewy texture and is an excellent substitute for rice dishes.

Melody Gentry

Buttered Green Beans

Serves 8

INGREDIENTS:

1 pound green beans, cut
 diagonally in 3″ lengths (or
 long beans, cut diagonally in 3″
 lengths, or haricots verts,
 trimmed)

1 tablespoon unsalted butter
salt to taste
freshly ground black pepper to
 taste

PROCEDURE:

Bring water to boil in a 10″ skillet. Add the beans and cook 15 seconds for haricots verts (or 30 seconds for green or long beans). Pour beans into a strainer and run cold water over them to stop the cookng. Pat dry. Heat butter in a 10″ skillet. Add beans, salt and freshly ground pepper to taste. Toss to coat beans evenly with butter.

*The beans may be made up to 2 hours before serving. Five minutes before serving,
heat beans on low. Do not overcook. They should be crunchy and retain
the bright green color they had when you ran cold water over them.*

Lyn Heller

Dilly Beans

Yields 4 pints

INGREDIENTS:

2 pounds green beans
4 garlic cloves
4 sprigs flowering dill
2 tablespoons mustard seed

½ cup plain salt
alum
2½ cups cider vinegar
2½ cups water

PROCEDURE:

Pack beans lengthwise into hot pint jars, leaving a ¼" space. Add 1 garlic clove, 1 dill sprig, ½ teaspoon mustard seed, 2 tablespoons salt and a inch of alum to each jar. Combine vinegar and water in a saucepan. Bring to a boil. Pour boiling vinegar/water mixture over beans leaving a ¼" space. Seal. Process in a water bath for 10 minutes. Allow to mellow for at least 6 weeks.

Dill weed or seed can be substituted for flowering dill.

Anne Coleman

Mom's Baked Beans

Serves 10-12

INGREDIENTS:

2 cups navy (or small white) beans, washed
¼ pound salt pork, halved
2 teaspoons salt
¼ teaspoon pepper
¼ cup brown sugar

½ teaspoon dry mustard
½ teaspoon thyme
½ cup catsup
¼ cup dark molasses
1 medium onion, diced

PROCEDURE:

Cover beans with water and soak overnight. Simmer beans until skins bust or until tender, about 45 minutes. Drain and reserve bean liquid. Preheat oven to 300°. Place ½ of the beans in a bean pot or 2-quart casserole. Bury half of the salt pork in the beans. Fill with remaining beans. Combine remaining ingredients with 1 cup of the bean liquid. Top with remaining salt pork. Add bean liquid to cover. Cover pot and bake for 4 hours. Add more bean liquid during cooking if all of the liquid is absorbed.

Great with a barbecued main course.

Beverly Fipp

Calico Beans

Serves 8

INGREDIENTS:

½ pound bacon, diced
1 pound groud beef
1 cup onions, chopped
1 #2 can pork n' beans

1 #2 can Kidney beans, drained
1 #2 can lima beans, drained
1 #2 can butter beans, drained

PROCEDURE:

Preheat oven to 350°. Cook the bacon, beef and onions in a frying pan until the onions are translucent. Drain off the fat. Stir in all of the beans. Place the bean mixture in a casserole. Bake for 1 hour.

Wonderful for a barbecue.

Linda Smith

Sweet N' Sour Limas

Serves 8-12

INGREDIENTS:

3 10-ounce packages frozen Ford-
    hook lima beans
4 ounces margarine, softened
1 teaspoon salt

¾ cup brown sugar
2 tablespoons molasses
1 teaspoon dry mustard
1 cup sour cream

PROCEDURE:

Preheat oven to 350°. Cook limas, according to package directions, until almost tender. Mix remaining ingredients and combine with drained limas. Transfer mixture to a beanpot or deep baking dish and bake for ½ hour. Let rest 5-10 minutes before serving.

Linda Goodwin

Broccoli Casserole

Serves 18

INGREDIENTS:

6 10-ounce packages frozen, chopped broccoli
1 cup sharp cheddar cheese, grated
1 can mushroom soup
¾ cup evaporated milk
1 cup Monterey jack cheese, grated

½ cup Pepperidge Farm herb dressing
2 tablespoons butter, melted
½ cup bread crumbs

PROCEDURE:

Preheat oven to 350°. Butter a 2-quart casserole. Cook broccoli according to package directions and drain. Combine cheese, soup and milk in a saucepan. Cook until cheese is melted. Mix broccoli, dressing and soup mixture together. Transfer to the prepared casserole. Combine butter and bread crumbs. Top casserole with bread crumbs. Bake for 30 minutes.

Linda Bird

Cheese-Broccoli Bake

Serves 6

INGREDIENTS:

1½ pounds of brocccoli
1 cup cottage cheese
⅓ cup cheddar cheese, grated
2 eggs, beaten
1 green onion, minced

½ teaspoon salt
¼ teaspoon pepper
3 dashes of Tabasco sauce
2 tablespoons butter, melted
⅓ cup bread crumbs

PROCEDURE:

Preheat oven to 350°. Butter a 9″ by 13″ glass baking dish. Peel and trim the broccoli stem. Blanch in boiling water for 5 minutes. Drain. Lay in the baking dish. Combine cheeses, eggs, onion and seasonings. Pour over broccoli. Combine butter and bread crumbs. Sprinkle over the top. Bake for 25 minutes.

Great company dish that takes little time to prepare.

Louise Lewis

Glazed Baked Carrots

Serves 4

INGREDIENTS:

2 pounds carrots, cut in 2″ sticks
3 tablespoons butter
½ teaspoon salt

⅛ teaspoon cinnamon
½ teaspoon sugar
¼ cup unseasoned bread crumbs

PROCEDURE:

Preheat oven to 400°. Parboil carrots for 2 minutes. Drain. Toss with 2 tablespoons butter, salt, cinnamon and sugar. Spoon into a 1½-quart casserole. Melt remaining tablespoon of butter and mix with bread crumbs. Sprinkle over carrots. Bake for 45 minutes.

Patti Hall

Grated Baked Lemon Carrots

Serves 6

INGREDIENTS:

3 cups carrots, grated
2 tablespoons margarine, melted
1 tablespoon lemon juice
½ teaspoon salt

2 tablespoons dry sherry
1 tablespoon chives, chopped
 (for garnish)

PROCEDURE:

Preheat oven to 350°. Place carrots in a casserole. Mix margarine, lemon juice, salt and sherry. Pour over carrots. Bake for 30 minutes. Cover with foil when the surface is golden. Garnish with chives.

Michelle Benson

211

Chiles Rellenos I

Serves 4

INGREDIENTS:

1 can green chiles, seeded and cut
   in strips
⅓ pound Monterey jack cheese,
   sliced
4 eggs
⅓ cup milk

½ cup flour
½ teaspoon baking powder
1 cup cheddar cheese, grated
black olives (for garnish)
1 can marinara sauce (or
   homemade, p.00)

PROCEDURE:

Preheat oven to 375°. Butter a casserole large enough to hold the chiles in one layer. Wrap jack cheese slices with chile strips. Place on casserole. Combine eggs, milk and baking powder. Beat until smooth. Pour over chiles. Top with cheddar cheese and bake for 30 minutes. Garnish with olives. Serve the marinara sauce separately.

Great with refried beans and tortillas.

Gayl Foshée

Chiles Rellenos II

Serves 8

INGREDIENTS:

2 7-ounce cans green chiles,
   drained, seeded and dried
1 pound Monterey jack cheese,
   grated
1 pound cheddar cheese, grated

8 eggs
1 pint sour cream
freshly ground black pepper to
   taste

PROCEDURE:

Preheat oven to 375°. Line the bottom of a 3-quart casserole with a layer of chiles. Combine the cheeses. Top the chiles with ½ the cheese mixture. Repeat the layers ending with the remainder of the cheese. Beat eggs and fold in sour cream. Pour over the chiles and cheese. Sprinkle with freshly ground pepper to taste. Bake for 45-60 minutes. Allow to rest 5 minutes before serving.

Serve with a green salad topped with thinly sliced red onion, orange sections
dressed with vinaigrette and refried beans.

Elizabeth Wheelock

Chiles Rellenos III

Serves 4

INGREDIENTS:

1 7-ounce can chiles, seeded
½ pound cheddar cheese, grated
½ pound Monterey jack cheese,
   grated

2 eggs
1 can evaporated milk
black olives (for garnish)

PROCEDURE:

Preheat oven to 350°. Line a baking dish with ½ the chiles. Cover with the cheddar cheese. Repeat the chile layer. Top with the jack cheese. Beat eggs and evaporated milk together. Pour over the chiles and cheeses. Bake for 40 minutes. Garnish with black olives.

Serve with an avocado and tomato salad and French bread.

Candy Perry Wiedemann

Chiles Rellenos IV

Serves 8

INGREDIENTS:

2-3 4-ounce cans whole green
   chiles, seeded and sliced in
   strips
1 pound Monterey jack cheese,
   grated

4 eggs
2 cups milk
½ cup flour
½ teaspoon salt

PROCEDURE:

Preheat oven to 350°. Place chiles in a single layer in a 8″ by 4″ ovenproof dish. Top with the cheese. Repeat layers ending with the cheese. Whip eggs, milk, flour and salt together. Pour over the chiles and cheese. Bake for 40-60 minutes or until golden brown.

Terrific accompanied by a green salad, crusty bread and white wine.
Try substituting green peppers for the chiles and adding
a layer of ham. Children love it.

Eva Schachter

Souffléed Corn

Serves 6-8

INGREDIENTS:

½ cup butter
½ cup sugar
1 tablespoon flour
½ cup evaporated milk, undiluted
2 eggs, well beaten
1½ teaspoons baking powder

2 12-ounce cans whole kernel corn, drained
1 tablespoon butter, melted
¼ cup sugar
½ teaspoon cinnamon

PROCEDURE:

Preheat oven to 350°. Butter a 1-quart casserole. Melt butter with sugar. Stir in flour until well blended. Remove from heat. Gradually stir in milk. Add eggs and baking powder. Mix well. Fold in corn. Tansfer to casserole. Bake for 40 minutes or until a knife inserted in the center comes out clean. Brush with melted butter. Sprinkle with sugar and cinnamon.

Anne Coleman

Mexican Eggplant Casserole

Serves 8

INGREDIENTS:

1 large unpeeled eggplant, sliced
    ½″ thick
¼ cup salad oil
1 15-ounce can tomato sauce
1 4-ounce can chopped chiles
½ cup green onions, sliced

1 teaspoon ground cumin
1 teaspoon garlic salt
1 2½-ounce can sliced ripe olives, drained
1½ cup cheddar cheese, shredded
½ cup sour cream

PROCEDURE:

Preheat oven to 450°. Brush both sides of the eggplant slices with oil. Arrange in a single layer on a rimmed baking sheet. Bake, uncovered, for 20 minutes or until soft. Combine tomato sauce, chiles, onions, cumin, garlic salt and olives in a saucepan. Simmer, uncovered, for 10 minutes. Reduce oven to 350°. Arrange a single layer of eggplant in the bottom of a 1½-quart casserole. Spoon on half the sauce. Sprinkle on half the cheese. Repeat the layers, ending with the cheese. Bake, uncovered, for 25 minutes or until the cheese is bubbly. Pass the sour cream separately.

Sally Jones

Turkish Fried Eggplant

Serves 8

INGREDIENTS:

2 eggplants, sliced ½" thick
2 green peppers, seeded and sliced
    lengthwise ¼" thick
olive oil

3 cups plain yogurt
2 garlic cloves, minced
salt to taste

PROCEDURE:

Preheat oven to 375°. Brush both sides of eggplant slices with oil. Arrange in a single layer on a rimmed baking sheet. Bake for 15-20 minutes or until tender. Fry green pepper slices in a skillet in olive oil until lightly browned. Arrange the cooked eggplant in overlaping slices on a platter. Garnish with the cooked green pepper. Refrigerate. Combine the yogurt, garlic and salt to taste. Serve, separately, with the cold eggplant.

A festive side dish for a hot summer evening.

Ayse Underhill

Ratatouille I

Serves 6

INGREDIENTS:

2 unpeeled eggplants, sliced
salt to taste
¼ cup olive oil
2 large onions, chopped
2 green peppers, seeded and cubed
2 red peppers, seeded and cubed
4 small zucchini, sliced ½" thick

6 large tomatoes, peeled and
    seeded
2 garlic cloves, minced
parsley to taste
basil to taste
½ cup white wine
black olives (optional)

PROCEDURE:

Sprinkle eggplant slices with salt. Let stand ½ hour. Dry. Heat the oil in a large skillet. Add the onions and peppers. Cook over medium heat for 15 minutes or until they are soft but not browned. Add the zucchini, eggplant, tomatoes, garlic, parsley and basil. Pour the wine over the vegetables and cook over low heat for 30-45 minutes. Adjust seasoning and serve.

May be served cold decorated with black olives.

Janine Ryder

Ratatouille II

Serves 8

INGREDIENTS:

1½ pound unpeeled eggplant,
    sliced crosswise, ¼" thick
garlic salt to taste
1 large green pepper, seeded and
    sliced crosswise ¼" thick

1 large onion, peeled and thinly
    sliced
1 1½-pound can plum tomatoes,
    drain and reserve juice
¼ cup olive oil

PROCEDURE:

Preheat oven to 300°. Arrange eggplant in a solid layer in a heavy casserole. Sprinkle generously with garlic salt. Add, separately, layers of green pepper, onion and tomatoes. Press to make more compact. Pour the juice from the canned tomatoes over the vegetables. Drizzle the oil over the top. Place the casserole in the oven and reduce to 275°. Bake for 4-5 hours.

*Ratatouille can be made 1-2 days in advance and reheated
in a 300° oven for 20 minutes.*

Darla Cox

Greek Marinated Mushrooms

Serves 6-8

INGREDIENTS:

1½ pounds small mushrooms
1 cup water
½ cup olive oil
1 lemon, juiced
¼ cup vinegar
2 garlic cloves
½ teaspoon rosemary

½ teaspoon sage
¼ teaspoon thyme
2 bay leaves
10 peppercorns
1 teaspoon salt
½ teaspoon tarragon

PROCEDURE:

Combine all ingredients and bring to a boil. Simmer, stirring occasionally, for 5 minutes. Pour into a glass bowl. Cover and marinate overnight.

Great served as an hors d'oeuvre, side dish or as part of
a platter of cold vegetables.

Catherine van Sonnenberg

Mushroom-Black Olive Casserole

Serves 8

INGREDIENTS:

1 cup cheddar cheese, shredded
1 pound mushrooms, thinly sliced
¼ cup black olives, pitted and
    chopped
1½ tablespoons flour
½ teaspoon Accent

⅓ cup half and half
dash of pepper
½ cup bread crumbs (or Pepperidge
    Farm herbed seasoned stuffing
    mix, crumbled)
2 tablespoons butter, melted

PROCEDURE:

Preheat oven to 350°. In a 2-quart casserole, layer consecutively cheese, mushrooms and olives. Combine flour, Accent, half and half and pepper. Drizzle over mushroom mixture. Top with bread crumbs. Drizzle butter over bread crumbs. Bake for 30 minutes.

Served with a green salad or fruit cup, it makes a great lunch.

Eleanor Munt

Onion Soufflé

Serves 4

INGREDIENTS:

1 10-ounce can cream of onion
   soup
1 cup sharp cheddar cheese, grated

2 tablespoons parsley, minced
6 eggs, separated

PROCEDURE:

Preheat oven to 400°. Grease a 2-quart soufflé dish. In a saucepan heat onion soup, cheese and parsley until the cheese melts. Do not boil. Remove from heat. Stir in slightly beaten egg yolks. In a large bowl or mixer beat egg whites until stiff. Fold into soup mixture. Pour into soufflé dish and bake for 30 minutes or until puffed and browned.

Sally Jones

Au Gratin Potatoes

Serves 6

INGREDIENTS:

10 red potatoes, sliced ¼″ thick
1 garlic clove, peeled and halved
7 tablespoons butter
¼ cup Parmesan cheese, grated

pepper to taste
basil to taste
1 10-ounce can beef broth

PROCEDURE:

Preheat oven to 400°. Rub the inside of a 9″ by 13″ glass baking dish with the garlic and 1 tablespoon butter. Place a single layer of the potatoes in the prepared baking dish. Sprinkle with ¼ cup Parmesan. Dot with 2 tablespoons butter. Season with pepper and basil. Repeat layers ending with cheese layer. Bring beef broth to boil and pour it over the potatoes. Bake for 1 hour or until the potatoes are browned.

Terrific with roast pork, beef and lamb.
Can be reheated.

Phyllis Queen Healy

Duchess Potatoes

Serves 8

INGREDIENTS:

3 pounds potatoes, boiled and
  mashed
3 eggs
2 tablespoons heavy cream
3 tablespoons butter
1½ teaspoons salt
dash of white pepper

dash of cayenne pepper
dash of nutmeg
3 tablespoons Parmesan, (romano
  or Swiss) cheese, finely grated
2 tablespoons parsley, minced (for
  garnish)

PROCEDURE:

Preheat oven to 425°. Butter a cookie sheet. Beat warm mashed potatoes and eggs in the bowl of a mixer until the eggs are incorporated. Add the remaining ingredients and mix until smooth. Pipe rosettes, using a pastry bag, the size of a medium flower onto the cookie sheet. Bake for 10 minutes or until browned. Garnish with parsley.

A wonderful accompaniment for beef.

Estelle Graff

Natural French Fries

Serves 6

INGREDIENTS:

5 large baking potatoes, wedged
  into eighths
2 egg whites

grated Parmesan cheese, to taste
black pepper to taste

PROCEDURE:

Preheat oven to 350°. Grease a cookie sheet. Brush potatoes with egg whites that have been beaten until frothy. Sprinkle with Parmesan and pepper. Place potatoes on the cookie sheet skin side down and bake for 40 minutes or until golden brown.

Tyler Emblem

Patrician Potatoes

Serves 8

INGREDIENTS:

4 cups mashed potatoes
3 cups cream style cottage cheese, sieved
¼ cup sour cream
1½ tablespoons onions, grated

2½ teaspoons salt
⅛ teaspoon pepper
¼ cup butter, melted
½ cup almonds, chopped (for garnish)

PROCEDURE:

Preheat oven to 350°. Butter a shallow baking dish. Mix potatoes, cottage cheese, sour cream, onion, salt and pepper. Spoon into baking dish. Brush with melted butter. Bake for 30 minutes. Garnish with almonds.

Can be assembled in the morning and baked just before serving.

Cherry Lee

Swiss Potatoes

Serves 4-6

INGREDIENTS:

1 garlic clove, peeled and halved
2½ tablespoons butter (or margarine)
3 tablespoons lemon juice
3 cups water
6 medium potatoes, peeled
salt to taste

pepper to taste
ground nutmeg to taste
¼ cup green onions, thinly sliced
2 cups Swiss cheese, shredded
1½ cups milk (or light cream)
1 egg yolk, slightly beaten

PROCEDURE:

Preheat oven to 350°. Rub the inside of a 2-quart baking dish with garlic and ½ tablespoon butter. Mix water and lemon juice in a bowl. Add potatoes to the bowl as you slice them. Drain. Arrange ¼ of the slices in an even layer in the prepared baking dish. Sprinkle lightly with salt and pepper and nutmeg. Top with ¼ of the onions and ¼ of the cheese. Repeat layers ending with the cheese. Scald milk and pour slowly into egg yolk, beating constantly until blended. Pour slowly over the potatoes. Dot with remaining butter. Bake uncovered for 1½ hours or until potatoes are tender when pierced with a fork.

Great with eggs for breakfast.

Betty Stewart

Carol's Sweet Potatoes

Serves 6-8

INGREDIENTS:

4 medium sweet potatoes
½ cup brown sugar
1 generous tablespoon cornstarch
¼ teaspoon salt
1 cup orange juice

½ teaspoon orange peel, grated
¼ cup raisins
3 tablespoons sherry
¼ cup butter

PROCEDURE:

Preheat oven to 350°. Cook potatoes in salted water until tender. Peel and halve. Arrange the potatoes in a single layer in a glass baking dish. Bring sugar, cornstarch, salt, orange juice, orange peel and raisins to a boil. Cook until thickened. Stir in sherry and butter. Pour over potatoes. Bake for 20 minutes.

Teresa Worsch

Orange-Glazed Sweet Potatoes

Serves 8

INGREDIENTS:

2 pounds sweet potatoes (or yams
    or 2 1-pound 10-ounce cans)
½ cup dark corn syrup

½ cup butter
½ cup orange juice
½ teaspoon salt

PROCEDURE:

Cook fresh potatoes in jackets in boiling water or drain canned potatoes. Cut in half or slice. Mix corn syrup, butter, orange juice and salt in a skillet. Bring to a boil and cook 3 minutes. Add the potatoes. Cook slowly, turning to coat the potatoes with the glaze, for 12-15 minutes.

Barbara Cherry

Baked Yams In Orange Sauce

INGREDIENTS:

Serves 12-14

4 pounds fresh yams (or sweet potatoes), peeled and sliced ½" thick
1¼ cups sugar
2 tablespoons cornstarch

1 teaspoon salt
2 cups orange juice
4 tablespoons butter (or margarine)
½ teaspoon orange peel
1 orange, thinly sliced

PROCEDURE:

Preheat oven to 400°. Overlap yam slices in parallel rows in a 7" by 14" baking dish. Combine sugar, cornstarch and salt in a saucepan. Stir in orange juice until well blended. Bring mixture to a boil. Boil for 1 minute, stirring, until sauce is thick and clear. Off heat, stir in butter and orange peel until butter melts. Pour sauce over yams and cover baking dish with foil. (Can be made ahead and refrigerated at this point). Place foil covered casserole in the oven and bake for 45 minutes. Remove baking dish from oven. Baste potatoes thoroughly with sauce. Return to the oven uncovered and bake for 15 minutes, basting every 5 minutes, until yams are tender when pierced with a fork and well glazed. Garnish with orange slices.

A perfect accompaniment for ham.

Susan Rantzow

Spinach-Apple Stuffing Patties

INGREDIENTS:

Serves 4

3 tablespoons onion, chopped
¼ cup celery, chopped
2 tablespoons cooking oil
3 bunches fresh spinach, cooked, chopped and drained (or 1 cup chopped frozen spinach, cooked and drained)

2 cups packaged seasoned bread dressing (or 2 cups packaged cornbread dressing)
½ cup chopped apple
½ cup apple juice
¼ teaspoon garlic powder
salt to taste

PROCEDURE:

Preheat oven to 350°. Grease a 9" by 13" baking pan. Sauté onion and celery in oil. Combine onion/celery mixture, spinach, dressing, apple, apple juice, garlic powder and salt in a bowl. Form stuffing mixture into 8 patties. Place in prepared baking pan and bake for 15 minutes.

Won first place in the vegetarian division of a cooking contest!

A nutritious dish to accompany a holiday turkey.

Ann R. Colby

Spinach-Artichoke Casserole

Serves 10-12

INGREDIENTS:

2 12-ounce packages of chopped
   frozen spinach
½ pound fresh mushrooms
4-5 tablespoons butter
1 tablespoon flour
½ cup milk
½ teaspoon salt
⅛ teaspoon garlic powder or 1
   garlic clove, minced)

2 14-ounce cans artichoke hearts,
   drained
1 cup sour cream
⅛ cup lemon juice
¼ cup mayonnaise
paprika to taste

PROCEDURE:

Preheat oven to 375°. Cook spinach according to package directions and drain. Remove the stems from 10 mushrooms. Reserve the caps. Chop the stems and remaining mushrooms. Melt 2 tablespoons of butter in a skillet. Sauté the reserved mushroom caps in the butter until browned. Remove caps from the skillet and set aside. Add 1 tablespoon butter to the skillet. Sauté the chopped stems and mushrooms in the butter until browned. Melt 2 tablespoons butter in a sauce pan. Add flour to the pan and cook until bubbly. Add milk and stir until smooth. Stir in salt, garlic, spinach and chopped mushrooms. Combine sour cream, lemon juice and mayonnaise in a bowl. Place artichokes in the bottom of a 2-quart casserole. Cover with the spinach mixture. Cover the spinach mixture with the sour cream mixture. Top with the reserved mushroom caps. Bake for 25 minutes. Garnish with paprika.

May be prepared in the morning and baked just before serving.

Lucy Smith

Spinach Cheese Custard

Serves 6-8

INGREDIENTS:

¼ cup butter
1 large onion, chopped
½ pound mushrooms, sliced
1 10-ounce package frozen chopped
   spinach, thawed and drained
1 cup small curd cottage cheese
1 cup sour cream

8 eggs
½ teaspoon salt
½ teaspoon pepper
¼ teaspoon ground nutmeg
1 cup Monterey jack cheese,
   shredded
1 cup cheddar cheese, shredded

PROCEDURE:

Preheat oven to 325°. Butter a 7" by 11" baking pan. Melt butter in a frying pan over medium heat. Sauté onion and mushrooms until most of the liquid has evaporated. Spread the onion/mushroom mixture on the bottom of the prepared pan. Combine spinach, cottage cheese and sour cream. Beat eggs, salt, pepper and nutmeg together. Add eggs to spinach mixture. Spread over mushroom/onion layer. Bake uncovered for 30 minutes. Remove from oven and sprinkle on jack and cheddar. Continue baking for 10-15 minutes or until custard is set. Let rest 10 minutes before serving.

Good brunch entrée.

Walda Brooks

Spinach Casserole I

Serves 6

INGREDIENTS:

16 ounces cottage cheese
4 eggs, beaten
4 tablespoons butter, cut in pieces
1 10-ounce package frozen
   spinach, thawed and drained

3 tablespoons flour
¼ pound cheddar cheese, grated

PROCEDURE:

Preheat oven to 350°. Grease a 2-quart casserole. Combine all ingredients, thoroughly, in a mixing bowl. Transfer to the casserole and bake for 1 hour.

Judy Levine

Spinach Casserole II

Serves 8

INGREDIENTS:

4 10-ounce packages frozen
   chopped spinach, thawed
3 teaspoons minced onion
8 ounces tomato sauce
16 ounces sour cream

1 8-ounce can chopped
   mushrooms, drained
2 cups sharp cheddar cheese,
   grated
2 tablespoons butter, melted
½ cup bread crumbs

PROCEDURE:

Preheat oven to 350°. Grease a 2½-quart casserole. Combine spinach and onions. Cook according to package directions. Drain. Combine spinach mixture, tomato sauce, sour cream, mushrooms and cheese. Spoon into casserole. Mix butter and bread crumbs. Top spinach mixture with bread crumbs. Bake for 20 minutes or until hot, bubbly and toasted.

Even non-spinach eaters have been known to take seconds. May be assembled 1-2 days in advance and baked just before serving. Extend cooking time to 45-55 minutes if taken directly from the refrigerator to the oven.

Susan K. Nagy

Spinach Casserole III

Serves 6

INGREDIENTS:

3 bunches fresh spinach, washed,
   cooked and drained
1 6-ounce can marinated artichoke
   hearts
2 tablespoons onion, chopped

½ teaspoon salt
¼ teaspoon pepper
1 3-ounce package cream cheese
½ cup sour cream
⅓ cup Parmesan cheese, grated

PROCEDURE:

Preheat oven to 350°. Combine spinach, artichokes, onion, salt and pepper. Spread in a glass baking dish. Mix cream cheese and sour cream together. Spread over spinach. Sprinkle with Parmesan cheese. Bake for 20-25 minutes.

Jennifer Howard

Spinach Dumplings

Serves 4-6

INGREDIENTS:

1 10-ounce package frozen
   spinach, thawed and
   squeezed dry
1 garlic clove, minced
1 pound ricotta cheese
½ cup Parmesan cheese, grated
½ teaspoon salt
1 egg
¾ cup flour

SAUCE
2 tablespoons butter
2 tablespoons flour
⅛ teaspoon salt
⅛ teaspoon ground red pepper
2 cups milk
½ cup Swiss cheese, grated

PROCEDURE:

Prepare dumplings. Combine spinach, garlic, ricotta, Parmesan, salt, egg and flour. Roll into 1″ balls. Coat lightly with flour. Bring water to boil in a pan large enough to hold the dumplings. Boil for 10 minutes or until puffed and set. Heat broiler. Prepare sauce. Melt butter. Stir in flour, salt and pepper. Cook for 1 minute. Stir in milk. Simmer until smooth and thickened. Add cheese and cook until cheese melts. Line a baking dish with a small amount of sauce. Place dumplings in dish. Top with remaining sauce. Broil 7-9″ from heat for 10-15 minutes or until hot and bubbly.

Carrie Grether

Spinach Fantasy

Serves 6

INGREDIENTS:

3 10-ounce packages frozen
   spinach, thawed and drained
1½ cups sour cream

1 package dry onion soup mix
cheddar cheese, grated
almonds, sliced

PROCEDURE:

Preheat oven to 350°. Grease a 1½-quart casserole. Combine spinach, sour cream and soup mix. Transfer to prepared casserole. Sprinkle with cheese and top with almonds. Bake for 30 minutes.

Can be prepared the day before.

226

Jan Friedman

Spinach Pie

Serves 6-8

INGREDIENTS:

1 prebaked 9″ pie shell
1 10-ounce package frozen
    chopped spinach
4 eggs
¾ teaspoon salt
½ teaspoon pepper

½ teaspoon nutmeg
1 cup sour cream
¼ cup bread crumbs
3 tablespoons butter, melted
¾ cup Swiss cheese, grated

PROCEDURE:

Preheat oven to 350°. Cook spinach according to package directions. Squeeze dry. Spread over bottom of pie shell. Beat together eggs, salt, pepper, nutmeg and sour cream. Pour over spinach. Toss bread crumbs with butter and cheese. Sprinkle over the top. Bake for 25-30 minutes or until set.

Sherry Cook

Baked Acorn Squash and Sausage

Serves 4

INGREDIENTS:

2 medium acorn squash, halved
    lengthwise and seeded
onion powder to taste

1 teaspoon salt
1 pound sage pork sausage

PROCEDURE:

Preheat oven to 350°. Sprinkle onion powder on each squash half. Place the sausage in the hollow of each half. Bake for 1 hour.

An easy and delicious fall treat.

Lani H. Donohoe

Spinach Pie Amiel

Serves 4-6

INGREDIENTS:

PIE CRUST
1 stick salted margarine, melted
1 cup flour
1 tablespoon warm water
pinch of baking powder

FILLING
½ stick margarine
4 tablespoons flour
2 cups milk
½ cup plus 2 tablespoons Parmesan
    cheese, grated
1 egg, beaten
1 10-ounce package chopped
    frozen spinach, drained

PROCEDURE:

Preheat oven to 350°. Grease an 8″ pie plate. Prepare the pie crust. Mix all ingredients together. Form a ball with the dough and spread in the prepared pie plate. Set aside. Prepare the filling. Melt margarine in a saucepan. Stir in flour. Cook for 2 minutes. Stir in milk slowly. Simmer for 5 minutes or until sauce has thickened. Off heat, stir in ½ cup cheese and egg. Mix half the sauce with spinach. Pour into pie crust. Cover with remaining sauce. Sprinkle with 2 tablespoons cheese. Bake for 35-45 minutes or until browned.

Accompany with a composed vegetable salad. Try substituting an equal amount of cooked, chopped broccoli for the spinach. Filo dough may be substituted for the pie crust.

Nancy Amiel

Sour Cream Spinach Ring

Serves 8-10

INGREDIENTS:

1 envelope Knox gelatine
1 cup cold milk
1 10-ounce package frozen chopped
  spinach, defrosted and drained
½ cup green onions, chopped

16 ounces sour cream
1½ teaspoon salt
dash of onion powder
½ teaspoon basil
¼ cup lemon juice

PROCEDURE:

Soften gelatine in ½ cup milk. Dissolve, in a double boiler, over low heat, stirring. Combine spinach, onions, sour cream, salt, onion powder, basil, remaining milk, and gelatine mixture. Pour into a 6-cup mold and chill until set.

May substitute broccoli for spinach. Excellent with beef or pork.

Sally Jones

Swiss Chard Enchiladas

Serves 6

INGREDIENTS:

2 pounds Swiss chard, washed (or fresh spinach)
vegetable oil
2 large garlic cloves
salt to taste
¼ teaspoon pepper
3 medium tomatoes, peeled (or 1 1-pound can tomatoes, drained)
1 small onion
2 hot fresh chiles, seeded

1 cup water (or juice from drained tomatoes)
18 corn tortillas
1 cup plus 2 tablespoons sour cream
1 cup mild cheddar cheese, shredded
1 large onion, thinly sliced and separated into rings

PROCEDURE:

Cook chard in a small amount of water, stirring for 5 minutes. Drain and chop. Heat 3 tablespoons oil in a saucepan. Mince 1 garlic clove and sauté in oil without browning. Add chard and cook gently for 3 minutes. Add 1 teaspoon salt and pepper. Combine tomatoes, small onion, remaining garlic and chiles in a blender. Do not over blend. Heat 3 tablespoons oil in a skillet. Add tomato sauce. Cook over medium/low heat, stirring for 5 minutes. Add salt to taste and continue to cook for 1 more minute. Keep warm. Heat ¼" oil in a skillet. Fry tortillas briefly on each side on low heat. They should be limp. Drain. Heat broiler. Spread sauce on each tortilla. Place 2-3 tablespoons chard filling and 1 tablespoon sour cream on the edge of each tortilla. Roll. Place in a warm 13" by 9" by 2" baking dish. Reheat remaining sauce and pour over enchiladas. Sprinkle with cheese and broil until cheese melts. Garnish with onions.

A great vegetarian fiesta dish. Cilantro, olives and more chiles may be added.

Jennifer Howard

Yellow Squash Casserole

Serves 10

INGREDIENTS:

1 can creamed chicken soup
1 cup sour cream
2 cups cooked yellow (or
    butternut) squash in ½″ slices
1 cup carrots, grated

¼ cup onion, chopped
1 stick margarine, melted
1 package Pepperidge Farm
    dressing mix

PROCEDURE:

Preheat oven to 350°. Grease a 9″ by 11″ baking dish. Mix soup and sour cream. Add squash, carrots and onions. Combine margarine and dressing. Place ½ the dressing in the baking dish. Cover with the squash mixture. Top with the remaining dressing. Bake for 45-50 minutes.

Carol Vadnais

Tomato Aspic

Serves 4-6

INGREDIENTS:

1 large package lemon Jello
½ cup water, boiling
1 14-ounce can Hunts stewed
    tomatoes containing celery and
    onion

1 teaspoon salt
2 tablespoons cider vinegar
½ cup green (or red) pepper,
    chopped
½ cup celery, chopped

PROCEDURE:

Dissolve Jello in water. Add tomatoes, salt, vinegar, pepper and celery. Pour into a 4-cup mold and chill until firm.

A different and delicious aspic.

Mrs. Lewis Pollak

Tomato Duxelles

Serves 4

INGREDIENTS:

2 medium tomatoes, halved, juiced
    and seeded
12 medium mushrooms, finely
    chopped
4 green onions, finely chopped
4 tablespoons butter

¼ cup dry sherry
1 teaspoon lemon juice
¼ teaspoon salt
dash of pepper
1 tablespoon Parmesan cheese,
    grated

PROCEDURE:

Preheat oven to 350°. Place the tomato halves in a pie plate. Sauté
mushrooms and onions in butter. Add sherry, lemon juice, salt and pepper
to the pan. Simmer 5-10 minutes or until liquid is absorbed. Mound
mushroom mixture in the tomato halves. Sprinkle with cheese. Bake for 10
minutes. Turn oven to broil. Broil until browned.

This colorful dish is a good accompaniment for beef, lamb or chicken.

Ann Poovey

Tomatoes Jablecki

Serves 1-2

INGREDIENTS:

1 large tomato, peeled and halved
½ cup cottage cheese
½ cup sour cream

salt to taste
pepper to taste
paprika to taste

PROCEDURE:

Combine cheese, sour cream, salt and pepper to taste. Mound the cheese
mixture on the tomato halves. Garnish with paprika.

Elizabeth Jablecki

Stuffed Tomatoes

Serves 8

INGREDIENTS:

4 large tomatoes, halved, juiced
    and seeded
½ cup bread crumbs
2 small garlic cloves, minced
¼ teaspoon parsley
1 teaspoon basil

1 teaspoon oregano
½ teaspoon salt
¼ cup Parmesan cheese, grated
¼ cup oil
pinch of pepper

PROCEDURE:

Preheat oven to 350°. Oil a 9″ by 13″ baking pan. Combine bread crumbs, garlic, parsley, basil, oregano, salt, cheese, oil and pepper. Spoon a generous amount of stuffing into each tomato. Bake 15 minutes. Turn oven to broil. Broil for 7 minutes or until brown.

Simple and delicious.

Estelle Graff

Marinated Vegetables

Serves 10

INGREDIENTS:

2 17-ounce cans green peas,
    drained
1 16-ounce can whole string beans,
    drained
1 15½-ounce can wax beans,
    drained
1 4-ounce can pimiento, chopped
1 4-ounce can mild chile peppers

5 celery stalks, chopped
5 green onions, chopped
1 garlic clove, mashed
1¼ cups salad oil
¾ cup vinegar
2 teaspoons honey
¼ teaspoon salt

PROCEDURE:

Combine green beans, string beans, wax beans, pimiento, chiles, celery, onions and garlic. Whisk together oil, vinegar, honey and salt. Pour dressing over vegetables and stir. Marinate, stirring occasionally, 1 day before serving.

Laurie Marcus

Romanian Vegetable Casserole

Serves 12

INGREDIENTS:

1 cup olive oil
6 garlic cloves, minced
¼ cup fresh parsley, minced
1 tablespoon thyme
2 tablespoons marjoram
2½ tablespoons salt
½ teaspoon crushed, dried red
    pepper flakes
1 medium unpeeled eggplant,
    cubed
3 medium zucchini, sliced ½" thick
3 red (or green) peppers, cut in 1"
    squares.
3 large white onions, sliced

1 cup celery, sliced
2 cups white cabbage, shredded
1 cup green beans, in 2" pieces
1 cup carrots, sliced
3 potatoes, peeled and sliced
1 celery root, peeled and thinly
    sliced
1 acorn squash, peeled, seeded and
    sliced
1 small cauliflower, in flowerets
3 medium ripe tomatoes, peeled,
    seeded and sliced
¼ pound seedless grapes
½ cup fresh peas (or frozen peas,
    defrosted)

PROCEDURE:

Preheat oven to 350°. Lightly grease a heavy 7-8 quart casserole. Beat together oil, garlic, parsley, thyme, marjoram, 2 tablespoons salt and pepper flakes. Layer vegetables in the following order, sprinkling each layer with the oil mixture, eggplant, zucchini, peppers, onions, celery, cabbage, beans, carrots, potatoes, celery root, squash and cauliflower. Cover tightly and bake for 1½ hours. Place tomatoes, grapes and peas on top. Sprinkle with remaining salt and cover. Bake an additional 15 minutes.

May substitute any vegetables except beets and spinach. An unusual and tasty way to serve vegetables. Delicious the following day at room temperature.

Laura S. Jemmer

234

Vegetable Medley Laced With Sherry

Serves 8

INGREDIENTS:

1 pound small new
potatoes, scrubbed and
quartered
½ pound small white onions
3 cups boiling salted water
1 10-ounce package frozen sliced
carrots
2 10-ounce packages frozen brussel
sprouts

¾ cup orange juice
¼ cup dry sherry
4 teaspoons cornstarch
¼ teaspoon nutmeg
¼ teaspoon salt
2 chicken bouillon cubes
½ cup water
⅓ cup butter (or margarine)

PROCEDURE:

Cook potatoes and onions in boiling water for 5 minutes. Add carrots and brussel sprouts. Simmer until all vegetables are tender. Drain. Stir orange juice, sherry, cornstarch, nutmeg and salt together in a bowl. Bring bouillon cubes and ½ cup water to boil in a saucepan. Stir until cubes dissolve. Add butter and stir until melted. Stir in orange juice mixture and simmer until thickened. Pour glaze over vegetables and toss lightly until coated.

Judie Dresser

Zucchini Bake

Serves 6

INGREDIENTS:

3 cups unpared zucchini, thinly
sliced
1 cup packaged baking mix
½ cup onion, grated
½ cup Parmesan cheese, grated
2 tablespoons parsley, snipped

½ teaspoon salt
½ teaspoon oregano
dash of pepper
4 eggs, slightly beaten
1 garlic clove, finely minced
½ cup oil

PROCEDURE:

Preheat oven to 350°. Grease a 9″ by 13″ by 2″ pan. Mix all ingredients together. Spread in pan. Bake for 25 minutes or until golden brown.

Delicious as a side dish or cut in 1″ by 2″ pieces as an appetizer.

Matilde Pelaez

Zucchini Herb Casserole

INGREDIENTS:

Serves 4-6

2 tablespoons salad oil
1½ pounds zucchini, cut in ¼" dice
1 cup green onions, sliced
1 garlic clove, minced
2 medium tomatoes, peeled, seeded
   and chopped

1¼ teaspoon garlic salt
½ teaspoon dry basil
½ teaspoon paprika
½ teaspoon oregano leaves
1 cup cooked rice
2 cups sharp cheddar cheese,
   shredded

PROCEDURE:

Preheat oven to 350°. Heat oil in a large frying pan, over medium/low heat. Stir in zucchini, onions and garlic. Cover and cook for 5-7 minutes or until vegetables are barely tender when pierced. Remove from heat. Stir in tomatoes, garlic salt, basil, paprika, oregano, rice and 1 cup cheese. Spoon mixture into shallow 1½ quart baking dish. Sprinkle with remaining cheese. Bake, uncovered, for 25 minutes or until mixture is hot throughout and the cheese is bubbly. Let stand 5 minutes before serving.

Can be assembled in the morning and baked just before serving. Bake for 35 minutes if placed in the oven directly from the refrigerator.

Janine Ryder

Zucchini Pie

INGREDIENTS:

Serves 8

8 medium zucchini, sliced ⅛" thick
¼ teaspoon pepper
½ teaspoon garlic salt
½ teaspoon oregano
¼ teaspoon sweet basil

½ pound cheddar cheese, grated
½ pound Monterey jack cheese,
   grated
2 eggs
½ cup half and half (or cream)
¼ teaspoon cream of tartar

PROCEDURE:

Preheat oven to 350°. Steam or cook zucchini until tender. Layer half the zucchini in an 8" square pan. Sprinkle with half the pepper, garlic salt, oregano and basil. Top with a layer of half the cheese. Arrange the remaining zucchini over the cheese. Sprinkle with the remaining pepper, garlic salt, oregano and basil. Top with the remaining cheese. Blend eggs, half and half and cream of tartar until light. Pour over zucchini mixture and bake for 35 minutes.

Delicious the first day, better the second.

Gleneva Belice

236

$40,000 Zucchini Pie

Serves 6

INGREDIENTS:

4 cups unpared zucchini, thinly
   sliced
1 cup onion, coarsely chopped
½ cup butter (or margarine)
½ cup chopped parsley
½ teaspoon salt
½ teaspoon black pepper

¼ teaspoon garlic powder
¼ teaspoon oregano leaves
2 eggs, well beaten
8 ounces mozzarella, shredded
1 8-ounce can refrigerated dinner
   rolls
2 teaspoons Dijon mustard

PROCEDURE:

Preheat oven to 375°. In a 10″ skillet cook zucchini and onion in butter until tender, about 10 minutes. Stir in parsley, salt, pepper, garlic and oregano. Blend eggs and cheese in a large bowl. Stir into vegetable mixture. Separate dough into 8 triangles. Place in an 11″ quiche pan, a 10″ pie plate or a 12″ by 8″ baking dish. Press dough over bottom and up sides to form crust. Spread with mustard. Pour vegetable mixture evenly over crust. Bake for 18-20 minutes or until a knife inserted into the pie comes out clean. Cover edges of crust with foil the last 10 minutes of baking if it becomes too brown. Let stand 10 minutes before serving.

Won first prize in the Pillsbury Bake-Off. A hearty vegetarian main course.

Michelle Benson   Helen Froeb

Zucchini Slippers

Serves 3

INGREDIENTS:

3 medium zucchini
2 eggs, well beaten
1½ cups sharp cheddar cheese,
   shredded

½ cup small curd cottage cheese
2 tablespoons parsley, chopped
½ teaspoon salt
½ teaspoon pepper

PROCEDURE:

Preheat oven to 350°. Steam zucchini until just tender. Mix eggs, cheddar, cottage cheese, parsley, salt and pepper. Halve the zucchini. Scoop out a small portion of the inside. Fill the hollow with the cheese mixture. Place in a glass baking dish. Bake for 15 minutes. Turn oven up to 450°. Continue to bake for 5 more minutes.

Tasty the following day. Reheat by browning under the broiler for 5 minutes.

Jennifer De Silva

Southern Cornbread Dressing

Serves 10-12

INGREDIENTS:

1 recipe cornbread, crumbled (see
  page 372)
3 cups Pepperidge Farm herb
  bread stuffing
3 tablespoons butter
1 tablespoon vegetable oil
1 cup scallions, chopped
2 cups celery, sliced on the
  diagonal

6-8 water chestnuts, (fresh or
  canned) sliced
½ pound mushrooms (optional)
¾ cup parsley, chopped
2 teaspoons poultry seasoning
2½ cups turkey (or chicken) stock,
  degreased
2 eggs, beaten

PROCEDURE:

Preheat oven to 375°. Butter a 3-quart soufflé dish or casserole. Crumble
cooled cornbread and mix with herb stuffing. Heat butter and oil. Sauté
scallions, celery, water chestnuts and mushrooms until translucent. Stir
in bread mixture, parsley and poultry seasoning. Can be prepared a day
ahead to this point. Stir in broth and eggs. Bake for 30-35 minutes until
browned.

Perfect holiday fare with poultry or ham.
Martha McCardell

Hot Curried Fruit

Serves 8

INGREDIENTS:

1 20-ounce can pineapple
1 16-ounce can pears
1 16-ounce can peaches
1 16-ounce can apricots

1 cup brown sugar
1 tablespoon cornstarch
½ teaspoon curry powder
2 tablespoons butter

PROCEDURE:

Preheat oven to 350°. Drain pineapple, pears, peaches and apricots.
Combine sugar, cornstarch and curry powder. Place fruit in a single layer
in a large glass baking dish. Dot with butter. Spread sugar mixture over
fruit. Bake for 30 minutes.

A good accompaniment for turkey, chicken and ham.

Phyllis Queen Healy

238

Bread And Butter Pickles

Yields 4 pints

INGREDIENTS:

12 pickling cucumbers (or 4-5
    Armenian cucumbers), washed,
    scrubbed and sliced crosswise
    ½" thick
6 white onions, sliced in slivers
2 quarts plus 1 cup water
1 cup salt

3½ cups cider vinegar
2 cups sugar
1 teaspoon celery seed
1 teaspoon mustard seed
1 teaspoon turmeric
alum

PROCEDURE:

Put cucumbers and onions into 2 quarts water mixed with 1 cup salt. Let stand 3 hours. Rinse. Bring 1 cup water, vinegar, sugar, celery seed, mustard seed and turmeric to a boil. Add cucumbers and onions and bring to a boil. They will change color. Fill sterilized pint jars with mixture and cover with the liquid. Add pinch alum on top. Seal jars in the regular manner. Allow to mellow for 3 weeks.

Vickie Briggs

Baked Pineapple Custard

Serves 4-6

INGREDIENTS:

½ cup butter
¾ cup sugar
dash of salt

3 extra large eggs, beaten
1 #2 can crushed pineapple
5 slices white bread, cubed

PROCEDURE:

Cream butter and sugar together. Add eggs and beat until incorporated. Fold in pineapple, not drained, and bread cubes. Mixture will look curdled. Transfer to a 1½-quart casserole. Bake for 40-50 minutes.

Perfect served with ham or pork instead of potatoes.

Susan Nagy

239

Notes

9

Cakes

BAKING TIPS

Use well rounded measurements of flour, but level sugar measurements. Too much sugar is the main cause of cakes falling.

Grease cake pans with butter, not margarine, as margarine causes cakes to stick.

Use fresh, large eggs, always at room temperature.

Bake in a draft-free kitchen, with windows and doors closed.

Folding should always be done by hand using a large metal spoon, with a gentle, repetitive cutting and lifting motion.

Black Magic Cake

Serves 8-10

INGREDIENTS:

1¾ cups flour
2 cups sugar
¾ cup cocoa
2 teaspoons baking soda
1 teaspoon baking powder
1 teaspoon salt

2 eggs
1 cup strong black coffee
1 cup sour milk (add 1 tablespoon vinegar to 1 cup milk)
½ cup oil
1 teaspoon vanilla extract

PROCEDURE:

Preheat oven to 350°. Grease and flour 13″ by 9″ by 2″ pan or 2 layer cake pans. Combine flour, sugar, cocoa, baking soda, baking powder and salt in a large bowl. Add eggs, coffee, sour milk, oil and vanilla. Batter will be thin. Pour into prepared pan(s). Bake 35-40 minutes for oblong pan, or 30-35 minutes for layer pans. Ice with favorite chocolate icing.

From "Peace Corps Volunteer Cookbook", Zaire 1976. This is a very moist, very good cake.

Virginia Erickson

241

Chocolate Chip Cake

Serves 12

INGREDIENTS:

1 box yellow cake mix
1 box instant chocolate pudding
   mix
½ cup cooking oil

4 eggs
8 ounces sour cream
1 cup chopped nuts
1½ cups chocolate chips

PROCEDURE:

Preheat oven to 350°. Grease a 10″ tube pan. Place all ingredients except the nuts and chocolate chips into a mixing bowl and mix on medium speed for approximately 3 minutes. Pour half the batter into the tube pan. Sprinkle with half the nuts and chocolate chips. Pour over remaining batter and sprinkle with remaining nuts and chips. Bake for 50-60 minutes. Cool for 1 hour before removing from pan.

This cake is simple yet delicious. It will keep well for several days if wrapped in foil and refrigerated. It travels well in a cooler for picnics.

Barbara Emblem

Chocolate Chocolate Chip Cake

Serves 16

INGREDIENTS:

½ cup oil
½ teaspoon cinnamon
2 heaping tablespoons Quik
   chocolate mix
2 eggs
1½ cups sugar

2 cups applesauce
1½ teaspoons baking soda
2 cups flour
TOPPING
3 tablespoons sugar
1 12-ounce package chocolate
   chips

PROCEDURE:

Preheat oven to 350°. Grease a 9″ by 13″ baking pan. Mix the cake ingredients thoroughly in a large mixing bowl. Pour into the baking pan. Sprinkle the topping over the batter. Bake for 40 minutes.

Won a first place Blue Ribbon at the Southern California Exposition, Del Mar Fair.

242

Samantha Dresser

Chocolate Brownie Cake

Serves 12-15

INGREDIENTS:

2 cups flour
2 cups sugar
1 teaspoon baking soda
2 sticks butter
4 tablespoons cocoa
1 cup water
2 eggs, beaten
½ cup buttermilk
1 teaspoon vanilla extract

TOPPING
1 stick butter
4 tablespoons cocoa
6 tablespoons buttermilk
1 box powdered sugar
1 teaspoon vanilla extract
1 cup chopped nuts

PROCEDURE:

Preheat oven to 350°. Grease and flour a 9″ by 12″ pan. Sift together flour, sugar and baking soda. Combine butter, cocoa and water in a saucepan and bring to a boil. Cool slightly then pour into dry ingredients and stir. Add eggs, buttermilk and vanilla. Pour into pan and bake for 30 minutes, or until toothpick inserted in center is clean. For the topping, combine the butter, cocoa and buttermilk in a saucepan and bring to a boil, stirring constantly. Remove from heat. Add powdered sugar, vanilla and nuts, and stir to combine. Pour over hot cake.

Nancy Doyne   *Sharon Krubel*

Chocolate Bundt Cake

Serves 8-12

INGREDIENTS:

1 package dark chocolate cake mix
1 package instant chocolate
   pudding
4 eggs
½ cup oil

½ cup warm water with 1 tablespoon instant coffee
1 cup sour cream
1 6-ounce package chocolate chips
½ teaspoon baking soda
powdered sugar (for garnish)

PROCEDURE:

Preheat oven to 350°. Grease a bundt pan well. Combine all ingredients except for chocolate chips. Mix well. Stir in the chocolate chips. Pour into bundt pan. Bake for 35-40 minutes. Set on rack to cool. Do not remove cake from pan until cool. Dust with powdered sugar.

Betty Stewart

Chocolate Cake

Serves 10-12

INGREDIENTS:

1 cup unsweetened cocoa, unsifted
2 cups boiling water
2¾ cups all-purpose flour, sifted
2 teaspoons baking soda
½ teaspoon salt
½ teaspoon baking powder
1 cup butter (or margarine),
   softened
2½ cups granulated sugar
4 eggs
1½ teaspoons vanilla extract

FROSTING
1 6-ounce package semisweet
   chocolate pieces
½ cup light cream
1 cup butter (or margarine)
2½ cups confectioner's sugar
FILLING
1 cup heavy cream, chilled
¼ cup confectioner's sugar
1 teaspoon vanilla extract

PROCEDURE:

In a medium bowl combine cocoa with boiling water, mixing with a wire whisk until smooth. Cool completely. Sift flour with soda, salt and baking powder. Preheat oven to 350°. Grease well and lightly flour 3 9″ by 1½″ round layer cake pans. In large bowl of electric mixer, at high speed, beat butter, sugar, eggs and vanilla, scraping bowl occasionally, until light — about 5 minutes. At low speed blend in flour mixture in fourths, alternately with cocoa mixture in thirds, beginning and ending with flour mixture. Do not overbeat! Divide evenly into pans and smooth tops. Bake for 25-30 minutes or until surface springs back when pressed with fingertip. Cool in pans 10 minutes. Carefully loosen sides with spatula; remove from pans and cool on racks. For the frosting, combine chocolate pieces, cream and butter in a medium saucepan. Stir over medium heat until smooth. Remove from heat. With whisk, blend in confectioner's sugar. In bowl set over ice, beat until it holds shape. For the filling, whip cream with sugar and vanilla. Refrigerate. To assemble cake, place a layer, top side down on serving plate. Spread with half of the cream. Place second layer top side down and spread with remaining cream. Place third layer, top side up. With a spatula, frost sides first, covering whipped cream. Use rest of frosting on top, swirling decoratively. Refrigerate at least 1 hour before serving. Cut with a thin-edged sharp knife using a sawing motion.

This cake takes a lot of time to prepare but is well worth the effort. Make room
in your refrigerator before you assemble the cake, it's tall!
Follow the directions carefully for an outstanding success.

Nita Young

Sue's Gooey Chocolate Nut Cake

Serves 10-12

INGREDIENTS:

2 extra-large eggs, separated
2 cups sugar
1¾ cups cake flour
1¾ teaspoons baking powder
¼ teaspoon baking soda
1 teaspoon salt
¼ cup oil
1½ cups milk
1 teaspoon vanilla extract
4 squares unsweetened chocolate,
  melted and cooled
1 cup blanched almonds, finely
  chopped

FILLING
¾ cup sugar
3 ⅝ ounce package chocolate fudge
  regular pudding mix
1½ cups milk
1 tablespoon butter, at room
  temperature
1 cup shredded coconut
1 cup chopped pecans
fresh whipped cream (or Cool
  Whip)

PROCEDURE:

Preheat oven to 350°. Beat egg whites until frothy. Gradually add ½ cup sugar. Beat until very glossy. Set aside. Blend remainder of sugar, flour, baking powder, baking soda and salt into another bowl. Add oil and 1 cup milk. Beat 1 minute on medium speed, scraping bowl often. Add remainder of milk, egg yolks, vanilla and chocolate. Beat 1 more minute, scraping bowl regularly. Fold in egg whites. Fold in chopped almonds. Bake in 2 9″ cake pans which have been well greased and floured, for 35-40 minutes. Test with toothpick. Cool in pans 10 minutes then turn layers out onto racks to cool completely before frosting. To make filling, combine sugar, pudding mix and milk. Cook until it boils and thickens. Remove from heat, blend in butter. Stir in coconut and pecans. Cool completely. To assemble cake, place a generous amount of filling between layers and over top layer, leaving a ¼″-½″ rim of bare cake at perimeter of top layer. Slather whipped cream or Cool Whip liberally around outside of cake and over the rim of the top layer to cover the edge and meet the filling. Refrigerate until ready to serve.

If using real cream the cake is best served within a few hours. If using Cool Whip the cake can be refrigerated overnight or longer. Either way this is a beautiful and impressive party dessert.

Susan Nagy

245

Chocolate Cream Cake

Serves 10-12

INGREDIENTS:

5 large eggs, separated
1 cup sugar
1 16-ounce can Hershey chocolate
   syrup

1 teaspoon salt
1 teaspoon vanilla extract
¾ cup unsifted flour
½ pint heavy cream

PROCEDURE:

Preheat oven to 325°. Beat egg yolks until thickened. Gradually beat in sugar until ivory color. Beat in half (¾ cup) of the chocolate syrup. Fold in salt, vanilla and flour. Beat egg whites until stiff and fold into chocolate mixture. Bake in ungreased 9″ springform pan for about 1 hour, or until a cake tester inserted in center comes out clean. Invert on rack and cool. Remove from pan and cut in half horizontally. Beat cream until almost stiff; gradually beat in remaining chocolate syrup until very stiff. Spread a little less than half the cream between cake layers and frost top and sides with rest. Refrigerate.

This is my family's favorite cake and I have to bake it for each of their birthdays.

Gleneva Belice

Chocolate Dream Torte

Serves 10-12

INGREDIENTS:

1 cup cake flour
¼ teaspoon salt
10 egg whites (1¼ cups)
2 teaspoons cream of tartar
1 cup sugar
1 teaspoon vanilla extract
½ pound sweet chocolate, grated

10 egg yolks
FROSTING
1 cup powdered sugar
6 tablespoons cocoa
2 cups heavy cream
1 teaspoon vanilla extract

PROCEDURE:

Preheat oven to 325°. Sift flour, add salt. Beat egg whites until frothy, add cream of tartar. When still moist but beginning to form soft peaks turn mixer to low speed and gradually add sugar. Continue beating until sugar is dissolved. Add vanilla. Fold in flour gently. Add grated chocolate. Beat egg yolks until thick and fold into egg white mixture. Bake in ungreased tube pan for about 1 hour. Invert and cool. For the frosting, combine sugar and cocoa. Add cream. Chill for 2-3 hours. Whip to spreading consistency. Add vanilla.

This is a fabulous cake. The only real work is to grate the chocolate.
For best results, we recommend doing this by hand.

Nancy Field Stork

Chocolate Mousse Cake I

Serves 8-10

INGREDIENTS:

7 ounces semisweet chocolate
¼ pound unsalted butter
8 extra-large eggs, separated
1 cup sugar
1 teaspoon vanilla extract

⅛ teaspoon cream of tartar
FROSTING
½ pint whipping cream
⅓ cup powdered sugar
1 teaspoon vanilla extract

PROCEDURE:

Preheat oven to 325°. In a small saucepan melt the chocolate and butter over low heat. In a large bowl beat egg yolks and ¾ cup sugar until very light and fluffy, about 5 minutes. Gradually beat in warm chocolate mixture and vanilla. In another large bowl beat egg whites with cream of tartar until soft peaks form. Add remaining ¼ cup sugar, 1 tablespoon at a time, beating continuously until stiff. Fold egg whites carefully into chocolate mixture. Pour three quarters of the batter into a 9" by 3" ungreased springform pan. Cover remaining batter and refrigerate. Bake cake for 35 minutes. Remove cake from oven and cool. Expect cake to drop as it cools. Stir the refrigerated batter and spread over the cake. Refrigerate until firm. (Cake may be frozen at this stage). Remove outside rim of springform pan and spread frosting over top and sides of cake. For the frosting, beat the cream in a small bowl until soft peaks form. Add powdered sugar and vanilla. Beat until stiff.

This cake never fails. It freezes beautifully, or can be made a day ahead of time
and kept in the refrigerator. Serve it straight from the refrigerator.

Betty Shaffer

Chocolate Mousse Cake II

Serves 16-20

INGREDIENTS:

14 eggs, separated
1 pound unsalted butter minus 2
   tablespoons
1 cup sugar minus 2 tablespoons
12 ounces semisweet chocolate,
   melted

1 teaspoon rum (or vanilla extract)

GARNISH
whipped cream
shaved chocolate

PROCEDURE:

This cake can only be made using a Kitchen Aid mixer. Mix egg yolks with all other ingredients, except for the egg whites, in your Kitchen Aid bowl. Beat this mixture for 40 minutes at speed number 6. Preheat oven to 325°. Beat egg whites until stiff. Fold egg whites into chocolate mixture. Pour half of the batter into a 10″ springform pan. Bake for 30 minutes. Refrigerate second half of batter. Allow baked half to cool in its pan, and expect it to fall in the center. When cool, pour the refrigerated mixture on top of the baked half, then place in freezer. When ready to serve, remove outside rim of pan and cover the cake with whipped cream and shaved chocolate. Allow to stand one half hour before serving.

Simple to make and tastes luscious. May be kept in the refrigerator. Leftovers may be frozen.

Bettye Ulevitch

Chocolate-Pistachio Cake

Serves 8

INGREDIENTS:

1 package white (or yellow) cake
   mix
1 package pistachio instant
   pudding mix
½ cup vegetable oil

¾ cup water
4 eggs
¼ cup crème de menthe
5½ ounce can chocolate syrup
powdered sugar (for garnish)

PROCEDURE:

Preheat oven to 350°. Grease and flour a bundt or tube pan. Mix cake mix and pudding. Add oil, water and eggs. Mix well. Add creme de menthe. Pour one quarter of this batter into another bowl, and add the chocolate syrup to it. Set aside. Pour the green mixture into the baking pan, then carefully pour in the chocolate mixture, keeping about 1″ away from the side of the pan. Bake for 45-55 minutes. Cool and sprinkle lightly with powdered sugar

This cake is easy to make and lovely to look at with its two colors. Freezes well.

Vina Saycocie

Frozen Chocolate Mousse Cake

Serves 14-16

INGREDIENTS:

1½ boxes Nabisco Chocolate Wafers, crumbed	2 cups whipping cream
1 stick butter, melted	6 tablespoons powdered sugar
1 pound bittersweet chocolate	4 egg whites
2 eggs	GARNISH
4 egg yolks	2 cups cream
	6 tablespoons powdered sugar

PROCEDURE:

For the crust, combine crumbs with butter. Press over bottom and completely up sides of 10″ springform pan. Refrigerate or freeze for 30 minutes. For the filling, soften chocolate in top of double-boiler over simmering water or melt in microwave oven for 3 minutes on high setting. Stir and cool to lukewarm. Add whole eggs and mix well. Add yolks and mix until thoroughly blended. Whip cream with powdered sugar until soft peaks form. Beat egg whites until stiff but not dry. Stir a little of the cream and whites into chocolate mixture to lighten. Fold in remaining cream and whites until completely incorporated. Pour into crust and freeze. For the garnish, whip the cream with the powdered sugar. To serve, loosen crust on all sides using a sharp knife. Remove springform pan. Place on serving plate. Spread ½″ of whipped cream over top. Pipe remaining whipped cream in rosettes over top and along border. Cut cake into wedges with thin sharp knife dipped in hot water.

A great "do-ahead" dessert that will send the chocoholic into ecstasy.

Fran Jenkins

Bacardi Rum Cake

Serves 10

INGREDIENTS:

1 cup chopped pecans (or walnuts)
1 18½-ounce Duncan Hines yellow
   cake mix
1 3¼-ounce package instant vanilla
   pudding mix
4 eggs
½ cup cold water
½ cup vegetable oil
½ cup Bacardi dark rum, 80 proof

GARNISH
whipped cream

GLAZE
¼ pound butter
1 cup granulated sugar
¼ cup water
½ cup rum

PROCEDURE:

Preheat oven to 325°. Grease a 10″ tube or bundt pan. Sprinkle nuts over bottom of pan. Mix all cake ingredients and beat for 4 minutes. Pour over nuts. Bake for 1 hour. Cool. Invert onto serving plate. Prick top. Drizzle and smooth glaze evenly over top and sides. Repeat until glaze is used. For the glaze, melt the butter in a saucepan. Stir in sugar and water. Boil 5 minutes, stirring constantly. Remove from stove. Stir in rum. To serve, slice and put a spoonful of whipped cream on each individual serving.

Billy Simms

Cointreau Fudge Torte

Serves 8

INGREDIENTS:

4 ounces Cointreau orange liqueur
1 16.5-ounce can Pillsbury Fudge
   Frosting Supreme

1 Sara Lee frozen pound cake
1 small package pecan halves

PROCEDURE:

Blend 1 ounce Cointreau into the frosting. Slice frozen cake horizontally into 4 or 5 slices. Place slices on a sheet of aluminum foil and drizzle with remaining Cointreau. Place one slice on a serving platter and frost lightly. Repeat until all layers have been placed and frosted. Frost all sides. Top with pecan halves. Chill before serving.

Dorothy Dickinson

Kahlua Cake

Serves 8-12

INGREDIENTS:

3½ cups cake flour, sifted before
    measuring
4 teaspoons double acting baking
    powder
½ teaspoon salt
2 cups sugar
1 cup butter

⅔ cup Kahlua
⅓ cup water
2 teaspoons vanilla extract
1 small bottle almond extract
3 eggs
powdered sugar (for garnish)

PROCEDURE:

Preheat oven to 375°. Grease and flour a small (mini) bundt pan. Resift the flour twice with the baking powder and salt. Cream sugar with butter. Add the flour mixture to the butter mixture in 3 parts alternately with the Kahlua and water. Stir the batter well after each addition. Beat in vanilla and almond extract. Beat in eggs. Pour into bundt pan and bake for 45 minutes or until toothpick inserted into cake comes out clean. Cool in pan for about 5 minutes before turning out on rack to cool. Sprinkle with powdered sugar.

A very rich and elegant dessert.
Julie Liss

Marie's Zabaglione Cake

Serves 8-10

INGREDIENTS:

approximately 25 lady fingers
2 cups milk
3 packages vanilla instant dessert
    mix

¾ cup Marsala
1 pint whipping cream

PROCEDURE:

Line lightly buttered springform pan bottom and sides with lady fingers halved lengthwise. Beat 2 cups milk into vanilla mixes. Slowly add Marsala. Beat ½ pint cream until stiff and fold into vanilla mixture. Spoon carefully into pan and chill overnight. Before serving, top with ½ pint whipped cream (optional).

Good and easy.
Linda Morefield

Elegant Spanish Sherry Cake

Serves 8-10

INGREDIENTS:

1½ cups sugar
¾ cup water
¾ cup cream sherry
1 12-ounce pound cake, cubed
¾ cup pecan halves
4 egg yolks

1 teaspoon almond extract (optional)
¼ teaspoon salt

GARNISH
whipped cream
pecan halves
chocolate syrup

PROCEDURE:

Preheat oven to 350°. Butter a 1-quart mold. Combine sugar and water in saucepan. Bring to boil. Reduce heat and simmer uncovered 10 minutes. Cool. Combine half the syrup with sherry and cake cubes, tossing lightly just to mix. Grind pecans in grinder. Add pecans, egg yolks, almond extract and salt to remaining half of syrup. Cook over medium heat, stirring often, until mixture begins to bubble, about 5 minutes. To assemble cake, layer one third of cake cube mixture in bottom of mold. Top with one third of pecan mixture. Repeat layering twice. Bake for 1 hour or until top is golden and crusty. Cool for ½ hour, then loosen sides with a knife and invert cake onto a plate. Cover with a cake dome or plastic wrap. Allow to stand for several hours or overnight. To serve, use puffs of whipped cream, pecan halves and even chocolate swirls for decoration.

Cake develops flavor as it ages. It may even be held for 2-3 days before serving, which is a good "make ahead" feature. This is a luscious dessert!

Joy Charney

Almond Sherry Cake

Serves 8-10

INGREDIENTS:

2 frozen 10¾-ounce pound cakes
3 cups sugar
1½ cups water
1½ cups cream sherry
3 tablespoons Amaretto

1½ cups almonds
6 egg yolks
2 teaspoons almond extract
½ teaspoon salt

252

PROCEDURE:

Follow directions for previous recipe, Elegant Spanish Sherry Cake, using a 1½-quart mold, as this recipe is larger than the other.

S. Brooke Miller

Piña Colada Cake

Serves 10-12

INGREDIENTS:

1 white cake mix
1 coconut (or vanilla) instant
  pudding mix
4 eggs
½ cup water (¾ cup water if using
  vanilla pudding)
¼ cup oil
⅓ cup dark rum

FROSTING
1 8-ounce can crushed pineapple
  with juice
1 coconut (or vanilla) instant
  pudding
⅓ cup dark rum
1 9-ounce Cool Whip

PROCEDURE:

Preheat oven to 350°. Mix ingredients and beat well. Pour into 9″ by 13″ baking pan. Bake for 25-30 minutes. Cool. For the frosting, mix the pineapple and juice with the pudding and rum. Fold in Cool Whip. Spread frosting over cake and refrigerate.

Mary Landa

Applesauce Cake

Serves 8

INGREDIENTS:

½ cup shortening
1 cup packed, light brown sugar
1 cup applesauce
2¼ cups flour
½ teaspoon baking soda

½ teaspoon salt
1 teaspoon baking powder
¾ teaspoon apple pie spice
1 cup chopped nuts

PROCEDURE:

Preheat oven to 325°. Grease 9″ by 5″ by 3″ loaf pan. Cream shortening and sugar. Add applesauce. Sift together flour, soda, salt, baking powder and spice. Add to applesauce mixture. Fold in nuts. Bake for 1 hour.

Frost with sugar and water icing if desired.

Sally Peters Davidson

253

Carrot Cake

INGREDIENTS:

2 cups flour
2 teaspoons baking powder
1½ teaspoons baking soda
1 teaspoon salt
1-2 teaspoons cinnamon
2 cups sugar
1¼-1½ cups oil
4 eggs
2 cups grated carrots
1 8-ounce can crushed pineapple,
    drained

FROSTING
½ cup margarine
8 ounces cream cheese
2 teaspoons vanilla extract
1 box powdered sugar
lemon juice (optional)
chopped nuts (optional)
ADD-IN OPTIONALS
2 teaspoons vanilla extract
1 cup shredded coconut
1 cup chopped nuts
instead of 1½ cups oil use ¾ cup oil
    with ¾ cup buttermilk

PROCEDURE:

Mix dry ingredients with oil and eggs; beat thoroughly. Fold in remaining ingredients. Pour into a greased 9″ by 13″ pan. Bake in a 350° oven for 45-55 minutes. Or bake in 2 9″ layer pans, well-greased, for 35 minutes. Or bake as cupcakes at 375° for 20-25 minutes. Cool before frosting. For the frosting, soften the margarine and cream cheese. Add the sugar, vanilla and lemon juice and beat. Ice cake and sprinkle with nuts.

Gina L. Bulen
Sherry Cook
Edna Gentry
Jana Lucic Paget
Susan Slesinger Ulevitch

Delicate Lemon Squares

Serves 10-12

INGREDIENTS:

2 eggs
¾ cup sugar
3 tablespoons lemon juice plus a
    little zest
2 tablespoons flour

½ teaspoon baking powder
CRUST
1 cup all-purpose flour
¼ cup powdered sugar
½ cup softened butter

PROCEDURE:

Preheat oven to 350°. For crust, stir flour and sugar together. Cut in butter and mix until mixture clings together. Pat into an ungreased 8″ by 8″ by 2″ baking pan. Bake for 10-12 minutes. For the filling, place eggs in mixing bowl and beat until frothy. Add sugar and lemon and beat until thick and smooth, about 10 minutes. Add flour mixed with baking powder to egg mixture and blend. Pour over hot baked layer and return to oven for 20-25 minutes. Sift powdered sugar over top. Cool and cut.

This recipe originates from the Zodiac Restaurant of Neiman Marcus. For a larger crowd, the recipe doubles well.

Bonnie Holmer

Fresh Plum Cake

Serves 16

INGREDIENTS:

2 cups flour
1 teaspoon baking soda
1 teaspoon salt
1 teaspoon cinnamon
3 eggs

1¾ cups sugar
1 cup oil
1 cup chopped nuts
2 heaping cups blue Italian plums, cut into eighths

PROCEDURE:

Preheat oven to 350°. Grease 9″ by 13″ baking dish. Sift together flour, baking soda, salt and cinnamon. Set aside. In mixmaster bowl, place eggs, sugar, oil and beat very well. Add flour mixture to egg mixture. Fold in chopped nuts and plums. Bake until golden and edges are pulling away from dish. Cut when cool. Sprinkle with confectioner's sugar.

Everybody loves this!

Bettye Ulevitch

Orange Fruit Loaf

Serves 12

INGREDIENTS:

juice of 2 oranges
rind of 2 oranges, finely grated
¼ cup raisins
¼ cup chopped almonds (or
    walnuts)
2 tablespoons butter (or
    margarine), melted

1 egg, beaten
¼ cup lemon juice
2½ cups flour, sifted
1 cup sugar
1 teaspoon baking soda
2 teaspoons baking powder
½ teaspoon salt

PROCEDURE:

Preheat oven to 350°. Grease an 8″ by 4″ loaf pan. Combine the orange rind, raisins, nuts, butter, egg and lemon juice. Add enough water to reserved orange juice to make up to ¾ cup liquid. Add to other ingredients. Sift together flour, sugar, baking soda, baking powder and salt. Add to fruit mixture, stirring just until blended. Pour into loaf pan and bake 1 hour 15 minutes or until done. Cool before slicing.

Theresa Worsch

Rave Reviews Coconut Cake

Serves 10

INGREDIENTS:

1 package yellow cake mix
1 package vanilla instant pudding
1⅓ cups water
4 eggs
¼ cup oil
2 cups angel flake coconut
1 cup chopped walnuts (pecans or
    almonds)

FROSTING
4 tablespoons butter (or margarine)
2 cups angel flake coconut
8 ounces cream cheese
2 teaspoons milk
3½ cups confectioner's sugar
½ teaspoon vanilla extract

PROCEDURE:

Preheat oven to 350°. Grease and flour 3 9″ layer pans. Blend cake mix, pudding mix, water, eggs and oil in a large mixer bowl. Beat at medium speed for 4 minutes. Stir in coconut and walnuts. Pour into layer pans and bake for 35 minutes. Remove from oven and cool in pans for 15 minutes. Turn layers out onto racks and cool completely. For the frosting, melt 2 tablespoons butter in a skillet, add coconut and stir constantly over low heat until golden brown. Spread coconut on absorbent paper to cool. Cream 2 tablespoons butter with the cream cheese. Add milk. Gradually beat in sugar. Blend in vanilla. Stir in 1¾ cups of the coconut. Spread over tops of cake layers. Stack and sprinkle with remaining coconut.

Pat Dean

Melt In Your Mouth Blueberry Cake

Serves 8

INGREDIENTS:

2 eggs, separated
1 cup sugar
½ cup shortening
¼ teaspoon salt
1 teaspoon vanilla extract

1½ cups flour, sifted
1 teaspoon baking powder
⅓ cup milk
1½ cups fresh blueberries
granulated sugar

PROCEDURE:

Preheat oven to 350°. Grease an 8″ by 8″ pan. Dust blueberries lightly with flour to prevent them from settling to the bottom of cake. Beat egg whites, gradually adding ¼ cup sugar, until stiff. Set aside. Cream shortening. Add salt and vanilla. Add remaining sugar gradually. Add unbeaten egg yolks and continue to beat until light and creamy. Add sifted flour and baking powder alternately with milk. Fold in beaten whites. Fold in blueberries. Turn into prepared pan. Sprinkle sugar lightly over batter. Bake for 50-60 minutes.

Good for breakfast as well as dessert.

Margi Bingham

Lemon Jello Cake

Serves 12

INGREDIENTS:

1 box yellow cake mix
¼ cup oil
4 eggs
1 3-ounce box lemon Jello

1 cup boiling water
GLAZE
3 tablespoons lemon juice with 1
   cup powdered sugar

PROCEDURE:

Preheat oven to 350°. Grease either a bundt pan or a 9″ by 12″ cake pan. Mix Jello with boiling water and allow to cool. Blend cake mix and oil. Add eggs one at a time, beating well after each addition. Add cooled Jello mixture, beat until smooth. Bake for 45 minutes in bundt pan or for 35 minutes in cake pan. Cool for 15-20 minutes, then remove from pan and glaze.

Very simple and delicious. May substitute lemon Jello with orange Jello for change of flavor.

Alice Yu

Carmel Cream Cake

Serves 12

INGREDIENTS:

1 cup butter, softened
2½ cups sugar
3 cups flour
4 teaspoons cocoa
1 teaspoon baking soda
pinch of salt
5 eggs, separated
1 cup buttermilk

5 tablespoons strong coffee
2 teaspoons vanilla extract
ICING
½ cup butter, softened
1 box powdered sugar, sifted
1 egg yolk
2 teaspoons cocoa, sifted
3 tablespoons strong coffee
1 teaspoon vanilla extract

PROCEDURE:

Preheat oven to 375°. Grease and flour 3 8″ layer cake pans. Cream butter. Add sugar and cream until fluffy. Sift dry ingredients together. Add egg yolks to butter and sugar; beat. Add dry ingredients alternately with buttermilk. Add coffee and vanilla, mixing on low speed. Beat egg whites until stiff and fold into mixture. Pour evenly into prepared pans and bake for 25-30 minutes For the icing, cream the butter and sugar. Add rest of ingredients and beat until fluffy.

258   *Connie W. Griffith*

Aunt Biddie's Gingerbread

Serves 10

INGREDIENTS:

2 eggs
¼ cup brown sugar
¼ cup molasses
¼ cup melted shortening (or salad
　　oil)
1 cup buttermilk
2½ cups flour

2 teaspoons baking soda
1½ teaspoons cinnamon
2 teaspoons ginger
¼ teaspoon cloves
¼ teaspoon nutmeg
½ teaspoon baking powder

PROCEDURE:

Preheat oven to 350°. Grease a 9" by 9" by 2" pan. Mix eggs, sugar and molasses and beat. Add rest of ingredients and mix until well blended. Bake for 45 minutes or until center is done.

Absolutely delicious sliced and buttered, or topped with freshly whipped cream.

Anne Coleman

Walnut Torte

Serves 6-8

INGREDIENTS:

6 eggs, separated
1½ cups sugar
2½ tablespoons flour
1 teaspoon baking powder
3 cups walnuts (or pecans), finely ground

2-3 cups whipped cream (for
　　garnish)
whole walnuts (for garnish)

PROCEDURE:

Preheat oven to 350°. Grease 2 9" layer pans with removable bottoms. Beat 6 egg yolks on medium to low speed of mixer, gradually adding sugar until light yellow and foamy. Sift together flour and baking powder and gradually add it to egg mixture. Stir in ground nuts. Fold in 6 stiffly beaten egg whites. Divide the batter between the 2 pans and bake for 25-30 minutes. Cool in pans. Turn out carefully. Frost between layers and over cake with whipped cream to cover completely. Decorate with walnuts.

Freezes well.

Susan Plazak

Coca Cola Cake

Serves 12

INGREDIENTS:

2 cups flour
2 cups sugar
2 sticks margarine
3 tablespoons cocoa
1 cup Coca Cola
2 eggs, beaten
1 teaspoon vanilla extract
½ cup buttermilk

1 teaspoon soda
1½ cups mini marshmallows

ICING
1 stick butter
3 tablespoons cocoa
6 tablespoons Coca Cola
1 box powdered sugar

PROCEDURE:

Preheat oven to 350°. Grease and flour a 13″ by 9″ by 2″ pan. Mix flour and sugar in a large bowl. In a saucepan, combine margarine, cocoa and Coca Cola, and bring to a boil. Pour over flour and sugar while hot. Stir. Add eggs, vanilla, buttermilk, baking soda and marshmallows and mix well. Pour into prepared pan and bake for 35 minutes. For the icing, bring the butter, cocoa and Coca Cola to a boil. Pour over powdered sugar and beat. It will be like fudge. Pour over warm cake.

Ruth E. Lischke

Crumb Cake

Serves 18

INGREDIENTS:

½ cup butter
8 ounces cream cheese
1¼ cups sugar
2 eggs
2 cups all purpose flour
2 teaspoons baking powder
½ teaspoon baking soda
½ teaspoon salt

½ cup milk
1 teaspoon vanilla extract
½ teaspoon almond extract
TOPPING
½ cup flour
½ cup granulated sugar
¼ cup margarine
½ cup chopped pecans

PROCEDURE:

Preheat oven to 350°. Grease and flour a 13″ by 9″ pan. Cream butter and cheese. Add sugar and cream. Add eggs. Sift flour, baking powder, soda and salt together. Add flour mixture alternately with milk to egg mixture. Add flavorings. Spread evenly in greased pan. For the topping, cut the margarine into the flour and sugar until mixture resembles coarse crumbs. Add pecans. Sprinkle over cake batter. Bake for 40 minutes. Serve warm.

Freezes well. Great with tea or coffee for brunch, or served alongside a scoop of ice cream for dessert.

Mrs. James Regan

Devil's Food Cake I

Serves 8-10

INGREDIENTS:

2 cups sugar
1 cup shortening
2 eggs
1 cup sour milk (1 cup milk plus 1
    tablespoon lemon juice or
    vinegar)
2½ cups flour
2 teaspoons soda
½ teaspoon salt
½ cup cocoa

1 cup hot water
1 teaspoon vanilla extract

ICING
1½ cups sugar
½ teaspoon salt
¼ teaspoon cream of tartar
5 tablespoons water
2 egg whites
1 teaspoon vanilla extract

PROCEDURE:

Preheat oven to 350°. Grease well and flour 2 9″ layer cake pans. Cream sugar and shortening. Add eggs and sour milk. Sift dry ingredients 3 times and add to mixer bowl together with water and vanilla. Bake for 35-40 minutes. For the icing, place all the ingredients except vanilla in a double boiler over simmering water. Beat with a hand-held electric beater until icing will hold a peak. Add vanilla. Use to fill and frost cooled layers.

Lenna Brown

Devil's Food Cake II

Serves 8-10

INGREDIENTS:

⅓ cup butter
1 cup sugar
2 egg yolks
1½ squares chocolate, melted
¼ cup buttermilk

1 cup cake flour
1 teaspoon baking powder
1 teaspoon baking soda
¾ teaspoon vanilla extract
2 egg whites, stiffly beaten

PROCEDURE:

Preheat oven to 350°. Grease (generously) and flour 2 9″ layer cake pans. Mix ingredients together well at one time, and fold in egg whites by hand. Bake for 20-25 minutes. Frost as desired.

Catherine R. Glass

"Easy True" Pound Cake

Serves 10

INGREDIENTS:

½ pound unsalted butter, softened
8 ounces cream cheese, softened
2 cups sugar
2 teaspoons lemon juice
2 teaspoons vanilla extract

6 eggs
2 cups flour
3 teaspoons baking powder
1 teaspoon salt
powdered sugar (for garnish)

PROCEDURE:

Preheat oven to 350°. Butter and flour a bundt pan. Cream butter, cheese and sugar until light and fluffy. Add lemon juice and vanilla. Beat in eggs one at a time. Add sifted dry ingredients. Pour into prepared pan and bake for 50-60 minutes. Cool and sprinkle powdered sugar on top.

This is a rich and tasty cake. It freezes well. Your house will smell wonderful as it bakes!

Edna Pollak

Friendship Cake

If ever you are lucky enough to be given the mysterious starter batter by a special friend, here is the simple day-by-day procedure to a light and delicious cake.

DAY 1
When you receive the base pour it into a large bowl (not metal). Stir, cover and place on counter. Do not refrigerate.
DAYS 2-3-4
Stir each day, cover and leave on counter
DAY 5
Add 1 cup sugar, 1 cup flour, 1 cup milk. Stir, cover and leave on counter
DAYS 6-7-8-9
Stir once each day. Cover and leave to rest on counter.
DAY 10
Add 1 cup sugar, 1 cup flour, 1 cup milk. Stir well. Take out 3 cups of this base and give 1 cup each to 3 friends, with these directions! Preheat your oven to 350°. Grease a tube or pan of your choice. To remaining batter add:

⅔ cup oil	2 teaspoons baking powder
3 eggs	½ teaspoon salt
2 cups flour	1½ teaspoons baking soda
1 cup sugar	2 teaspoons vanilla extract (or
1½ teaspoons cinnamon (or	other flavoring)
nutmeg)	

Beat until smooth. Fold in ⅓ cup of any combination of the following suggested ingredients:

nuts	apples
raisins	pineapple (drained)
currants	cherries
dates	chocolate chips

. . . or anything that tickles your fancy.

Bake for 55-60 minutes.

Pauline Batties

263

Faye's Ice Box Cake

Serves 6

INGREDIENTS:

1 box ladyfingers
2 squares bitter chocolate, melted
1 cup sugar
½ cup butter
4 eggs

PROCEDURE:

Butter a small bread pan. Place a layer of ladyfingers along bottom. Cream sugar and butter, and add chocolate. Add eggs 1 at a time beating for 3 minutes after each addition. Continue to beat until stiff. Cover ladyfingers with some frosting and repeat layers of ladyfingers and frosting ending with ladyfingers. Cover and refrigerate for 24 hours. To serve, loosen sides with knife by running knife along sides of pan. Invert onto serving plate. Slice.

Good after a light meal.

Mrs. Frederick M. Owens, Jr.

Geneva Coffee Cake

Serves 10

INGREDIENTS:

3 eggs, separated
1 cup sugar
½ cup Crisco
1⅓ cups plus 2½ tablespoons cake
    flour
1½ teaspoons baking powder
1 teaspoon cinnamon
¼ teaspoon ginger
¼ teaspoon cloves
½ cup milk
TOPPING
1 cup chopped nuts
2 teaspoons cinnamon
½ cup sugar

PROCEDURE:

Preheat oven to 325°. Grease an 8" by 12" by 2" pan. Beat egg whites until they will hold a peak. Add ⅓ cup sugar and continue to beat until stiff. In mixer bowl cream Crisco, remaining sugar and yolks. Sift flour, baking powder and spices together, and add alternately with milk to Crisco mixture, beginning and ending with flour. Fold in egg whites by hand. Pour into prepared pan. Combine topping ingredients and spread over top of batter in pan. Bake for 35-40 minutes. Cut and serve while warm.

This is my mother's recipe and the best coffee cake I have ever eaten.

Elinor Merideth

Italian Sour Cream Cake

Serves 16

INGREDIENTS:

2 tablespoons shortening	GLAZE
2 eggs, separated	1 cup powdered sugar, sifted
½ cup brown sugar, firmly packed	2 tablespoons cocoa
1 cup coconut	2 tablespoons Amaretto
½ cup ground pecans	1 tablespoon margarine, softened
yellow butter cake mix with	1 tablespoon corn syrup
pudding included	2-4 teaspoons water
1 cup sour cream	2 teaspoons ground pecans
½ cup Amaretto liqueur	6 maraschino cherries
½ cup water	

PROCEDURE:

Heat oven to 350°. Use the 2 tablespoons shortening to generously grease a large bundt pan. Beat 2 egg whites until foamy. Gradually add brown sugar and beat for about 3 minutes until stiff. Fold in coconut and ground pecans. Spread meringue over bottom and up sides of pan to within 1" of top. Set aside. In large bowl, blend cake mix, sour cream, Amaretto, water, eggs and 2 yolks at low speed until moistened. Beat for 2 minutes at high speed. Pour batter into prepared pan. Bake for 55-60 minutes or until toothpick inserted comes out clean. Cool upright in pan for 10 minutes, then gently loosen sides and invert onto serving plate. Cool completely. For the glaze, blend powdered sugar, cocoa, Amaretto, margarine, corn syrup and water until smooth. Spoon over top of cake, allowing some to run down sides. Sprinkle with ground pecans and decorate with cherries.

This cake is beautifully moist and attractive. It can be made a day in advance.

Carol Vadnais

Hot Milk Sponge Cake

Serves 10

INGREDIENTS:

1 cup milk
¼ pound butter
2 cups flour, sifted
1 teaspoon baking powder
¼ teaspoon salt

4 eggs
2 cups sugar
1 teaspoon vanilla extract
powdered sugar (for garnish)

PROCEDURE:

Preheat oven to 375°. Grease and flour a tube pan. Place milk and butter in a saucepan and heat over moderate heat until butter melts, but do not allow milk to boil. Sift flour with baking powder and salt. Beat eggs well. Add sugar and continue to beat until thick. Add vanilla. Fold in dry ingredients. Fold in hot milk with butter. Pour into prepared pan and bake 35-45 minutes. Invert to cool. Serve with powdered sugar sifted over top.

Jane Hubler

Italian Cream Cake

Serves 14-16

INGREDIENTS:

2 cups sugar
1 cup shortening
1 stick butter (or margarine)
5 eggs, separated
1 teaspoon soda
1 teaspoon vanilla extract
1½ teaspoons salt
1 cup buttermilk
2 cups flour

1 3½-ounce can flaked coconut
1 cup chopped nuts (black walnuts)

ICING

8 ounces cream cheese
1 stick butter
1 box powdered sugar
1 teaspoon vanilla extract
black walnuts (for garnish)

PROCEDURE:

Preheat oven to 350°. Grease and flour 3 9″ pans and line them with wax paper. Cream sugar, shortening and margarine. Add egg yolks. Stir soda, vanilla and salt into buttermilk and add alternately with flour to creamed mixture. Beat egg whites until stiff. Fold coconut, nuts and egg whites into other ingredients. Pour in equal amounts into 3 prepared pans and bake for 25-30 minutes. Cool completely before icing. For the icing, cream the cheese and butter. Gradually add powdered sugar. Beat until fluffy. Beat in vanilla.

Marilyn Sarlin

Pumpkin Cake Roll

Serves 8

INGREDIENTS:

3 eggs
1 cup sugar
⅔ cup cooked, mashed pumpkin
   (preferably canned)
1 teaspoon lemon juice
¾ cup flour
1 teaspoon baking powder
2 teaspoons cinnamon
1 teaspoon ginger

½ teaspoon nutmeg
½ teaspoon salt
1 cup walnuts, finely chopped
powdered sugar
FILLING
1 cup powdered sugar
6 ounces cream cheese, softened
4 tablespoons margarine
½ teaspoon vanilla extract

PROCEDURE:

Preheat oven to 375°. Grease and flour a 15″ by 10″ by 1″ jelly roll pan. Sprinkle a clean kitchen towel with sugar and leave ready on counter. Beat eggs on high speed of mixer for 5 minutes. Gradually beat in sugar. Stir in pumpkin and lemon juice. Combine dry ingredients and fold into pumpkin mixture. Spread into pan and sprinkle evenly with nuts. Bake for 15 minutes. Turn out onto tea towel and starting at narrow end, roll up towel and cake together. Cool. Unroll and spread filling over inside of cake. Roll up and refrigerate. For the filling, combine all four ingredients and beat until smooth. Sprinkle with powered sugar.

Really different and delicious!

Jean Popoff

267

Rich Butter Cake

Serves 12-15

INGREDIENTS:

1 box pound cake mix
2 eggs
1 stick of butter

FROSTING
1 box powdered sugar
8 ounces cream cheese
2 eggs

PROCEDURE:

Preheat oven to 350°. Grease and flour a 13″ by 9″ pan. Mix all ingredients for cake thoroughly. Spread in pan and bake for 40-50 minutes until golden brown. Beat ingredients for frosting until fluffy and spread over cake.

This is a very rich cake, so serve small portions.

Jean Klaber

Sour Cream Coffee Cake

Serves 10

INGREDIENTS:

1 package yellow cake mix
1 package vanilla instant pudding
4 eggs
¾ cup water
1 cup sour cream
1 teaspoon vanilla extract

¼ cup cooking oil
FILLING
¾ cup sugar
2 tablespoons cinnamon
1 cup chopped nuts (optional)

PROCEDURE:

Preheat oven to 350°. Grease and flour a bundt pan. In large bowl combine cake mix, pudding mix, eggs, water, sour cream, vanilla and oil. Beat well. Combine ingredients for filling. Sprinkle bottom and sides of pan with some of the filling. Alternate layers of batter and filling in pan. Bake for 45 minutes or until done. Cool in pan 15 minutes and then turn out to cool completely. Wrap in foil and allow to stand for 2-3 days to improve the flavor.

This also freezes well.

Karen Stewart

20-Minute Angel Food Cake

Serves 10

INGREDIENTS:

1 cup cake flour
1½ cups fine sugar
1½ cups egg whites
½ teaspoon salt

2 tablespoons water
1 teaspoon vanilla extract
½ teaspoon almond extract
1½ teaspoons cream of tartar

PROCEDURE:

Preheat oven to 450°. Sift flour. Sift again with ½ cup sugar. Place egg whites in large bowl with salt, water and flavoring. Whip eggs until foamy; add cream of tartar and whip them until stiff, but not dry. Fold in remaining 1 cup sugar, 2 tablespoons at a time. Fold in the flour mixture in 4 equal parts. Pour batter into ungreased 9″ tube pan. Bake for 20 minutes. (The high temperature will cause the cake to crack. This is of no consequence as the cake will be inverted to serve). Invert cake when taken from the oven and remove from pan 1½ hours later.

ICING
1 tablespoon unflavored gelatine
¼ cup cold water
2 tablespoons bourbon

8 egg yolks
1 cup confectioner's sugar
1 pint heavy cream, whipped

PROCEDURE:

Slice cake crosswise into 3 layers. Soak gelatine in cold water and then dissolve over hot water. Add bourbon. Beat egg yolks until thick and beat in sugar. Add gelatine mixture. Fold in whipped cream; chill until mixture begins to stiffen. Spread between cake layers. Cover entire cake with cream mixture. Chill for several hours.

This recipe was given to me by an aunt many years ago, and I have been making this cake for over thirty years. I think it is the best angel food cake I have ever eaten. It is so light, fluffy and moist.

Mildred Shelton

269

Best Chocolate Chip Cheesecake

Serves 10

A food processor is needed for this recipe.

INGREDIENTS:

1 box Nabisco Chocolate Wafers
up to ¼ pound butter, softened
1 pound cream cheese, softened
½ cup dairy sour cream
1 teaspoon vanilla extract
4 eggs

¾ cup sugar
1 6-ounce package chocolate chips
TOPPING
½ pint dairy sour cream
½ cup sugar
1½ teaspoons lemon juice
1½ teaspoons vanilla extract

PROCEDURE:

Preheat oven to 325°. Butter a 9″ by 3″ springform pan. In food processor fitted with metal blade, process sufficient wafers to fill 1 8-ounce cup. Add 1 tablespoon of butter at a time to wafer crumbs and process until crumbs are heavy enough and buttery enough to be compacted and hold their form. Press into bottom and ½″ up sides of springform pan. Refrigerate. In a large mixer bowl, beat cream cheese until fluffy. Gradually add sugar, beating until smooth. Add sour cream, vanilla and eggs. Mix well. Set aside. In food processor fitted with metal blade, process chocolate chips for 30 seconds until they have been chopped to small pieces. Stir chocolate chip pieces into cheese mixture. Pour batter into chocolate wafer crust. Bake for 40 minutes or until a 3″ circle in center of cheesecake jiggles when pan is shaken. Remove cake from oven. Cheesecake will become firm as it cools. Turn oven heat up to 475°. Cool cheesecake for 20 minutes. Prepare topping by blending all ingredients in food processor bowl fitted with plastic mixing blade. Spoon topping gently over cooled cake. Return to oven for 5 minutes only. Cool thoroughly. Cake may be refrigerated for up to 4 days, or frozen. To serve, remove outside ring of springform pan and allow to stand at room temperature for 1 hour before slicing.

Ellen Charo

Cheese Cake I

Serves 8-10

INGREDIENTS:

16 ounces cottage cheese
16 ounces cream cheese
1½ cups sugar
4 eggs, lightly beaten
juice of ½ lemon

1 teaspoon vanilla extract
3 tablespoons flour
3 tablespoons cornstarch
¼ pound butter, melted
1 pint sour cream

PROCEDURE:

Preheat oven to 325°. Butter a 9" by 3" springform pan. In a mixer bowl, cream the cottage cheese with the cream cheese. Gradually add sugar and then the eggs. Beat well. Stir in the lemon juice, vanilla, flour and cornstarch. Add butter and mix until smooth. Blend in sour cream. Pour into pan and bake for 1 hour. Without opening oven door, turn heat up to 375° and bake for 10 minutes longer to brown top. Turn off heat and leave in oven for at least 2 hours. If desired, sprinkle with powdered sugar when cool.

A family recipe that has lasted four generations.

Lillian Classon

Cheese Cake II

Serves 12

INGREDIENTS:

1 box Sunshine vanilla wafers, crushed
¼ pound butter, at room temperature
2 pounds natural cream cheese
4 egg yolks

4 teaspoons flour
1 cup sugar
1 pint heavy whipping cream
½ teaspoon vanilla extract (optional)
4 egg whites, stiffly beaten

PROCEDURE:

Preheat oven to 325°. Butter a 9" by 13" pyrex dish. Mix wafer crumbs with butter to form crust. Press over bottom of dish. Refrigerate. In large mixmaster bowl, cream the cream cheese until fluffy. Add egg yolks, flour and sugar. Mix to blend. With motor running at lowest speed, slowly pour in cream until incorporated. Vanilla may be added at this time. Fold in egg whites. Pour mixture over crust and bake for 35-40 minutes, but not for longer. Expect cake to crack. Remove from oven. Cool on a rack for 1½ hours, then cover with foil and refrigerate for at least 4 hours before serving. The taste actually improves after 24 hours of refrigeration. Serve from pyrex dish.

I often serve this with a fresh berry sauce spooned over individual portions of cake.

Helen Mayer

271

Chocolate Cheesecake

Serves 16

INGREDIENTS:

1 cup crushed Graham crackers or chocolate chip cookies
¼ cup butter, melted
¾ cup sugar
3 eggs
1½ pounds cream cheese, softened

8 ounces semisweet chocolate, melted
2 tablespoons vanilla (or Kahlua)
2 tablespoons cocoa
3 cups sour cream
1¼ cups melted butter

PROCEDURE:

Preheat oven to 350°. Butter a 10″ springform pan. For the crust, mix cracker crumbs with melted butter and press into pan. In large mixer bowl, blend sugar and eggs until light and thick. Gradually add cream cheese. Beat until smooth. Stir in melted chocolate, Kahlua and cocoa. Mix in sour cream. Fold in melted butter. Bake for 45 minutes. Cool and then refrigerate. Remove outer rim of pan to serve.

Anne Page

Kahlua Cheesecake

Serves 14-16

A food processor is needed for this recipe

INGREDIENTS:

24 ounces cream cheese
4 eggs
1 cup sugar
⅓ cup Kahlua (or Bailey's Irish Cream)
1 teaspoon vanilla extract

CRUST
1 box Nabisco Famous Chocolate Wafers
½ cup toasted chopped almonds
¾ stick margarine
½ cup sugar

TOPPING
16 ounces sour cream
½ cup sugar
1 teaspoon vanilla extract

PROCEDURE:

Preheat oven to 350°. Butter a 9″ springform pan. To food processor bowl fitted with metal blade, add chocolate wafers and chop. Add toasted almonds. Chop. Add margarine and sugar and process untill combined. Pat into springform pan. Combine ingredients for filling and pour over crust. Bake for 45 minutes to 1 hour. Cool for 5 minutes. Blend topping and spoon over cake. Return to oven for 5 minutes only.

Can be made 1 or 2 days ahead.

Jan Friedman

My Secret Cheesecake

Serves 10-12

A food processor is required for this recipe.

INGREDIENTS:

10 Graham crackers
3-4 tablespoons butter, melted
6 ounces dry cottage cheese
1 pound cream cheese, softened

¾ cup sugar
6 eggs
1 cup sour cream
1 cup half and half

PROCEDURE:

Preheat oven to 200°. Butter a 9″ springform pan. In food processor bowl fitted with metal blade, crush crackers finely. Pour in butter and process. Pat crust into springform pan and bake for 10 minutes. Remove from oven and cool. Turn oven temperature up to 350°. In food processor bowl fitted with steel blade, process cottage cheese until smooth. Blend in cream cheese. Empty cheese mixture into a large mixing bowl. Add sugar gradually, stirring well with a wooden spoon. Beat in eggs one at a time, by hand, beating well after each addition. Stir in sour cream and half and half. Pour mixture gently and slowly over crust. Bake for 1½ hours. Remove from oven and cool. Cake may crack but this will not spoil the delicious taste.

Farmer's cheese may be substituted for cottage cheese. This cake has New York flavor with California lightness, and is delicious plain or with puréed fruit topping. It's better if made the day before serving. You'll love it!

Susan Slesinger Ulevitch

273

Sinful Cheesecake

Serves 10

INGREDIENTS:

1 cup Graham cracker crumbs
¼ cup firmly packed light brown
    sugar
¼ cup butter(or margarine), melted
¼ teaspoon ground nutmeg
2 pounds cream cheese, softened
8 ounces ricotta cheese, at room
    temperature
1¼ cups sugar

3 tablespoons flour
1½ teaspoons vanilla extract
1½ teaspoons grated orange rind
¼ cup milk
1 tablespoon Amaretto liqueur
6 eggs
GLAZE
1 cup strawberry jelly
1 tablespoon Kirsch

PROCEDURE:

Butter a 9″ springform   pan. Preheat oven to 275°. In medium bowl, toss cracker crumbs, brown sugar, butter and nutmeg together. Press mixture onto bottom of pan. Bake for 10 minutes. Cool in pan on rack. Turn oven temperature up to 500°. In large bowl of an electric mixer, at high speed, beat together the two cheeses with sugar until fluffy. Blend in flour, vanilla, orange rind, milk and Amaretto until mixture is smooth. Beat in eggs, one at a time, beating thoroughly after each addition. Pour mixture over baked crumb crust. Bake at 500° for 15 minutes, then reduce heat to 250°. Bake for 1 hour longer. Leave cake in oven with heat turned off and door shut for 20 minutes. Remove from oven. Cool on rack until room temperature and then refrigerate cake for at least 3 hours and up to 8 hours before serving. For the strawberry glaze, which is optional, combine melted jelly with Kirsch. Cool slightly and pour over warm cake.

This recipe was passed on to me by my dear friend Jo Anna and is guaranteed to please the most discriminating New Yorker.

Rosario Reyes Kurtz

Rocky Road Cheesecake

Serves 8

INGREDIENTS:

2 cups chocolate wafer crumbs
½ cup confectioner's sugar
½ cup butter, melted
2 envelopes unflavored gelatine
½ cup cold water
⅓ cup all-purpose flour
¾ cup granulated sugar
½ cup milk

4 egg yolks, slightly beaten
1 6-ounce package semisweet
 chocolate pieces
1 cup whipping cream
2 cups cottage cheese
1 teaspoon vanilla extract
½ teaspoon almond extract
4 egg whites

PROCEDURE:

Butter a 9" springform pan. Combine crumbs and sugar. Stir in butter. Press mixture firmly and evenly against the bottom and halfway up the sides of pan. Chill. For filling, sprinkle gelatine over water to soften. Set aside. Combine flour and ¼ cup sugar. Stir in milk. Cook over medium heat, stirring constantly, until mixture thickens. Add small amount of hot mixture to egg yolks. Return all to saucepan. Cook 1 additional minute. Add softened gelatine, stir until dissolved. Cook to lukewarm. In a separate saucepan melt chocolate pieces with ⅓ cup whipping cream over low heat, stirring constantly, until chocolate is melted. Remove from heat. Cool. Beat cottage cheese for 5 minutes on highest speed of mixer. Blend in vanilla, almond extract and the gelatine mixture. Beat egg whites until foamy and gradually add remaining ½ cup sugar, beating until stiff peaks form. Fold beaten egg whites into gelatine mixture. Whip remaining ⅔ cup cream in a chilled bowl with chilled beaters until stiff. Fold into gelatine mixture. Spoon about ⅓ of filling into crust; drizzle thin stream of chocolate over filling. Swirl with spoon in marble pattern. Repeat until filling and chocolate are used. Chill 6 hours or more. Remove outside rim of pan to serve.

Anne Coleman

Original Philadelphia Cream Cheese Cake

Serves 12-16

INGREDIENTS:

1 cup Graham cracker crumbs
3 tablespoons sugar
3 tablespoons melted butter
2 8-ounce packages plus 1 3-ounce
   package cream cheese
¾ cup sugar
2 tablespoons flour

¼ teaspoon salt
1 teaspoon vanilla extract
4 egg yolks
1 cup whipping cream
4 egg whites, well beaten but not
   dry

PROCEDURE:

Preheat oven to 325° or 350°.   Butter a 9"springform pan . Mix cracker crumbs with sugar and melted butter. Press into bottom of pan. Set aside. Cream cheese with sugar, flour and salt. Mix well. Add vanilla and egg yolks, mixing thoroughly. Add cream slowly. Lastly fold in egg whites. Bake for 1 hour or until a knife comes out clean. Leave in oven to cool with door slightly ajar. Then refrigerate. Cake will drop in center while cooling.

This is supposed to be "the" original New York recipe. I had a Kraft
Cheese book about 40 years ago from which I took this recipe.
It has remained a family favorite.

Evelyn P. Landa

Sour Cream Cheesecake

Serves 6-8

A food processor or a blender is recommended but not essential.

INGREDIENTS:

15 Graham crackers
½ cup sugar
½ teaspoon cinnamon
¼ cup butter, melted
2 eggs
½ cup sugar

2 teaspoons vanilla extract
1½ cups sour cream
16 ounces cream cheese, softened.
SAUCE
1 small box frozen raspberries (or
strawberries)

PROCEDURE:

Preheat oven to 325°. Butter a 9″ square baking dish. Grind crackers into crumbs. Empty crumbs into a bowl and add sugar, cinnamon and melted butter. Stir well and press into pan. Chill, or bake at 400° for 6 minutes and cool before filling. Blend eggs, sugar, vanilla and sour cream well. Cut cream cheese into small pieces and add while motor is on, add a little at a time, until smooth. Pour mixture into crust and bake at 325° for 35 minutes or until center is set. Filling will be a little soft but will firm up when cake cools. Serve with berry sauce. For the sauce, pour partially defrosted berries of your choice into processor and purée.

Charlotte Chandler

New York Cheesecake

Serves 15-20

INGREDIENTS:

1 box zweibach crackers, crushed
¼ cup sugar
½ cup melted butter (or margarine)
1 teaspoon cinnamon
1¼ pounds creamed cottage cheese
1¼ pounds cream cheese
1 cup sugar

1 tablespoon flour
juice of ½ lemon
grated lemon rind (optional)
1 teaspoon vanilla extract
1 pint sour cream
½ teaspoon salt
dash of nutmeg
dash of cinnamon
6 eggs

PROCEDURE:

Preheat oven to 325°. Butter a 10″ springform pan. For the crust, mix crushed crackers, sugar, melted butter and cinnamon and pat into bottom of pan. Cream the two cheeses together. Add sugar, flour, lemon juice and rind. Mix. Add vanilla, sour cream, salt, spices and eggs. Beat everything together. Pour into pan over crust and bake for 1 hour. Turn off oven and leave cake to stand inside, with oven door open, for 1 more hour. Remove and cool.

This is a genuine "New York Cheese Cake" recipe and makes an excellent dessert for a large group of people. I receive raves when I serve it.

Mildred Kramer

Chocolate Roll With Hot Fudge Sauce

Serves 6

INGREDIENTS:

4 eggs, separated
1 cup minus 1 tablespoon
   granulated sugar
½ teaspoon vanilla extract
3 tablespoons Droste's cocoa, sifted
FILLING
½-¾ pint heavy cream
¼ cup powdered sugar
½ teaspoon vanilla extract

SAUCE
½ cup Droste's cocoa
1 cup sour cream
1½ cups powdered sugar
½ teaspoon vanilla extract
GARNISH
powdered sugar

PROCEDURE:

Preheat oven to 350°. Grease a 9″ by 13″ jelly roll pan well, taking care to grease corners as well. Prepare a large sheet of waxed paper by dusting with powdered sugar. Set aside. Beat egg whites until stiff, adding sugar gradually. Set aside. Beat egg yolks until thick and lemon-colored. Fold into whites. Add vanilla. Fold in cocoa. Pour into pan, spreading into corners. Bake for 20-30 minutes or until toothpick tests clean. Remove from oven and cool for 5 minutes. Using a spatula, gently loosen cake from sides and bottom of pan and invert onto prepared wax paper. Cool. Whip cream, adding powdered sugar and vanilla. Spread evenly over cake and tilt wax paper to roll up. Chill for 2 hours before serving. Garnish with powdered sugar. For the sauce, combine all the ingredients listed and cook in top of double boiler over boiling water for 1 hour, stirring occasionally. This sauce will be thick and will keep well if stored in a jar in the refrigerator.

Unbelievably delicious; a chocolate lover's dream!

Nancy Gordon

Easy Chocolate Chip Cake

Serves 12

INGREDIENTS:

1 package Devil's Food cake mix
eggs — number called for in mix
1 large package regular (not
   instant) chocolate pudding

milk — amount to make pudding
chocolate chips
nuts

278

PROCEDURE:

Heat oven according to directions on cake box. Grease and flour 13″ by 9″ pan. Add eggs to cake mix. Make pudding, following directions on box and add to cake mix. Combine well. Pour into pan. Sprinkle chocolate chips and nuts over top and bake according to cake mix instructions. Serve from pan.

Judith Rosenberg

Mrs. Herder's Cheesecake

Serves 12

INGREDIENTS:

2 individual packets Graham
   crackers, crushed
8 tablespoons butter
⅓ cup sugar
1 cup cold water
½ cup sugar
1½ packages gelatine

½ cup cold water
4 egg yolks
12 ounces cream cheese
2½ tablespoons lemon juice
½ pint whipping cream
4 egg whites, stiffly beaten

PROCEDURE:

Butter a 10″ springform pan. Combine crushed crackers, butter and sugar and pat into pan. In top of a double boiler mix cold water, sugar and gelatine. Mix ½ cup cold water and egg yolks and beat lightly just to blend. Add egg mixture to double boiler. Cook over gently boiling water, stirring constantly until thick. Blend cream cheese with lemon juice and add to mixture in double boiler. Continue stirring until thickened. Remove from heat. Fold in whipping cream. Fold in beaten egg whites. Pour into graham cracker crust. Refrigerate 3-4 hours before serving.

From an old hunting and sports catalog comes this light, smooth cheesecake.

Mrs. Robert Terlaak

Michelle's Cheesecake

Serves 10

INGREDIENTS:

⅓ cup butter, melted
1¾ cups crushed Graham crackers
dash of cinnamon
8 eggs
1¼ cups sugar
2 pounds cream cheese, softened
1 tablespoon vanilla extract
1 tablespoon lemon extract (or
    juice with rind)

TOPPING

1½ cups sour cream
5 tablespoons sugar
1 teaspoon vanilla extract
1 teaspoon lemon extract (or juice
    and rind)
Strawberry or blueberry glaze
    (optional)

PROCEDURE:

Preheat oven to 375°. Butter a 9″ springform pan. Combine butter, crushed crackers and cinnamon and pat into pan. In a large bowl, beat eggs and sugar until creamy. Add cream cheese, vanilla and lemon. Beat well. Pour over crust and bake for 35-40 minutes. Remove from oven and cool for 1 hour. Preheat oven to 375°. Mix topping ingredients and spread over cooled cake. Bake for 15 minutes. Cool completely. May leave plain, or top with glazed berries.

Michelle Benson

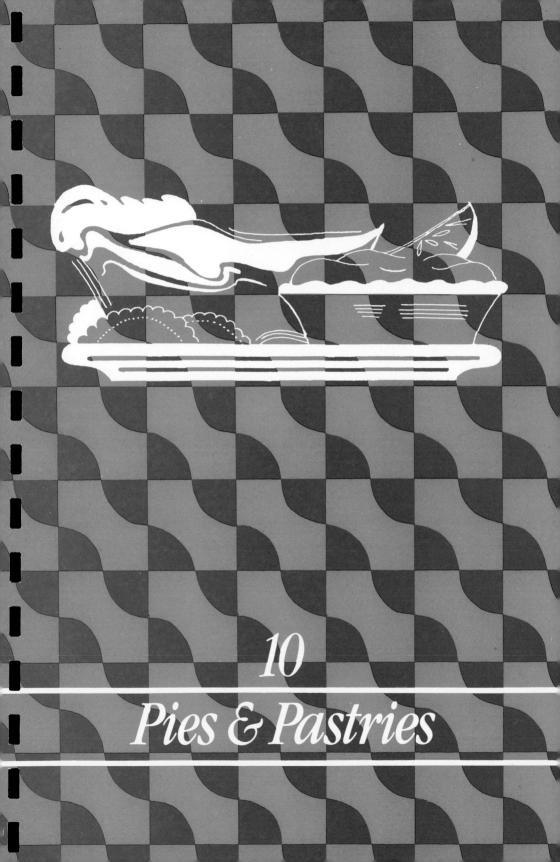

10
Pies & Pastries

PROCEDURE:

Cream margarine and sugar until fluffy. Beat in chocolate. Beat in eggs one at a time, beating well after each addition. Add vanilla and almond extract. Pour into pie crust. Chill for several hours.

Serve with whipped cream.

David and Sarah Burton

Ambassador Black Bottom Pie

Serves 6-8

INGREDIENTS:

1 9" pie crust shell, baked
1¼ tablespoons cornstarch
1 cup sugar
4 egg yolks
2 cups milk, scalded
1½ ounces chocolate, melted
1 teaspoon vanilla extract
1 envelope Knox gelatine, slaked
   in ½ cup cold water

4 egg whites
¼ teaspoon cream of tartar
1 teaspoon vanilla extract (or rum)
1 cup cream, whipped with 2 teaspoons powdered sugar
shaved chocolate or chocolate
   sprinkles (for garnish)

PROCEDURE:

In a small bowl combine cornstarch with ½ cup sugar. In another bowl beat the egg yolks and add the milk. Slowly add the cornstarch and sugar, stirring with a wooden spoon. Cook this in a double boiler, stirring constantly, until custard barely coats the spoon. Remove 1 cup of the custard and add the melted chocolate. Beat well. Set aside to cool. When cool add vanilla and pour into crust. Add gelatine to the remaining hot custard and allow it to cool, but not to stiffen. Make a meringue by beating the egg whites until soft peaks form, then add ½ cup sugar, cream of tartar and vanilla, and beat until stiff. Fold meringue into the cooled custard, and pour it over the chocolate layer. Chill until set. Spread with whipped cream and sprinkle with shaved chocolate.

My mother made this recipe throughout my childhood. It was, at my request, my "birthday cake" each year.

Cherry Lee

Chocolate Mousse Torte

Serves 10

INGREDIENTS:

1 8-ounce package semisweet
   chocolate squares
6 eggs, separated, at room
   temperature

2 teaspoons vanilla extract
1 8-ounce package chocolate wafers
¼ cup orange juice
½ cup whipping cream, whipped

PROCEDURE:

In a double boiler, over hot but not boiling water, melt 7 squares of chocolate. Remove from heat. With rubber spatula, stir in egg yolks until well mixed. Stir in vanilla. Beat egg whites until stiff peaks form. Gently fold into chocolate mixture. Set aside. With a pastry brush, brush half of chocolate wafers with orange juice and arrange wafers on bottom of a 9″ springform pan, overlapping slightly, in one layer. Spoon half of chocolate mixture evenly over wafers. Repeat brushing and layering with remaining juice and wafers. Top with remaining chocolate mixture. Cover pan with plastic wrap or foil and refrigerate for at least 5 hours or until set. Dip small spatula in warm water and use it to loosen cake from side of springform pan. Carefully remove side of pan. Coarsely grate remaining chocolate square. With hand, press grated chocolate on side of torte. Spoon cream into medium rosette tube and decorate top of torte. Refrigerate. To slice, dip a sharp knife in hot water and cut torte into small wedges.

Britt Lundberg

Sinful Chocolate Pie

Serves 8-10

INGREDIENTS:

CRUST
1⅓ cups vanilla wafer crumbs
½ stick butter
½ cup chopped pecans

FILLING
¾ cup butter
1 cup + 1 tablespoon sugar
1 teaspoon vanilla extract
2 squares unsweetened chocolate,
   melted
3 eggs

PROCEDURE:

Preheat oven to 350°. For the crust, mix wafer crumbs, butter and pecans. Pat ⅔ of mixture into a 9″ pie plate. Spread remaining mixture onto a small cookie sheet. Bake pie crust for 15 minutes. Toast crumbs on cookie sheet for 10 minutes in same oven. Cool both. For the filling, cream butter and sugar. Add vanilla and chocolate. Beat in eggs, one at a time, beating for 4 minutes on medium speed after each addition. Pour into crust. Sprinkle toasted crumbs over top. Refrigerate.

This is best served in thin wedges (it's rich!) with a teaspoon of Grand Marnier or Triple Sec drizzled over each slice.

Beverly Fipp

Chocolate Mousse Pie

Serves 10

INGREDIENTS:

24 Oreo cookies (or chocolate wafers), finely ground
½ cup margarine, softened
8 ounces cream cheese, softened
½ cup + 1 tablespoon sugar
2½ teaspoons vanilla extract

3 eggs, separated
½ pint whipping cream
1 cup chopped nuts
6 ounces semisweet chocolate, melted

PROCEDURE:

For the crust, combine the cookie crumbs with the margarine. Press into a 9″ pie plate. Chill. For the filling, beat cream cheese with ¼ cup sugar and 2 teaspoons vanilla. Add 3 egg yolks. Beat again. Add chocolate. Blend. In a separate bowl, beat egg whites until firm but not dry. Gradually add ¼ cup sugar, beating constantly. In a third bowl, whip the cream with 1 tablespoon sugar and ½ teaspoon vanilla. Gently fold beaten egg whites into cream cheese mixture. Gently fold in whipped cream. Gently fold in nuts. Pour filling into pie crust and refrigerate for 6 hours.

This is very rich! Guests often ask for the recipe. You can decorate the pie with rosettes of whipped cream if you wish.

Susan M. Plazak

285

Chocolate Pie

Serves 8

INGREDIENTS:

CRUST
18 Graham crackers (or 24 chocolate wafers), crumbled
½ cup butter, melted
¼ cup sugar (only if using Graham crackers)

FILLING
4 eggs, separated
1 cup sugar
¼ cup (Ghiradelli) chocolate chips
1 tablespoon milk
1 teaspoon vanilla extract
whipped cream (for garnish)

PROCEDURE:

Preheat oven to 325°. For the crust, combine cracker crumbs, butter and sugar and pat into a 9″ pie plate. Refrigerate. For the filling, beat egg yolks with sugar until thick and creamy. In a saucepan over medium heat, combine chocolate, milk and vanilla and cook until chocolate melts, stirring constantly. Cool. Stir into egg yolk mixture. In a separate bowl, beat egg whites until stiff. Gently fold into chocolate mixture. Pour into pie crust. Bake for 40 minutes. Cool and then chill. Serve with whipped cream.

Mrs. Joseph Davis

Tart Elizabeth

Serves 6-8

INGREDIENTS:

1 9″ pie shell, baked and cooled
¼-⅓ cup seedless raspberry jam
1½ cups heavy cream
10 ounces semisweet chocolate pieces

¼ cup dark rum (or brandy)
1 teaspoon vanilla extract
whipped cream (for garnish)

PROCEDURE:

Spread jam over bottom of pie shell. For the filling, combine cream and chocolate pieces in a small saucepan. Stir over medium heat until chocolate is completely melted. Over very low heat, simmer until mixture thickens slightly to original consistency of heavy cream. Chill for 1 hour. Add rum and vanilla. Beat until soft peaks form. Spoon into pie shell. Chill. Serve cold, garnished with whipped cream.

Elizabeth Jablecki

Caramel Pie

Serves 8

INGREDIENTS:

1 14-ounce can condensed milk
2 bananas

1 9″ Graham cracker crust
1 cup cream, whipped

PROCEDURE:

Place unopened can of condensed milk in pot of water and gently boil for 3 hours. Freeze for 2 hours. Slice bananas into crust. Pour caramel (formerly milk) over bananas. Garnish with whipped cream. Serve chilled.

So easy and so good!

Retta Dwyer

Mocha Pie

Serves 6

INGREDIENTS:

SHELL
2 egg whites
pinch of salt
¼ teaspoon vanilla extract
½ teaspoon vinegar
⅔ cup sugar
2½-ounce package slivered almonds

FILLING
1 12-ounce package chocolate
  chips
1 tablespoon instant coffee
¼ cup boiling water
1 cup whipping cream
¼ teaspoon almond extract
1 teaspoon vanilla extract

PROCEDURE:

Preheat oven to 300°. Grease a 9″ pie plate well. Combine egg whites, salt, vanilla and vinegar in a mixing bowl. Beat until it will hold soft peaks. Gradually add sugar, beating constantly. Continue to beat until stiff. Spread evenly over bottom and sides of pie plate. Sprinkle half of the almonds over meringue. Bake for 45 minutes. For the filling, melt chocolate chips over hot water. Stir in coffee and water. Beat until creamy, then allow to cool. Whip cream with almond and vanilla extracts. Fold chocolate mixture into cream. Pour filling into shell. Sprinkle reserved almonds over filling. Refrigerate for at least 2 hours or overnight.

Sarah Vander Laan

287

Mocha Ice Cream Pie

Serves 6

INGREDIENTS:

20 single Graham crackers,
  crushed
¼ cup brown sugar
¼ teaspoon cinnamon
¼ cup butter, melted

1½ quarts coffee ice cream
1 square unsweetened chocolate,
  grated

PROCEDURE:

Preheat oven to 350°. Grease a 9″ glass pie plate well. Combine cracker crumbs, sugar, cinnamon and butter. Press onto bottom and up sides of pie plate. Bake for 8 minutes. Cool. Allow ice cream to stand at room temperature only until soft enough to spread. Half-fill shell with ice cream and sprinkle generously with chocolate. Add remaining ice cream and sprinkle remaining chocolate over top. Freeze. Remove from freezer 10 minutes before serving.

Linda Goodwin

Date Pie with Ice Cream

Serves 8-10

INGREDIENTS:

15 soda crackers, finely ground
1 cup seeded dates, chopped small
½ cup finely ground nuts
1 cup sugar

¼ teaspoon baking powder
3 egg whites
1 teaspoon almond extract
vanilla ice cream

PROCEDURE:

Preheat oven to 300°. Grease a 9″ pie plate. Mix cracker crumbs, dates, nuts, sugar and baking powder. Beat egg whites with almond extract until firm. Fold in dry ingredients. The meringue will be sticky and hard to handle. Use a spoon to pick it up and a rubber spatula to push it off the spoon. Place tablespoonsful of the meringue touching one another around the sides of the plate and over the bottom and spread uniformly to make a shell. Bake for 30 minutes. Cool and fill with vanilla ice cream or any other favorite flavor. Chill for 6 hours or overnight in freezer.

Libby Clemmer

Grasshopper Glace Pie

Serves 8-10

INGREDIENTS:

CRUMB CAKE
1½ cups chocolate wafers, crumbled
¼ cup melted butter (or margarine)
2 tablespoons sugar
⅛ teaspoon cinnamon

FILLING
¼ cup crème de cacao
¼ cup green crème de menthe
1 quart vanilla ice cream, softened
whipped cream (for garnish)

PROCEDURE:

Preheat oven to 375°. Butter an 8″ or 9″ pie plate. For the chocolate crumb cake, mix the ingredients together. Press into pie plate. Bake for 8 minutes. Cool completely before filling. For the filling, mix creme de cacao with creme de menthe. Gradually add softened ice cream and blend thoroughly. Pour into prepared crust. Freeze, uncovered, until firm, then cover with freezer paper or foil. Place in refrigerator for 15 minutes before serving. Garnish with whipped cream.

Britt Lundberg

Frozen Chocolate Cream Cheese Pie

Serves 8

INGREDIENTS:

1½ cups crushed chocolate wafers
⅓ cup butter, melted
8 ounces cream cheese
½ cup sugar
1 teaspoon vanilla extract

2 eggs, separated
6 ounces chocolate chips, melted
  and cooled
1 cup heavy cream, whipped
¾ cup chopped pecans

PROCEDURE:

Preheat oven to 325°. For the crust, combine chocolate wafers and butter. Press over bottom of a 9″ or 10″ springform pan. Bake for 10 minutes. Cool. For the filling, beat cream cheese with ¼ cup sugar and vanilla until blended. Stir in beaten egg yolks and chocolate. In a separate bowl, beat egg whites until peaks form. Gradually add ¼ cup sugar and beat until stiff. Gently fold meringue into chocolate mixture. Gently fold in whipped cream. Gently fold in pecans. Pour over crust and freeze until firm. Remove from freezer 10 minutes before serving.

Decorate with whipped cream lattice-work and shaved chocolate curls. Everybody loves this!

Suzanne Watkins

Cheesecake Pie

Serves 8-10

INGREDIENTS:

CRUST
1½ cups Graham cracker crumbs
⅓ cup butter, melted
¼ cup sugar

¾ cup sugar
2 teaspoons vanilla extract
dash of cinnamon

FILLING
1 pound cream cheese, at room
  temperature
2 eggs, beaten

TOPPING
1 pint sour cream
1½ teaspoons vanilla extract
3½ tablespoons sugar

PROCEDURE:

Preheat oven to 350°. For the crust, combine crumbs, butter and sugar. Press into bottom of 9″ springform pan or 9″ pie plate. Bake for 5-10 minutes. Set aside. For the filling, combine all ingredients and beat until light and frothy. Pour into crust and return to oven for 15-20 minutes. Cool slightly. For topping, blend sour cream, vanilla and sugar. Pour over pie. Return to oven for 10 minutes. Cool, and then freeze for 5 hours or overnight. Serve frozen or thawed.

Top with canned cherry pie filling if you want to pull out all the stops.

Estelle Graff

Cream Cheese Pie

Serves 8

INGREDIENTS:

CRUST
¼ pound butter (or margarine), at room temperature
1 cup flour, sifted
2 tablespoons powdered sugar, sifted

FILLING
1 cup whipping cream
3 ounces cream cheese
½ cup powdered sugar, sifted
1 teaspoon vanilla extract
1 can fruit pie filling of your choice

PROCEDURE:

Preheat oven to 350°. For the crust, combine butter, flour and sugar using an electric mixer. Press into an 8″ pie plate. Bake for 15 minutes until golden brown. Cool to room temperature. For the filling, whip the cream only until it has begun to thicken. In a separate bowl, beat the cream cheese with an electric mixer. Add the cheese to the cream and continue beating. Do not overbeat. Should be firm but not buttery. Add sugar and vanilla. Mix to blend. Spread into crust. Cover with fruit topping. Refrigerate before serving.

Kelly Schalm

Cannoli

Serves 40

INGREDIENTS:

4 dozen wonton skins
vegetable oil
2 pounds ricotta cheese, beaten
    until smooth, or sieved
1 cup powdered sugar
2 teaspoons vanilla extract

⅔ cup semisweet chocolate
    shavings
ground pistachio nuts (for garnish)
powdered sugar (for garnish)
sprigs of fresh mint (for garnish)

PROCEDURE:

Heat vegetable oil in deep pot. Place cannoli tubes (or 1″ aluminum tubing cut into 6″ lengths or 6″ wooden dowels) diagonally across center of wonton squares and wrap skins around, securing tips with water. Lower a few at a time into deep hot vegetable oil seam side down. Fry for 30 seconds or until just golden. Remove and drain on paper towels. While still hot, gently push out tubes. Cool completely before storing in airtight container. May be frozen or stored at room temperature for a day or so. For the filling, combine cheese, powdered sugar, vanilla and chocolate. Cover and chill. Just before serving, fill cannoli shells. Dip ends in pistachio nuts and sprinkle cannoli with powdered sugar. Decorate with mint.

Filling variation: omit vanilla and use liqueur or rum. Sprinkle with powdered sugar mixed with instant espresso or dark cocoa.

Suzie Desmarais

Banana Cheese Pie

Serves 6-8

INGREDIENTS:

1⅓ cups Graham cracker crumbs
¼ cup margarine, melted
¼ teaspoon cinnamon
1 cup lowfat cottage cheese
1 cup plain (or flavored) yogurt
3 egg whites

juice of ½ lemon
1 teaspoon vanilla extract
¼ cup wheat flour
3 tablespoons honey
2 ripe bananas, sliced

PROCEDURE:

Preheat oven to 350°. For the crust, combine the cracker crumbs with the margarine and cinnamon and press into a 9″ pie plate. For the filling, use either a blender or a hand mixer to blend the cottage cheese, yogurt, egg whites, lemon juice and vanilla. Add flour and mix at low speed. Blend in honey slowly, a tablespoon at a time. Gently add the bananas, stirring by hand. Pour filling into crust and bake for 20-25 minutes. Serve warm sprinkled with cinnamon, or chilled decorated with berries.

This is a highly nutritious, low cholesterol dessert which is also suitable for brunch.

Ann R. Colby

Apple Custard Pie

Serves 6-8

INGREDIENTS:

1 cup flour	½ teaspoon cinnamon
½ cup brown sugar	3 cups tart apples, peeled and
½ teaspoon salt	sliced
¼ teaspoon baking powder	1 egg yolk
⅓ cup butter, softened	½ cup whipping cream
⅓ cup sugar	½ cup chopped nuts

PROCEDURE:

Preheat oven to 350°. For the crust, combine flour, brown sugar, salt and baking powder and cut in butter until mixture is crumbly. Press into bottom and up sides of an 8″ or 9″ pie pan. For the filling, combine sugar and cinnamon. Place half the apples in the crust and sprinkle with half the sugar/cinnamon mixture. Repeat. Bake for 15 minutes. Beat the egg yolk with the cream. Sprinkle the nuts over the apples and then pour over the cream. Bake an additional 20-25 minutes or until custard is set and apples are tender. Cool to room temperature.

Serve with cheddar cheese, whipped cream or ice cream.

Beverly Fipp

Apple Strudel

Serves 6

INGREDIENTS:

1 tablespoon butter
1 cup fine bread crumbs
6 sheets filo dough
1 stick sweet butter, melted

4-5 apples, thinly sliced
1½ cups chopped walnuts
2 teaspoons cinnamon
1 cup golden raisins
powdered sugar (for garnish)

PROCEDURE:

Preheat oven to 375°. Grease a baking sheet lightly. Melt the tablespoon of butter in a frying pan and cook the bread crumbs until golden brown. Cool. On a flat surface, arrange the sheets of filo dough, one on top of another, brushing each sheet with melted butter. Sprinkle the bread crumbs over the top sheet. Place the filling over the filo dough, leaving 1″ clear from all edges. Roll up like a jelly roll and tuck the open sides under. Place the pastry roll, seams down, on the baking sheet. Using a serrated knife, cut diagonal slits into top of roll. Bake for 35 minutes or until golden brown.

This can be prepared in advance and frozen. Remove from freezer and place directly in oven and bake for about 1 hour.

Roswitha Marouf

Tarte Aux Pommes En Sac

INGREDIENTS:
1 9″ pie crust, unbaked

FILLING
6-7 cups pippin apples, peeled and
    thinly sliced
½ cup sugar
2 tablespoons flour
2 tablespoons lemon juice
½ teaspoon nutmeg, freshly grated
½ teaspoon cinnamon (optional)

TOPPING
½ cup sugar
½ cup flour
½ cup butter

A large, heavy brown paper bag that has not been recycled. Check before using.

PROCEDURE:

Preheat oven to 425°. For the filling, combine all ingredients in a large mixing bowl and stir gently with a wooden spoon to distribute flavorings evenly. Arrange in pie crust, mounding in center. Apples will "cook down" in baking. For the topping, combine sugar and flour. Rub in butter. Sprinkle over apple filling. Place pie in brown bag. Fold bag over twice to close, and staple to secure. Bake for 1 hour. Even though bag may seem to burn, oven will not catch fire! Serve warm or at room temperature, with whipped cream passed separately.

Judy Rosenblatt

Peaches And Cream Pie

Serves 8

INGREDIENTS:

1 9" pie shell, unbaked
3-4 medium size ripe peaches,
   peeled and halved
1 cup light cream

2 eggs
1 teaspoon vanilla extract
⅓ cup sugar
2 tablespoons butter

PROCEDURE:

Chill pie shell. Preheat oven to 350°. Arrange peach halves, cut side up, in the pie shell. Beat cream, eggs, vanilla and ¼ cup sugar well together. Pour around peaches. Dot butter over peaches. Sprinkle with remaining sugar. Bake for 1 hour or until crust is golden and filling is set. Cool on a rack.

You may substitute green seedless grapes or pitted fresh cherries for peaches in this luscious pie.

Betty Vale

Peach Pecan Pie

Serves 8

INGREDIENTS:

1 9" pastry shell, unbaked
4 cups fresh peaches, peeled and
   sliced
½ cup sugar
2 tablespoons tapioca
2 teaspoons lemon juice

¼ teaspoon almond extract
1 teaspoon brandy (optional)
¼ cup brown sugar
¼ cup flour
½ cup chopped pecans
¼ cup butter

PROCEDURE:

Preheat oven to 425°. Combine peaches, sugar, tapioca, lemon juice, almond extract and brandy. Allow to stand for 15 minutes. Combine sugar, flour, pecans and butter. Sprinkle half of pecan mixture over bottom of pie crust. Pour entire peach mixture into pie crust. Sprinkle remaining pecan mixture over peaches. Bake for 10 minutes then lower heat to 325° and continue baking for another 20 minutes.

Ann Poovey

Peach Cream Puff Pie

Serves 6-8

INGREDIENTS:

PASTRY
6 tablespoons butter (or margarine)
¾ cup water
¾ cup flour
3 eggs
FILLING
1 3-ounce regular vanilla pudding
   mix

12 ounces peach nectar, heated
1½ teaspoons unflavored gelatine
1 tablespoon cold water
1 cup whipping cream
2 tablespoons sugar
1½ cups fresh peach slices

PROCEDURE:

Preheat oven to 425°. For the pastry, combine butter and water in medium saucepan and boil until butter has melted. Remove from heat. Immediately add flour all at once, beating rapidly with wooden spoon until batter leaves the sides of the saucepan to form a ball. Beat in eggs, one at a time, beating very well after each addition. Spread into an 8" pie plate, building up an outer edge of 1". Bake for 30 minute or until golden brown and puffed. Cool. For the filling, prepare the vanilla pudding using peach nectar instead of milk. Sprinkle gelatine over water to soften. Add to hot pudding and stir to dissolve completely. Cool. Whip cream with sugar and fold into pudding. Pour half of the pudding into pastry shell, then arrange a layer using half of the peach slices. Repeat layers. Cover with waxed paper and chill for 8-10 hours or until set.

Sherri S. Lightner

Lemon Chess Pie

Serves 6

INGREDIENTS:

1 8" pie crust, unbaked
¾ stick butter
1½ cups sugar

3 eggs
juice of 1 lemon

PROCEDURE:

Preheat oven to 400°. Melt butter. Add sugar. Mix. Stir in eggs. Add lemon juice. Pour into pie crust. Bake approximately 20 minutes or until light brown and crusty.

This old Southern recipe is easy and absolutely delicious. If you don't have the time to make your own pie crust, use a ready-made.

Kiki Henry

Lemon-Sour Cream Pie

Serves 6-8

INGREDIENTS:

1 deep dish 9″ pie shell, baked

FILLING
1 cup sugar
4 rounded tablespoons cornstarch
pinch of salt
1 cup milk
3 egg yolks, lightly beaten
4 tablespoons butter
1 teaspoon lemon peel, grated

¼ cup lemon juice
1 cup sour cream

MERINGUE
3 egg whites
¼ teaspoon cream of tartar
½ teaspoon vanilla extract
6 tablespoons sugar

PROCEDURE:

Preheat oven to 350°. For the filling, combine sugar, cornstarch and salt in a saucepan. Slowly stir in milk. Cook over medium heat until thickened, stirring constantly with a wooden spoon. Add egg yolks and cook for 2 minutes longer, stirring slowly. Remove from heat and stir in butter, peel and juice. Allow to cool. Fold in sour cream. Pour into pie shell. For the meringue, beat egg whites with cream of tartar and vanilla. Slowly add sugar, beating until stiff. Spread meringue over lemon filling to cover completely. Bake for 12-15 minutes or until light golden color. Cool well.

Nina Calhoun
Loisanne Mitchell

Pavlova Torte

Serves 8-10

INGREDIENTS:

4 egg whites
¾ cup sugar
1 teaspoon white vinegar
1 teaspoon cornstarch

few drops vanilla extract
⅛ teaspoon salt
1 cup cream, whipped
1 pint berries in season

PROCEDURE:

Preheat oven to 400°. Line a 9″ or 10″ pie plate with buttered or oiled brown paper, or with parchment paper. Beat egg whites and slowly dribble in sugar. Add vinegar, cornstarch, vanilla and salt. Beat until stiff and glossy. Spread pavlova into prepared pie plate. Place in oven and immediately turn off heat. Torte should remain in oven until oven is cool. Carefully remove paper. Spread whipped cream over top of torte and cover with berries.

Easy to make, impressive to look at, scrumptious to eat! If you make torte early in the day, top with cream and berries right before serving.

Judy Lewis

Macademia Cream Pie

Serves 8

INGREDIENTS:

1 9″ pie shell, baked
½ cup sugar
pinch of salt
3½ tablespoons cornstarch
3 egg yolks

1 teaspoon vanilla extract
2 cups milk
1 cup raw macademia nuts,
    crushed (or bananas, sliced)
whipped cream (for garnish)

PROCEDURE:

In a small bowl, mix sugar, salt, cornstarch, egg yolks and vanilla. In a saucepan, scald the milk. Add paste in small bowl to the milk, and cook over medium heat until thickened, stirring constantly. Remove from heat and cool completely. Sprinkle nuts (or bananas) over bottom of pie shell. Pour over filling. Decorate with whipped cream. Refrigerate.

Nina Calhoun

Louisiana Pecan Pie

Serves 6-8

INGREDIENTS:

1 9" pie crust, unbaked
½ cup dark Karo corn syrup
½ cup light Karo corn syrup
1 tablespoon butter, softened
⅛ teaspoon salt

½ cup sugar
1 teaspoon vanilla extract
3 eggs
1 cup pecan pieces

PROCEDURE:

Preheat oven to 300°. Mix all ingredients, except pecan pieces, in a bowl. Beat well. Stir in pecan pieces. Pour into pie crust. Bake for 1 hour.

This recipe, although a typical Southern pecan pie, is less sweet than most. This is a family favorite in our home, and can be baked a day ahead of serving.

Martha McCardell

Miss Beach's Nut Pie

Serves 6-8

INGREDIENTS:

14 double Graham crackers,
    crumbled
1 cup chopped pecans
1 cup sugar
1 teaspoon baking powder
1 teaspoon vanilla extract
3 eggs, well beaten

CRÈME CHANTILLY
1 cup whipping cream
1 tablespoon sugar
½ teaspoon vanilla extract

PROCEDURE:

Preheat oven to 300°. Mix all ingredients together. Bake in ungreased pie plate for 45-50 minutes. Serve each slice with a dollop of Crème Chantilly. For the Crème Chantilly, beat all ingredients until thick.

This recipe was given to me about 35 years ago by the Dean of Women of the college I had attended in North Louisiana. She was such a lovely lady! This pie has been a favorite of ours throughout the years. It can be made a day in advance.

Martha McCardell

Pretzel Tart

Serves 12

INGREDIENTS:

1 cup butter
1 cup granulated sugar
2 cups pretzels, crushed
8 ounces cream cheese, softened

1 cup powdered sugar
1 envelope Dream Whip
2 cans pie filling of your choice

PROCEDURE:

Melt butter, add granulated sugar and mix well with crushed pretzels. Spread half on bottom of 13" by 9" by 2" baking dish. Set aside. Blend cream cheese with sugar until creamy. Make Dream Whip following directions on box. Mix with cream cheese using a fork. Spread over pretzel mixture in dish. Refrigerate for at least 1 hour before sprinkling remaining pretzel mixture over filling. Top with fruit pie filling.

Delicious and requires no baking.!

Lucia Pérez

Glazed Fruit Tartlets

Serves 24

INGREDIENTS:

PASTRY
¼ pound butter, softened
½ cup sugar
1 egg yolk
1 tablespoon orange juice
1 teaspoon vanilla extract
1 tablespoon grated orange peel
1¾ cups all purpose flour

GLAZE
½ cup sugar
1½ tablespoons cornstarch
dash of salt
1 cup orange juice
2 teaspoons grated orange peel
1 tablespoon liqueur (optional)

FILLING
3-4 cups fresh fruit in season
(sliced bananas, strawberries,
seedless grapes, kiwi fruit,
blueberries, raspberries, orange
sections)

PROCEDURE:

Preheat oven to 350°. In a medium bowl, beat butter until fluffy. Gradually mix in sugar, beating until light. Add egg yolk, orange juice, vanilla and orange peel. Mix in flour. Press dough into 2″ or 3″ tart molds. Bake for 15-20 minutes or until lightly browned. Cool in molds 10 minutes. Insert tip of knife between edge of crust and mold and invert crusts one at a time into your hand. Cool completely on wire racks. May be frozen at this point. For the orange glaze, mix the sugar, cornstarch and salt in a small saucepan. Gradually add orange juice, stirring until smooth. Heat to boiling, stirring constantly. Boil and stir for 2 minutes. Add orange peel. Cover and cool. Stir in optional orange liqueur. To assemble, fill tart shells with fruit. Carefully spoon cooled orange glaze over the top, covering fruit completely. May be refrigerated for up to 8 hours.

Fun for children to assemble.

Betty Vale

Pear Tart

Serves 10

INGREDIENTS:

PASTRY
1½ cups cake flour
8 tablespoons butter, very cold
6-8 tablespoons ice water
FILLING
½ cup + 1 tablespoon sugar
2 tablespoons flour
3 tablespoons butter, melted
1 large egg
1 egg yolk

GLAZE
¼ cup apricot preserves
2 tablespoons water
2½ ounces ground almonds
3 tablespoons heavy cream
1½ teaspoons almond extract
1 large can pear halves, drained

PROCEDURE:

Preheat oven to 425°. For the pastry, cut the butter into the flour until the mixture resembles rolled oats. Sprinkle over ice water and work in with a fork just until dough will adhere if you try to form a ball. With floured hands, gently knead the dough 5-6 times, adding more flour or water if necessary. Place on a floured surface and roll out with rolling pin. Lightly flour a loose-bottom 12″ tart pan. Fit dough into pan. Adjust rack to top third of oven. In a mixing bowl, combine all ingredients for the filling except the pear halves. Using a wire whisk, blend filling. Pour into pastry shell. Arrange pears over filling. Bake for 25 minutes, watching closely. The filling should be quite dark. Remove from oven. Cool on rack for 5 minutes, then carefully remove tart from pan. For the glaze, mix apricot preserves and water over low heat until warm and quite runny. Using a pastry brush, gently paint tart with the glaze. Serve tart at room temperature.

A show stopper! Well worth the cook's time and effort!

Joyce Aftahi

303

Ribbon Pumpkin Pie

Serves 8-10

INGREDIENTS:

SHELL
1 9" deep dish pie shell (or 1 10"
    pie shell), not fully baked
⅓ cup butter
⅓ cup brown sugar, packed
½ cup chopped pecans
FILLING
1 envelope unflavored gelatine
¼ cup cold water

3 eggs, separated
⅓ cup sugar
1¼ cups pumpkin, cooked or
    canned
½ cup sour cream
½ teaspoon salt
1½ teaspoons pumpkin pie spice
1 tablespoon candied ginger,
    chopped
¼ cup sugar
1 cup whipping cream

PROCEDURE:

Preheat oven to 425°. For the crunchy praline pie shell, combine butter and sugar in a saucepan. Cook and stir until sugar melts and mixture bubbles vigorously. Remove from heat, stir in pecans. Spread over bottom of pie shell. Bake for 5 minutes or until bubbly. Remove from oven. Cool completely. For the filling, soften gelatine by sprinkling it over the water. Set aside. Beat egg yolks well with sugar. Add pumpkin, sour cream, salt, spice and ginger. Cook and stir over medium heat until mixture comes to a boil. Reduce heat and simmer for 2 minutes, stirring constantly. Remove from heat. Add gelatine, and stir until dissolved. Cool. Beat egg whites until frothy. Gradually add sugar. Continue to beat until stiff. Fold meringue into pumpkin mixture. Spoon half the filling into pie shell. Chill in refrigerator until almost set, about 1 hour. Refrigerate remaining pumpkin mixture. Whip cream and spread half of it over pumpkin layer. Top with remaining pumpkin mixture. Chill until almost set. Cover with remaining whipped cream.

I sprinkle chopped pecans over whipped cream topping. Even people who are not fond of pumpkin pie will eat this one!

Suzie Desmarais

Pumpkin Pie

Serves 12

INGREDIENTS:

PASTRY
2 cups flour
1 teaspoon salt
⅔ cup Crisco
2 tablespoons butter, melted
5 tablespoons cold water
1 tablespoon vinegar
FILLING
1 cup sugar
1 tablespoon flour
½ teaspoon salt

1 teaspoon ginger
1 teaspoon cinnamon
½ teaspoon nutmeg
⅛ teaspoon pepper
⅛ teaspoon cloves
3 large eggs
1 can (or 1½ cups mashed)
    pumpkin
1 cup light cream (or evaporated
    milk)

PROCEDURE:

For the flaky pastry, mix flour and salt. Cut in Crisco and butter until mixture resembles coarse crumbs. Add water and vinegar mixing with a fork. Form into ball and chill for at least 1 hour. Roll out to line 2 9″ pie plates. Refrigerate while making filling. Preheat oven to 400°. For the filling, mix all dry ingredients together. Beat in eggs. Stir in pumpkin and cream. Pour into pie shells. Bake for 50 minutes, or until knife inserted in center of pie comes out clean. Cool completely before serving.

We have made these pies for Thanksgiving for years with repeated success.

Dick and Patricia Carlson

Minnie's Rhubarb Pie

Serves 6

INGREDIENTS:

1 9" pie shell, unbaked
1½ tablespoons tapioca
1¼ cups granulated sugar
¼ teaspoon salt
1 tablespoon butter, melted

3½ cups rhubarb, cut into ½"
    lengths
2 egg yolks, lightly beaten
2 egg whites
¼ cup sugar

PROCEDURE:

Preheat oven to 350°. Combine tapioca, sugar, salt, butter and rhubarb. Allow to stand for 15 minutes to draw juices. Add egg yolks to rhubarb mixture. Pour into pie shell. Bake for 35-40 minutes. Beat egg whites until stiff. Gradually add sugar. Continue beating until stiff. Cover pie with meringue and return to oven until pale golden.

This is an old recipe from Baden-Baden in the Black Forest.

Wilhelmina Himmelspach

Republican Dessert

Serves 15

INGREDIENTS:

CRUST
1 cup flour
1 stick margarine, softened
½ cup chopped nuts
FILLING
8 ounces cream cheese, softened
1 cup powdered sugar

12 ounces Cool Whip
2 small boxes instant pudding mix,
    any flavor
2½ cups milk
grated chocolate (for garnish)
chopped nuts (for garnish)
flaked coconut (for garnish)

306

PROCEDURE:

Preheat oven to 350°. For the crust, cut margarine into flour until mealy. Add nuts and incorporate. Press into bottom of 9″ by 13″ dish. Bake for 10 minutes. Cool. For the first layer of filling, beat cream cheese with sugar until fluffy. Fold in 8 ounces of Cool Whip. Spread over crust. For the second layer mix instant puddings with milk, using an electric beater. Beat for 2 minutes. Spread over first layer. For the third layer, spread 4 ounces of Cool Whip over pudding. Sprinkle with grated chocolate, chopped nuts or coconut. Refrigerate for 4 hours, or freeze. Remove from freezer 45 minutes before serving.

Marilyn Greco

Booze 'n Berry Pie

Serves 6-8

INGREDIENTS:

CRUST
1½ cups vanilla wafer crumbs
¼ cup butter, melted
FILLING
½ cup cold water
2 envelopes unflavored gelatine
⅔ cup sugar

3 large eggs, separated
⅛ teaspoon salt
½ cup Crème de Cassis
1 cup whipping cream
2 cups boysenberries, fresh or canned

PROCEDURE:

Preheat oven to 350°. For the crust, combine crumbs with butter, and press into 9″ pie plate. Bake for 10 minutes, then remove from oven and cool. If using canned boysenberries for the filling, drain the berries well and reserve ½ cup of juice for use in place of the cold water. For the filling, pour water (or boysenberry juice) into a saucepan. Sprinkle gelatine over it. Add ⅓ cup sugar, egg yolks and salt. Stir well. Cook over low heat, stirring constantly, until mixture thickens. Do not boil. Remove from heat and stir in Crème de Cassis. Chill until custard begins to set. Beat egg whites until stiff, then add remaining ⅓ cup sugar and beat to form a stiff meringue. Fold into custard. Fold in berries. Fold in whipped cream. Spoon into crust, mounding in center. If mixture is too soft to mound, chill until it is firmer and then fill crust. Chill for several hours before serving.

Other berries and liqueurs can be substituted with pleasing results. Try Mandarin oranges and curaçao in a chocolate wafer crust.

Arlene S. Kavanaugh

Basic Pie Shell

Yields 1 9" shell

INGREDIENTS:

1 cup all-purpose flour, sifted
½ teaspoon salt
3 tablespoons Crisco, cold

3 tablespoons sweet butter, cold,
    cut into small pieces
3 tablespoons (or less) ice water

PROCEDURE:

Place flour and salt in large mixing bowl. Add Crisco and butter. Use a pastry blender to cut in until mixture resembles coarse crumbs. Sprinkle 1 tablespoon of ice water all over surface. Do not dump water in one place. Mix and toss with a fork. Continue adding water in small amounts just until all flour is barely moistened. The mixture will still be lumpy. Form a ball with it. If dough is too dry to hold together, return it to bowl. Use a knife to cut it into small pieces again, and sprinkle over a little more water, starting with 1 teaspoonful. Shape into a ball; flatten to a disk. Wrap in foil. Refrigerate at least 2 hours or overnight. (If using a food processor, add flour and salt to beaker. Add Crisco and butter. Process on and off until mixture resembles coarse crumbs. Add water through feed tube, a few drops at a time, until ball of dough forms on blades. Flatten to a disk and refrigerate). Roll out to line a pie plate and prick at ¼" intervals with a fork. For a recipe that calls for a ready baked shell, place pastry-lined pie plate in freezer for 20-25 minutes until frozen firm. This helps prevent shrinking. Preheat oven to 450°. Place a 12" square of foil, shiny side down in the frozen shell. Let the corners of the foil stand up. Fill with dried beans or rice. Bake for 13 minutes. Remove from oven. Reduce temperature to 400°. Remove foil and beans and bake for 7-10 minutes longer. Cool on a rack.

Handle dough as little as possible. Do not knead. Keep in mind that too much water makes pastry soggy to work with and tough when baked. Practice makes perfect!

Helen Mayer

11
Other Desserts

Fruit Delight

Serves 12

INGREDIENTS:

1 package frozen blackberries,
  unsweetened
1 package frozen strawberries
1 package frozen mixed fruit
1 package frozen blueberries
2 oranges, peeled, thinly sliced

2 apples, thinly sliced
2 bananas, sliced
1 11-ounce can pineapple chunks
8 ounces orange juice
4 ounces Triple Sec

PROCEDURE:

Defrost frozen fruit and mix all ingredients.

Very refreshing!

Laurie Marcus

Strawberry Angel

Serves 24

INGREDIENTS:

2 3-ounce packages strawberry
  gelatin
2 cups boiling water
1 pint frozen strawberries
½ cup sugar

juice of 1 lemon
1 pint whipping cream (or Cool
  Whip)
1 large angel food cake

PROCEDURE:

Dissolve gelatin in boiling water. Add strawberries, sugar and lemon juice. Whip cream and add to mixture. Crumble half of the cake. Sprinkle crumbs over bottom of two 13" by 9" by ½" glass baking dish. Pour half of the gelatin mixture over cake crumbs. Crumble remaining cake and sprinkle over filling. Chill in refrigerator 24 hours.

Connie and Jennifer Reins

Strawberries In Liqueur

Serves 6

INGREDIENTS:

2 pints strawberries
¼ cup confectioner's sugar
3 tablespoons rum

3 tablespoons Cointreau
1½ cups whipping cream
3 tablespoons Kirsch

PROCEDURE:

Wash, hull and slice strawberries. Combine in bowl with sugar. Pour rum and Cointreau over the berries. Chill for at least 2 hours. Whip cream, flavor with Kirsh, mix well with strawberries. Serve very cold.

Serve in crystal goblets with a whole strawberry or crystallized rose petals.

Jean Scott

Strawberry Dainty

Serves 6-8

INGREDIENTS:

½ cup milk
½ pound marshmallows
1 cup whipping cream

2 cups strawberries, crushed
¾ cup sugar
⅓ pound vanilla wafers, crushed

PROCEDURE:

Melt marshmallows in milk in double boiler. Whip slightly with fork. Let cool. Whip cream until stiff. Crush berries well; add sugar and half of crushed wafers. Combine all ingredients. Cover with remaining wafer crumbs. Freeze for 6 hours.

Anne Coleman

Peppermint Ice Cream

Yields 4 cups

INGREDIENTS:

1 egg
½ cup sugar
1½ pints whipping cream
1 teaspoon vanilla extract
½ cup crushed peppermint candy

peppermint extract to taste
1 1-pound coffee can with lid
1 3-pound coffee can with lid
ice
rock salt

PROCEDURE:

Lightly beat egg; slowly add sugar. Stir in cream, vanilla, candy, and peppermint extract. Pour mixture into 1-pound can and cover with lid. Place can inside 3-pound can, fill space between cans with alternating layers of ice and rock salt. Put lid on 3-pound can and roll on hard surface for approximately 1 hour, opening can every 15-20 minutes to stir ice cream. Pour out excess water, adding more rock salt and ice as necessary.

Brooke Peterson

Broiled Ice Cream

Serves 10

INGREDIENTS:

½ gallon ice cream, softened (your favorite flavor)
4 egg whites, at room temperature

pinch of cream of tartar
8 tablespoons white sugar
8 ounces slivered almonds

PROCEDURE:

Spread ice cream in 9″ by 13″ by 2″ aluminum pan. Beat egg whites with cream of tartar until very stiff. Gradually beat in sugar. Spread meringue over ice cream. Sprinkle with almonds. Freeze for several hours. Just before serving, place under broiler until meringue turns golden brown. Serve immediately.

Uva Márquez Sterling

Rich Vanilla Ice Cream

An ice cream maker is required for this recipe.

Yields 1 quart

INGREDIENTS:

2 cups whipping cream
1 vanilla bean

6 jumbo egg yolks
¾ cup sugar

PROCEDURE:

Scald 1 cup cream; freeze 30 minutes to chill. Bring remaining 1 cup cream and vanilla bean to boil in heavy small saucepan over medium heat. Remove from heat. Split vanilla bean and scrape seeds into cream. Beat egg yolks and sugar with electric mixer until pale yellow and slowly dissolving ribbon forms when beaters are lifted. Beat in ⅓ cup hot cream; return mixture to saucepan. Cook over low heat until mixture leaves path on back of spoon when finger is drawn across, and registers 180° F. on candy thermometer. Stir constantly for about 5 minutes; do not boil. Strain custard through fine sieve into bowl set into larger bowl of ice water. Stir occasionally until cool. Strain in scalded cream. Process vanilla mixture in ice cream maker according to manufacturers instruction. Freeze in covered container overnight to mellow flavors.

Lyn Heller

Peanut Brittle Ice Cream

Serves 8

INGREDIENTS:

1 recipe vanilla ice cream
  (See above)
2 cups granulated sugar

¼ teaspoon lemon juice
1 tablespoon butter
1¼ cups salted peanuts

PROCEDURE:

In small saucepan, melt ¼ cup sugar. Continue to add sugar, ¼ cupful at a time, until all the sugar is dissolved. Stir in lemon juice. Cook the caramel until golden brown. Remove pan from heat, add butter and peanuts. Mix until nuts are coated with caramel. Pour mixture onto an oiled cookie sheet; with an oiled spatula, spread until thickness of a peanut. Cool for 15 minutes then store in tin. Break ¼ of brittle into small pieces. Process in food processor or blender until coarsely ground. Stir ⅓ cup of coarsely ground peanut brittle into vanilla ice cream. Store in freezer. Serve with hot caramel sauce.(Recipe on p. 317)

Lyn Heller

Chocolate Chocolate Chip Ice Cream

Serves 12

INGREDIENTS:

8 ounces Belgium chocolate
    (bittersweet)
8 tablespoons Hershey's
    unsweetened cocoa
2 cups half and half
2 cups cream
2 eggs, at room temperature

¾ cup white sugar
⅛ teaspoon salt
2 tablespoons chocolate extract
1 tablespoon vanilla extract
1 teaspoon cinnamon
4 ounces Belgium chocolate

PROCEDURE:

Over double boiler melt 8 ounces Belgium chocolate. As soon as melted remove from heat and stir with spoon. Let cool. Add cocoa. Combine half and half, cream, eggs, sugar, salt, chocolate extract, vanilla extract and cinnamon, and put in ice cream can. Chop 4 ounces of Belgium chocolate into chips. Add to ice cream can; process for 30 minutes or until firm. Remove from can when finished processing; pour into freezer container. Freeze 24 hours. Serve alone or over cake.

This recipe is original and won a blue ribbon at The Del Mar Fair Exposition.

Natalie P. Pike

Halva Ice Cream

Yields 2½ quarts

INGREDIENTS:

2 quarts quality vanilla ice cream, 1-ounce package halva
   slightly softened

PROCEDURE:

Chop halva, stir into softened ice cream. Freeze in an attractive container.

Very simple, yet delicious! Best with homemade ice cream.

Helen Mayer

Choco-Mint Ice Cream Dessert

Serves 12

INGREDIENTS:

2 cups vanilla wafer crumbs,   1 cup powdered sugar
   buttered   chopped nuts (optional)
½ cup butter   3 egg whites, beaten
2 squares chocolate (unsweetened) ½ gallon peppermint (or mint)
3 egg yolks, beaten   chocolate ice cream, softened

PROCEDURE:

Butter a 9″ by 13″ glass dish. Sprinkle over the bottom 1½ cups vanilla wafer crumbs, moistened with butter. Melt ½ cup butter with chocolate. Add the beaten egg yolks, then the sifted powdered sugar. Cook slowly for a few minutes. Add chopped nuts if desired. Remove from heat; add beaten egg whites. Spread this mixture over the crumbs and cool. Layer ice cream over cooled chocolate mixture. Sprinkle remaining crumbs over top. Cover with foil and freeze until time to serve.

Linda Goodwin

Kentucky Ice Cream Pudding

Serves 8

INGREDIENTS:

1 cup Graham cracker crumbs
½ cup maraschino cherries,
  chopped
2 tablespoons creamy peanut
  butter

½ cup chopped raisins
1 quart vanilla ice cream, softened

PROCEDURE:

Mix well the crumbs, peanut butter, cherries and raisins. Spread half of mixture in bottom of ice tray; spread softened ice cream over crumb mixture; sprinkle remaining crumbs on top. Freeze. Cut into squares to serve.

An old Kentucky recipe used in our family for 40 years!

Mrs. Dallas M. Lancaster

Ambrosia Dressing

Yields 1 cup

INGREDIENTS:

⅔ cup sugar
1 teaspoon dry mustard
1 teaspoon celery seed
1 teaspoon paprika
¼ teaspoon salt

⅓ cup honey
5 tablespoons vinegar
1 tablespoon lemon juice
1 teaspoon grated onion
1 cup salad oil

PROCEDURE:

Mix dry ingredients. Add honey, vinegar, lemon juice and grated onion. Pour oil into mixture very slowly. Beat continually with electric beater.

This is a perfect blend of seasonings to bring out the luscious flavor of fruits.
Serve over summer fruits for dessert at a picnic or barbecue.

Susie Desmarais

Raspberry Sauce

Serves 6-8

INGREDIENTS:

1 quart fresh raspberries   powdered sugar

PROCEDURE:

Force raspberries through sieve. Place raspberry purée in saucepan over low heat; whisk in powdered sugar to taste. (Amount of sugar depends on tartness of berries). Let mixture cool. Serve over vanilla ice cream.

Lyn Heller

Rum Custard Sauce

Yields 2 cups

INGREDIENTS:

6 egg yolks   ½ cup dry sherry
1 cup granulated sugar   1 cup heavy cream
1 teaspoon fresh lemon juice   ¼ cup light rum

PROCEDURE:

Combine egg yolks, sugar and lemon juice in top of double boiler over moderate heat. Beat well. Add sherry; continue beating until sauce thickens. Remove from heat and cool. Whip 1 cup cream until stiff. Fold cream into sauce. Add rum. Chill 1 hour before serving.

Suzie Desmarais

Caramel Sauce

Serves 4-6

INGREDIENTS:

1 cup granulated sugar
⅛ cup lemon juice

¾ cup whipping cream

PROCEDURE:

In small saucepan over medium heat, melt ¼ cup sugar. Continue to add sugar, ¼ cupful at a time, stirring until smooth. Stir in lemon juice. Cook until caramel is golden brown. Remove from heat. After 5 minutes, add boiling cream, little by little, stirring constantly until smooth. Serve hot over peanut brittle ice cream. (Recipe on p. 312).

Lyn Heller

Chocolate Sauce

Serves 4-6

INGREDIENTS:

6 ounces semisweet chocolate
2 tablespoons unsalted butter

⅓ cup hot water
1 teaspoon vanilla extract

PROCEDURE:

Melt chocolate in double boiler. Add the butter, stir until well blended. Whisk while adding hot water. Add vanilla. Store in glass jar. Reheat in double boiler.

Serve warm over ice cream.

Lyn Heller

Hot Fudge Sauce

Yields 1 cup

INGREDIENTS:

½ cup whipping cream
3 tablespoons butter, unsalted
⅓ cup white sugar

⅓ cup brown sugar
pinch of salt
½ cup Dutch cocoa

PROCEDURE:

Heat cream and butter over low heat. Add sugars with whisk. Whisk in salt and cocoa.

Refrigerate indefinitely. Serve warm over ice cream or fruit.

Melody Gentry

Chocolate Mousse I

Serves 8-10

INGREDIENTS:

½ cup strong coffee
1 12-ounce package chocolate
  chips

6 eggs, separated
3-4 tablespoons rum

PROCEDURE:

Bring coffee to boil. Add chocolate chips. Stir until melted. Gradually stir in well beaten egg yolks and rum. Fold in stiffly beaten egg whites. Pour into individual bowls or 1 large bowl. Refrigerate 12 hours. Top with whipped cream.

Judith Rosenberg

Chocolate Mousse II

Serves 8

INGREDIENTS:

6 ounces semisweet chocolate
4 tablespoons water
4 eggs, separated
¾ cup plus 1 tablespoon sugar

⅓ cup Grand Marnier
10 teaspoons butter, softened
⅛ teaspoon salt
1 cup heavy cream, whipped

PROCEDURE:

Melt chocolate with water in top of double boiler over hot but not boiling water. In small pan mix egg yolks with ¾ cup sugar. Heat gently, stirring until mixture thickens. Do not allow to boil. Remove from heat and immediately add liqueur. Beat butter into chocolate mixture; when smooth add to cooked yolks. Fold in whipped cream. Beat egg whites with remaining sugar until stiff but not dry. Fold into chocolate mixture. Pour into individual dishes or large bowl. Chill 4-6 hours. Serve with whipped cream.

This dessert can be made a day ahead. It also freezes well.

Joan Schultz

Super Easy Chocolate Mousse

Serves 4

INGREDIENTS:

6 ounces semisweet chocolate chips
2 whole eggs
3 tablespoons hot coffee

2 tablespoons rum (or Cointreau)
¾ cup scalded milk
chocolate shavings (for garnish)

PROCEDURE:

Place all ingredients in blender. Blend at high speed for two minutes. Pour into 4 dessert cups. Chill. Top with whipped cream and shaved chocolate.

Mary Helen Cahill

319

The World's Easiest Chocolate Mousse

Serves 3-4

INGREDIENTS:

6 ounces semisweet chocolate
2 tablespoons Kahlua
1 tablespoon orange juice
2 extra large egg yolks

2 extra large eggs
1 teaspoon vanilla extract
¼ cup sugar
1 cup heavy cream

PROCEDURE:

Melt chocolate in the Kahlua and orange juice over very low heat. Set aside. Put egg yolks, eggs, vanilla and sugar in blender for 2 minutes at medium high speed. Add heavy cream; blend for another 30 seconds. Add melted chocolate mixture; blend until smooth. Pour into small individual cups. Refrigerate until ready to serve.

Susan Nagy

Quick Chocolate Mousse

Serves 4

INGREDIENTS:

2 pints heavy cream
2 tablespoons Hershey's baking
    powder
1 teaspoon vanilla extract

1 teaspoon almond extract
¼ cup sugar
1 square semisweet chocolate,
    shaved or in curls

PROCEDURE:

Combine first five ingredients in large mixing bowl stirring only until powder dissolves and mixture resembles chocolate milk. Do not beat. Refrigerate for at least 1 hour. Whip until peaks form. Spoon into individual ramekins and top with shaved or curled chocolate. Serve chilled.

Effortless and delicious!

Julie Bertini

Chocolate Rum Mousse

Serves 4-6

INGREDIENTS:

6 ounces sweet chocolate
5 eggs, separated
1 tablespoon vanilla extract
1 teaspoon instant coffee

1 tablespoon hot water
½ pint double cream
2 tablespoons rum

PROCEDURE:

Melt chocolate in top of double boiler over hot, not boiling water. Remove from heat, allow to cool. Beat egg yolks lightly; gradually beat them into melted chocolate. Flavor to taste with vanilla extract and instant coffee diluted in hot water. Beat cream until thick. Stir in rum. Fold in chocolate mixture. Beat egg whites until stiff; fold into mixture a little at a time. Pour into serving dish. Chill for at least 2 hours.

Eva Sonnenberg Lewin

Grand Marnier Mousse

Serves 6

INGREDIENTS:

4 eggs, separated
½ cup sugar
½ envelope unflavored gelatine
⅓ cup cold water

⅓ cup Grand Marnier
1½ cups whipping cream
16 lady fingers (optional)

PROCEDURE:

Beat egg yolks with sugar until very thick. Sprinkle gelatine over water in a small pan. Let set for 5 minutes; heat to dissolve. Add Grand Marnier. Fold in egg whites. Pour into a mold or 1-quart soufflé dish. Refrigerate for 4 hours.

The soufflé dish may be lined with lady fingers. An elegant and delicious dessert.

Jean Scott

Orange Mousse

Serves 6

INGREDIENTS:

1 tablespoon plus 1 teaspoon
   unflavored gelatine
⅓ cup cold water
⅓ cup boiling water
1 cup sugar
3 tablespoons lemon juice
1 cup fresh orange juice

3 tablespoons grated orange peel
3 egg whites, stiffly beaten
fresh strawberries
Mandarin orange slices
½ pint whipping cream
sliced almonds (for garnish)

PROCEDURE:

Soak gelatine in cold water, then dissolve in hot water. Add sugar, juices and orange peel. Chill in pan of ice water. When it begins to jell, fold in stiffly beaten egg whites. Turn into ring mold. Chill until firm. Unmold on tray; surround with fruits. Fill center with whipped cream. Sprinkle almonds over all.

Betty Vale

Frozen Lemon Mousse

Serves 12

INGREDIENTS:

2 packages lady fingers
4 egg yolks
½ cup fresh lemon juice
¼ cup sugar
1½ tablespoons grated lemon zest

4 egg whites
⅛ teaspoon cream of tartar
⅛ teaspoon salt
¾ cup sugar
1½ cups whipping cream

PROCEDURE:

Line bottom and sides of 8″ or 9″ springform pan with lady fingers. Combine next 4 ingredients in large bowl, blending well. Let mixture stand at room temperature. Beat egg whites until foamy, add cream of tartar and salt; continue beating until soft peaks form. Gradually add remaining sugar, beating constantly until stiff and glossy. Whip cream until stiff. Gently fold whites and cream into yolk mixture. Carefully spoon into pan. Cover with foil and freeze overnight. Let mousse soften in refrigerator about 1 hour before serving. Serve with additional whipped cream.

Elizabeth Wheelock

Crème Brûlé

Serves 4-6

INGREDIENTS:

6 egg yolks
½ cup sugar
2 cups heavy cream

1 cup half and half
2 teaspoons vanilla extract
½ cup light brown sugar

PROCEDURE:

Preheat oven to 325-350°. Beat egg yolks and sugar together thoroughly. Scald cream and half and half. Slowly beat egg yolks and sugar into cream mixture. Add vanilla extract. Pour into individual soufflé dishes. Place dishes in shallow pan of hot water; bake for 30 minutes, or until a silver knife inserted in center comes out clean. Cool thoroughly (overnight if desired). Sprinkle surface with light brown sugar. Put under broiler. Watch carefully; sugar will melt to thin crust in a minute or two and burn in another few seconds. May be served immediately or chilled.

Martha G. Dennis

Summer Delight

Serves 6

INGREDIENTS:

1 7-ounce box vanilla wafers
½ cup butter
1½ cups powdered sugar

2 eggs
1 pint whipping cream
1 20-ounce can crushed pineapple
   bits

PROCEDURE:

Crush wafers. Set aside. Cream together butter and sugar. Lightly beat eggs; blend with butter/sugar mixture. Spread cookie crumbs in a 9″ by 12″ dish, reserving ½ cup. Pour butter/sugar/egg mixture over crumbs. In bowl blend whipped cream and pineapple bits. Spoon over layer of crumbs. Sprinkle remaining crumbs over top. Refrigerate overnight. Cut into squares.

Light, refreshing and so easy!

Sally Peters Davidson

323

Mocha Soufflé

Serves 6

INGREDIENTS:

2 squares (2 ounces) unsweetened
   chocolate
¼ cup butter (or margarine)
3 tablespoons flour
⅓ cup sugar
1 teaspoon instant coffee
1 cup hot milk

3 egg yolks, well beaten
1 teaspoon vanilla extract
¼ teaspoon salt
4 egg whites
⅓ cup sugar
½ teaspoon cream of tartar

PROCEDURE:

Melt chocolate in top of double boiler or in microwave. Melt butter in
saucepan over low heat. Blend in flour; cook for 2 or 3 minutes. Remove
from heat. Add ⅓ cup sugar and instant coffee; mix well. Slowly add hot
milk; stir to a smooth mixture. Cook, stirring, over medium heat until sauce
thickens and comes to a boil. Remove from heat. Blend in melted chocolate
and vanilla. Cool 10 minutes. Gradually add beaten egg yolks, stirring
briskly. (Can be prepared to this point and refrigerated. Keep at room
temperature 2 hours before completing recipe). Preheat oven to 350°.
Combine egg whites, salt and cream of tartar. Beat to soft peaks. Gradually
add ⅓ cup sugar until stiff glossy peaks form. Egg whites will not slip out of
bowl. Gently, but thoroughly, fold chocolate mixture into egg whites. Pour
into a 1½ quart ungreased soufflé dish. Place in a shallow pan containing 1″
of hot water. Bake for 60-70 minutes.

Serve with a bowl of whipped cream on the side.

Estelle Graff

Old Fashioned Bread Pudding

Serves 4

INGREDIENTS:

1 cup dark brown sugar
3 slices of bread
2 tablespoons butter, softened
1 cup raisins
2 eggs

2 cups milk
⅛ teaspoon salt
¼ teaspoon vanilla extract
whipped cream (optional)

324

PROCEDURE:

Pour brown sugar into top of double-boiler. Butter bread, cube and sprinkle it over sugar. Add raisins. In separate bowl beat eggs, milk, salt and vanilla. Pour over bread cubes. Cook over simmering water for 1 hour. Do not stir. Serve warm or chilled with whipped cream.

Martha Shea

Chocolate Brownie Pudding

Serves 8-10

INGREDIENTS:

1 cup flour	2 tablespoons butter, melted
¼ teaspoon salt	1 teaspoon vanilla extract
¾ cup sugar	½ cup nuts, chopped
2 teaspoons baking powder	½ cup white sugar
3 tablespoons cocoa	½ cup brown sugar
½ cup milk	2 tablespoons cocoa
	1 cup water

PROCEDURE:

Preheat oven to 375°. Sift together first 5 dry ingredients. Mix with milk, melted butter, vanilla and nuts. Pour into a 9" by 12" pan. Top with sugars and 2 heaping tablespoons cocoa. Pour 1 cup water over all; do not stir. Bake for 45 minutes. Top with whipped cream if desired.

Children can make this easily.

Mildred Branard

Banana Split Dessert

Serves 12

INGREDIENTS:

2 cups Graham crackers, crushed
5 tablespoons melted butter
3 bananas, sliced
2 cups crushed pineapple, drained
½ cup nuts, chopped

maraschino cherries to taste,
  halved
2 cups powdered sugar
2 eggs
¼ pound butter
Dream Whip (for garnish)

PROCEDURE:

Combine crushed Graham crackers and melted butter to make crust; press into a 13″ by 9″ pan. Beat together the remaining ingredients; layer over the Graham cracker mixture. Garnish with Dream Whip. Refrigerate 3 hours before cutting to serve.

Bernadine A. Terlaak

Orange Dessert And Custard Sauce

Serves 8

INGREDIENTS:

1 package unflavored gelatine
¼ cup cold water
1 cup boiling water
½ cup orange juice
1 tablespoon lemon juice
1 cup sugar
3 egg whites, stiffly beaten

SAUCE
¾ cup milk
3 egg yolks
½ cup sugar
1 teaspoon vanilla extract

PROCEDURE:

Soak gelatine in cold water. Add boiling water to dissolve. Add juices and sugar. Stir occasionally. When almost set, beat; fold in beaten egg whites. Pour in serving dishes. Top with custard sauce. For sauce, heat milk in double boiler. Beat egg yolks and sugar together, add to milk. Cook until mixture thickens to coat a spoon. Add vanilla just before serving.

Mrs. Frederick M. Owens, Jr.

Persimmon Pudding

Serves 6-8

INGREDIENTS:

½ cup butter, melted
1 cup sugar
1 cup flour, sifted
¼ teaspoon salt
1 teaspoon cinnamon
1 cup persimmon pulp (3-4 ripe
   persimmons)

2 teaspoons baking soda
2 teaspoons warm water
3 tablespoons brandy
1 teaspoon vanilla extract
1 cup golden raisins
½ cup walnuts, chopped
2 eggs, slightly beaten

PROCEDURE:

Stir sugar into melted butter; add flour, resifted with salt and cinnamon; add persimmon pulp, baking soda dissolved in warm water, brandy and vanilla; add eggs. Mix lightly but thoroughly. Add raisins and nuts, stirring only until mixed. Put in buttered steam-type covered mold; steam 2½ hours. Serve topped with whipped cream; or flame at table with brandy and serve with brandy flavored hard sauce.

Can be frozen when unmolded. Wrap tightly in foil, then in plastic. Reheat by steaming in foil wrapping.

Elizabeth Wheelock

Almond Float

Serves 6-8

INGREDIENTS:

2 packages unflavored gelatine
1¾ cups cold water
4 tablespoons sugar

1½ cups milk
1 tablespoon almond extract
1 large can peaches (or mixed fruit)

PROCEDURE:

Add unflavored gelatine to ½ cup water; let it soften for 5 minutes. Bring the remaining water to boil; stir in sugar and softened gelatine until completely dissolved. Add milk and almond extract; mix well. Pour into shallow pan. Refrigerate until firm. Cut into small squares with sharp knife. Place in individual dessert bowls; top with fruit.

Josie Kan

Chantilly

Serves 8

INGREDIENTS:

12 egg whites
1 cup granulated sugar
1 cup confectioner's sugar
2 teaspoons cream of tartar

2 teaspoons vanilla extract
2 teaspoons cider vinegar
1 pint heavy cream
1 pint of your favorite berry

PROCEDURE:

Preheat oven to 275°. Beat egg whites until frothy; gradually add granulated sugar, beating continually. Slowly add confectioner's sugar, beating as before. Add vanilla, cream of tartar and vinegar. Continue to beat until stiff. Dust a 10″-tube pan or 12-cup bundt pan with flour. Spoon meringue mixture into pan. Place in pan of hot water 2″ deep. Bake for 3½ hours. Remove from oven, unmold, cool and refrigerate for 2-4 hours. An hour before serving, whip 1 pint cream until stiff. Frost sides and top of meringue with cream. Return to refrigerator. Serve garnished with whole berries, accompanied by rum custard sauce on p. 316.

Suzie Desmarais

Meringue Kisses

Serves 10-12

INGREDIENTS:

3 egg whites, at room temperature
½ teaspoon cream of tartar
1 cup sugar
1 teaspoon vanilla extract

1½ cups heavy cream, whipped
    with sugar to taste
berries in season

PROCEDURE:

Preheat oven to 400°. Beat egg whites with cream of tartar until frothy. Gradually beat in sugar until stiff and glossy. Slowly add vanilla. Drop small spoonsful onto wax paper on a baking sheet. Place in oven, turn it off and leave overnight. Do not open oven! (Meringues may be stored in airtight container until ready to serve). Place two meringues, sideways, in an attractive paper cupcake/muffin tin. Fill with whipped cream (or vanilla ice cream) and top with berries.

Eva Schacter

Russian Cream Dessert

Yields 3 cups

INGREDIENTS:

¾ cup superfine sugar
1 envelope Knox gelatine
½ cup water
1 cup whipping cream

1½ cup sour cream
1 teaspoon vanilla extract
fresh strawberries

PROCEDURE:

Oil a 3-cup mold. In small pan, blend sugar and gelatine. Add water, mix and let stand for 5 minutes. Bring to full boil, stirring constantly. Remove from heat; gently pour in whipping cream; stir without causing bubbles. In small bowl, mix sour cream and vanilla. Slowly combine hot and cold mixtures. Pour into mold. Cover with plastic wrap. Chill 4 hours. Unmold on plate. Surround with fresh strawberries.

Serve with wafers or crisp cookies.

Sally Peters Davidson

Swedish Cream Dessert

Serves 6-8

INGREDIENTS:

2⅓ cups heavy cream
1 cup sugar
1 package unflavored gelatine
1 pint sour cream

1 teaspoon vanilla extract
fresh raspberries, strawberries or
 blueberries

PROCEDURE:

Mix together heavy cream, sugar and gelatine. Heat gently, stirring until gelatine is completely dissolved. Cool until slightly thickened. Fold in sour cream and vanilla. Pour into individual serving dishes and chill until firm. Top with unsweetened fruit.

Kathy Glick

Huckleberry Dessert

Serves 8-10

INGREDIENTS:

1 4-ounce stick butter
1½ cups flour
1 3⅛-ounce package vanilla
   pudding (not instant)
1¾ cup milk

1 pint canned, fresh, or frozen
   huckleberries (raspberries, blue
   or blackberries)
3 tablespoons cornstarch
½ cup sugar
1 cup heavy cream

PROCEDURE:

Preheat oven to 350°. Mix butter and flour. Pat into 8″ by 8″ pan. Bake for 25 minutes until pie crust comes away from sides of pan. Cool. Mix vanilla pudding with milk. Cook until thick. Pour into pie crust. Drain berries, saving juice. Add enough water to juice to make 1½ cup. Mix small amount with 3 tablespoons cornstarch. Combine remaining juice, ½ cup sugar and cornstarch mixture in saucepan. Cook until thick. Cool. Add berries, and pour over pudding mixture. Whip cream, with small amount sugar to taste. Spread over pudding/berry layers. Refrigerate. Cut into squares.

Attractive and tasty, always a crowd-pleaser!

Joan Terry

Rodgrod

Serves 10-12

INGREDIENTS:

2 cans fruit — preferably berries
   or cherries
1 can purple plums, pitted

1 tablespoon cornstarch
¼-½ teaspoon cinnamon

PROCEDURE:

Reserve juice from fruit. Mix cornstarch with a small portion of juice. Bring remaining juice to boil; add cornstarch and cinnamon, stirring constantly until mixture thickens. Add fruit; bring to boil. Remove from heat, cool, and place in glass bowl. Chill. Serve over ice cream or cheese cake.

330

Denise Selati

Benjie's Pink Pudding

Serves 4

INGREDIENTS:

15 ounces loganberries (or
    raspberries)
1 package raspberry Jello

1 6-ounce can evaporated milk
1 teaspooon lemon juice
whipped cream (for garnish)

PROCEDURE:

Strain juice from loganberries into measuring cup and add water to make ½ pint. Put juice in pan, bring to boiling point. Add to Jello and stir until dissolved. Leave in cold place until just beginning to set. Purée loganberries. Combine evaporated milk and lemon juice and whisk until soft peaks form. Fold in loganberry purée and half-set Jello. Mix well, spoon into serving dish. Refrigerate until set, then decorate with whipped cream and, if desired, fresh loganberries.

Anne Page

Gingersnap Ice Box Pudding

Serves 6-8

INGREDIENTS:

12 ounces gingersnap cookies
8 tablespoons butter
2 cups powdered sugar
2 eggs

1 pint heavy whipping cream
3 firm bananas, sliced
1 cup pineapple tidbits, drained
1 cup pecans (or walnuts)

PROCEDURE:

Crush cookies into fine crumbs. Cream butter and sugar; add eggs and cream again. Whip cream. Fold in sliced bananas, pineapple tidbits and nuts. Butter a 10″square pan, line with ⅓ crumbs. Pour in butter mixture, spreading evenly. Cover with half remaining crumbs. Spread with cream mixture; cover with remaining crumbs. Chill. Cut into squares.

Theresa Worsch

Blueberry Mold

Serves 8-10

INGREDIENTS:

1 3-ounce package lemon Jello
1 cup boiling water
1 8-ounce package cream cheese
1 cup sour cream
2 heaping tablespoons powdered
   sugar

1 teaspoon vanilla extract
2 3-ounce packages raspberry (or
   blackberry) Jello
2 cups boiling water
1 can Maine wild blueberries with
   juice

PROCEDURE:

Dissolve lemon Jello in 1 cup water. Cool to room temperature. Combine cream cheese, sour cream, powdered sugar and vanilla; add to cool lemon Jello; blend well. Pour into large Pyrex dish. Refrigerate. Dissolve raspberry Jello in 2 remaining cups water. Add blueberries with juice. Pour over jelled lemon mixture. Refrigerate until entire mold is set.

Joan Marvil

Apple Crisp

Serves 12

INGREDIENTS:

5 pounds pippin apples, peeled and
   sliced
1 cup whole wheat flour

1 stick butter (or margarine)
1¼ cup brown sugar
cinnamon to taste

PROCEDURE:

Preheat oven to 350°. Place apples in 13"by 9"inch pan. Sprinkle with cinnamon. Mix flour, butter and sugar until crumbly. Sprinkle over apples. Bake for 45 minutes. Serve with ice cream or whipped cream.

Judith Rosenberg

Pineapple Meringue Torte

Serves 12

INGREDIENTS:

6 egg whites, at room temperature
2 cups sugar
1 tablespoon vinegar
1 teaspoon vanilla extract
¼ teaspoon cream of tartar

1 pint whipping cream
1 #2 can crushed pineapple
1 tablespoon powdered sugar
¾ cup chopped pecans (or walnuts)

PROCEDURE:

Preheat oven to 275°. Beat egg whites into soft peaks; gradually add sugar, then vinegar, vanilla and cream of tartar. Beat until stiff peaks form. Shape two pieces of foil into 6"-7" rounds to make two layers; spray with Pam. Spread egg white mixture in each. Bake one hour. Cool slightly, then carefully remove foil. Don't worry if meringue cracks slightly. Whip the cream until stiff. Gently fold in nearly drained pineapple, sugar and nuts. Spread between meringue layers, on top, and sides. Refrigerate overnight.

Helen Russell

Fruit Nut Torte

Serves 8

INGREDIENTS:

1 egg
¾ cup sugar
1 cup fruit cocktail, undrained
1 cup flour
1 teaspoon baking soda
½ cup walnuts, chopped

¼ cup brown sugar
¾ cup sugar
½ cup evaporated milk
⅓ cup butter
½ cup vanilla extract

PROCEDURE:

Preheat oven to 350°. Beat egg well, add sugar and fruit cocktail. Slowly add flour and baking soda. Mix well. Pour into greased 9" round pan. Combine walnuts and brown sugar. Sprinkle over batter. Bake for 30 minutes. Just before cake is done, prepare icing. Mix sugar, milk, and butter. Boil 3 minutes stirring constantly. Remove from heat. Stir in vanilla. Pour hot icing over warm cake. Serve with whipped cream.

Nina Calhoun

Lemon Bars

Yields 16 squares

INGREDIENTS:

1 cup flour
⅓ cup powdered sugar
½ cup butter
3 eggs, beaten
3 tablespoons lemon juice

1 teaspoon grated lemon rind
1 capful lemon extract
1½ cups sugar
¾ teaspoon baking powder
3 tablespoons flour

PROCEDURE:

Preheat oven to 350°. Cream flour, powdered sugar and butter together. Spread in an 8″ by 8″ glass baking dish. Bake for 25 minutes. Beat remaining ingredients together; pour over baked mixture. Bake for an additional 25 minutes or until custard is set. Remove from oven; loosen edges. Remove squares to paper toweling. Generously sprinkle with additional powdered sugar, dusting top of squares as well.

Glass baking dish is a must. Squares freeze nicely, and are good straight from the freezer, too.

Kathy Draz

Amaretto Cheese

Serves 4-6

INGREDIENTS:

2 8-ounce packages cream cheese
4 egg yolks
1 tablespoon Knox gelatine (1 envelope)

¼ cup water
½ cup sugar
2 tablespoons Amaretto

PROCEDURE:

Whirl softened cheese in food processor or mixer. Add egg yolks to blend. Sprinkle gelatine over ¼ cup water in saucepan; heat to dissolve. Add gelatine water to cheese mixture; mix in sugar and Amaretto. Pour into small molds or cups. Chill several hours. Serve with fresh fruit, nuts, or unsalted crackers.

Keeps 3 to 4 days covered in refrigerator. A dessert of cheese and fruit is often a welcome change!

Nancy Knox

Cheesecake Squares

Yields 16 squares

INGREDIENTS:

1 cup minus 2 tablespoons whole
   wheat pastry flour
2 tablespoons soy flour
⅓ cup finely ground unsweetened
   coconut
¼ cup butter, softened
½ cup walnuts, chopped

8 ounces cream cheese, softened
¼ cup honey
2 tablespoons milk
1 teaspoon vanilla extract
1 teaspoon grated lemon rind
scrapings of nutmeg to taste

PROCEDURE:

Heat oven to 350°. Combine the flours and ground coconut. Using pastry blender or 2 knives, cut butter into mixture. Add nuts. Reserve ¾ cup of mixture. Spread remaining mixture over bottom of buttered 8″by 8″baking dish. Bake for 15 minutes. Combine cream cheese and remaining ingredients in blender until smooth. Spread cream cheese mixture over baked crust. Top with reserved ¾ cup crust mixture. Bake for another 30 minutes. Cool slightly. Cut into squares.

Great for lunch boxes or just snacking.

Josephine Green

Café Brûlot Diabolique

Serves 6

INGREDIENTS:

2 lemons
4 cinnamon sticks
8 cloves

2 tablespoons sugar
1½ cups cognac (or brandy)
3 cups hot coffee

PROCEDURE:

Cut outside rind from lemon and remove white underskin. Retain rind. In chafing dish, combine rind, cinnamon, cloves, sugar and brandy. Heat. Carefully light liquid with match. Stir with ladle for 30 seconds to distribute alcohol. Add hot coffee and serve in demitasse cups.

Joy Charney

Notes

12
Cookies & Candy

Chocolate "Melt In Your Mouth" Cookies

Yields 2 dozen

INGREDIENTS:

1½ cups brown sugar
½ cup shortening
1 egg, well beaten
2 cups cake flour
1 teaspoon baking soda
1 cup sour milk (1 tablespoon
  vinegar to 1 cup milk)
2 tablespoons vanilla extract
1 cup pecans
3 squares semisweet chocolate,
  melted

FROSTING
6 tablespoons butter
1 tablespoon shortening
1¾ cups powdered sugar
2 squares semisweet chocolate,
  melted
1 teaspoon vanilla extract
milk, to make frosting spreadable

PROCEDURE:

Preheat oven to 450°. Flour and grease cookie sheet. Cream brown sugar and shortening; add egg. Mix in flour and soda, then sour milk. Add vanilla, pecans and chocolate; mix well. Bake 5 minutes. Do not overbake. Cookies should be soft. In small bowl, combine butter, shortening, sugar, chocolate, vanilla and milk. Mix until smooth. Spread over warm cookies and serve.

Susan Bennett

Lace Cookies

Yields 4 dozen

INGREDIENTS:

3 cups quick cooking oats
1½ cups sugar
1 teaspoon salt
6 tablespoons flour
1 cup margarine, melted

2 eggs, slightly beaten
1 tablespoon orange juice
3 teaspoons vanilla extract
12 ounces semisweet chocolate
  chips, melted

PROCEDURE:

Preheat oven to 375°. Line cookie sheet with aluminum foil. Combine dry ingredients in large bowl. Add margarine, mixing with large spoon. Add remaining ingredients and blend well. Drop by ½ teaspoons, well apart. Bake 8-10 minutes. Do not overbake. Cool cookies, and then peel off foil. Taking 2 cookies the same size, spread chocolate on flat sides to make sandwich.

Arlene Berger

Unbaked Cookies

Yields 4 dozen

INGREDIENTS:

2 cups sugar
½ cup milk
½ cup butter (or margarine)
4 tablespoons cocoa

½ cup peanut butter
3 cups quick-cooking oatmeal
2 teaspoons vanilla extract
1 cup nuts, chopped

PROCEDURE:

Boil sugar, milk, butter and cocoa for 1-1½ minutes at full boil. Remove from heat. Add peanut butter, oatmeal, vanilla and nuts. Beat until blended. Drop by teaspoons on wax paper. Cool until set. Coconut or dates may be added if desired.

Janis Butcher

Healthy Chocolate Chip Cookies

Yields 7 dozen

INGREDIENTS:

1 cup margarine, softened
1½ cups dark brown sugar, packed
2 eggs
2 teaspoons vanilla extract
2 cups whole wheat pastry flour
1 teaspoon baking soda
1½ teaspoons cinnamon
1 teaspoon salt (optional)

1½ cups uncooked oats
½ cup bran flakes
1 cup corn flakes, crumbled
¼ cup wheat germ
¼ cup macaroon coconut
milk, as needed
1 cup walnuts, chopped
12 ounces chocolate chips

PROCEDURE:

Preheat oven to 375°. Grease cookie sheet. Beat margarine and sugar until creamy. Add eggs and vanilla. Beat. Stir in flour, soda, cinnamon and salt; mix well. Stir in oats, flakes, wheat germ and coconut. Blend well. If batter is too dry, add a small amount of milk. Stir in nuts and chocolate chips. Drop by rounded teaspoons. Bake 10 minutes. Best when a little soft, not cooked crisp.

Geri Caceres

Christy's Forgotten Unforgettables

Yields 3 dozen

INGREDIENTS:

2 egg whites, at room temperature
½ teaspoon cream of tartar
⅔ cup white sugar

pinch of salt
1 teaspoon vanilla extract
1 cup chocolate chips

PROCEDURE:

Preheat oven to 350°. Grease cookie sheets or line with foil. Beat egg whites with cream of tartar until frothy. Gradually add sugar, salt and vanilla beating until stiff and dry. Fold in chocolate chips. Drop by small teaspoons on cookie sheet approximately ½" apart. Put in oven and turn it off. Remove the following morning. Do not open oven!

Try using butterscotch or peanut butter chips, chopped nuts or a combination of these instead of the chocolate chips. Stored in an airtight container, these delicious meringues will stay fresh for a long time, but don't bake them in humid weather. Add a touch of food coloring for appropriate holiday hues!

Gayl Foshée
Christy Rantzow

Chocolate Munchies

Yields 4 dozen

INGREDIENTS:

½ cup butter
2 ounces unsweetened chocolate
2 cups sugar
2 eggs

½ cup pecans, chopped
2 cups flour
2 teaspoons baking powder

PROCEDURE:

Preheat oven to 350°. Grease cookie sheet. Melt butter and chocolate over low heat. In large bowl, blend sugar and eggs. Add nuts. Sift in flour, baking powder and chocolate mixture. Chill 15 minutes. Form into 1" balls. Place 2"-3" apart on cookie sheet. Bake 15 minutes. Remove from cookie sheet at once and cool.

For kids of all ages!

Laurie Marcus

Washington Cookies

Yields 3 dozen

INGREDIENTS:

1 cup margarine
¼ cup brown sugar
¼ cup white sugar
2 eggs
1 teaspoon vanilla extract
1½ cups flour

1 teaspoon baking soda
1 teaspoon salt
1 cup walnuts, chopped
2 cups oats
12 ounces chocolate chips

PROCEDURE:

Preheat oven to 350°. Cream margarine and sugars. Add eggs; mix well. Add vanilla. Stir in dry ingredients. Add nuts, oats and chocolate chips. Drop by spoonsful onto greased cookie sheet. Bake 12-15 minutes. For a different flavor you can use peanut butter instead of chocolate chips.

Carolyn Wood Fudge

Yugoslav Cookies

Yields 20

INGREDIENTS:

1 cup butter
1¼ cups sugar
1 egg yolk
¼ teaspoon salt

2½ cups flour
1 jar currant jelly
3 egg whites
¾ cup walnuts, chopped

PROCEDURE:

Preheat oven to 350°. Cream butter. Stir in ½ cup sugar. Add yolk and salt. Stir in flour and pat into bottom of 9″ by 13″ by 2″ pan. Beat jelly with fork. Spread on dough. Beat egg whites until stiff. Gradually add remaining sugar and beat until it stands in peaks. Spread over jelly. Sprinkle nuts on top. Bake 45 minutes. Cool well and cut into squares.

DiAnn Hjermstad

Mexican Wedding Cookies

Yields 2 dozen

INGREDIENTS:

½ cup butter
1 cup flour
¼ cup powdered sugar
½ cup pecans

½ teaspoon vanilla extract
pinch of salt
powdered sugar, for rolling

PROCEDURE:

Preheat oven to 425°. Combine ingredients. Roll into walnut-size balls. Bake on cookie sheet for 12 minutes or until light golden brown. Cool. Roll in powdered sugar.

Anne Holzer

Butter Pecan Turtle Cookies

Yields 2 dozen

INGREDIENTS:

2 cups flour
1 cup brown sugar, packed
½ cup butter, softened
1 cup whole pecan halves

⅔ cup butter
½ cup brown sugar, packed
1 cup milk chocolate chips

PROCEDURE:

Preheat oven to 350°. Combine flour, 1 cup brown sugar and ½ cup butter for crust. Mix at medium speed for 2-3 minutes until well mixed and particles are fine. Pat firmly into ungreased 13″ by 9″ by 2″ pan. Sprinkle pecans evenly over unbaked crust; set aside. In heavy saucepan, combine ½ cup brown sugar and ⅔ cups butter. Cook over medium heat, stirring constantly until entire surface begins to boil. Boil ½-1 minute, stirring constantly. Pour evenly over pecans and crust. Bake 18-22 minutes or until caramel layer is bubbly and crust is golden brown. Remove from oven. Immediately sprinkle with chips; allow chips to melt slightly and swirl. Leave some chips whole; cool. Cut into small squares.

Helen Magenheimer

Old Fashioned Molasses Cookies

Yields 2 dozen

INGREDIENTS:

½ cup shortening
½ cup sugar
1 egg
1 cup dark molasses
1 tablespoon lemon juice
3½ cups flour

1 teaspoon cinnamon
¼ teaspoon ground cloves
½ teaspoon ginger
2 teaspoons baking soda
½ teaspoon salt
⅓ cup boiling water

PROCEDURE:

Preheat oven to 350°. Cream shortening and sugar; beat in egg. Add molasses and lemon juice; blend well. Sift and mix dry ingredients; add to cream mixture. Add boiling water; mix well. Chill thoroughly. Drop by teaspoons on greased cookie sheets. Sprinkle with sugar to taste. Bake 8-12 minutes.

Mable Lehmann

Old Fashioned Sour Cream Cookies

Yields 5 dozen

INGREDIENTS:

½ cup shortening, softened
1½ cups sugar
2 eggs
1 cup sour cream
1 teaspoon vanilla extract
2¼ cups flour, sifted
½ teaspoon soda

½ teaspoon baking powder
½ teaspoon salt
2 cups powdered sugar
¼ cup butter
½ teaspoon vanilla extract
milk

PROCEDURE:

Preheat oven to 350°. Mix shortening, sugar and eggs; stir in sour cream and vanilla. Add flour, soda, baking powder and salt. Chill at least one hour. Drop by rounded teaspoon about 2″ apart on ungreased cookie sheet. Bake 8-10 minutes until delicately browned (until almost no imprint remains when lightly touched with finger). Cool. Mix powdered sugar, butter, vanilla and milk to right consistency and spread over cookies.

Olive Nordstrom

Old Fashioned Cut Out Sugar Cookies

Yields 12 dozen

INGREDIENTS:

2¼ cups sugar
2 cups shortening
4 eggs, lightly beaten
2 teaspoons vanilla extract

6 cups flour, sifted
1½ teaspoons salt
2 teaspoons baking powder

PROCEDURE:

Preheat oven to 400°. Cream sugar and shortening. Stir in eggs and vanilla. Sift flour, salt and baking powder. Add to sugar mixture and mix well. Chill several hours or overnight. Roll and cut out with assorted cookie cutters. Bake 10 minutes. For a change, divide dough into thirds. Leave ⅓ plain. Add 2 squares of melted chocolate to second third. Add 1½ teaspoons cinnamon, ½ teaspoon cloves and ½ teaspoon ginger to last third.

Cookies freeze very well.

Linda Altes

Oatmeal Drop Cookies

Yields 3 dozen

INGREDIENTS:

½ cup shortening, softened
1¼ cups sugar
2 eggs
6 tablespoons molasses
1¾ cups flour
1 teaspoon baking soda

1 teaspoon cinnamon
1 teaspoon salt
2 cups rolled oats (not instant)
1 cup raisins
½ cup nuts, optional

PROCEDURE:

Preheat oven to 350°. Mix shortening, sugar and eggs. Add molasses, flour, soda, cinnamon and salt. Mix thoroughly. Stir in rolled oats, raisins and nuts. Bake for 10-12 minutes on greased cookie sheets.

Grace Smith

Sugar Cutouts

Yields 6 dozen

INGREDIENTS:

½ cup butter
¾ cup sugar
¾ teaspoon vanilla extract
1 egg, lightly beaten
2 cups sifted flour
½ teaspoon baking soda

pinch of salt
FROSTING
4 egg whites
½ teaspoon cream of tartar
5 cups sifted powdered sugar
½ teaspoon vanilla extract

PROCEDURE:

Preheat oven to 375°. Cream butter and sugar. Add vanilla and egg. Sift flour, soda and salt together; mix into butter mixture (dough will be stiff). Working with a small amount of dough at a time, roll out very thin between sheets of floured wax paper. Cut into desired shapes and place on greased cookie sheet. Bake 10-12 minutes. Cool. In bowl, beat egg whites with cream of tartar until foamy. Gradually beat in powdered sugar until it stands in peaks. Add vanilla. Add more sugar if not stiff enough; add hot water if it hardens. Divide into small bowls or cups. Add food coloring to each one. Paint cookies with thin brushes.

Betty Vale
Lucy Smith

Tea Scones

Yields 10

INGREDIENTS:

2 cups unsifted, unbleached flour
4 teaspoons baking powder
⅛ teaspoon salt
1 heaped tablespoon sugar

3 ounces very cold butter
1 egg, lightly beaten
1 cup sour cream

PROCEDURE:

Preheat oven to 400°. Mix flour, baking powder, salt and sugar in large bowl. Add butter and rapidly mix, on and off, until the butter has been incorporated and mixture resembles fine cornmeal. Add egg and sour cream; mix until ball of sticky dough forms. Drop balls of dough into cupcake baking cups and bake for 15 minutes. Cool.

Split and top each half with jam and whipped cream. Delicious for afternoon tea!

Helen Mayer

Turtle Brownies

Yields 24

INGREDIENTS:

14 ounces caramels
⅔ cup evaporated milk
1 box dark chocolate cake mix

¾ cup soft margarine
1 cup nuts, chopped (optional)
12 ounces semisweet chocolate

PROCEDURE:

Preheat oven to 350°. Grease 13"by 9"by 2"pan. Combine caramels and ⅓ cup evaporated milk over low heat in double boiler. Stir until melted. Set aside. Combine in bowl cake mix, remaining evaporated milk and margarine. Stir in nuts. Press ½ of cake mixture into pan. Bake 6 minutes. Sprinkle chocolate pieces evenly on top. Pour melted caramels over chocolate, spreading evenly. Pour remaining cake mixture on top of caramels. Bake 15-18 minutes. (Should be soft). Cool completely, even overnight, and cut into squares.

Quite simple to make, yet different enough to serve to guests.

Joan Gass

Brownies

Yields 12-16

INGREDIENTS:

¾ cup butter (or margarine)
4 ounces unsweetened chocolate
3 eggs
1½ cups sugar

1½ teaspoons vanilla extract
¾ cup flour, sifted
½ cup pecans, coarsely chopped

PROCEDURE:

Preheat oven to 350°. Grease 8"by 8"by 2"pan. Melt butter and chocolate together; cool. Beat eggs, sugar and vanilla until thick and piled softly. Add cooled chocolate mixture and beat until blended. Mix in flour, then pecans. Turn into pan and spread evenly. Bake 35 minutes. Cool and cut into squares.

Mary Landa

My Boibe's Favorite Brownies

Yields 20-30

INGREDIENTS:

½ cup butter
3 or 4 1-ounce chocolate squares
1½ cups sugar
1 teaspoon vanilla extract
2 eggs

1½ cups flour
½ teaspoon baking powder
⅛ teaspoon salt
grated nuts

PROCEDURE:

Preheat oven to 350°. Melt butter in saucepan, add chocolate, sugar and vanilla; cool. Add eggs, one at a time. Add flour, baking powder and salt; mix well until smooth. Pour into greased 10"by 14"pan. Sprinkle top with nuts. Bake ½ hour; do not overbake. Place on rack; cool a few minutes then cut half way through into squares using sharp knife. Cut through completely when cooled.

Marissa Schwartz

Old World Raspberry Bars

Yields 2 dozen

INGREDIENTS:

2¼ cups flour
1 cup sugar
1 cup pecans, chopped

1 cup sweet butter
1 egg
1 10-ounce jar raspberry preserves

PROCEDURE:

Preheat oven to 350°. Grease 8"pan. Combine flour, sugar, pecans, butter and egg; mix on low speed until crumbly. Set aside 1½ cups for topping. Press rest in pan. Spread preserves to within ½"of pan. Top with crumbs. Bake 45 minutes. Cool completely. Cut into 1"by 4"bars.

Jackie Hassler

Peanut Butter Bars

Yields 24

INGREDIENTS:

1 cup chunky peanut butter
⅔ cup butter, softened
1 teaspoon vanilla extract
2 cups light brown sugar, firmly
   packed

3 eggs
1 cup all purpose flour, sifted
½ teaspoon salt
¾ cup powdered sugar
2 teaspoons water

PROCEDURE:

Preheat oven to 350°. Grease 13"by 9"by 2"pan. Combine peanut butter, butter, vanilla and brown sugar. Beat with mixer until well blended. Beat in eggs one at a time. Stir in flour and salt. Spread batter in pan and bake for 35 minutes. Glaze with mixture of powdered sugar and water.

Cindy Coleman

Chocolate Cherry Bars

Yields 24

INGREDIENTS:

1 package fudge cake mix
1 21-ounce can cherry fruit filling, unstrained
1 teaspoon almond extract
2 eggs, beaten

1 cup sugar
15 tablespoons butter (or margarine)
⅓ cup milk
6 ounces semisweet chocolate

PROCEDURE:

Preheat oven to 350°. Grease and flour 13″ by 9″ pan or 15″ by 10″ jelly roll pan. Combine cake mix, fruit filling, almond extract and eggs; stir by hand until well blended. Pour into prepared pan. Bake 25-30 minutes or until toothpick comes out clean. In small saucepan, combine sugar, butter and milk. Boil, stirring constantly for 1 minute. Remove from heat and stir in chocolate pieces until smooth. Pour over cake and slice into bars.

Virginia Frizzell

Seven Layer Bars

Yields 24

INGREDIENTS:

½ cup butter
1 cup Graham cracker crumbs
1 cup walnuts, coarsely chopped
6 ounces chocolate chips

6 ounces butterscotch chips
1 cup shredded coconut
1 8-ounce can condensed milk

PROCEDURE:

Preheat oven to 350°. In 9″ by 13″ pan, melt butter; scatter crumbs evenly over melted butter. Layer other ingredients in order listed. Over top layer of coconut, drizzle milk. Bake 25-30 minutes. Cool and cut into squares.

Jackie Hassler

Chocolate Malted Milk Bars

Serves 16

INGREDIENTS:

6 tablespoons butter (or margarine)
¾ cup brown sugar, packed
2 eggs, lightly beaten
½ teaspoon vanilla extract
¾ cup flour
½ teaspoon baking powder

½ cup instant chocolate malted
  milk powder
1 cup dates, snipped
½ cup walnuts, chopped
½ cup coconut
confectioner's sugar (optional)

PROCEDURE:

Preheat oven to 350°. Grease and flour 9"by 9"by 2"pan. In 3-quart saucepan, melt butter; remove from heat and blend in brown sugar. Beat in eggs one at a time. Add vanilla; stir in flour, baking powder and chocolate malted milk powder. Mix thoroughly; fold in dates, nuts and coconut. Turn into pan. Bake 25-30 minutes. Cool. Cut into bars, sprinkle with confectioner's sugar if desired.

Betty Ulevitch

Lemon-Cheese Bars

Yields 30

INGREDIENTS:

1 box yellow pudding cake mix
2 eggs
⅓ cup oil

8 ounces cream cheese
⅓ cup sugar
1 teaspoon lemon juice

PROCEDURE:

Preheat oven to 350°. Mix cake mix with 1 egg and oil until crumbly. Reserve 1 cup. Pour rest into 13"by 9"by 2"pan. Bake 15 minutes. Set aside. In bowl, beat cream cheese, sugar, lemon juice and egg until fluffy. Spread over baked mixture. Add reserved crumbs to top and bake 10-15 minutes longer. Cool and cut into bars.

Carol Vadnais

Chocolate Chip Bars

Yields 24

INGREDIENTS:

1 package white cake mix
½ cup cooking oil
2 tablespoons water

2 eggs
6 ounces chocolate chips
½ cup chopped walnuts (or pecans)

PROCEDURE:

Preheat oven to 350°. Grease 9″by 13″pan. Combine cake mix, oil, water and eggs by hand in large bowl. Add chocolate chips and nuts. Bake 15-20 minutes or until light brown. Cool, cut into squares.

This is a fun recipe that even your children can make!

Anita Strauss

Almond Squares

Serves 10-12

INGREDIENTS:

¾ cup margarine, softened
3 egg yolks
¾ cup flour
¾ cup brown sugar
2 teaspoons baking powder
1½ teaspoons vanilla extract

TOPPING
2 cups brown sugar
3 egg whites, beaten
1 cup almonds, chopped

PROCEDURE:

Preheat oven to 350°. Grease 13″by 9″pan. Beat margarine and egg yolks. Add flour, brown sugar and baking powder; beat until smooth. Add vanilla. Spread in pan. In bowl, mix brown sugar with beaten egg whites. Beat until combined. Spread on top of base mixture. Sprinkle with almonds. Bake 30 minutes. Cool and cut into squares.

This "old family recipe" could easily become "your old family recipe."

Judith Rosenberg

Rocky Road Squares

Yields 24

INGREDIENTS:

12 ounces semisweet chocolate
    morsels
1 14-ounce can sweetened con-
    densed milk
2 tablespoons butter (or margarine)

2 cups dry roasted peanuts
10½ ounces miniature white
    marshmallows

PROCEDURE:

In top of double boiler, over boiling water, melt morsels with milk and
butter; remove from heat. In large bowl, combine nuts and marshmallows;
fold in chocolate mixture. Spread in 13″by 9″pan lined with wax paper.
Chill 2 hours or until firm. Remove from pan, peel off wax paper; cut into
small squares. Cover and store at room temperature.

Jackie Hassler

Date Squares

Serves 16

INGREDIENTS:

¾ pound pitted dates, coarsely
    chopped
½ cup water
½ cup sugar
dash of salt
1½ cup oatmeal, uncooked

1½ cups flour
1 cup brown sugar
¾ cup shortening
½ teaspoon baking soda
¼ teaspoon salt

PROCEDURE:

Preheat oven to 375°. Grease 8″pan. Cook dates in water over medium
heat until tender, about 5 minutes. Add sugar and salt; blend. Cool. In large
bowl, mix dry ingredients together until evenly blended. Press slightly more
than ⅔ of mixture along bottom and sides of pan; cover with date mixture.
Sprinkle remaining crumb mixture over dates; pressing lightly. Bake 25-30
minutes. Cool and cut into squares. Serve plain or with vanilla ice cream.

Alice Sweeney

Chocolate Peanut Squares

Yields 24

INGREDIENTS:

1 cup butter (or margarine)
½ cup white sugar
½ cup brown sugar
2 egg yolks, lightly beaten
1 tablespoon cold water
1 teaspoon vanilla extract
2 cups flour

½ teaspoon salt
1 teaspoon baking soda
6 ounces chocolate chips
2 egg whites
1 cup brown sugar (additional)
1 cup salted peanuts, chopped

PROCEDURE:

Preheat oven to 375°. Grease and flour 12″by 8″by 1″cookie sheet. Cream butter and sugars. Add yolks, water and vanilla. Blend well. Sift flour, salt and soda together. Add to butter mixture. Blend thoroughly. Spread over cookie sheet. Pat down to smoothly fill the pan. Sprinkle with chocolate chips. Beat egg whites until stiff. Add 1 cup brown sugar slowly to form stiff meringue. Spread over chocolate chips. Sprinkle chopped nuts over meringue. Bake 25 minutes. Cool. Cut into 2″squares.

Arlene Kavanaugh

Chocolate Chip Kookie Brittle

Yields 1¼ pounds

INGREDIENTS:

1 cup butter
1 cup sugar
1 teaspoon vanilla extract

2 cups flour
1½ cups chocolate chips
½ cup pecans (optional)

PROCEDURE:

Preheat oven to 350°. Melt butter. Add sugar, vanilla and flour; stir well. Add chips and nuts. Dough will be dry. Press onto jelly roll pan or small cookie sheet. Bake 25-30 minutes. Cool and break apart.

Jackie Hassler

Chocolate Chip-Coconut Goodies

Serves 10

INGREDIENTS:

½ cup butter
1 package Graham crackers,
  crumbled
12 ounces semisweet chocolate
  chips

1½ cups coconut
⅔ cup sweetened condensed milk
8-10 ounces nuts, either pecans or
  almonds

PROCEDURE:

Preheat oven to 350°. Melt butter; mix with Graham cracker crumbs lining bottom of cake pan (any size), patting mixture flat. Add chocolate chips evenly on top of crust. Layer coconut, condensed milk and nuts. Bake until golden brown. Cut into small squares or wedges.

Ilene Wachsman

Pecan Meringues

Yields 225

INGREDIENTS:

pinch of salt
½ teaspoon lemon juice
4 egg whites, at room temperature

1 cup sugar
1 teaspoon vanilla extract
4 cups unsalted raw pecan halves

PROCEDURE:

Preheat oven to 175°. Butter and flour 4 teflon cookie sheets. Place salt and lemon juice in large bowl of electric mixer. Add egg whites and whip on medium-high until egg whites hold a peak. While beating, gradually add sugar and then vanilla. Beat until stiff and shiny. Measure approximately 4 cups of meringue and fold an equal amount of pecans into it. Place the individual coated nuts on cookie sheets. Bake 2-2½ hours. When meringues are beige and firm, they are ready. Store in airtight containers. Keeps for 7-10 days.

Lyn Heller

Caramel Corn

Yields 7 quarts

INGREDIENTS:

7 quarts freshly-popped corn
2 cups brown sugar
1 cup butter

½ cup light corn syrup
1 teaspoon salt
nuts (optional)

PROCEDURE:

Preheat oven to 225°. Put popcorn in very large bowl. Mix remaining ingredients in medium sauce pan. Cook over moderate heat, boiling for 5 minutes. Remove from heat and pour over popcorn; mix until completely coated. Spread caramel corn in shallow pans and bake 1 hour. Cool and break apart.

A wonderful holiday gift when packaged in a colorful canister.

Olivia Chier

Mixed Nut Cluster

Yields 24

INGREDIENTS:

1 cup sugar
½ cup light corn syrup
¼ cup water

¼ cup butter
2 cups mixed nuts
2 teaspoons baking soda

PROCEDURE:

Bring sugar, syrup and water to a boil. Add butter and nuts. Stir until amber color. Remove from heat and add baking soda. Stir well and pour in buttered cookie sheet; stretching it as it cools. Break into pieces.

Megan Hooker

Peanut Butter Bonbons

Yields 100

INGREDIENTS:

3 cups chunky peanut butter
½ cup butter (or margarine)
4 cups powdered sugar, sifted
3 cups Rice Krispies cereal

9 ounces butterscotch chips
9 ounces semisweet chocolate chips
4¼ tablespoons shortening

PROCEDURE:

Melt peanut butter with butter. In large bowl mix sugar and cereal. Pour melted mixture over sugar and cereal. Mix well by hand. Form ½"balls. Place on cookie sheets lined with wax paper. Chill until firm. Melt chips and add shortening. Dip and place balls back on waxed paper and chill again. These will keep for a few months in the refrigerator.

Place bonbons in individual candy cups for a special hostess or holiday gift.

Linda Clark

World's Best Fudge

Yields 5 pounds

INGREDIENTS:

4½ cups sugar
1 large can evaporated milk
½ cup butter
3 6-ounce packages chocolate chips

1 pint marshmallow cream
1 cup walnuts, chopped
2 teaspoons vanilla extract

PROCEDURE:

Bring sugar and milk to rolling boil. Boil for 9 minutes, stirring occasionally. Remove from heat. Add butter, chips, marshmallow cream, walnuts and vanilla. Pour into 13"by 9"greased pan. Let stand a few minutes before cutting into small squares.

Jackie Hassler

Candied Orange Peel

Yields 16

INGREDIENTS:

4 large thick-skinned oranges
4 cups sugar

1 cup water

PROCEDURE:

Quarter orange peel by cutting through skin and white underskin of each orange from top to bottom. Slice wedges of peel in four, lengthwise. Bring water to boil in saucepan. Add orange peel and boil for 5 minutes. Drain. Repeat 3 times, using fresh water each time. Place 2 cups sugar and water in frying pan. Boil until it reaches 230° on candy thermometer. Add orange peel. Over low heat, cook orange peel until tender, 30-45 minutes. Place peel in single layer on parchment paper. Roll warm peel in 2 cups of sugar. Dry peel on cake racks for 12-18 hours. Store in airtight tin.

Lyn Heller

Kara's Truffles

Yields 48

INGREDIENTS:

16 ounces semisweet chocolate
  chips
½ cup heavy whipping cream
2 egg yolks

½ cup sweet butter, softened
2 tablespoons brandy
Hershey's cocoa

PROCEDURE:

Melt chocolate chips with whipping cream in double boiler until smooth. Cool to just above room temperature. Add egg yolks, sweet butter and brandy and whisk together until well blended. Refrigerate at least 4 hours. Shape into 1"balls (mixture will be sticky). Roll in cocoa. Place in truffle cups and keep refrigerated. Keeps for two weeks in refrigerator.

Elizabeth Zongker

Chocolate Truffles

Yields 60

INGREDIENTS:

¾ cup hazelnuts, walnuts or pecans
6 ounces semisweet chocolate
⅓ cup heavy cream
1⅓ cup confectioner's sugar

1 egg white
2 tablespoons Grand Marnier,
  Cointreau or rum
chocolate sprinkles

PROCEDURE:

Grind nuts in blender, processor or Mouli grater. Line bottom of 9″by 5″by 3″loaf pan with waxed paper. In small saucepan, combine chocolate and cream. Heat over low heat just until chocolate is melted. Remove from heat. In medium bowl, combine nuts, sugar and egg white. With wooden spoon, stir until combined. Stir in chocolate mixture and liqueur; combine well. Turn into prepared pan. Refrigerate until firm. Shape into round balls, using rounded half-teaspoons for each. Roll each in chocolate sprinkles. Place in candy wrappers; refrigerate. Keeps for 2-3 weeks in refrigerator.

Use red and green chocolate sprinkles for a holiday gift.

Kerry Myers

357

Notes

13

Bread & Breakfast

Zucchini Bread I

Yields 2 loaves

INGREDIENTS:

3 eggs
1 cup oil
2 cups zucchini, peeled and grated
2 cups sugar
3 cups flour
1 teaspoon baking soda

1 teaspoon salt
½ teaspoon baking powder
2 teaspoons vanilla extract
2 teaspoons cinnamon
1 cup walnuts, chopped

PROCEDURE:

Preheat oven to 325°. Beat eggs in large bowl. Add oil, zucchini and sugar. Sift dry ingredients together. Add to egg mixture and mix well. Stir in nuts. Put in 2 well-greased and floured loaf pans. Bake for 1 hour.

Galen Cooper

Zucchini Bread II

Yields 2 loaves

INGREDIENTS:

3 eggs
1 cup brown sugar
1 cup white sugar
1 cup vegetable oil
1 tablespoon vanilla extract
2 cups sifted flour
1 tablespoon cinnamon

2 teaspoons baking soda
1 teaspoon salt
¼ teaspoon baking powder
2 cups zucchini, coarsely grated
1 cup nuts, chopped
1 teaspoon grated lemon rind

PROCEDURE:

Preheat oven to 350°. Beat eggs until fluffy. Beat in sugars, oil and vanilla until mixture is thick. Sift together dry ingredients. Add to egg mixture. Add remaining ingredients. Pour into 2 greased and floured loaf pans or paper molds in muffin tins. Bake for 50-60 minutes. Remove from pans and cool completely on rack.

Joyce Aftahi

Banana Bread

Yields 1 loaf

INGREDIENTS:

1 cup sugar
½ cup brown sugar
2 eggs, beaten
1 teaspoon baking soda
6 tablespoons sour milk

3 ripe bananas, mashed
2 cups flour
1 teaspoon vanilla extract
½ cup margarine, melted
½ cup chopped nuts (optional)

PROCEDURE:

Preheat oven to 325°. Cream sugars and eggs. Set aside. Mix soda with sour milk. Add bananas and mix well. Add to egg mixture. Beat in flour, vanilla and margarine, mixing well. Stir in nuts. Pour into greased loaf pan. Bake for 1 hour. Remove from pan onto cooling rack.

Katherine E. Hudzik

Lemon Tea Bread

Yields 1 loaf

INGREDIENTS:

⅓ cup butter, melted
1 cup sugar
3 tablespoons lemon extract
2 eggs
1½ cups flour
1 teaspoon baking powder

1 teaspoon salt
½ cup milk
1½ tablespoons grated lemon peel
½ cup pecans, chopped
¼ cup lemon juice
½ cup sugar

PROCEDURE:

Preheat oven to 350°. In a large bowl, cream butter, sugar and lemon extract until fluffy. Add eggs, beating until mixture is blended. In a medium bowl, sift flour, baking powder and salt. Add flour mixture and milk alternately to egg mixture. Stir until all is blended. Do not overmix. Fold in lemon peel and pecans. Pour batter into greased and floured loaf pan. Bake for 60 minutes or until wooden pick inserted in center comes out clean. Mix together lemon juice and sugar. Pour slowly over top of bread hot from the oven. Let stand 15-20 minutes. Turn onto rack to cool.

Wonderful with coffee or tea!

Linda Saxon

McFall Congo Banana Bread

Yields 1 loaf

INGREDIENTS:

1 cup honey
½ cup butter
2 eggs
3 ripe bananas, mashed
1½ cups whole wheat flour
¼ cup bran

1 teaspoon soda
pinch of salt
½ teaspoon baking powder
1 cup walnuts, chopped
½ cup raisins (optional)

PROCEDURE:

Preheat oven to 325°. Mix together honey, butter, eggs and bananas. Add remaining ingredients and mix well. Pour into greased loaf pan. Bake for 1 hour.

Sandra Angelo

Tropical Fruit Bread

Yields 1 loaf

INGREDIENTS:

2 cups flour
1 cup sugar, preferably raw
½ cup clover (or kiawe) honey
½ cup polyunsaturated oil
    (safflower)
½ cup butter (or margarine), melted
½ cup raisins

¼ cup nuts, chopped
3 eggs, beaten
½ cup Quaker oats
2 teaspoons cinnamon
2 teaspoons baking soda
1 teaspoon vanilla extract
½ teaspoon salt
½ cup shredded coconut (optional)

PROCEDURE:

Mix all ingredients thoroughly, making sure all dry ingredients are moistened. Let stand 20 minutes. Preheat oven to 350°. Stir. Pour into an oiled loaf pan. Bake for 50-60 minutes.

A delicious and wholesome after school snack.

Jane Jones

Coconut Bread

Yields 2 loaves

INGREDIENTS:

3 cups flour
1 cup sugar
3 teaspoons baking powder
½ teaspoon salt
1 egg

1½ cups milk
½ teaspoon vanilla extract
½ teaspoon almond extract
1 cup sweetened coconut

PROCEDURE:

Preheat oven to 350°. Mix dry ingredients together. Blend egg, milk and flavorings. Add liquid to dry ingredients. Mix well. Stir in coconut. Pour into 3 small or 2 large greased loaf pans. Bake for 1 hour 10 minutes.

Libby Clemmer

Joan's Key Lime Bread

Yields 2 loaves

INGREDIENTS:

⅔ cup butter, melted
2 cups sugar
4 eggs
½ teaspoon vanilla extract
2 key lime rinds, grated
3 cups flour

1 teaspoon salt
2½ teaspoons baking powder
1 cup milk
1 cup walnuts, chopped
3 tablespoons key lime juice
½ cup sugar

PROCEDURE:

Preheat oven to 350°. Blend butter and sugar. Add eggs and beat well. Stir in vanilla and grated rinds. Combine dry ingredients. Add alternately with milk. Fold in nuts. Turn into 2 well-greased 5" by 9" loaf pans. Bake for 50-60 minutes. (If key limes are unavailable, use part lemon and part lime). Mix lime juice and sugar. Spoon over hot bread in pans. Cool 15 minutes. Remove from pans. Do not slice for 18-20 hours.

A terrific holiday gift. Freezes well, too.

Joan Capen

Cranberry-Orange Bread

Yields 1 loaf

INGREDIENTS:

2 cups flour, sifted
¾ cup sugar
1½ teaspoons baking powder
1 teaspoon salt
½ teaspoon baking soda
1 cup fresh cranberries, coarsely
    chopped

½ cup walnuts, chopped
1 teaspoon grated orange peel
1 egg, beaten
¾ cup orange juice
2 tablespoons vegetable oil

PROCEDURE:

Preheat oven to 350°. Sift flour, sugar, baking powder, salt and soda together. Stir in cranberries, walnuts and orange peel. Set aside. Combine egg, orange juice and oil. Add to dry ingredients, stirring just until moistened. Pour into greased loaf pan. Bake for 50 minutes or until done. Remove from pan and cool on rack.

Perfect for holiday gift giving!

Alyce Gibbs

Banana Nut Bread

Yields 1 loaf

INGREDIENTS:

2 cups flour
1 teaspoon baking soda
½ teaspoon salt
3 ripe bananas, mashed

1 cup sugar
½ cup margarine, melted
2 eggs, beaten
¼ cup walnuts (or pecans), chopped

PROCEDURE:

Preheat oven to 325°. Sift together flour, soda and salt. Set aside. Mix bananas, sugar, margarine and eggs together. Add dry ingredients and mix well. Stir in nuts. Pour into greased loaf pan. Bake for 1 hour.

Easy and delicious snack in a hurry!

Anita Strauss

363

Pumpkin Nut Bread With Grand Marnier Glaze

Yields 3 loaves

INGREDIENTS:

2 cups pumpkin purée
4 eggs
1 cup oil
1 cup water
3 cups sugar
3⅓ cups flour
2 teaspoons salt
2 teaspoons baking soda

½ teaspoon baking powder
1 teaspoon ground cloves
1 teaspoon cinnamon
1 teaspoon nutmeg
1 teaspoon allspice
4 cups shelled, whole walnuts
2 cups powdered sugar
¼ cup Grand Marnier

PROCEDURE:

Preheat oven to 325°. Combine pumpkin, eggs, oil, water and sugar. Set aside. Mix together flour, salt, soda, baking powder and spices. Add to pumpkin mixture. Stir in nuts. Pour into 3 greased loaf pans. Bake for 1 hour and 10 minutes or until toothpick inserted in center comes out clean. Partially cool; then transfer from pans to cooling rack. Mix powdered sugar and Grand Marnier together. Drizzle over tops of loaves.

Perfect for holiday meals or as a gift!

Judie Dresser

Irish Soda Bread

Yields 1 loaf

INGREDIENTS:

2 cups flour
1 tablespoon sugar
1½ teaspoons baking powder
1 teaspoon baking soda
¼ teaspoon salt
¼ cup butter (or margarine),
    softened

¾ cup raisins
1½ teaspoons caraway seeds
    (optional)
1 cup buttermilk
1 egg, lightly beaten with 1 table-
    spoon water

PROCEDURE:

Preheat oven to 375°. Sift flour, sugar, baking powder, soda and salt into a large mixing bowl. Cut in butter with a pastry blender until mixture resembles coarse meal. Stir in raisins and caraway seeds. Add buttermilk. Blend to moisten the dry ingredients. Turn dough onto floured board. Knead for several minutes until smooth. Form dough into a round ball and place on greased baking sheet. Flatten ball until dough is about 1½" high. Brush top and sides with egg-water mixture. Cut a ½" deep cross in top of bread with sharp knife. Bake for 30-40 minutes or until toothpick inserted in center comes out clean. Transfer to wire rack to cool. Brush top with butter or margarine and cover with cloth.

Serve warm with lots of butter!

Valerie Bauer

Gingerbread

Serves 12

INGREDIENTS:

¾ cup margarine
½ cup sugar
1 egg
1 cup molasses
2½ cups flour
1½ teaspoons baking soda

½ teaspoon salt
1 teaspoon ginger
½ teaspoon cloves
½ teaspoon cinnamon
1 cup boiling water

PROCEDURE:

Preheat oven to 350°. Cream margarine and sugar until light and fluffy. Add egg and molasses. Beat thoroughly. Sift together dry ingredients. Add to molasses mixture alternately with boiling water, beating after each addition. Bake in well-greased 9" by 9" pan for 30-40 minutes.

Delicious served warm with whipped cream!

Theresa Worsch

Beer Bread

Yields 1 loaf

INGREDIENTS:

3 cups self-rising flour
2 eggs
3 tablespoons sugar

1 teaspoon salt
1 12-ounce bottle beer, at room
    temperature
melted butter (optional)

PROCEDURE:

Mix all ingredients together. Let rise for 20 minutes. Pour into greased loaf pan. Put in cold oven for 20 minutes, then bake at 350° for 60 minutes. If desired, spoon melted butter over bread halfway through cooking time.

Great toasted in slices with butter and jam for breakfast! Also makes a welcome hostess gift.

Kiki Henry
Polly M. Wolf

Popovers

Serves 6

INGREDIENTS:

1¼ cups sifted flour
½ teaspoon salt

1¼ cups milk
3 jumbo eggs

PROCEDURE:

Preheat oven to 425°. Sift together flour and salt. Add milk and mix only until well-blended. Add one egg at a time, beating each in until completely blended. Do not overbeat. Pour batter into well-greased popover cups or muffin tins, filling each slightly more than half full. Bake for 20 minutes. Without opening oven door, reduce temperature to 325° and continue baking for 15-20 minutes longer or until golden brown. Serve immediately.

Delicious served hot with butter and honey!

Christy Rantzow

Zucchini Nut Muffins

Yields 18

INGREDIENTS:

2 eggs
½ cup brown sugar, packed
½ cup honey
½ cup butter, melted
1 teaspoon vanilla extract
1¾ cup flour
1 teaspoon baking soda

1 teaspoon salt
½ teaspoon baking powder
1 teaspoon ground nutmeg
3 teaspoons cinnamon
1 cup granola cereal
½ cup nuts, chopped
2 cups zucchini, grated

PROCEDURE:

Preheat oven to 350°. Beat eggs lightly in large bowl. Beat in brown sugar, honey, butter and vanilla. Add dry ingredients and stir until evenly moistened. Stir in granola, nuts and zucchini. Fill 18 well-greased muffin cups ¾ full. Bake for 25 minutes.

These freeze beautifully!

Connie Engelhardt

Lemon Muffins

Yields 18

INGREDIENTS:

¾ cup shortening
1 cup sugar
4 eggs, separated
2 cups flour, sifted

2 teaspoons baking powder
1 teaspoon salt
½ cup lemon juice
2 teaspoons grated lemon rind

PROCEDURE:

Preheat oven to 375°. Cream sugar and shortening. Beat egg yolks and blend in flour, baking powder and salt. Add to creamed mixture alternately with lemon juice. Beat egg whites until stiff. Fold egg whites and lemon rind into flour mixture. Place in greased muffin tins. Bake for 20 minutes until lightly browned.

Libby Clemmer

Raisin Bran Muffins

Yields 30

INGREDIENTS:

1 cup All Bran cereal
1 cup raisins
1 cup boiling water
½ cup oil
1 cup sugar
1¼ cup honey
2 cups buttermilk
2 eggs, beaten
1½ teaspoons vanilla extract
1 teaspoon brandy

2 tablespoons molasses
2 tablespoons grated orange rind
1½ cups whole wheat flour
1 cup white flour
1 tablespoon baking soda
1 teaspoon salt
1 teaspoon cinnamon
½ teaspoon nutmeg
¼ teaspoon allspice
2 cups bran buds

PROCEDURE:

Mix together All Bran, raisins and boiling water. Stir in oil, sugar, honey and buttermilk. Add eggs, vanilla, brandy, molasses and orange rind. Mix well. Stir flours, soda, salt and spices together. Add to first mixture, blending lightly and sprinkling in bran buds until all are moist. Cover bowl and let stand in refrigerator overnight. (Batter will keep up to 10 days in refrigerator). Preheat oven to 350°. Fill greased muffin tins ⅔ full. Bake for 25-30 minutes.

This is a recipe from Ireland, circa 1885, updated with today's bran products.

Anne Lee

Cheese Braids

Yields 32

INGREDIENTS:

1 cup sour cream
½ cup sugar
1 teaspoon salt
½ cup butter, melted
2 packages yeast
½ cup warm water
2 eggs, beaten
4 cups flour, white or wheat
16 ounces cream cheese, softened

¾ cup sugar
1 egg
⅛ teaspoon salt
2 teaspoons vanilla (or almond) extract
2 cups powdered sugar
4 tablespoons milk
2 teaspoons vanilla extract

PROCEDURE:

Heat sour cream over low heat. Stir in sugar, salt and butter. Cool to lukewarm. Sprinkle yeast over warm water in large bowl stirring until yeast is dissolved. Add sour cream mixture, eggs and flour and mix well. Cover tightly and refrigerate overnight. Next day, combine cream cheese and sugar in small mixing bowl. Add egg, salt and vanilla. Mix well and set aside. Divide dough into 4 equal parts. Roll out each on a well-floured board into 12″ by 8″ rectangles. Spread each with ¼ of the cream cheese mixture. Roll up, beginning at long sides. Pinch edges together and fold ends under. Place rolls seam side down on a greased baking sheet. Slit each roll to resemble braids. Cover and let rise in a warm place until doubled in size. Bake at 350° for 12-15 minutes. Combine powdered sugar, milk and vanilla. Mix well. Glaze warm rolls with mixture.

Terri Albritton

Cinnamon Rolls

Yields 30

INGREDIENTS:

2 packages dry yeast
2½ cups whole milk, warmed
1 teaspoon salt
¾ cup sugar
½ cup butter, softened
1 egg

4-6 cups flour
½ cup butter, softened
cinnamon to taste
nutmeats (optional)
candied fruits or dates (optional)

PROCEDURE:

Approximately 2 hours before ingredients are mixed, combine yeast with ½ cup lukewarm milk and set aside. (It will be ready for use when bubbles appear on surface). Mix thoroughly 2 cups warm milk, salt, ½ cup sugar, ½ cup butter and egg. Add yeast mixture. Begin adding flour gradually until mixture is neither sticky nor dry, working in more flour only when bubbles appear on surface of mixture. (Use only amount of flour necessary as too much flour makes rolls cakey). With buttered hands, place dough in large, greased bowl. Allow to rise until doubled in size, about 1½-2 hours. Butter hands and place half the dough on a well-floured pastry board. Shape into a 15″-18″ square. Spread ¼ cup butter over square. Sprinkle on ¼ cup sugar and cinnamon to taste. Nutmeats, candied fruits or dates can be added at this time, if desired. Roll up dough into a tight log. Cut into slices and place ½″ apart in buttered pie pans. Repeat with other half of dough. Allow to rise for 1 hour. Preheat oven to 350°. Bake for 20-25 minutes or until browned. Spread lightly with butter while warm. Add glaze or icing after cooled if desired.

Tim Burns

Dilly Casserole Bread

Serves 6

INGREDIENTS:

1 package active dry yeast
¼ cup warm water
1 cup creamed cottage cheese, warmed
2 tablespoons sugar
1 tablespoon instant minced onion

1 tablespoon butter, softened
2 teaspoons dill seed
1 teaspoon salt
¼ teaspoon baking soda
1 egg
2¼-2½ cups flour

PROCEDURE:

Soften yeast in water. Heat cottage cheese to lukewarm. Combine in mixing bowl warmed cottage cheese, sugar, onion, butter, dill seed, salt, soda, egg and softened yeast. Add flour to form stiff dough, beating well after each addition. Cover. Let rise in warm place (85°-90°F) until light and doubled in size, 50-60 minutes. Stir dough down. Turn into well-greased, 8" round, 1½-2 quart casserole. Let rise in warm place until light, 30-40 minutes. Bake at 350° for 40-50 minutes until golden brown. Brush with soft butter and sprinkle with salt.

Libby Clemmer

Herb Bread

Serves 20

INGREDIENTS:

1 loaf white sandwich bread, unsliced
¾ cup margarine
¼ teaspoon salt

½ teaspoon thyme
¼ teaspoon paprika
¼ teaspoon savory
dash of cayenne pepper

PROCEDURE:

Preheat oven to 375°. Cut off top crust, ends, and sides of bread, but leave bottom crust on. Cut bread in half lengthwise, being careful not to cut through the bottom crust. Cut crosswise into even slices, again being careful not to cut through bottom crust. Mix remaining ingredients together. Frost top, sides and between slices with margarine mixture. Place on cookie sheet. Bake for 15-20 minutes.

Beverly Fipp

Southern Spoon Bread

Serves 6

INGREDIENTS:

1¾ cup yellow cornmeal
¼ cup butter
1 teaspoon salt
boiling water

1 cup buttermilk
1 teaspoon baking soda
3 eggs, well beaten
½ teaspoon baking powder

PROCEDURE:

Preheat oven to 350°. To cornmeal, butter and salt add, while beating, enough boiling water to make a thick mush. (The amount varies according to hardness and milling of corn). Mix soda and buttermilk until foaming ceases. Pour over mush mixture. Add eggs and baking powder. Mix well. Pour into greased 1½-quart casserole. Bake for 45-60 minutes or until knife blade inserted in center leaves no batter residue.

Serve with butter and syrup to complement country ham or bacon.

Barbara Judy

Spoon Bread

Serves 6

INGREDIENTS:

3 cups milk
1¼ cups cornmeal
1 teaspoon salt

3 eggs, well beaten
2 tablespoons butter
1¾ teaspoons baking powder

PROCEDURE:

Preheat oven to 350°. Heat milk in saucepan. Add cornmeal and stir while bringing to a boil over medium heat. Let thicken and remove from heat. Cool for a few minutes. Add salt, eggs, butter and baking powder. Pour into buttered 1½-quart square glass baking dish. Bake for 30-40 minutes until firm.

Serve hot with a spoon. Eat with a fork!

Phyllis Queen Healy

Southern Corn Bread

Serves 6

INGREDIENTS:

2 tablespoons melted bacon grease
¾ cup plus 2 tablespoons yellow,
    stone-ground cornmeal
¼ cup flour
1 teaspoon sugar

1 teaspoon baking powder
1 teaspoon salt
¼ teaspoon baking soda
1 cup buttermilk
1 egg

PROCEDURE:

Preheat oven to 450°. Melt bacon grease in 8″ square pan. Coat pan with grease. Pour out excess and reserve. Dust pan with cornmeal. Mix dry ingredients together. Add buttermilk, egg and reserved bacon grease. Mix thoroughly. Put prepared pan in preheated oven for one minute. Remove and pour in the batter. Bake for 25 minutes or until golden brown.

This is a part of Southern Corn Bread dressing, (see p. 238) but can also be served hot out of the oven and cut into squares with butter.

Martha McCardell

Mexican Corn Bread

Serves 6

INGREDIENTS:

1 8½-ounce package corn bread
    mix
1 9-ounce can cream corn

2 tablespoons margarine, melted
1 4-ounce can whole green chiles
1½ cups cheddar cheese, grated

PROCEDURE:

Preheat oven to 375°. Prepare corn bread mix according to directions. Stir in corn and margarine. Put half of mixture in greased 9″ by 9″ pan. Cut chiles into strips. Place half of chiles and half of grated cheese over batter. Pour on remaining batter. Add remaining chiles and cheese. Bake for 30 minutes.

Melody Gentry

Corn Bread Casserole

Serves 16

INGREDIENTS:

2 large onions, chopped
6 tablespoons butter
2 eggs
2 tablespoons milk
2 17-ounce cans cream style corn

1 16-ounce package cornmeal
  muffin mix
8 ounces sour cream
2 cups sharp cheddar cheese,
  shredded

PROCEDURE:

Preheat oven to 425°. In a medium skillet, sauté onions in butter until golden. Set aside. In a medium bowl, mix eggs and milk until blended. Add corn and muffin mix. Mix well. Spread batter into buttered 13" by 9" baking dish. Spoon sautéed onions over top. Spread sour cream over onions and sprinkle with cheese. Bake for 35 minutes. Let stand 10 minutes before cutting into squares.

A wonderful accompaniment to any special meal!

Judy Levine

Moreen's Birthday Bread

Serves 10

INGREDIENTS:

2 packages dry yeast
½ cup warm water
1 cup milk, scalded
4 tablespoons honey

1 teaspoon salt
½ cup margarine, melted
3½ cups whole wheat flour
½ cup butter, melted

PROCEDURE:

In large bowl, mix yeast and warm water. Let stand 5 minutes. Scald milk and allow to cool to lukewarm. Stir yeast mixture gently. Add milk, honey, salt and margarine. Add ½ of the flour and stir well. Add second half of flour and beat well until all is evenly blended. (Dough will be like batter). Put bowl in a warm place, cover with a damp towel, and allow to rise until doubled in size (about 1 hour). Punch down and roll out of bowl on a lightly floured board. Let rest 10 minutes. Preheat oven to 400°. Roll dough out to ¼" thickness. Cut into diamond shapes about 2½" long. Dip each piece in melted butter and arrange in a 9" ring mold until ½ full. Cover and let rise until doubled in size (about 30 minutes). Bake for 30 minutes or until brown.

Geri Caceres

Puffed Apple Pancake

Serves 8

INGREDIENTS:

6 eggs
1¼ cups milk
1 cup flour
3 tablespoons sugar
1 teaspoon vanilla extract

½ teaspoon salt
¼ teaspoon cinnamon
½ cup butter
2 apples, peeled and thinly sliced
3 tablespoons brown sugar

PROCEDURE:

Preheat oven to 425°. In a blender, mix eggs, milk, flour, sugar, vanilla, salt and cinnamon until blended. Melt butter in a 12" quiche pan or a 13" by 9" baking dish in oven. Arrange apple slices in baking dish. Return to oven until butter sizzles. Do not let butter brown. Remove dish from oven and immediately pour batter over apples. Sprinkle with brown sugar. Bake in middle of oven for approximately 20 minutes or until puffed and brown. Serve immediately.

Great for Sunday brunch!

Marti Oliva

Mexicali Breakfast Stew

Serves 6

INGREDIENTS:

1 4-ounce can diced chiles
1 4-ounce can chopped black olives
2 green onions, chopped
3 fresh tomatoes, chopped
chopped parsley to taste

¼ cup wine vinegar
2 tablespoons oil
garlic salt to taste
2 avocadoes, diced

PROCEDURE:

Combine all ingredients except avocadoes. Add avocadoes just before serving over scrambled eggs or in cheese omelet. Best when prepared in advance (without avocadoes) and allowed to stand for flavors to blend.

Cindy Wise

Sunday Morning Pancakes

Serves 4

INGREDIENTS:

4 eggs
16 ounces sour cream
1 cup flour
½ teaspoon salt

½ teaspoon baking soda
½ teaspoon baking powder
1 tablespoon oil

PROCEDURE:

Blend eggs and sour cream. Sift together flour, salt, soda and baking powder. Add to egg mixture and blend well. Mix in oil until batter is smooth. Brown on lightly greased griddle over medium-high heat.

Also great as waffles.

Linda Goodwin

Oatmeal Pancakes

Serves 4

INGREDIENTS:

2 cups regular Quaker oats
2 cups buttermilk
2 eggs, lightly beaten
¼ cup margarine, melted
½ cup raisins
½ cup flour

2 tablespoons sugar
1 teaspoon baking soda
1 teaspoon baking powder
½ teaspoon cinnamon
½ teaspoon salt

PROCEDURE:

Mix oats and buttermilk. Soak in refrigerator overnight. Add eggs, margarine and raisins. Mix together dry ingredients and add to batter. Brown on lightly greased griddle over medium-high heat.

A healthy breakfast served with fresh fruit or applesauce!

Joan Marvil

Cottage Cheese Pancakes

Serves 4

INGREDIENTS:

1 cup cottage cheese
4 eggs
pinch of salt

6 tablespoons butter, melted
½ cup flour

PROCEDURE:

Place all ingredients in blender and process until nearly smooth. Brown on lightly greased griddle over medium-high heat.

Delicate flavor, great with jam!

Joan Marvil

Marv's Swedish Pancakes

Serves 4

INGREDIENTS:

6 eggs, well beaten
2 cups flour
1 teaspoon salt

2 tablespoons sugar
2 cups milk

PROCEDURE:

Beat together first 4 ingredients. Add milk and beat well. Put small amount of butter in pan before cooking each pancake. Swirl pan to coat entire bottom of pan thinly. Use about ½ cup or less per pancake. Do not overcook.

Also wonderful served as main dish or dessert crêpes.

Michelle Benson

Weightless Waffles

Serves 6

INGREDIENTS:

1 cup whole wheat flour
1 cup white flour
¼-½ cup soy flour
2 teaspoons baking powder
1 teaspoon baking soda

½ teaspoon salt (optional)
2 eggs, separated
2½ cups milk (or buttermilk)
2½ tablespoons vegetable oil

PROCEDURE:

Mix dry ingredients in large bowl. Beat egg whites until stiff. Mix egg yolks, milk and oil together. Combine with dry ingredients stirring just enough to eliminate lumps. Fold in egg whites being careful not to stir too much. Cook in waffle iron, using about ½ cup per waffle. Nuts, coconut or raisins can be added before cooking, if desired. Serve with fruit, whipped cream, jam, syrup or garnish of your choice.

Al E. Rubottom

Pumpkin Waffles

Serves 6

INGREDIENTS:

2¼ cups flour
4 teaspoons baking powder
2 teaspoons cinnamon
1 teaspoon allspice
1 teaspoon ginger
½ teaspoon salt

¼ cup brown sugar
4 eggs, separated
1 cup pumpkin (canned or fresh)
2 cups milk
¼ cup margarine, melted

PROCEDURE:

Combine dry ingredients. Beat egg whites until they form soft peaks. Set aside. Combine pumpkin, milk, egg yolks and margarine. Stir in dry ingredients. Fold in egg whites. Cook in waffle iron. Top with nut butter made by combining ½ cup soft butter, ½ cup chopped nuts and 1 teaspoon grated orange peel.

Spectacular for a holiday breakfast!

Helen Russell

377

Aunt Ann's Jelly

Yields 3 cups

INGREDIENTS:

3 cups fruit juice (apple, grape, etc).

1 teaspoon cream of tartar
3 cups white sugar

PROCEDURE:

Bring juice to a boil in saucepan. Stir in cream of tartar and sugar. Boil gently until syrupy and 2 heavy drops cling to a wooden spoon (approximately 1½-2 hours). Pour into mason jars, label and enjoy on warm bread.

Ann Perry Shepard

Lemon Jam

Yields 4 cups

INGREDIENTS:

1½ cups sugar
½ cup butter
4 eggs, lightly beaten

4 lemon rinds, grated
juice of 4 lemons

PROCEDURE:

Place sugar and butter in saucepan. Add eggs and mix well with whisk. Add lemon rind. Stir slowly over low heat until ingredients have melted. Add lemon juice. Cook slowly over medium heat, stirring constantly. Allow to boil for a few minutes. Cool before storing.

Excellent on toast for breakfast. Also a great cake filling or a lovely gift!

Theresa Worsch

14

Just For Kids

Orange Blossom Special

Serves 4-6

INGREDIENTS:

1 cup milk
6 ounces frozen orange juice

¼ cup sugar
1 teaspoon vanilla extract
20 ice cubes

PROCEDURE:

Combine all ingredients in blender, process.

Add a raw egg for a quick, nutritious breakfast.

Galen Cooper

Banana Smoothies

Serves 4

INGREDIENTS:

2 medium bananas, cut in 1"
    pieces
1½ cups milk

8 ounces plain yogurt
2 tablespoons sugar
1 teaspoon vanilla extract

PROCEDURE:

Wrap banana pieces in plastic wrap and freeze several hours. Place ½ of the frozen bananas in blender, along with the remaining ingredients. Blend until well mixed. Add remaining bananas and blend until smooth.

Melody Gentry

Sunshine

Serves 4

INGREDIENTS:

1½ cups freshly squeezed orange
    juice
1½ cups frozen unsweetened berries

1 medium banana, peeled
1 tablespoon protein powder
    (optional)

PROCEDURE:

Liquify all ingredients in a blender and serve with a straw.

Hedy Brehm

The Utmost In Lemonade

Serves 8

INGREDIENTS:

7 cups water
1⅓ cups sugar

1 cup lemon juice
juice of 1 orange

PROCEDURE:

Combine 1 cup of water with sugar. Bring to a boil and simmer 2 minutes.
Cool. Add remaining ingredients and serve chilled over ice.

Sandra Harding

Polka Dot Pancakes

Serves 4-6

INGREDIENTS:

1 8-ounce package Brown and
  Serve sausage links
1 cup all-purpose flour
2 tablespoons sugar
2 teaspoons baking powder

¼ teaspoon salt
¾ cup milk
1 egg
3 tablespoons butter, melted

PROCEDURE:

Preheat oven to 375°. Cut sausages into ½″ slices, cook until brown, stirring occasionally. Drain on paper towels and set aside. Mix dry ingredients in large bowl. In a small bowl combine milk, egg and butter. Pour egg mixture into flour mixture, stir until moist. Batter will be lumpy. Pour batter into greased 11″ by 7″ by 2″ baking pan. Sprinkle with sausage. Bake 25 minutes or until golden.

A wonderful Saturday morning treat.

Susan Bendon

Breakfast Pancake

Serves 4

INGREDIENTS:

½ cup flour
2 eggs
½ cup milk
pinch of nutmeg

¼ cup butter, melted
2 tablespoons confectioner's sugar
juice of ½ lemon

PROCEDURE:

Preheat oven to 425°. Mix flour, eggs, milk and nutmeg (leaving batter a bit lumpy). Pour butter into an 8″ pie plate and cover with batter. Bake 15-20 minutes until golden brown. Sprinkle with confectioner's sugar and return briefly to oven. Sprinkle with lemon juice. Cut into wedges and serve at once.

Nichole Fipp
Lucy Smith

381

Super Soup

Serves 6

INGREDIENTS:

6 cups boiling water
½ teaspoon salt
1 7¼-ounce package macaroni and
    cheese mixture
1 10-ounce package frozen mixed
    vegetables

¼ cup butter
¼ cup flour
2 13¾-ounce cans chicken broth
1½ cups milk

PROCEDURE:

Boil macaroni in salted water for 5 minutes. Add frozen vegetables, cover and simmer over medium heat for 5 more minutes. Drain well. Melt butter in 3-quart saucepan, add flour and stir until smooth. Pour in the powdered cheese sauce mix from macaroni package and blend well. Add the broth and milk, stirring until mixture comes to a boil. Stir in the macaroni and vegetables, cooking until soup is heated through.

Cindy Wise

Mini Pizzas

Serves 4

INGREDIENTS:

2 English muffins, split
1 8-ounce jar pizza sauce

8 ounces mozzarella cheese,
    shredded
16 slices pepperoni

PROCEDURE:

Cover each muffin half with pizza sauce. Sprinkle with cheese, pepperoni or topping of your choice. Broil or microwave until cheese melts.

An old time favorite that never fails.

Marilyn Greco

Tuna Dogs

Serves 10

INGREDIENTS:

2 6½-ounce cans of tuna, flaked
4 hard boiled eggs, chopped
½ pound cheddar cheese, grated
4 tablespoons sweet pickle relish

½ cup mayonnaise
10 hot dog rolls
butter, softened

PROCEDURE:

Preheat oven to 400°. Mix together the flaked tuna, chopped eggs, cheese, relish and mayonnaise. Split the rolls and carefully scoop out some of the bread. Butter both sides and stuff with tuna mixture. Wrap each bun in a long piece of foil, twisting the ends to look like a firecracker. Bake 15-20 minutes.

Gloria Andújar

Banana Dogs

Serves 4

INGREDIENTS:

¾ cup peanut butter
2 tablespoons honey
4 hot dog buns, split

2 small bananas
1 tablespoon lemon juice

PROCEDURE:

Combine peanut butter with honey. Spread 3 tablespoons on each bun. Cut bananas in half lengthwise and coat with lemon juice. Place on bun.

Ben Garcia
John Garcia

Tortilla Dogs

Serves 4

INGREDIENTS:

4 hot dogs
4 tortillas (medium size)

4 ounces cheddar cheese, grated
hot sauce (optional)

PROCEDURE:

Preheat oven to 350°. Place hot dogs on tortillas, sprinkle with cheese and hot sauce. Roll and secure with toothpicks. Bake 8-10 minutes.

Brent Clemmer

Spaghetti Pie

Serves 6

INGREDIENTS:

6 ounces spaghetti
6 cups boiling water
2 tablespoons butter
2 eggs
⅓ cup Parmesan cheese, grated

½ pound lean ground beef
1 medium onion, chopped
1 8-ounce can pizza sauce
8 ounces mozzarella cheese,
    shredded

PROCEDURE:

Preheat oven to 350°. Boil spaghetti in water until tender. Drain and toss with butter. Beat eggs lightly with fork, add cheese and mix well. Combine with spaghetti. Pour spaghetti mixture into buttered 9″ pie plate. Mold spaghetti into the shape of a pie crust. Brown ground beef and onions. Add pizza sauce, stirring well. Spoon meat mixture into the crust. Bake 20 minutes, sprinkle with cheese and return to oven for 5 minutes. Let stand for 5 minutes. Serve as you would a pizza.

Carol Garcia

Hot Diggity Apple Dogs

Serves 6

INGREDIENTS:

8 medium apples, peeled and sliced
 ¼" thick
juice of 1 lemon

½ cup brown sugar
12 hot dogs, sliced 1½" thick

PROCEDURE:

Preheat oven to 375°. Toss apples with lemon juice and sugar. Layer apples and hot dogs in buttered 3-quart casserole. Cover and bake 35-40 minutes.

Peggy Zimmerman

Porcupines

Serves 4

INGREDIENTS:

1 egg
1 10¾-ounce can tomato soup
¼ cup long grain rice
2 tablespoons parsley
1 teaspoon minced onion
¼ teaspoon seasoning salt

dash of pepper
1 teaspoon soy sauce
1 pound lean ground meat
½ cup water
1 teaspoon Worcestershire sauce

PROCEDURE:

Combine egg and ¼ cup soup. Add rice, parsley, onion, salt, pepper and soy sauce. Stir until well mixed. Add ground meat, mixing well. Shape into 1" meatballs. In a small bowl combine water, remaining soup and Worcestershire sauce. Pour over meatballs in skillet. Heat over medium heat until mixture begins to boil. Cover and simmer for 40 minutes, stirring occasionally.

Carolyn DeFever

Super Sandwich Filling

Serves 8

INGREDIENTS:

1 cup peanut butter (or cream
   cheese)
1 entire orange, cut in pieces (Yes!
   rind, sections, the works — just
   pop it in)

2 tablespoons carrot, grated
2 tablespoons raisins
2 tablespoons walnuts

PROCEDURE:

Combine all ingredients in food processor, blender or grinder. Process until smooth. Spread on whole wheat bread.

Brooke Suiter

Quick And Easy Sandwich

Serves 1

INGREDIENTS:

2 slices of bread (I like whole
   wheat, but almost any kind will
   do).
3-4 tablespoons Skippy Super
   Chunk peanut butter (I try to
   stay away from the organic
   stuff, it has to be stirred and
   gets oil all over the kitchen
   counter).

3-4 tablespoons boysenberry
   preserves (The kind with the
   seeds left in. The Knott's
   version, though expensive,
   offers an interesting history of
   the boysenberry on the label).

PROCEDURE:

Spread peanut butter on one slice of bread. Spread preserves on top of that and cover with remaining slice of bread. Cut in half, if you like, and serve. That's it. Delicious.

Particularly wonderful if served with love. Your thousandth will taste as good as your first.

Peter Becker

Vegetable Pastry Casserole

Serves 8

INGREDIENTS:

2 10-ounce packages frozen green
   beans
1 10¾-ounce can condensed cream
   of celery soup
¼ cup milk

1 cup cheddar cheese, shredded
½ teaspoon dried basil
1 8-ounce package refrigerated
   flakey dinner rolls

PROCEDURE:

Preheat 350°. Cook beans according to directions and drain. Combine soup and milk in large bowl. Stir in cheese, beans and basil. Place mixture in 10" by 6" by 2" baking dish. Bake for 20 minutes. Meanwhile separate dinner roll dough into 12 pieces, cut each in half. Place the halves around the outside of the casserole. Return to oven and bake 20 minutes longer.

For variety, other vegetables may be substituted for green beans.

Liz Haberman

Popovers

Serves 6

INGREDIENTS:

2 cups flour
2 cups milk

2 eggs
unsalted butter

PROCEDURE:

Preheat oven to 475°. Mix together flour, milk and eggs. Batter should be somewhat lumpy. Very thoroughly grease muffin tins and fill ⅔ full with batter. Bake 20-25 minutes until golden brown.

Michael Bliss

387

Soft Whole Wheat Pretzels

Serves 12

INGREDIENTS:

2 16-ounce loaves frozen
   wholewheat bread dough
1 egg white, slightly beaten

1 teaspoon water
coarse salt

PROCEDURE:

Preheat oven to 350°. Thaw bread in refrigerator overnight. Divide each loaf into 12 pieces. Roll into ½" snakes, then form into desired shapes. Arrange on greased cookie sheet and let stand for 20 minutes. Combine egg white with water and brush on pretzels, topping with coarse salt. Place shallow pan containing 1" of hot water on a lower rack in the oven. Place cookie sheet on rack above the water and bake for 20 minutes.

Raw pretzels may be topped with melted butter, cinnamon and sugar instead of egg and salt.

Julie Harris

Soft Pretzels

Serves 12

INGREDIENTS:

1½ cups warm water
1 package dry yeast
1 teaspoon salt
1 tablespoon sugar

4 cups flour
1 egg, beaten
coarse salt

PROCEDURE:

Preheat oven to 425°. Measure water into a large bowl and sprinkle with yeast. Mix in salt, sugar and flour. Turn out dough onto floured surface and knead until well blended. Roll bits of dough into ¾" snakes, then shape into letters, numbers or designs. Place pretzels on a greased cookie sheet. Brush pretzels with beaten egg and sprinkle with coarse salt. Bake 12-15 minutes.

A super small group cooking project.

Barbara Begg   Ginger Lynch

Snacks On A Stick

Serves 10

INGREDIENTS:

3 cups miniature marshmallows
¼ cup butter
¼ cup creamy peanut butter
3 cups Cheerios

½ cup raisins
⅓ cup roasted sunflower seeds
10 wooden popsicle sticks

PROCEDURE:

Combine marshmallows and butter in saucepan. Stir over low heat until smooth. Add peanut butter and blend. Remove from heat and add remaining ingredients. Mix and let stand 2 minutes. Shape into balls with buttered hands, insert sticks and allow to set for ½ hour on waxed paper.

A good alternative for a party treat.

Melody Gentry

Oyster Cracker Snacks

Serves 10-12

INGREDIENTS:

2 5-ounce packages oyster crackers
1 teaspoon dill weed
½ teaspoon lemon pepper

1 package Hidden Valley Ranch
    Dressing mix
½ cup salad oil, warmed

PROCEDURE:

Mix together dry ingredients. Pour warm oil over mixture tossing until oil is absorbed. Let stand ½ hour before serving.

Pat Lang

389

Marshmallow Popcorn Balls

Serves 8

INGREDIENTS:

6 tablespoons butter
3 cups miniature marshmallows
3 tablespoons raspberry Jello
    powder

3 quarts unsalted prepared popcorn

PROCEDURE:

Melt butter in large saucepan over low heat. Add marshmallows stirring until mixture is totally melted. Remove from heat and blend in Jello. Mix into popcorn, then form balls with buttered hands.

Walda Brooks

Peanut Butter Crunchies

Yields 4 dozen

INGREDIENTS:

4 cups cornflakes
1 cup butter, softened
½ cup peanut butter
½ cup white sugar
½ cup brown sugar

1 egg
2 teaspoons vanilla extract
1½ cup all-purpose flour
48 peanuts

PROCEDURE:

Preheat oven to 350°. Crush cornflakes into fine crumbs, set aside. In large bowl mix butter and peanut butter. Add the sugars, egg and vanilla. Beat thoroughly and stir in flour. Shape mixture into small balls and roll in cornflake crumbs. Place on greased baking sheet. Press a peanut into each ball. Bake for 15 minutes.

Gloria Andújar

Rice Krispies Cheese Balls

Serves 20-25

INGREDIENTS:

2 cups Rice Krispies
1 cup margarine, softened
2 cups flour
10 ounces sharp cheddar cheese,
    grated

½ teaspoon salt
½ teaspoon cayenne pepper

PROCEDURE:

Preheat oven to 350°. Crush Rice Krispies very fine. Blend together all ingredients. Shape into small balls (approximately 60-70). Bake 20 minutes or until light brown. Can be frozen indefinitely. Warm when ready to serve.

Kay Kirstein

Fruit Snowballs

Serves 8

INGREDIENTS:

1 16-ounce can fruit cocktail
½ cup miniature marshmallows
½ cup strawberry yogurt

2 tablespoons mayonnaise
1 cup whipping cream, whipped
    and sweetened to taste

PROCEDURE:

Drain fruit cocktail and place in large bowl. Add marshmallows, yogurt and mayonnaise, mixing well. Gently fold in whipped cream. Use an ice cream scoop to put fruit mixture into muffin tin lined with paper bake cups. Freeze 2 hours, then allow to soften slightly before serving. May be kept in freezer for weeks if wrapped in plastic.

Mary Miller

Frozen Grapes

INGREDIENTS:

Thompson seedless grapes, stems
    intact

PROCEDURE:

Place small bunches of grapes in baggies and put in freezer. May be eaten
after several hours or keeps for weeks in the freezer.

A refreshing, natural snack.

Dick Morgan

Knox Blox Finger Treats

Serves 12

INGREDIENTS:

4 envelopes Knox unflavored
    gelatine
3 3-ounce packages flavored
    gelatin

4 cups boiling water

PROCEDURE:

Combine gelatines and boiling water, stirring until completely dissolved.
Pour into 13" by 9" pan. Chill until firm. Cut into squares and serve or
shape with holiday cookie cutters for special occasions.

Candy Karas

Grape Finger Jello

Serves 12

INGREDIENTS:

3 envelopes unflavored gelatine
1 12-ounce can frozen grape juice
   concentrate, thawed

1½ cups boiling water

PROCEDURE:

Soften gelatine in juice concentrate. Combine with boiling water and stir until gelatine has completely dissolved. Pour into lightly buttered 9" by 13" glass pan and chill for three hours. Cut into squares and serve

An alternative to the traditional finger jello.

Hedy Brehm

Blueberry Yogurt Pops

Serves 10

INGREDIENTS:

2 8-ounce cartons blueberry yogurt
1 10-ounce package frozen
   blueberries, thawed

10 3-ounce cold drink paper cups
10 wooden popsicle sticks

PROCEDURE:

Combine yogurt and blueberries in a small bowl. Stir until blended. Fill cups ⅔ full. Place cups in freezer until partially frozen (about 1 hour). Insert sticks and freeze until hard. Peel off the paper cups before serving.

Other fruits or yogurt flavors may be substituted in the amounts listed above.

Moreen Fielden

393

Apple Graham Cracker Surprise

Serves 1

INGREDIENTS:

3 Graham crackers
¼ cup applesauce

¼ cup heavy cream, sweetened and
   whipped

PROCEDURE:

Layer 3 Graham crackers with applesauce in between. Frost with whipped cream. Refrigerate for ½ hour.

A wonderful, easy treat — ask any preschooler!

Anita Tashchian

Apple Crisp

Serves 8

INGREDIENTS:

6 medium apples, peeled and sliced
   in ¼" slices
¾ cup packed brown sugar
½ cup flour

½ cup rolled oats
¾ teaspoon cinnamon
¾ teaspoon nutmeg
⅓ cup butter

PROCEDURE:

Preheat oven to 350°. Place apples in buttered 8" square pan. Blend remaining ingredients until mixture is crumbly. Spread the mixture over apples. Bake 35 minutes.

Barbara Begg

Peanut Butter Kisses

Yields 3 dozen

INGREDIENTS:

½ cup honey
1 cup peanut butter
1 cup non-fat dry milk

½ cup raisins
wheat germ (or powdered sugar)

PROCEDURE:

Thoroughly mix honey, peanut butter, dry milk and raisins. Shape into 1″ balls with hands then roll in wheat germ. May be refrigerated in air-tight container for several weeks.

Judie Dresser
Chris Grasso

Peanut Butter Squares

Serves 8-12

INGREDIENTS:

1 5-ounce package Graham
   crackers
1 pound powdered sugar

1¾ cup creamy peanut butter
¾ cup butter, softened
8 ounces chocolate chips

PROCEDURE:

Crush Graham crackers and combine with powdered sugar. Add peanut butter and butter, mixing well. Firmly pack in 9f310by 12f310baking pan. Melt chocolate chips. Spread evenly over peanut butter mixture. Refrigerate 10 minutes. Cut into squares.

Sally Peters Davidson

Datenut Dainties

Yields 2 dozen

INGREDIENTS:

½ cup peanut butter
½ tablespoon butter
½ cup powdered sugar

½ cup dates, chopped
¼ cup walnuts, chopped
6 ounces chocolate chips, melted

PROCEDURE:

Cream peanut butter, butter and sugar together. Mix in dates and nuts. Form dough into 1″ balls and dip into melted chocolate. Set on wax paper to cool.

Sonya Olsen

Monster Cookies

Yields 20 dozen

INGREDIENTS:

12 eggs
2 pounds brown sugar
1 tablespoon vanilla extract
8 tablespoons baking soda

1 pound butter
3 pounds chunky peanut butter
18 cups oatmeal
1 pound chocolate chips

PROCEDURE:

Preheat oven to 350°. Mix ingredients in order given in large bowl. Drop by teaspoonsful onto ungreased cookie sheets. Flatten each with a fork. Bake 10-12 minutes. Do not overbake.

They freeze well, pack well. Much appreciated by kids at college — the whole dorm!

Carolyn Butler

Cookie Paint

INGREDIENTS:

3 egg yolks
1 teaspoon water
1 teaspoon sugar

food coloring
sugar cookie dough

PROCEDURE:

Blend together egg yolks, water and sugar. Divide into 3-4 small containers and add desired food coloring. Using small paint brushes, decorate your favorite unbaked, cut-out cookies. Bake as usual, according to cookie directions.

When baked, this paint turns into a hardened glaze. A fun change from frosting.

Rebecca Gentry
Ryan Gentry

Chocolate Cutouts

Yields 40

INGREDIENTS:

8 ounces semisweet chocolate

PROCEDURE:

Melt chocolate in a double boiler. Whisk to eliminate all of the lumps. Pour the chocolate onto a cookie sheet lined with waxed paper. Spread it with a spatula until it is ⅛" thick. Refrigerate for 2 hours. Remove from the refrigerator. Using hors d'oeuvre cutters, cut the desired shapes. Decorate with powdered sugar or cocoa, if desired.

Lyn Heller

Tin Roof Sundae Bars

Yields 3 dozen

INGREDIENTS:

1 22½-ounce package fudge
   brownie mix
½ cup very hot water
½ cup oil
1 egg

1 7-ounce jar marshmallow cream
1½ cups peanuts
6 1.45-ounce Hershey milk
   chocolate bars, coarsely
   chopped

PROCEDURE:

Preheat oven to 350°. In large bowl combine brownie mix, hot water, oil and egg. Beat 50 strokes with spoon, then spread in buttered 13" by 9" pan. Bake 30 minutes. Remove from oven immediately. Spread marshmallow cream on top. Sprinkle evenly with peanuts. Top with candy bar pieces. Return to oven for 2 minutes or until chocolate is melted. Spread evenly to cover. Cool completely, cut into bars.

Evelin Nagy

Oreo Special

Serves 6-8

INGREDIENTS:

½ gallon vanilla ice cream

6-8 oreo cookies (or to taste)

PROCEDURE:

Allow vanilla ice cream to soften. Meanwhile crush cookies into crumbs (by hand or with food processor). Combine the crumbs with the ice cream, mixing well. Place in air tight container and return to freezer for 1 hour.

Jeff Przonek

Doughables!

Non-edible

Yields 1 dozen

INGREDIENTS:

1 cup salt
1½ cups hot water

4 cups flour

PROCEDURE:

Preheat oven 325°. Combine salt and hot water. Stir occasionally until mixture is cooled. Add flour, mix with spoon and shape into a ball with your hands. Knead 6-8 minutes until dough reaches a smooth consistency. Form ornaments on individual squares of aluminum foil. Make Mr. Santa, Mrs. Santa, soldier, drummer boy, angel, child with a doll or bear, or rocking horse — use your imagination. Insert a paper clip for hanging and bake for at least 40 minutes. Ornaments should turn beige and be moisture free. Paint with acrylic paints and spray with an acrylic spray to seal and shine.

For younger children, roll out dough and use cookie cutters.

Galen Cooper

Playdoh

Non-edible

INGREDIENTS:

2½ cups flour
½ cup salt
1 teaspoon powdered alum

1¾ cups boiling water
2 tablespoons salad oil
food coloring of your choice

PROCEDURE:

Combine all ingredients in bowl. Turn out on flat surface and knead until smooth. Store in air tight container at room temperature.

Baby oil may be substituted for salad oil. It smells wonderful and does great things for your hands!

Galen Cooper

399

Goop!

INGREDIENTS:

1 1-pound box cornstarch   food coloring (optional)
1-2 cups of water   smock (recommended)

PROCEDURE:

Place cornstarch in a large flat plastic container. Slowly add water as child stirs and squishes mixture with his hands. Consistency will vary depending on amount of water used. This is used for free, unstructured play in the container.

A wonderful tactile experience for a rainy day.

Sara Mastroianni

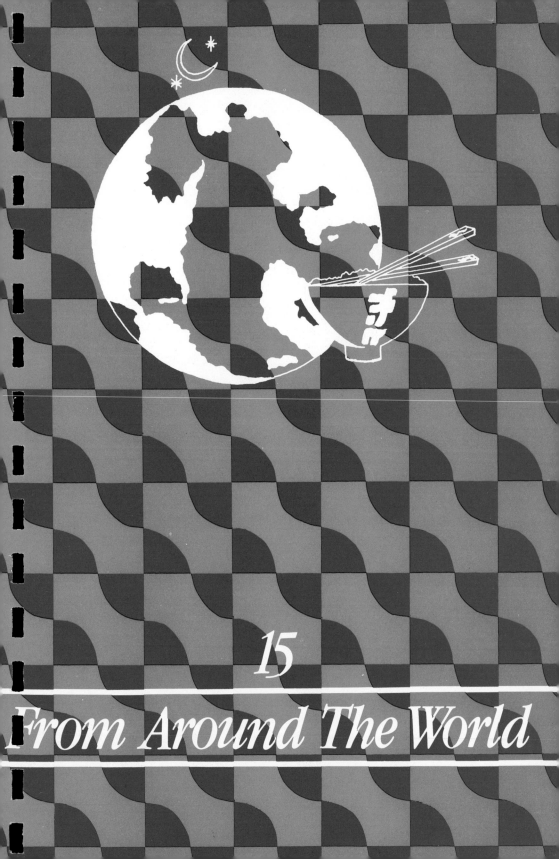

15
From Around The World

Spring Rolls

China
Serves 6-8

INGREDIENTS:

2-3 cups oil
½ cup Napa or head cabbage,
    shredded
6 black mushrooms, soaked and
    shredded
2 cups bean sprouts
½ cup carrots, shredded
3 green onions, shredded
2 cups cooked shrimp, shredded
¼ cup cooked ham, shredded

1 tablespoon light soy sauce
1½ tablespoons dry sherry
1 tablespoon sesame oil
½ teaspoon black pepper
1 tablespoon cornstarch
1½ tablespoons water
15 spring roll wrappers (Shanghai-
    style)
1 or 2 eggs, beaten

PROCEDURE:

Heat 2 tablespoons of oil. Stir fry cabbage, mushrooms, sprouts, carrots, and green onions. Add shrimp and ham and toss well. Pour in soy sauce, sherry, sesame oil and black pepper. Thicken with cornstarch and water. Transfer to large bowl and cool completely in refrigerator. Place 1 table-spoon of filling in one corner of the wrapper. Roll it once or twice. Fold in the sides and seal with beaten egg. Deep fry until golden brown.

Dolly Woo

Houmis

Middle East
Serves 12-15

INGREDIENTS:

2 16-ounce cans chick peas,
    drained
1 cup tahini (sesame seed paste)
1 cup lemon juice
⅓ cup cold water

4 garlic cloves
2 teaspoons salt
black olives (optional)
chopped parsley (optional)
cayenne pepper (optional)

PROCEDURE:

Purée all ingredients in food processor or blender. Spread ½" thick on serving platter and garnish with black olives, parsley or pepper. Chill and serve with small pieces of pita bread.

Allan Gall
Linda Kripke

Wonton

China
Yields 3 dozen

INGREDIENTS:

1 pound raw shrimp, shelled and
    chopped
½ pound lean ground pork
5 water chestnuts, chopped

1 tablespoon soy sauce
1 teaspoon cornstarch
3 cups oil
1 pound wonton wrappers

PROCEDURE:

Combine shrimp, pork, chestnuts, soy sauce and cornstarch. Place ½
teaspoon of filling in the center of each wrapper and moisten edges with
water. Fold in half to form a triangle. Moisten the two longer corners, bring
together and seal. Deep fry 8-10 wonton at a time over high heat until crisp
and golden brown. Serve with plum sauce and/or Chinese mustard.

*Fried wonton may be kept warm in a 250° oven for approximately 1 hour
or reheated for 5 minutes at 450°.*

Josie Kan

Ma Ho

Thailand
Serves 6-8

INGREDIENTS:

5 garlic cloves, crushed
4 fresh cilantro roots, crushed
2 tablespoons vegetable oil
8 ounces ground pork
3 tablespoons roasted peanuts,
    coarsely chopped
1½ tablespoons fish sauce (nuac
    mam)
⅛ teaspoon ground black pepper

2 tablespoons brown sugar
1 fresh chile (or green pepper),
    seeded and chopped
2 tablespoons fresh cilantro leaves,
    chopped
fresh Mandarin oranges (or
    pineapple), chilled
lettuce leaves (for garnish)

PROCEDURE:

Fry garlic and cilantro root in oil over low heat until slightly golden. Add pork, peanuts, fish sauce, pepper, sugar, chile and cilantro leaves. Stir fry over high heat until the mixture turns dark brown and dry. Discard any excess grease while cooking. Peel and separate oranges into segments and split each one open down the back. Lay flat on serving dish, skin up. (If using pineapple, cut into bite-size chunks). Pile pork mixture over chilled fruit pieces on platter and border with lettuce. Serve warm or at room temperature.

This interesting appetizer is also popular as a main course when served over white rice.

Vina Saycocie

Shau Mai

China
Serves 6

INGREDIENTS:

10 ounces pork loin, diced
4 black Chinese mushrooms, presoftened and diced
6 water chestnuts, diced
1 egg white
1 teaspoon salt

½ teaspoon sesame oil
½ teaspoon sugar
½ teaspoon sherry
1½ teaspoons cornstarch
30-40 wonton skins

PROCEDURE:

Combine pork, mushrooms and chestnuts in mixing bowl. Add egg white, salt, oil, sugar, sherry and cornstarch and mix well. Trim wonton skins into flat circles. Fill each one with approximately 1 teaspoon of pork mixture. Gather edges together with thumb and index finger to form a waist. Do not close completely. If necessary, use a spoon dipped in cold water to press down filling. Steam over high heat, ½" apart, for 8-10 minutes. Shrimp may be substituted for pork.

May be frozen raw and steamed just before serving.

Dolly Woo

Vichyssoise

France
Serves 8

INGREDIENTS:

1 pound leeks, washed and drained
¼ cup butter
½ cup onions, chopped
1 pound potatoes, cut into ½"
   cubes
½ teaspoon salt

white pepper to taste
2 13¾-ounce cans chicken broth
2 cups milk
1 cup light cream, chilled
½ cup chives, snipped
crushed ice

PROCEDURE:

Cut off roots, tips and dark green from leeks. Slice crosswise ¼" thick. Melt butter in a 5-quart Dutch oven. Sauté leeks and onions over medium heat until golden, not brown. Add potatoes, salt, pepper and chicken broth. Bring to a boil. Cover and simmer for 45 minutes. Purée potato/leek mixture in blender or food processor, 2 cups at a time. Set aside in large bowl. Heat milk in small saucepan until bubbles form. Add to potato/leek mixture and mix well with wire whisk. Cover and refrigerate overnight, or at least 6 hours. Before serving, gradually add chilled cream and mix well. Pour into chilled soup bowls, top with chives and surround with crushed ice.

Beverly Wulfeck

Egg Flower Soup

China
Serves 4

INGREDIENTS:

¼ pound lean pork, shredded
2 teaspoons soy sauce
1 tablespoon cornstarch
1 tablespoon sherry
1 egg white

1 large can chicken broth
2½ cups water
¼ cup bamboo shoots, shredded
2 eggs, beaten
1 stalk green onion, minced

PROCEDURE:

Season pork with soy sauce, cornstarch, sherry and egg white. Bring chicken broth and water to a boil. Add pork and bamboo shoots. Slowly stir in eggs until they separate into threads. Pour into soup bowls and garnish with green onion. Chicken may be substituted for pork.

Josie Kan

Fried Noodles

China

INGREDIENTS:

1 package wonton wrappers 2-3 cups cooking oil

PROCEDURE:

Heat oil in deep fryer. Slice wrappers into ¼″ strips. Drop small amounts into hot oil and stir until just slightly brown. Drain.

These are the perfect complement to so many Chinese soups and dishes. Try them once . . . you'll never use canned ones again!

Wanda Fleischaker

Black Bean Soup

Brazil
Serves 6

INGREDIENTS:

2 cups dried black beans
3½ cups water
2 teaspoons salt
2 tablespoons oil
3 garlic cloves, crushed
1 large onion, finely chopped
1 large green pepper, finely
    chopped
1 large carrot, chopped
1 celery stalk, chopped

1 teaspoon ground coriander
1½ teaspoons cumin
½ cup orange juice
1 tablespoon dry sherry
2 oranges, seeded and sectioned
    (optional)
½ teaspoon red pepper
½ teaspoon black pepper
½ teaspoon lemon juice

PROCEDURE:

Rinse beans and cover with water. Soak overnight, or at least 4 hours. Drain. Place beans in large saucepan with 3½ cups water and salt. Boil, cover and simmer for 1½ hours over low heat. Sauté garlic, onion, pepper, carrot, celery, coriander and cumin in oil. Add to the beans and continue to simmer for 30 minutes. Add orange juice, sherry, oranges, pepper and lemon juice. Simmer for 10 more minutes. Serve piping hot topped with cold sour cream. If you prefer a thicker consistency, purée 1 cup of beans in the blender and stir back into soup.

Always tastes best the next day . . . freezes beautifully, too.

Kelly Schalm

Spring Chicken Soup

Japan
Serves 6

INGREDIENTS:

6 cups chicken broth
3 1″ squares kombu
1½ teaspoons salt
½ teaspoon soy sauce
1 teaspoon sake

½ 5.2-ounce package harusame
6 quail eggs, boiled, shelled and
   halved
6-8 snow peas, very thinly sliced

PROCEDURE:

Warm broth with kombu. Remove the kombu as soon as the broth begins
to boil. Season broth with salt, soy sauce and sake. Boil harusame until
tender (approximately 3 minutes). Place harusame and eggs in soup bowls.
Pour in broth and garnish with snow peas. Serve immediately.

Mineko Takane Moreno

Hot And Sour Soup

China
Serves 4

INGREDIENTS:

⅔ cup pork, chicken or beef,
   shredded
3 tablespoons soy sauce
1½ teaspoons sherry
6½ tablespoons water
5½ tablespoons cornstarch
2 tablespoons vinegar
1 teaspoon pepper

2 teaspoons sesame oil
2 tablespoons scallions, shredded
6 cups chicken stock
1 teaspoon salt
6 wood ears (tree fungus)
½ cup bamboo shoots, shredded
2 squares bean curd, shredded
2 eggs, lightly beaten

PROCEDURE:

Marinate meat in 1 tablespoon soy sauce, sherry, ½ tablespoon water and 1
tablespoon of cornstarch for 15 minutes. Mix 2 tablespoons soy sauce,
vinegar, pepper, oil and scallions in a bowl and set aside. Boil chicken stock
and salt. Add meat, bamboo shoots and wood ears. Bring to a boil. Add
bean curd and boil again. Add 4½ tablespoons cornstarch and 6 tablespoons
water. Boil again. Slowly stir in beaten eggs and turn off heat. Pour into
soup bowls and serve at once.

Dolly Woo

Misoshiru

Japan
Serves 6

INGREDIENTS:

6 cups cold water
2 1″ square kombu (dried kelp),
    wiped and diced
½ cup katsuobushi (dried bonito)
½ cup miso

½ package tofu, diced
handful wakame (dried seaweed),
    soaked, drained and chopped
1 scallion, finely chopped

PROCEDURE:

Pour water into large saucepan. Add kombu and bring to a boil. Immediately remove kombu and add enough cold water to stop the boiling. Add katsuobushi and heat again. Place miso in small strainer and dip into the soup, stirring until completely dissolved. Reduce heat. Gently insert tofu and wakame. Return to a near boil. Garnish with scallions and serve immediately.

Mineko Takane Moreno

Raw Kibbi

Lebanon
Serves 8

INGREDIENTS:

3 cups lean ground lamb (leg
    portion only)
1 cup bulgar wheat, finely cracked

1 medium onion, chopped
salt to taste
pepper to taste

PROCEDURE:

Keep all ingredients as cold as possible. Soak wheat in water and remove excess water by pressing between the palms of your hands. Mix lamb with wheat, onion, salt and pepper kneading well. When mixture becomes stiff, dip your hands in ice water and knead to soften. Run mixture through grinder. Arrange on serving platter garnished with onion slivers. Serve immediately.

Melia Cory

Mu-Shu Pork

China
Serves 4

INGREDIENTS:

25 dried tiger lily buds
2 tablespoons dried wood ears
4 scallions, shredded
1 teaspoon salt
½ pound boneless pork, shredded
1 tablespoon soy sauce

1 teaspoon dry sherry
1 teaspoon sugar
1 teaspoon cornstarch
4 tablespoons cooking oil
3 eggs, lightly beaten
1 teaspoon sesame oil

PROCEDURE:

Soak lily buds, wood ears, scallions and salt in water for 30 minutes. Break wood ears into small pieces. Soak pork in soy sauce, sherry, sugar and cornstarch. Scramble eggs in 2 tablespoons of hot oil and transfer to plate. Heat remaining 2 tablespoons of oil to stir fry pork. Add drained lily buds, wood ears and scallions for 4 minutes. Add eggs and sesame oil. Mix well and serve with Mandarin pancakes (recipe follows).

Dolly Woo

Mandarin Pancakes

China
Yields 2 dozen

INGREDIENTS:

¾ cup boiling water
2 cups all-purpose flour

2 tablespoons sesame oil

PROCEDURE:

Pour water in flour and mix well. Knead until smooth, cover and let stand for 15 minutes. Divide dough in half. Roll each half into 12 balls and flatten each ball by hand. Lightly grease tops on 12 pancakes and cover with the remaining 12 ungreased pancakes. Roll out to 6″ circles. Set a flat bottom pan over low heat. Cook pancakes on one side until bubbles form. Turn over and cook until lightly browned. Remove from heat and carefully separate the two layers of each pancake.

Dolly Woo

Picadillo

Cuba
Serves 8

INGREDIENTS:

½ cup cooking oil
3 garlic cloves, minced
2 onions, minced
1 green pepper, minced
1 large can stewed tomatoes
salt to taste
pepper to taste

1 pound lean ground beef
1 pound ground pork
¼ cup vinegar
¾ cup green olives, chopped
½ cup raisins
2 tablespoons capers

PROCEDURE:

Sauté garlic, onions and pepper in hot oil. Add tomatoes, salt and pepper. Add meat and stir to break up completely. Combine all remaining ingredients, cover and simmer over low heat for 1 hour. Serve over white rice accompanied by baked bananas (recipe follows) and a green salad.

Picadillo seems to taste better the next day. It freezes well and also makes a tasty filling for a 9" pie.

Janet Brunet

Plátanos En Tentación

Cuba
Serves 8

INGREDIENTS:

8 ripe bananas, sliced lengthwise
1 tablespoon lemon juice
½ cup brown sugar

1 tablespoon cinnamon
½ cup dry sherry
2 tablespoons butter

PROCEDURE:

Preheat oven to 350°. Arrange bananas in single layer across baking pan. Sprinkle with lemon juice, sugar, cinnamon and sherry. Dot with butter. Bake for approximately 20 minutes.

Janet Brunet

Kebab With Yogurt

Turkey
Serves 12

INGREDIENTS:

2 pounds ground beef
1 cup Crisco oil
2 onions, finely chopped
6 garlic cloves, minced
½ cup fresh parsley, chopped
1 teaspoon allspice
2 eggs, beaten
3 slices French bread
1 teaspoon paprika
1 teaspoon cayenne pepper

salt to taste
black pepper to taste
1 teaspoon oregano
1 teaspoon thyme
3 slices pita bread, quartered
3 cups plain yogurt
2 tablespoons tomato paste
2 fresh tomatoes, cubed
1 green pepper, finely chopped

PROCEDURE:

Thoroughly mix meat, 2 tablespoons of oil, onions, 3 minced garlic cloves, parsley, allspice, eggs, French bread, paprika, salt, pepper, oregano and thyme. Shape into 5″ long by ¼″ wide patties and broil. Spread pita pieces in single layer across a Pyrex or similar serving dish. Slice each cooked meat patty into approximately 5 pieces and layer over pita. Mix yogurt, 3 minced garlic cloves and salt. Spread over meat slices. In remaining oil, cook tomato paste, tomatoes and pepper until tender. Pour over the yogurt. Serve hot or warm.

Since this crowd-pleasing dish is quite filling, it is best accompanied by a fresh green salad and a light dessert.

Aysegul Underhill

Five Spice Chicken

China
Serves 4

INGREDIENTS:

1 large chicken, cut into 10 serving
   pieces
1 jar five-spice powder
1 garlic head, minced
1 bunch green onions, chopped

3 tablespoons sesame oil
1 bottle dark soy sauce
Pam
honey

410

PROCEDURE:

Pat chicken dry. Coat each piece with five-spice powder and place in single layer in deep bowl. Sprinkle generously with half the garlic and onion. Drizzle with 1½ tablespoons of sesame oil and half the soy sauce. Layer more chicken on top and repeat process. Marinate overnight stirring occasionally. Preheat oven to 350°. Spray roasting pan with Pam and line with foil. Spray rack, place chicken on top and drizzle with honey. Bake for 30 minutes or until done.

This simple recipe can be doubled or tripled as a party dish using all wings or small legs.

Sally Wang

Tourtière À Pierette

France
Serves 6

INGREDIENTS:

¾ pound ground pork
¼ pound ground veal
1 large onion, minced
½ cup chopped celery
2 garlic cloves, minced
½ cup water
½ cup tomato sauce

½ teaspoon savory
2 bay leaves
2 clove heads
1 teaspoon salt
¼ teaspoon pepper
pastry for a 2-crust 9″ pie

PROCEDURE:

Cook all ingredients stirring constantly until meat loses red color. Cover and simmer over low heat for 30 minutes. Preheat oven to 425°. Line a 9″ pie pan with pastry. Pour in the meat mixture and cover with remaining pastry. Seal and flute edges. Lightly prick top. Bake at 425° for 10 minutes. Reduce heat to 350° and bake 20 minutes longer.

Rachel Gorski

Szechwan Prawns

China
Serves 4

INGREDIENTS:

1½ pounds prawns, washed and deveined
3 teaspoons salt
3 tablespoons oil
2 tablespoons dry sherry
1 shallot, sliced in 2″ lengths
1 garlic clove, minced
3 slices fresh ginger
2 red peppers, seeded and shredded
1 green pepper, seeded and shredded

½ cup chicken stock
1 tablespoon Worcestershire sauce
2 tablespoons catsup
1 teaspoon sugar
4 green onions, sliced in 2″ lengths
1 teaspoon cornstarch
2 teaspoons cold water
2 parsley sprigs

PROCEDURE:

Trim swimmerettes off prawns, rub with 2 teaspoons of salt and rinse under cold running water. Heat 2 tablespoons of oil in large skillet. Lay prawns flat with all heads pointing towards center of skillet. Cook each side for 5 minutes over medium heat. Sprinkle with 1 tablespoon sherry and set aside. Add another tablespoon of oil to heated skillet and stir fry shallot, garlic, ginger slices and peppers for 20 seconds. Sprinkle with 1 tablespoon of sherry and chicken stock. Season with Worcestershire sauce, catsup, 1 teaspoon salt and sugar. Add green onions and prawns. Thicken with cornstarch dissolved in water. Stir quickly until sauce thickens and transfer to heated platter. Garnish with parsley and serve at once with steamed white rice.

Pearl Yu

Chow Mein

China
Serves 6

INGREDIENTS:

1 pound dry Chinese noodles
9 tablespoons cooking oil
1 cup shredded meat, chicken or pork
3½ tablespoons cornstarch
1 teaspoon sherry

2 cups cabbage, shredded
¼ cup celery, shredded
1 cup canned mushrooms
1 cup bamboo shoots
1½ cups chicken broth

PROCEDURE:

Place noodles in rapidly boiling water for 3 minutes stirring to avoid sticking. Rinse in cold water and drain completely. Place noodles in large bowl and coat with 2 tablespoons of oil. Heat 5 tablespoons of oil in large skillet. Add greased noodles flattening them to shape a large pancake. Fry over medium heat until golden brown. Turn over to brown both sides. Keep browned noodle pancake in a warm oven until ready to use. Mix the meat with ½ tablespoon cornstarch and sherry. Heat 2 tablespoons oil. Stir fry meat over medium heat for 2 minutes. Add cabbage, celery, mushrooms, bamboo shoots and 1 cup of broth. Cook until tender. Mix 3 tablespoons of cornstarch with ½ cup of broth. Stir into meat and vegetable mixture until it thickens. Pour over browned noodles and serve immediately.

Josie Kan

Tonkatsu

Japan
Serves 6

INGREDIENTS:

½ fresh cabbage, very thinly sliced
6 ½-pound pork sirloin cutlets
salt to taste
white pepper to taste
½ cup flour
2 eggs, lightly beaten
1 cup bread crumbs

1½ quarts vegetable oil
1 small piece pork fat
½ cup tonkatsu sauce
½ cup catsup (optional)
2 tablespoons white roasted sesame
seeds

PROCEDURE:

Place cabbage in ice water until it becomes very crisp. Drain and set aside. Trim fat from cutlets and cut into 1″ slices. Season with salt and pepper. Coat pork with flour, dip in egg and coat thoroughly with bread crumbs. Heat oil with pork fat in deep, heavy frying pan or wok. Gently place coated pork into hot oil and reduce heat. Fry until pork floats to the surface. Drain on paper towel or wire rack. Mix tonkatsu sauce, catsup and sesame seeds. Slice pork into bite-size pieces and serve alongside cold cabbage accompanied by sauce in a separate bowl.

Mineko Takane Moreno

413

Coquilles Saint-Jacques

France
Serves 6-8

INGREDIENTS:

2½ pounds scallops
1½ cups white vermouth (or dry sherry)
24 small mushrooms
1 bay leaf
salt to taste
pepper to taste
4 tablespoons shallots, minced
6 tablespoons butter

8 tablespoons flour
4 egg yolks
2 cups liquid from scallops
1½ cups milk
½ cup cream
lemon juice to taste
1 cup Swiss cheese, grated
parsley (or dill)

PROCEDURE:

Blanch scallops in boiling water and drain. Place in saucepan adding vermouth and enough water to cover scallops. Add mushrooms, bay leaf, salt, pepper and shallots. Cover and simmer for 5 minutes. Remove scallops and mushrooms and boil remaining liquid down to 2 cups. Melt butter in medium size frying pan. Gradually stir in flour, egg yolks, liquid from scallops, milk, cream and lemon juice. Cook until slightly thickened. Add scallops and mushrooms. Pour into 8 large shells (or ramekins) and sprinkle with cheese and parsley. Bake at 350° for 15 minutes until golden brown.

Great with half a broiled tomato, crisp green salad and fresh rolls.

Nina Calhoun

Ternera Sevillana

Spain
Serves 4

INGREDIENTS:

2 pounds sliced veal
3 tablespoons flour
1 onion, thinly sliced
12 large mushrooms, sliced
10 string beans, quartered
1 red pimiento, chopped

6 tablespoons oil
½ pound butter
4 garlic cloves, minced
salt to taste
pepper to taste
6 ounces white wine

PROCEDURE:

Coat veal in flour. Sauté onion, mushrooms, string beans and pimiento in oil, butter and garlic for approximately 5 minutes. Add veal and cover with wine. Simmer until veal is done (7-10 minutes depending on the thickness of fillets). Serve with saffron or yellow rice.

Gloria Andújar

Shrimp With Cashew Nuts

China
Serves 4

INGREDIENTS:

⅔ pound medium shrimp
½ egg white
1½ tablespoons dry sherry
1 tablespoon cornstarch
1½ teaspoons salt
3 cups cooking oil

5 ounces cashew nuts
8 green onions, in 1″ lengths
8 slices ginger
¼ teaspoon black pepper
1 teaspoon sesame oil

PROCEDURE:

Shell and devein shrimp. Marinate in egg white, 1 tablespoon dry sherry, cornstarch and 1 teaspoon of salt for 30 minutes. Over low heat, deep fry cashews until golden brown. Drain and set aside. Deep fry shrimp for 30 seconds. Remove quickly. Heat 2 tablespoons of oil. Stir fry green onions and ginger. Add shrimp, ½ teaspoon salt, ½ tablespoon sherry, pepper and sesame oil. Mix thoroughly over high heat. Turn off and stir in cashews. Serve immediately.

Dolly Woo

Kung Pao Chicken

China
Serves 6

INGREDIENTS:

1 egg white
2 teaspoons cornstarch
5 boneless chicken breasts, cubed
1½ cups cooking oil
1 tablespoon hoisin sauce
2 tablespoons soy sauce

½ teaspoon chile pepper flakes
2 tablespoons dry sherry (or wine)
2 teaspoons sugar
1 cup peanuts
4 green onions, sliced

PROCEDURE:

Combine egg white with cornstarch. Add chicken cubes and 1 tablespoon of oil. Let stand 30 minutes. Fry chicken mixture until opaque. Remove and drain. Heat hoisin sauce, soy sauce, chile flakes, sherry and sugar in pan for 1 minute. Toss in chicken, peanuts and green onions. Stir and cook a few more minutes until chicken is done.

Melody Gentry

Parrillada De Mariscos

Spain
Serves 4

INGREDIENTS:

1 lobster, halved
4 pieces fresh cod fish
12 mussels
8 clams
16 shrimp
12 scallops
4 tablespoons olive oil

½ pound butter
salt to taste
4 tablespoons garlic powder
4 tablespoons Spanish "pimentón"
    or paprika
5 ounces white wine

PROCEDURE:

Preheat oven to 400°. Wash all fish and place in baking pan. Sprinkle all remaining ingredients over fish. Bake for 25 minutes uncovered. Serve immediately with saffron rice.

Café Español
New York

Kushi Katsu

Japan
Serves 6

INGREDIENTS:

½ cabbage, finely shredded
15 scallions, in 1″ lengths
36 cubes pork tenderloin
18 bamboo skewers
1 cup flour

2 eggs, lightly beaten
1½ cups French bread crumbs
1½ quart vegetable oil
½ cup tonkatsu sauce
2 tablespoons roasted sesame seeds

PROCEDURE:

Place cabbage in ice water until it becomes very crisp. Drain and set aside. Skewer onion/pork/onion/pork/onion pieces. Coat each skewer with flour, egg and bread crumbs. Deep fry and serve immediately accompanied by cold cabbage and a bowl of tonkatsu sauce mixed with sesame seeds.

Mineko Takane Moreno

Crab And Mushroom Stirfry

China
Serves 6

INGREDIENTS:

5 tablespoons sesame oil
1½ pounds broccoli, chopped
2 tablespoons water
2 teaspoons salt
6 1″ strips green onion
6 slices ginger root
2 cans straw mushrooms, boiled
    and drained

1 teaspoon rice wine (or dry
    sherry)
¼ teaspoon black pepper
1 cup stock
4 ounces crabmeat
1 tablespoon cornstarch

PROCEDURE:

Heat 4 tablespoons sesame oil and briefly stir fry broccoli with 1 tablespoon water and 1 teaspoon salt. Arrange around outer edge of serving platter. Stir fry onion and ginger root until fragrant. Add mushrooms, rice wine, 1 teaspoon salt, pepper, 1 tablespoon oil and stock. Bring to a boil and add crabmeat. Continue to stir fry briefly and thicken with cornstarch and 1 tablespoon water. Arrange inside broccoli border and serve immediately with white rice.

Dolly Woo

417

Paella

Spain
Serves 6

INGREDIENTS:

1 3-pound chicken, cut into serving
   pieces
¼ cup oil
1 pound Italian sausage (hot or
   mild), cut in 1″ lengths
1 large onion, chopped
2 garlic cloves, minced
5 mushrooms, sliced
1 teaspoon paprika
1 tablespoon parsley, chopped
¼ teaspoon saffron
salt to taste

pepper to taste
1½ cups tomato juice
1½ cups beer
1½ cups long grain rice
1 red pimiento, sliced
1 small can sliced olives
1 package frozen artichoke hearts
12 clams
½ pound lobster, cooked and cut
12 large shrimp, cooked
1 8-ounce package frozen peas

PROCEDURE:

Brown chicken in oil. Brown sausages lightly. Remove. Sauté onion, garlic
and mushrooms. Add paprika, parsley, saffron, salt, pepper, tomato juice
and beer. Bring to a boil. Add rice, chicken, pimiento and olives. Cover and
simmer for 25 minutes. Add sausage, artichokes, clams, lobster, shrimp and
peas. Cover and simmer for 10 minutes.

Valerie Bauer

Kai Yang

Thailand
Serves 4

INGREDIENTS:

2 tablespoons fresh garlic, minced
½ teaspoon ground pepper
2 tablespoons sugar
¼ teaspoon salt
3 tablespoons Chinese parsley (or
   coriander), chopped
2 tablespoons soy sauce
3 pounds chicken, cut into serving
   pieces

SAUCE
3 tablespoons water
1 tablespoon cornstarch
¼ cup apple cider vinegar
2 tablespoons fresh chile, finely
   chopped
½ cup sugar
¼ teaspoon salt
1 tablespoon fresh garlic, minced
1 tablespoon Chinese parsley,
   chopped

PROCEDURE:

Mix first 6 ingredients and marinate chicken for 2-3 hours. Barbecue. In a medium saucepan dissolve starch in water until crystal clear. Pour in vinegar, chile, sugar, salt and garlic. Stir until well mixed and cool slightly. Stir in parsley. Pour sauce over barbecued chicken when serving.

Susan Bennett

Ropa Vieja

Cuba
Serves 8

INGREDIENTS:

2½ pounds flank steak
⅓ cup olive oil
1 large onion, cut into thin strips
1 large green pepper, cut into thin strips
4 garlic cloves, minced

8 ounces tomato sauce
salt to taste
pepper to taste
2 bay leaves
¾ cup cooking sherry
1 small jar red pimientos

PROCEDURE:

Boil flank steak until tender. Cool slightly and shred into thin strips. Sauté onion, pepper and garlic in hot olive oil. Add the meat, tomato sauce, salt, pepper, bay leaves and sherry. Cover and cook over medium heat for 20 minutes. Garnish with pimientos. Serve with white rice and sliced avocadoes vinaigrette.

Gloria Andújar

Tabbouli

Lebanon
Serves 10

INGREDIENTS:

1 cup fine bulgar wheat
2 cups green onions, finely
  chopped
3 cups parsley, finely chopped
4 tomatoes, peeled and chopped
½ cup fresh mint, finely chopped

½ cup olive oil
½ cup lemon juice
½ teaspoon cinnamon
dash of allspice
tomato wedges (for garnish)
mint leaves (for garnish)

PROCEDURE:

Soak wheat in water and squeeze dry. Set aside. Combine all vegetables. Beat oil, lemon, cinnamon and allspice. Fold into vegetables. Add wheat and mix until well blended. Garnish with tomato wedges and mint leaves.

This colorful salad is a particularly good accompaniment to all lamb dishes.

Thomas Tuchscher

Wang's Tofu

China
Serves 4

INGREDIENTS:

1 package Chinese-style bean curd,
  cut into ½" cubes
3 cups cooking oil
8 garlic cloves, minced
3 green onions, minced

dried red peppers to taste
2 tablespoons soy sauce
1 tablespoon cornstarch
1½ tablespoons water

PROCEDURE:

In hot oil deep fry drained bean curd ⅓ at a time. (Fry until you feel no sponginess when picking up with tongs or chopsticks). Drain. Retain 2 tablespoons of oil in pan and stir fry garlic, onions, and peppers for about 1 minute. Gently press peppers into oil as you fry. Add soy sauce. Dissolve cornstarch in water and add until a thick, clear sauce forms. Pour over fried bean curd and serve immediately.

Sally Wang

420

Gratin Douphinois

France
Serves 4

INGREDIENTS:

1½ pounds potatoes, peeled
½ ounce butter
3 garlic cloves, minced
salt to taste

pepper to taste
nutmeg to taste
2 ounces Swiss cheese, grated
1¼ cups cream

PROCEDURE:

Preheat oven to 325°. Cut potatoes into ⅛″ slices and dry thoroughly. Grease a shallow, ovenproof dish. Spread half the potatoes in a single layer and sprinkle with seasonings, half the garlic and 1 ounce of cheese. Spread the remaining potatoes on top and sprinkle with additional seasonings, garlic and cheese. Carefully pour in the cream. Bake uncovered for 1½ hours until creamy and golden brown.

Janine Ryder

Szechwan Eggplant

China
Serves 4

INGREDIENTS:

1 eggplant, peeled and cut into
    thumb-size pieces
3 cups cooking oil
2 tablespoons green onion,
    chopped
1 tablespoon ginger, chopped
2 teaspoons garlic, minced

1 tablespoon hot bean paste
2 teaspoons soy sauce
1 teaspoon sugar
½ cup soup stock
½ tablespoon Worcestershire sauce
½ tablespoon sesame oil

PROCEDURE:

Deep fry eggplant until soft. Press to squeeze out excess oil and set aside. In 3 tablespoons of oil, stir fry 1 tablespoon green onion, ginger, garlic and bean paste. Add soy sauce, sugar and stock. Bring to a boil. Add eggplant cooking until all liquid is absorbed. Add Worcestershire sauce and sesame oil. Mix well and sprinkle with remaining tablespoon of green onion.

Dolly Woo

Wheat Pilaf

Turkey
Serves 10

INGREDIENTS:

2 cups large grain bulgar wheat
1 pound butter
2 large onions, chopped

2 tomatoes, peeled and diced
3 cups chicken broth
salt to taste

PROCEDURE:

Rinse wheat in a bowl and set aside. In heavy skillet melt butter and saute onions until soft. Add tomatoes, broth and salt. Cook for a few minutes before adding drained wheat. Cover and bring to a boil. Reduce heat and simmer for 20 minutes. Remove from heat. Cover skillet with a cloth, replace lid and let stand for 10 minutes. Serve hot.

A different and delicious accompaniment to your meat dishes.

Aysegul Underhill

Fried Rice

China
Serves 4

INGREDIENTS:

8 tablespoons cooking oil
2 eggs, lightly beaten
½ cup small shrimp
½ cup roast pork (or ham), diced
3 tablespoons green peas

2 tablespoons green onions,
    chopped
4 cups cooked rice
1 teaspoon salt
2 teaspoons soy sauce

PROCEDURE:

Scramble eggs in 2 tablespoons of hot oil. Set aside. Add 3 tablespoons of oil to stir fry shrimp, pork, peas and onion. Set aside. Heat remaining 3 tablespoons of oil. Stir fry cold rice, salt and soy sauce until thoroughly heated. Add pork/shrimp mixture and eggs. Mix well and serve immediately.

Josie Kan

Crème Brûlée

France
Serves 4-6

INGREDIENTS:

5 egg yolks
2 cups heavy cream, scalded
¼ cup sugar

1 tablespoon vanilla extract
½ cup light brown sugar

PROCEDURE:

Preheat oven to 300°. Beat egg yolks and cream. Add sugar and vanilla. Pour into a baking dish or individual ramekins. Place in a pan containing 1″ of hot water. Bake for 1 hour. Refrigerate. Before serving spread thin layer of brown sugar over the custard. Set on a bed of cracked ice and broil carefully until the sugar is brown and completely melted. Serve hot or chilled.

Elizabeth Wilder

Pavlova

Australia
Serves 8

INGREDIENTS:

3 egg whites, at room temperature
3 tablespoons cold water
1 cup granulated sugar
¼ cup confectioner's sugar
pinch of salt
½ teaspoon vanilla extract

1 teaspoon vinegar
3 teaspoons cornstarch
fresh whipped cream
fruit of your choice (kiwi, berries, pineapple, etc).

PROCEDURE:

Preheat oven to 275°. Beat eggs whites until very stiff. Gradually add water beating between teaspoons. Then add the sugar gradually. Fold in salt, vanilla, vinegar and cornstarch. Shape meringue into a large circle on unglazed paper on a baking sheet. Build up the sides by laying coils of meringue one on top of the other to approximately a 1″ depth. Bake for 1 hour. Turn off oven and leave tart inside for another hour. Gently peel off paper. Fill with whipped cream and top with fruit.

Brenda Kerr

Trifle

England
Serves 8-10

INGREDIENTS:

2 packages lady fingers
2 10-ounce packages red raspberries
3 tablespoons cooking sherry
2 envelopes Birds custard

2 bananas, sliced
2 small cartons whipping cream
fresh strawberries (for garnish)

PROCEDURE:

Spread lady fingers across bottom and sides of clear serving bowl. Place raspberries and sherry on top. Make 1 custard according to package directions. Pour semi-set custard over berries. Refrigerate for 10 minutes and spread layer of 1 sliced banana. Make second package of custard. Pour semi-set custard over bananas and refrigerate for 10 minutes. Layer second sliced banana on top. Cover with whipped cream and garnish with fresh strawberries.

Best made a day ahead and well-chilled. Add whipped cream and strawberries before serving. The perfect dessert on a hot day.

Jennifer De Silva

Orange Flan

Spain
Serves 4

INGREDIENTS:

4 teaspoons granulated sugar (to caramelize 4 muffin molds or ramekins)
½ cup frozen orange juice concentrate

½ cup water
2 tablespoons sugar
2 whole eggs, at room temperature
½ teaspoon powdered ginger

PROCEDURE:

Glaze the four separate muffin molds or ramekins. Let cool completely. Preheat oven to 325°. Reconstitute frozen orange juice with ½ cup water at room temperature. Add whole eggs, sugar and ginger; mix well without beating. Strain into glazed molds. Place, bain-marie, in shallow pan. Bake for 45 minutes or until set. Cool completely. Draw knife around edges and unmold onto dessert dish. For a festive look, edge dish in a wreath of loose, even, seedless grapes.

Keeps for days covered in refrigerator, but should be taken out one hour before serving.
This is the Andalusian relief for the ever-present flan on Spanish tables.

Tana de Gámez

Clafouti

France
Serves 10

INGREDIENTS:

4½ ounces flour
2 eggs
2 tablespoons rum (or kirsch)
pinch of salt
1 tablespoon oil

4 ounces sugar
1½ cups milk
12 ounces fruit (pitted cherries,
  apricots, sliced pears or apples,
  etc).
1 ounce butter

PROCEDURE:

Preheat oven to 400°. Place flour in large bowl and form a well. In the center, drop in eggs, liquor, salt, oil and 3 ounces of sugar. Mix from the center towards the outside until all liquid is absorbed and there are no lumps. Gradually add the milk. Mix in fruit of your choice. Pour into a 10″ oven-to-table dish. Sprinkle with 1 ounce of sugar and dot with butter. Bake for approximately 1 hour or check for doneness with toothpick or skewer. Serve warm or cold.

Janine Ryder

Marie's Bonetto

Italy
Serves 8

INGREDIENTS:

6 tablespoons sugar
1 quart milk
1 package Amaretti cookies
8 eggs, lightly beaten

2 tablespoons cocoa
2 teaspoons almond extract
2 ounces vermouth (or brandy)

PROCEDURE:

Preheat oven to 350°. Heat 4 tablespoons of sugar slowly in small, heavy skillet. Stir constantly until sugar melts and is free of lumps. Pour into baking dish coating bottom and sides. Set aside. Soak cookies in milk until softened. Break up into smaller pieces. Combine eggs, cocoa, almond extract, vermouth and 2 tablespoons of sugar. Blend in soaked cookie mixture. Pour into baking dish and set in a pan of hot water. Bake for approximately 45 minutes or until knife inserted in center comes out clean. Chill thoroughly. Run sharp knife around sides and turn into a flat, lipped serving dish. Serve cold.

Linda Morefield

425

Madeleines

France
Yields 14-18

INGREDIENTS:

3½ ounces sugar
3 eggs, at room temperature
3½ ounces flour
3½ ounces butter, melted

pinch of salt
½ teaspoon baking powder
1 teaspoon vanilla (or lemon)
   extract

PROCEDURE:

Preheat oven to 350°. Thoroughly butter madeleine mold. Mix sugar and eggs. Add flour, butter, salt and baking powder stirring well after each addition. Blend in the extract. Spoon the batter into molds until they are ⅔ full. Bake for 25 minutes. Unmold immediately and cool completely on racks.

These plump little cakes, proclaimed by some as the finest complement to tea, are best when freshly baked but can also be kept for several days in an airtight container.

Wiener Kipfesl

Austria
Yields 48

INGREDIENTS:

1½ stick butter, softened
¾ cup almonds, peeled and finely
   ground
⅓ cup granulated sugar

2 egg yolks
¾ cup flour
confectioner's (or vanilla) sugar

PROCEDURE:

Cream butter. Beat in almonds, sugar and egg yolks. Gradually add the flour beating and scraping bowl until thoroughly mixed. Refrigerate for 1 hour. Preheat oven to 350°. Divide dough into 4 pieces. Roll out each quarter into a 10″ log. Cut each log into 12 pieces. Roll each into a 3″ cigar shape tapered on both ends and slightly thicker in the middle. Place on cookie sheet curving ends to form crescent shape. Bake for 12-15 minutes until golden. Cool for 2 minutes. Gently transfer crescents to racks set over paper. While still warm, generously sprinkle crescents with confectioner's or vanilla sugar (available at German food stores).

Marilies Schoepflin

Suspiros

Mexico
Yields 48

INGREDIENTS:

1 cup powdered sugar
2 tablespoons lemon peel, grated
2 ounce blanched almonds, toasted
    and finely ground
2½ cups flour
1 cup unsalted butter, softened

¾ cup granulated sugar
2 egg whites
1½ teaspoon vanilla extract
pinch of salt

PROCEDURE:

Combine powdered sugar with lemon peel. Cover and let stand overnight at room temperature. Preheat oven to 325°. Combine almonds with ⅔ cup of flour and set aside. Cream butter and granulated sugar at high speed until light and creamy. Beat in egg whites, vanilla and salt until smooth. Gradually stir in remaining flour. Blend in almond/flour mixture. Line rimless cookie sheets with parchment paper. Gently roll dough into walnut-size balls between the palms of your hands, but do not squeeze while rolling. Bake, 1″ apart, until cookies spring back when touched (approximately 10-12 minutes). Transfer to racks set over paper. Sift lemon/sugar generously over cookies while they are still warm.

Best when freshly baked, but can be made a day ahead and stored in airtight container between layers of wax paper.

Yolanda Sustaeta

Langues De Chat Au Chocolat

France
Yields 12

INGREDIENTS:

½ cup sweet butter, softened
½ cup sugar
1 teaspoon vanilla extract
3 eggs whites, at room temperature

½ cup cocoa
½ cup flour
6 tablespoons heavy cream

PROCEDURE:

Preheat oven to 425°. Cream butter, sugar and vanilla for 5 minutes. Gradually add egg whites. Fold in cocoa, then flour, then heavy cream. Butter langues de chat mold, miniature cupcake mold or madeleine mold. Press the batter through a pastry bag onto mold. Bake for 5 minutes until edges are slightly brown. Remove carefully (these are quite fragile) and serve warm.

Susan Shuckett

Bowknots

China
Yields 50-70

INGREDIENTS:

1 1-pound package wonton skins
3-4 cups peanut oil
4 cups granulated sugar

2 cups water
½ cup clear corn syrup
sesame seeds, toasted

PROCEDURE:

Cut stack of wonton skins in half. Using double layers, make 2-3″ long parallel slits down the middle of each stack avoiding edges. Hold the double layers in your left hand and push the right end through the left slit. Reach around the back and pull the right end through to end up with a bow shape. Lay on a cookie sheet under a slightly damp towel until all knots are shaped. Heat oil until a haze forms and deep fry 6 bows at a time turning once until light brown. Drain well on paper towels. Heat sugar, corn syrup and water until thick enough to coat a spoon. Dip each twist into the syrup and place on cake rack to drain. Sprinkle immediately with sesame seeds and dry thoroughly. If syrup begins to harden add ½ cup more water and heat through.

Liz Fong Wills

Scones

England
Yields 16

INGREDIENTS:

2 cups sifted flour
2 tablespoons sugar
1 teaspoon cream of tartar
1 teaspoon baking soda
½ teaspoon salt

⅓ cup butter
1 egg, lightly beaten
¾ cup milk
¾ cup raisins

PROCEDURE:

Preheat oven to 400°. Sift together all dry ingredients. Cut in the butter until particles form that resemble coarse bread crumbs. Stir in egg and milk. Add raisins. Knead dough gently on floured surface. Cut in half and roll each half into a ball. Flatten each ball into a ½″-thick round and slice into 8 wedges. Place on greased cookie sheet. Brush with beaten egg and sprinkle with sugar. Bake for 15 minutes or until golden brown. Serve immediately with honey, jams or lemon butter.

Jennifer Howard

Toad In The Hole

England
Serves 4

INGREDIENTS:

1½ cups flour
1 egg
½ cup milk

salt to taste
pepper to taste
1 package breakfast sausage

PROCEDURE:

Mix flour, egg, milk, salt and pepper. Cover and refrigerate for 1 day. Preheat oven to 450°. Brown sausages in oven and drain. Add sufficient milk to flour mixture to obtain consistency of thick cream. Transfer sausages to baking dish and pour mixture over them. Bake at 400° for 45 minutes.

Typically served with mashed potatoes whipped with sour cream, green peas and a bovril-base brown sauce.

Janet Loomis

Banukukua

Finland
Serves 6

INGREDIENTS:

6 eggs, lightly beaten at room
    temperature
2 cups milk, at room temperature
1 cup flour

pinch of salt
cinnamon (or nutmeg) to taste
½ cup butter

PROCEDURE:

Preheat oven to 400°. Gradually add milk, flour, salt and cinnamon to eggs beating thoroughly after each one. Melt butter in large shallow baking dish in oven. Coat evenly and pour in egg mixture. Bake for 20 minutes. Serve immediately with honey, syrup, jams and jellies.

The traditional company breakfast . . . quick and so easy yet always receives rave reviews.

Beatrice Stanley

Notes

16

From Around The Town

Ceviche

Serves 6-8

INGREDIENTS:

1 pound bay scallops, halved
¾ pound onions, chopped
1 tablespoon parsley, chopped
juice of 3 lemons
½ cup orange juice
3 ounces lime juice with 1 ounce sugar
1 teaspoon salt
⅛ teaspoon pepper
1 teaspoon Worcestershire sauce
2 drops Tabasco sauce
¼ cup water

½ bunch cilantro, chopped
½ large bell pepper, diced
10 stuffed olives, sliced
2 tomatoes, diced
2 marinated jalapeño peppers, diced
1 tablespoon parsley, chopped
1 avocado, diced
¼ cup orange juice
½ cup catsup
juice of 1 lemon
¾ ounce olive oil

PROCEDURE:

Combine first 11 ingredients in glass, wood or plastic bowl. Refrigerate. Combine next 10 ingredients in separate bowl. Chill both mixtures for 24 hours. Drain scallop mixture (without squeezing) and incorporate into second mixture. Add olive oil and serve as an appetizer.

The Sea Thief
La Jolla

Grilled Oysters With Cilantro

Serves 1

INGREDIENTS:

4 fresh oysters, opened
2 ounces fresh cilantro
4 ounces fresh spinach
juice of ½ lemon
1 teaspoon garlic, chopped

1 teaspoon cayenne pepper
1 ounce Parmesan cheese, freshly grated
¼ cup salad oil
rock salt

PROCEDURE:

Preheat oven to 375°. Open oysters and loosen. Reserve liquid in shell. In blender or food processor purée cilantro, spinach, lemon juice, garlic and pepper. Add cheese and oil in slow, steady stream. Spread evenly over oysters and place them in a pan with rock salt base to hold them steady. Bake 4-6 minutes until liquid bubbles. Serve immediately.

Bob Brody
Sheraton Harbor Island West

431

Chicken Liver Pâté

Serves 12-14

INGREDIENTS:

1 pound chicken livers
⅔ cup onions, thinly sliced
1 garlic clove
2 bay leaves, crushed
¼ teaspoon thyme leaves

2 teaspoons salt
1½ cups butter, softened
freshly ground black pepper
2 teaspoons cognac (or Scotch)

PROCEDURE:

Sauté livers, onions, garlic, bay leaves and 1 teaspoon salt in fry pan over high heat for 7-8 minutes. (Livers will still be pink and soft). Remove from heat. Take out solids with slotted spoon. Place in food processor bowl fitted with metal blade. Start processing liver adding butter piece by piece. Add second teaspoon of salt, pepper to taste and cognac. Process 2 more minutes until creamy and smooth. Pour into mold. Refrigerate to set. Garnish as desired before serving. Best if prepared a day ahead.

Patty Murray Catering
La Jolla

Shrimp Toast

Serves 48

INGREDIENTS:

¼ pound ground pork
¾ pound fresh shrimp, peeled,
    deveined and chopped
8 water chestnuts, chopped
4 stalks green onion, chopped
½ bunch cilantro, chopped
1 teaspoon salt
½ teaspoon light soy sauce

1 teaspoon Hsiao Hsing rice wine
2 teaspoons cornstarch
2 egg whites, stiffly beaten
12 bread slices
1 package panko (Japanese bread
    crumbs)
2 ounces sesame seeds
peanut oil

PROCEDURE:

Chop or blend together first 10 ingredients. Remove crust from bread slices. Mix panko and sesame seeds. Spread generous amount of shrimp mixture on single side of each bread slice. Press into tray of panko/seeds mix. Cut to form 4 triangles. Deep fry in hot peanut oil over high heat, shrimp side down, for 1 minute. Turn and fry for 1 additional minute.

These may be made in advance and frozen. Do not thaw. Place on cookie sheet and heat for 12 minutes at 350°.

Woo Chee Chong
San Diego

Chilled Cucumber Soup

Serves 6-8

INGREDIENTS:

4 ounces butter
2 leeks, chopped
1 white onion, chopped
3 cucumbers, peeled and seeded
2 quarts chicken stock

1 teaspoon dill
salt to taste
pepper to taste
1 potato, diced
2 cups milk

PROCEDURE:

Melt butter and sauté leeks and onion. Simmer while adding remaining ingredients except milk. When cooked, blend until smooth in food processor or blender. Stir in milk. Refrigerate several hours. Serve in chilled bowls topped with chopped cucumbers.

Hotel del Coronado
Coronado

Cream Of Artichoke And Chestnut Soup

Serves 8-10

INGREDIENTS:

1 teaspoon shallots, minced
½ cup sherry
4 artichoke bottoms, freshly
    cooked (or water-packed,
    drained)
8 fresh chestnuts, peeled (or 1 cup
    chestnut purée)

1 quart chicken stock
1 quart whipping cream
1 sprig fresh (or dried) thyme
salt to taste
freshly ground white pepper to
    taste

PROCEDURE:

Cook shallots and sherry in 1-gallon pot over moderately high heat until reduced to approximately 1 tablespoon. Add the artichoke, chestnuts and stock. Simmer for 15 minutes. Purée this mixture, in batches, in food processor fitted with metal blade for 10 seconds. Return to pot and bring to a boil. Stir in cream and thyme. Reduce to desired consistency. Season with salt and pepper.

Dan Belajack
Piret's
San Diego

433

Shellfish Soup

Serves 6

INGREDIENTS:

1 onion, chopped
2 tablespoons shallots, minced
1 tablespoon garlic, minced
2 tablespoons sweet butter
1 cup shrimp (or lobster) shells, chopped
2 cups white wine
3 cups fish stock
1 bouquet garni

1 cup heavy cream
2 tablespoons tomato paste
sherry to taste
salt to taste
pepper to taste
18 mussels (steamed open)
12 oytsters (shucked)
18 scallops
minced parsley or chives (for garnish)

PROCEDURE:

Sauté onion, shallots and garlic in butter until golden. Add shells and white wine. Reduce by half. Add fish stock and bouquet garni. Cover and simmer until good flavor develops. Stir in heavy cream and continue to simmer approximately 1 hour or until desired consistency . Strain. Stir in tomato paste and sherry. Season with salt and pepper. Place 3 mussels, 2 oysters and 3 scallops each into 6 heated bowls. Pour boiling soup over shellfish. Garnish with parsley or chives and serve at once.

Sheppard's
San Diego

Shrimp Bisque

Serves 10-15

INGREDIENTS:

1 pound medium-size shrimp
½ gallon water
1 tablespoon lemon juice
pinch of pickling spice
½ cup butter
¾ cup flour

½ teaspoon Spanish "pimentón" (or paprika)
1½ ounces sherry
salt to taste
pepper to taste

PROCEDURE:

Bring shrimp to a boil in ½ gallon of water with lemon juice and pickling spice. Remove shrimp immediately when water begins to boil. Peel and devein. Rinse off spices. Return shells to water and reduce 15-20 minutes. Make a roux with butter, flour and paprika. Strain stock and gradually stir into roux. Bring to a gentle boil stirring constantly. Season with sherry, salt and pepper. Chop shrimp coarsely. Add to bisque and serve.

The Inn
Rancho Santa Fe

Sopa De Tortilla

Serves 4

INGREDIENTS:

4 medium-size tomatoes, chopped
2 garlic cloves, chopped
½ onion, chopped
1 tablespoon salad oil
2 cups chicken consommé
2 cups beef consommé
1 teaspoon salt
½ teaspoon pepper

1 avocado, diced
½ bunch cilantro, chopped
8 ounces sour cream
8 corn tortillas, cut into thin strips
    and deep fried
Monterey jack cheese to taste,
    grated

PROCEDURE:

Sauté tomatoes, garlic and onion in oil. Add 1 cup of the combined stocks and bring to a boil. Purée in blender and add to remaining stock. Boil until broth is thin. Season with salt and pepper. Pour broth into heated bowls. Add avocado, cilantro, sour cream and tortilla strips to each one. Top with grated cheese.

Pancho Wellington's
La Jolla

Grilled Lamb Shanks With Lentils

Serves 6-8

INGREDIENTS:

1 pound lentils
2 tablespoons vegetable oil
4 ounces Canadian bacon, in 1"
    cubes
5 lamb shanks
2 carrots, in 2" chunks

1 4" celery branch
2 onions, coarsely chopped
2 bay leaves
1 garlic head
1 quart beef stock (or canned
    consommé)

PROCEDURE:

Soak lentils in water overnight. Preheat oven to 375°. Place oil and bacon in an oven casserole, stovetop. When most of the fat has been rendered from the bacon, add lamb and brown on all sides. Add the carrots, celery, onions and bay leaves. When onions become translucent, add garlic and stock. Bring to a boil then transfer to oven. Add lentils after 1 hour. Continue roasting for another hour. Remove when lentils are tender and lamb almost falls off bone.

Bob Brody
Sheraton Harbor Island West

Duck Lasagne With Porcini Mushrooms And White Truffles

Serves 6

INGREDIENTS:

4 tablespoons butter
4 tablespoons olive oil
3 ducks, quartered
2 yellow onions, chopped
4 celery stalks, chopped
3 carrots, chopped
12 cups water
2 oranges, sectioned
minced shallots to taste
thyme to taste
salt to taste

white pepper to taste
1 cup porcini mushrooms soaked
    in 1 cup Madeira
¼ pound flour
¼ pound butter
2 cups whipping cream
12 lasagne noodles, cooked al
    dente and drained
¾ cup Parmesan cheese, grated
2 white truffles, slivered

PROCEDURE:

Heat butter with oil in large pot. Brown duck. Brown onion, celery and carrots. Cover with water. Add oranges, shallots and spices. Gently boil until reduced to half (approximately 2 hours). Strain and reserve stock. Chop duck meat and combine with porcinis in Madeira. Set aside. Make roux by whisking flour into ¼ pound melted butter. Whisk in duck stock. Stir in cream. Bring to a boil and remove from heat. Preheat oven to 350°. Layer lasagne noodles, creamed stock and duck/porcini mixture in lasagne pan. Sprinkle cheese over all. Top with truffles. Cover and bake for 30 minutes or until bubbly.

Avanti
La Jolla

Fettucini Abruzzese

Serves 6

INGREDIENTS:

12 bacon pieces, diced
2 medium-size onions, diced
12 tomatoes, skinned
3 bunches fresh basil, finely
    chopped
salt to taste

pepper to taste
1 tablespoon butter
2 pounds fettucini
2 cups Parmesan cheese, freshly
    grated

PROCEDURE:

In a large pan, fry bacon until almost crisp. Stir in onions until soft. Add tomatoes, basil, salt and pepper. With handmasher, purée into a smooth sauce. (The tomatoes will mash easier if added immediately after skinning). Add butter and simmer over very low heat. Boil fettucini. Drain and toss in sauce. Sprinkle with cheese and toss again. Serve immediately.

Use all fresh ingredients for best results. Also, if the fettucini aren't cooked long enough, they will not absorb the sauce's flavor.

Taste of Rome
La Jolla

Tagliarini Frutti Mare

Serves 4

INGREDIENTS:

2 tablespoons butter
3 tablespoons garlic, chopped
8 littleneck clams
salt to taste
freshly ground pepper to taste
1 teaspoon oregano, fresh if
    possible
1 tablespoon Spanish "pimentón"
    (or paprika)
1 cup dry white wine
½ cup clam juice
3 tablespoons anchovy fillets,
    crushed

2 ground pear tomatoes, chopped
½ teaspoon fresh basil, chopped
½ cup olive oil
8 small shrimp
8 fresh mussels, steamed
4 crab claws
½ pound eastern scallops
1 cup clams, chopped
1½ pounds tagliarini
fresh parsley, chopped (for garnish)

PROCEDURE:

Melt butter. Sauté garlic and whole clams for 5 minutes. Add spices, wine, clam juice and anchovies. Simmer for 10 minutes. Add the tomatoes, basil and olive oil and simmer further. Add shrimp, mussels, crab, scallops and chopped clams. Simmer another 5 minutes. Boil tagliarini in salted water. Drain thoroughly and transfer to warm serving dish. Spoon fish mixture on top. Add whole pieces of fish to platter in a decorative, appealing manner. Sprinkle with parsley and serve at once. Pass additional sauce in gravy boat.

Di Canti
La Jolla

Boneless Breast Of Chicken Saltimbocca

Serves 6

INGREDIENTS:

6 whole chicken breasts, boned
   and halved
flour for dredging
butter
12 slices Monterey jack cheese
12 slices prosciutto
3 large shallots, finely chopped
3 large garlic cloves, finely
   chopped

½ pound mushrooms, sliced
½ cup dry white wine
1 cup chicken stock
thyme to taste
oregano to taste
salt to taste
pepper to taste
½ cup sherry
½ cup cream

PROCEDURE:

Preheat oven to 400°. Dredge chicken breasts with flour and brown both sides in butter. Remove from pan and place in casserole. Top each breast with cheese and prosciutto slice. In pan with butter, braise shallots and garlic. Add mushrooms. Cook quickly. Stir in wine, stock and seasonings. Bring to a boil and simmer for 15 minutes. Stir in sherry and cream. Pour over chicken breasts and bake for 20 minutes.

The Inn
Rancho Santa Fe

Pollo San Remo

Serves 4

INGREDIENTS:

1 red pepper
1 green pepper
15 large dried porcini mushrooms
   soaked in 1 cup hot water
4 tablespoons olive oil
4 chicken breasts, rib bones-
   removed and wings trimmed at
   second joint from tip

flour for dredging
3 garlic cloves, crushed
15 mushrooms, sliced
15 sundried tomatoes, sliced
1 cup chicken stock
salt to taste
pepper to taste

PROCEDURE:

Roast whole peppers under broiler until skin is black and blistered. Put in small paper bag for 20 minutes. Peel off blackened skin. Top and core peppers. Cut into large slices. Cut softened porcinis into large slices. Heat skillet with olive oil. Dredge chicken in flour. Sauté chicken, skin side down, for 2 minutes. Turn chicken, add garlic and sauté for additional minute. Add peppers, mushrooms, tomatoes and stock. Season with salt and pepper. Cover and simmer for 15 minutes. Remove chicken to warm serving platter. Reduce sauce by one third. Adjust seasonings. Spoon sauce over chicken and serve.

PAX
La Jolla

Fresh Rabbit With Wild Mushroom Sauce

Serves 6

INGREDIENTS:

1 fresh rabbit, cut into serving pieces
2 tablespoons vegetable oil
½ cup water
1 ounce oyster (or morel) mushrooms, sliced
8 tablespoons unsalted butter
½ pound domestic mushrooms, sliced

½ pound fresh shitake mushrooms, sliced
2 medium shallots, finely chopped
salt to taste
pepper to taste
2 cups heavy cream

PROCEDURE:

Preheat oven to 350°. Trim rabbit of all fat. Heat skillet with oil and sauté rabbit until brown on all sides. Transfer to casserole, add water, cover and roast for 1-1½ hours. (Add more water as needed). Saute morels in 1 tablespoon melted butter until they are well coated, about 1 minute over medium/high heat. Reduce heat to low, cover and cook for 5 minutes or until morels are very soft. Transfer to a 1-quart mixing bowl with a slotted spoon. Melt the remaining butter and sauté other mushrooms until light brown, about 5 minutes over medium heat. Add the shallots, salt and pepper and cook 1 more minute. Reduce to low and stir in reserved morels and 1 cup cream. Cover and simmer for 5 minutes. Add the remaining cream, stir, cover and simmer until cream has thickened enough to coat a spoon, about 10 minutes over low heat. Spoon over rabbit when ready to serve.

Accompany with blanched broccoli sautéed in garlic butter and fresh angelhair pasta.

Patty Murray Catering
La Jolla

Rabbit Liver With Rich Cream Mustard Sauce

Serves 1

INGREDIENTS:

4-5 ounce rabbit liver
flour for dredging
2 tablespoons clarified oil
4 tablespoons brandy
½ cup raw certified cream

pepper to taste
salt to taste
2 teaspoons mustard
2 teaspoons Dijon mustard

PROCEDURE:

Dry liver in paper towels and lightly flour one side. Heat oil over medium heat in shallow sauté pan. Brown liver, on floured side, for 30-60 seconds. Turn and cook to reach desired doneness, 1-2 minutes. Remove liver from pan and keep hot. Drain oil and pat pan dry leaving cooking remains. Add brandy off heat (careful of flame) and reduce to a quarter over high heat. Add cream and pepper to taste. Reduce to sauce consistency. Season with salt and pepper. Turn off heat, add mustards and mix well. Pour over liver and enjoy!

Gustaf Anders
La Jolla

Calamari Cordon Bleu

Serves 1

INGREDIENTS:

1 egg, well beaten
2 tablespoons milk
salt to taste
pepper to taste
2 calamari steaks, well pounded
1 thin slice Provolone (or Swiss)
   cheese

1 thin slice prosciutto
½ cup flour
vegetable oil
4 ounces champagne
1 8-ounce can crushed pineapple,
   drained
paprika (for garnish)

PROCEDURE:

Preheat oven to 400°. Combine egg, milk, salt and pepper in shallow bowl. Place cheese and ham between well-pounded calamari steaks. Dip in egg mixture then dredge in flour. Repeat. Sauté in vegetable oil on medium/low heat until lightly brown on both sides. Bake for 8 minutes. Heat champagne and pineapple on stovetop or in oven. Pour over calamari, garnish with paprika and serve at once.

This recipe was created for abalone steaks, rather than calamari. Since high-grade abalone has become very costly and difficult to obtain, we have substituted calamari with excellent results.

The Sea Thief
La Jolla

Shrimp Cabrillo

Serves 4

INGREDIENTS:

24 extra large raw shrimp, peeled
    and deveined
½ pound bacon, in 1″ pieces
2 bell peppers, in 1″ chunks
8 large mushroom caps, stems
    removed

3 tablespoons oil
2 tablespoons butter, melted
Cabrillo Sauce (recipe follows)
8 skewers

PROCEDURE:

Prepare barbecue. Assemble shrimp/bacon/pepper/mushroom on each skewer. Repeat using 3 shrimp per skewer. Baste lightly with oil and cook over charcoal for 8-10 minutes or until shrimp turns pink. Remove to warm serving platter. Baste with melted butter to keep moist. Spoon Cabrillo Sauce on top and serve.

Cabrillo Sauce

Yields 2 cups

INGREDIENTS:

½ cup butter
1 teaspoon dry English mustard
12 ounces catsup

juice of 1 lemon
½ teaspoon Worcestershire sauce
6 drops Tabasco sauce

PROCEDURE:

Melt butter in large skillet but do not brown. Add mustard and cook 3-4 minutes over low heat. Add remaining ingredients and bring to a boil, stirring occasionally. Simmer over low heat for 20 minutes to combine flavors. Refrigerate unused portion for another time.

Lubach's
San Diego

Mama Ghio's Shellfish Cioppino

Serves 4

INGREDIENTS:

¼ cup oil
½ cup butter
1 large onion, chopped
4 garlic cloves, chopped
3 tablespoons parsley, finely
   chopped
¾ cup dry sherry
1 #2 can solid pack plum
   tomatoes, chopped
8 ounces tomato sauce
2 bay leaves
1 teaspoon salt

½ teaspoon pepper
dash of Tabasco sauce
½ teaspoon thyme
2 cups water (more if needed)
1 Dungeness crab, cut up
2 lobster tails, cut up
8 large shrimp (shell on), split
12 clams, in shell
8 ounces scallops
8 ounces halibut or baguetta
   (optional)

PROCEDURE:

Heat oil and butter in large kettle. Brown onion, garlic and parsley. Add sherry. Sauté 5-7 minutes. Add tomatoes, tomato sauce, bay leaves, salt, pepper, Tabasco and thyme. Stir frequently while cooking 15-20 minutes. Add water. Cover and simmer 30 minutes. Into simmering sauce add crab, lobster, shrimp, clams and scallops. Cook, covered, 15 minutes. Add optional fish fillets after 5 minutes. When clams have opened, cioppino will be done and ready for serving. Divide shellfish into large, shallow soup bowls or serve family style from a community pot.

Don't forget crusty sourdough rolls, wine, nut crackers for the shells and bibs!

Anthony's
San Diego

Lobster Thermador

Serves 1

INGREDIENTS:

1¼-1½ pound lobster, cooked
4 small garlic cloves
2 tablespoons shallots, minced
2 ounces butter
2 ounces sherry

1 ounce brandy
1 cup whipping cream
1 teaspoon Dijon mustard
4 ounces Gruyére cheese

PROCEDURE:

Preheat oven to 450°. Split a precooked local lobster in two and wash out guts with cold water. Carefully remove meat and cut into bite-size pieces. Reserve shells. Sauté garlic and shallots in butter until shallots become clear. Add sherry, brandy, cream and mustard. Bring to a boil cooking until it begins to thicken. Spoon the lobster out of the pan and into shells. Pour sauce over lobster meat into shells. Top with cheese and bake for 4-5 minutes.

Harbor House
San Diego

Lobster With Herbs And Vegetables

Serves 4

INGREDIENTS:

1 gallon salted water	½ quart heavy cream
1 medium onion, diced	4 ounces fresh butter, softened
2 carrots, diced	salt to taste
1 celery stalk, diced	white pepper to taste
5 parsley sprigs	½ pound Chinese peas, julienned
2 tablespoons cracked pepper	and steamed
2 ounces vinegar	½ pound carrots, julienned and
1 garlic head, halved	steamed
4 live lobsters (1½ pounds each)	1 small bunch chives, chopped
1 quart white wine	4 small crayfish (for garnish)

PROCEDURE:

Bring salted water to a boil. Add onion, carrots, celery, parsley, pepper, vinegar and garlic. Boil for 30 minutes. Add lobsters and return to a boil. Simmer 10 minutes. Remove lobsters from pot. Remove arms and tail then add to stock. Quarter torsos and put in another pot. Add wine and 3 ounces of lobster stock. Boil until reduced by half. Add heavy cream. Boil vigorously until cream reaches sauce consistency. Strain through a fine strainer. Add butter. Season with salt and pepper. Remove lobster arms and tails from stock. Remove meat from shells. (Halve tail lengthwise for easiest removal). Sauté peas and carrots with lobster meat. Add chives. Transfer to serving platter, pour sauce over top and garnish with crayfish.

El Bizcocho
Rancho Bernardo Inn
San Diego

Marinated Seabass With Cilantro And Ginger

Serves 4

INGREDIENTS:

⅓ cup olive oil
1 tablespoon fresh lemon juice
1 teaspoon ginger, finely grated
½ cup cilantro, coarsely chopped

1 teaspoon grated lemon rind
1 teaspoon salt
½ teaspoon pepper
2 pounds fresh seabass fillets

PROCEDURE:

Mix all ingredients together and marinate fish in mixture for 4 hours. Grill fillets on hot griddle. Baste with marinade on both sides until fish is cooked.

Pancho Wellington's
La Jolla

Scampi Bonaparte

Serves 4

INGREDIENTS:

16 large shrimp, peeled and
    deveined
salt to taste
white pepper to taste
2 tablespoons olive oil
¼ cup brandy

⅓ cup dry white wine
2 teaspoons green peppercorns
juice of 1 lime
3 tablespoons sweet butter
fresh parsley, chopped (for garnish)

PROCEDURE:

Preheat oven to 400°. Season shrimp with salt and pepper. Sauté in olive oil then bake for 10 minutes. Return shrimp to fry pan over open flame. Pour in brandy and flame. Let brandy evaporate. Add white wine and set aside. Remove shrimp to serving platter. Add peppercorns and lime juice to pan. Return to fire and reduce slightly. Mix in the sweet butter a little at a time. Do not boil. Pour sauce over shrimp and garnish with parsley.

Elarios
La Jolla

Crab Stuffing

Yields 3 cups

INGREDIENTS:

8 ounces snow or king crab
6 ounces Monterey jack cheese, shredded
1 cup bread crumbs, toasted (sourdough or French)
½ pound butter, melted
3 tablespoons Parmesan cheese

2 eggs, beaten
1 bunch green onions, tops finely minced
1 cup Chablis
½ teaspoon oregano
salt to taste

PROCEDURE:

Combine all ingredients and mix thoroughly. Use in the following ways: **Wontons:** Fill skins with stuffing, fold and deep fry until golden brown. Serve with sweet and sour sauce or hot mustard. **Mushrooms:** Clean fresh mushrooms and pull out stems. Fill with stuffing, top with little mounds of grated Monterey jack cheese and bake at 350° for 10-15 minutes. **Enchiladas:** Fry small corn tortillas in oil. Drain. Dip in enchilada sauce. Fill tortillas with stuffing, sour cream and shredded cheese. Form into enchiladas. Place in baking dish. Cover with more sauce and bake at 350° until cheese is slightly brown. **Fish fillets:** Bone small fillets and place layer in bottom of buttered dish. Add layer of stuffing over fillets. Add another layer of fillets on top. Lace with butter, favorite seasonings and white wine. Bake until fish is done. Top with Hollandaise, fish sauce or butter sauce. **Trout:** Bone trout, dehead and cut off tail. Fill with stuffing. Finish same as fish fillets above.

El Crab Catcher
La Jolla

Machaca Sonorense

Serves 4

INGREDIENTS:

8 ounces beef (flank preferred), boiled and shredded
1 tablespoon vegetable oil
salt to taste
pepper to taste

2 garlic cloves, minced
2 tomatoes, diced
1 white onion, diced
2 green bell peppers, diced
4 eggs, well beaten

PROCEDURE:

Brown beef in oil until golden. Season with salt and pepper. Add vegetables. Stir in eggs and cook over low heat for approximately 5 minutes. Serve with refried beans and red chilaquiles (tortilla filled with tomatoes, cheese, chiles and herbs).

Casa de Bandini
San Diego

Mongolian Hot Pot

Serves 6

Mongolian Hot Pot, also known as Hot Pot, Fire Pot or Shabu Shabu is a guest participation table cooking dish. Provide each guest with chopsticks and a wire dipping basket for cooking his own choice of ingredients. Place the "hot pot" at center table (filled with chicken broth) over sterno. Arrange the following, artistically, on a large tray or trays accompanied by garnishes and sauces:

1 pound prime quality cut beef (marbleized sukiyaki type is best), cut paper thin

1 pound chicken breast, in large paper-thin slices, marinated in 1 tablespoon cornstarch, 1 teaspoon salt, 1 tablespoon thin soy sauce and ¼ cup chicken broth

½ pound scallops, halved, marinated in 1 tablespoon grated ginger, 1 tablespoon cornstarch, 1 teaspoon salt, 1 tablespoon thin soy sauce and ¼ cup chicken broth

½ pound medium shrimp, shelled and deveined. Marinate together with scallops but separate to display on tray

1 bunch green onions (or leeks), in 2″ diagonal strips

12 dried black mushrooms, soaked and stems removed

1 bunch shungiku or kikuna (edible chrysanthemum leaves)

8 nappa cabbage leaves, in 2″ pieces

8 ounces bamboo shoots, sliced

1 pound tofu, in 1″ cubes

½-1 pound fresh Chinese noodles, parboiled

12 freshly-frozen fish/shrimp balls

GARNISHES

½ cup green onions, chopped

1 cup daikon oroshi (grated Japanese radish)

½ cup ginger, grated

SAUCES

Sesame: 3 tablespoons white sesame seeds (ground and toasted), 1 tablespoon sugar, 2½ tablespoons soy sauce, ½ cup dashi (or chicken broth), 2 tablespoons mirin (Japanese sake with glucose)

Ginger Miso: 1 tablespoon grated ginger, 3 tablespoons sugar, 1 tablespoon wine (or mirin), 5 tablespoons red miso (Japanese bean sauce). Simmer this sauce before serving.

Hot Mustard: ½ cup soy sauce, ½ cup chicken broth, 2 tablespoons dry mustard, 2 tablespoons white sesame seeds (ground and toasted)

Oyster: blend 2 parts bottled oyster sauce to 1 part salad oil
Black Bean Chile: available, premixed, from oriental foods stores
Ponzu: ½ cup lemon juice, ½ cup lime juice, ¼ cup unseasoned rice vinegar, 1 cup dark soy sauce, 2 tablespoons mirin, ¼ cup dried bonito flakes, 2" kelp kombu. For best flavor age this mixture in refrigerator for 1 month. Use within 3 months.

Woo Chee Chong
San Diego

Carbonnades À La Flamande

Serves 4

INGREDIENTS:

2 pounds beef stew, fat trimmed
salt to taste
pepper to taste
goose or duck fat (butter or lard
    will do)
2 large onions, sliced
¼ cup flour
1 tablespoon brown sugar

thyme to taste
bay leaves to taste
12 ounces strong beer (Belgian
    "Gueuze" is best)
2 tablespoons red wine vinegar
2 tablespoons Dijon mustard
1 slice bread

PROCEDURE:

Season meat with salt and pepper. Brown in fat. Otherwise use butter or lard. Remove meat from pot. Add onions and cook slowly for 10 minutes without browning them. Return meat to pot. Add flour and mix well. (This step is critical because proper cooking of the flour before adding liquid will guarantee a lumpless sauce). Preheat oven to 350°. Add remaining ingredients except mustard and bread. Mix well. Bring to a light boil stirring frequently. Liquid should have thickened. Add a little more beer if too thick. Roast, covered, for approximately 2 hours or until meat is tender. Spread mustard on bread slice and float on top of meat (it will slowly dissolve). The mustard could be added to meat, but any Belgian grandmother would tell you that "it just won't be the same."

A popular variation calls for adding prunes soaked in Genever (a Flemish gin) a few minutes before the meat is done. This is an excellent dish to make the day ahead. The more you make it, the better you'll become at adapting it to your taste. Maybe a little more mustard, a little less of this or that. Don't be afraid to experiment.

The Belgian Lion
San Diego

447

Salade Suzanne

Serves 4

INGREDIENTS:

1 radicchio lettuce
1 bunch spinach
1 bunch curly endive
1-2 bunches arugula (optional)
2 large red onions, thinly sliced
8 small zucchini, halved and sliced
    lengthwise
4 large mushroom caps

8 large prawns, peeled, deveined,
    tails intact
8 large scallops
8 small crab claws
virgin olive oil
1 cup Mustard Vinaigrette (recipe
    follows)

PROCEDURE:

Prepare barbecue until coals glow red (broiler may also be used). Break all greens into bite-size pieces. Wash, dry carefully and refrigerate in sealed containers until ready to serve. Grill onions, zucchini and mushrooms. Then add prawns, scallops and crab claws. Brush with olive oil. Seafood should be moist and succulent; do not overcook. Total grilling time should be 5-8 minutes. Transfer seafood, vegetables and greens to large bowl. Toss with vinaigrette. Divide evenly on dinner plates and serve immediately.

Mustard Vinaigrette

Yields 2 cups

INGREDIENTS:

3 teaspoons meaux mustard
2 teaspoons fresh tarragon, minced
4 tablespoons sherry wine vinegar
1 egg yolk

pinch of salt
freshly ground pepper to taste
1½ cups salad oil (almond or
    safflower)

PROCEDURE:

Whisk all ingredients together except oil. Then add oil in slow, steady stream until dressing thickens. Be careful not to overwhisk.

California Cuisine
San Diego

Summer Chicken Salad

Serves 4

INGREDIENTS:

2 chicken breasts
2 ripe honeydew melons
1 tablespoon ginger
2 tablespoons scallions, chopped
juice of 1 lime
¼ cup carrots, grated
1 red apple, diced
1 small bunch seedless grapes

salt to taste
pepper to taste
1 iceberg lettuce, washed and dried
1 romaine lettuce, washed and
   dried
1 avocado, sliced
1 small can Mandarin oranges
Curry Salad Dressing (recipe
   follows)

PROCEDURE:

Poach chicken until tender. Dice and chill in refrigerator. Halve melons, seed and scoop out small balls. Scrape away any remaining flesh and drain hollowed-out shells. Mix cooled chicken pieces, melon balls, ginger, scallions, lime juice, carrots, apple and grapes. Season with salt and pepper. Tear lettuces into bite-size pieces. Line bottoms and sides of melon shells with mixed lettuce pieces. Spoon in chicken mixture. Garnish with avocado and orange slices. Top with chilled curry dressing.

Curry Salad Dressing

Yields 1 cup

INGREDIENTS:

1 cup mayonnaise
1 tablespoon lemon juice
1½ tablespoon curry
1 scallion (green part only), finely
   chopped
1 tablespoon fresh parsley,
   chopped

1 tablespoon honey
dash of dry mustard
dash of cayenne pepper
salt to taste
pepper to taste

PROCEDURE:

Blend all ingredients and chill to blend flavors.

Putnam's
La Jolla

Caesar Salad

Serves 2

INGREDIENTS:

4 anchovy fillets
1 teaspoon crushed pepper
2 garlic cloves, minced
1 egg
1 cup olive oil
2 tablespoons Worcestershire sauce
2 teaspoons Poupon mustard

juice of 1 lemon
1 romaine lettuce (inner leaves
    only), cut in bite-size pieces
1 cup Parmesan cheese, freshly
    grated
1 cup croutons

PROCEDURE:

Combine anchovies and pepper in large salad bowl. Crush into a paste. Add garlic, egg, oil, Worcestershire, mustard and lemon. Whip until creamy. Add lettuce, cheese and croutons. Toss and serve immediately on chilled plates.

The Westgate Hotel
San Diego

Blue Cheese Dressing

Yields 2½ cups

INGREDIENTS:

¾ cup sour cream
½ teaspoon dry mustard
½ teaspoon black pepper
½ teaspoon salt
⅓ teaspoon garlic powder

1 teaspoon Worcestershire sauce
1⅓ cups mayonnaise
4 ounces Danish blue cheese,
    crumbled into very small bits

PROCEDURE:

Blend first 6 ingredients at low speed. Add mayonnaise and blend another half minute at low speed, then 2 minutes at medium speed. Incorporate crumbled cheese and continue to blend for 3 more minutes. Refrigerate for 24 hours before serving.

The Chart House
La Jolla

Magic Pan Mustard Sauce

Yields 2 cups

INGREDIENTS:

4 egg yolks
4 teaspoons vinegar
1 tespoon salt
⅛ teaspoon white pepper

2 cups salad oil
1 tablespoon lemon juice
3 ounces prepared mustard
2 tablespoons honey

PROCEDURE:

Beat yolks lightly with electric mixer. Add 3 teaspoons vinegar, salt and pepper. Blend thoroughly. Slowly pour in oil, beating continuously at medium speed. Add last teaspoon of vinegar, lemon juice, mustard and honey. Blend until well mixed.

Especially good with ham palascintas, cheese fritters or assorted deep fried vegetables.

The Magic Pan
San Diego

Fär Breton

Serves 6-8

INGREDIENTS:

DOUGH
1 pound flour
¼ teaspoon salt
8 ounces butter, softened
2 eggs
1 tablespoon water

CREAM CUSTARD
8 eggs
10 ounces sugar
5 ounces flour
4 cups milk, boiled with 1 vanilla
    bean, split
6¾ ounces butter
pitted prunes to taste

PROCEDURE:

Mix all dough ingredients in a mixer.   Shape into a ball, wrap in a dishcloth and refrigerate for 2 hours. Roll dough out into a circle and pat into a floured tart pan. Preheat oven to 475°. Mix eggs with sugar. Add flour, boiled milk and butter. Cool completely. Arrange pitted prunes over crust in tart pan, cover with cream and bake 30-40 minutes. Cool at room temperature before serving.

The French Pastry Shop
La Jolla

Michel's Chocolate Mousse

Serves 6-8

INGREDIENTS:

2½ cups heavy cream
3 tablespoons sugar
1 pound sweet chocolate, melted
6 egg yolks

6 egg whites
pinch of salt
dash of cream of tartar

PROCEDURE:

Whip cream with sugar and chill. Beat egg yolks, one at a time, into melted chocolate. Set aside to cool. Beat egg whites with salt and cream of tartar until soft peaks form. Stir a quarter of the whites into chocolate mixture. Fold in remaining whites. Fold in whipped cream. Chill until ready to serve.

French Gourmet
La Jolla

Mud Pie

Serves 8

INGREDIENTS:

½ package Nabisco chocolate
   wafers, crushed
2 ounces butter

1 gallon coffee ice cream, softened
1½ cup fudge sauce, cooled slightly

PROCEDURE:

Mix wafers and butter well. Press into a 9″ pie plate. Cover with ice cream and freeze until firm. Top with cold fudge sauce and refreeze for 10 hours. Slice into eighths and serve on chilled dessert plates with chilled forks. If desired, top with whipped cream and slivered almonds.

The Chart House
La Jolla

Le Poire Meringue À La Sauce Chocolat

Serves 6

INGREDIENTS:

3 cups water
1½ cups sugar
1 tablespoon fresh lemon juice
3 medium-ripe pears, peeled,halved
　and cored

4 large egg whites
⅛ teaspoon cream of tartar
Rum Mocha Chocolate Sauce
　(recipe follows)

PROCEDURE:

Bring water, ¾ cup sugar and lemon juice to a boil in a pan which will accommodate all pear halves in a single layer. When sugar dissolves completely, add pears and simmer uncovered for 10-12 minutes or until tender. Drain pears on paper towels and cool completely. Position rack in upper third of oven and preheat to 475°. Transfer pear halves to buttered baking sheet, cut-side down, 4″ apart. Beat egg whites with cream of tartar until soft peaks form. Gradually incorporate remaining sugar beating until stiff and shiny. Using pastry bag with large star tip, pipe meringue over each pear and bake until lightly browned, approximately 2 minutes. Cool or serve immediately with sauce.

Rum Mocha Chocolate Sauce

Yields 2½ cups

INGREDIENTS:

4 ounces butter
2 tablespoons dark rum
1 cup sugar
⅓ cup unsweetened cocoa powder,
　strained

1 cup heavy cream
⅛ teaspoon salt
1 teaspoon dry instant coffee
1 teaspoon vanilla extract

PROCEDURE:

Melt butter in a saucepan over low heat. Add rum, sugar, cocoa, cream and salt. Stir and bring to a boil over moderate heat. Add coffee, stirring to dissolve. Simmer for 5 minutes over low heat. Remove from heat and stir in vanilla. You can refrigerate any unused portion for weeks.

Patty Murray Catering
La Jolla

Grand Marnier Soufflé

Serves 4

INGREDIENTS:

2 cups milk
2½ ounces butter
4 ounces flour

8 ounces Grand Marnier
5 egg yolks
5 egg whites, stiffly beaten

PROCEDURE:

Preheat oven to 500°. Boil milk. Make roux by combining butter and flour in another pan. Mix into milk. Add Grand Marnier and cool. Add egg yolks and mix well. Add stiffly beaten whites. Butter individual soufflé molds, sprinkle with sugar and fill to rim with soufflé mixture. Bake for ·15 minutes.

If desired, swirl some Grand Marnier into softened vanilla ice cream and serve on the side.

Le Papillon Cafe
La Jolla

Harry's Helpful Hints

To get more juice out of lemons and limes ... bring them to room temperature and roll them firmly on countertop before squeezing.

To top apple pie ... soften vanilla ice cream, swirl it with cinnamon and refreeze until firm enough to scoop.

A low calorie dessert that even a non-dieter would love ... orange slices, a spoonful of yogurt and a sprinkling of crystallized ginger.

As good as Bearnaise, but lots easier ... top hamburgers with sour cream and onion dip.

Leftover coffee won't taste stale if you add a cinnamon stick to the pot when you reheat it.

Flavor hot popcorn with grated Parmesan cheese. Skip the butter if you are watching your weight.

Harry's Coffee Shop
La Jolla

INDEX

POULTRY & GAME

SEAFOOD

VEGETABLES & ACCOMPANIMENTS

CAKES

PIES & PASTRIES

OTHER DESSERTS

COOKIES & CANDY

BREAD & BREAKFAST

JUST FOR KIDS

FROM AROUND THE WORLD

FROM AROUND THE TOWN

Notes

Notes

Notes

Notes

Notes

Notes

La Jolla Cooks
La Jolla Country Day School
9490 Genesee Avenue
La Jolla, California 92037

Please send me _____ copies .... $14.95 each _____
Postage and handling .... 2.00 each _____
California residents add 6% sales tax .... .90 each _____
Enclosed is my check or money order   TOTAL _____

Make checks payable to LJCDS Parents Association. Proceeds from the sale
of this cookbook are contributed to La Jolla Country Day School.

NAME _____

ADDRESS _____

CITY_____ STATE _____ ZIP _____

La Jolla Cooks
La Jolla Country Day School
9490 Genesee Avenue
La Jolla, California 92037

Please send me _____ copies .... $14.95 each _____
Postage and handling .... 2.00 each _____
California residents add 6% sales tax .... .90 each _____
Enclosed is my check or money order   TOTAL _____

Make checks payable to LJCDS Parents Association. Proceeds from the sale
of this cookbook are contributed to La Jolla Country Day School.

NAME _____

ADDRESS _____

CITY_____ STATE _____ ZIP _____

La Jolla Cooks
La Jolla Country Day School
9490 Genesee Avenue
La Jolla, California 92037

Please send me _____ copies .... $14.95 each _____
Postage and handling .... 2.00 each _____
California residents add 6% sales tax .... .90 each _____
Enclosed is my check or money order   TOTAL _____

Make checks payable to LJCDS Parents Association. Proceeds from the sale
of this cookbook are contributed to La Jolla Country Day School.

NAME _____

ADDRESS _____

CITY_____ STATE _____ ZIP _____

La Jolla Cooks
La Jolla Country Day School
9490 Genesee Avenue
La Jolla, California 92037

Please send me _____ copies .... $14.95 each _____
Postage and handling .... 2.00 each _____
California residents add 6% sales tax .... .90 each _____
Enclosed is my check or money order   TOTAL _____

Make checks payable to LJCDS Parents Association. Proceeds from the sale
of this cookbook are contributed to La Jolla Country Day School.

NAME _____

ADDRESS _____

CITY_____ STATE _____ ZIP _____